The Afterlife of Used Things

Recycling is not a concept that is usually applied to the eighteenth century. “The environment” may not have existed as a notion then, yet practices of reuse and transformation obviously shaped the early modern world. Still, this period of booming commerce and exchange was also marked by scarcity and want. This book reveals the fascinating variety and ingenuity of recycling processes that may be observed in the commerce, crafts, literature, and science of the eighteenth century. Recycling is used as a thought-provoking means to revisit subjects such as consumption, the scientific process, or novel writing, and cast them in a new light where the waste of some becomes the luxury of others, clothes worn to rags are turned into paper and into books, and scientific breakthroughs are carried out in old kitchen pans.

Ariane Fennetaux is a senior lecturer at the University of Paris Diderot. She specialises in eighteenth-century material culture.

Amélie Junqua is a senior lecturer at the University of Amiens. She specialises in eighteenth-century literature.

Sophie Vasset is a senior lecturer at the University of Paris Diderot. She specialises in eighteenth-century literature and medicine.

Routledge Studies in Cultural History

1 **The Politics of Information in Early Modern Europe**
Edited by Brendan Dooley and Sabrina Baron

2 **The Insanity of Place/ The Place of Insanity**
Essays on the History of Psychiatry
Andrew Scull

3 **Film, History, and Cultural Citizenship**
Sites of Production
Edited by Tina Mai Chen and David S. Churchill

4 **Genre and Cinema**
Ireland and Transnationalism
Edited by Brian McIlroy

5 **Histories of Postmodernism**
Edited by Mark Bevir, Jill Hargis, and Sara Rushing

6 **Africa after Modernism**
Transitions in Literature, Media, and Philosophy
Michael Janis

7 **Rethinking Race, Politics, and Poetics**
C. L. R. James' Critique of Modernity
Brett St Louis

8 **Making British Culture**
English Readers and the Scottish Enlightenment, 1740–1830
David Allan

9 **Empires and Boundaries**
Rethinking Race, Class, and Gender in Colonial Settings
Edited by Harald Fischer-Tiné and Susanne Gehrmann

10 **Tobacco in Russian History and Culture**
From the Seventeenth Century to the Present
Edited by Matthew P. Romaniello and Tricia Starks

11 **History of Islam in German Thought**
From Leibniz to Nietzsche
Ian Almond

12 **Israeli-Palestinian Conflict in the Francophone World**
Edited by Nathalie Debrauwere-Miller

13 **History of Participatory Media**
Politics and Publics, 1750–2000
Edited by Anders Ekström Solveig Jülich, Frans Lundgren, and Per Wisselgren

14 **Living in the City**
Urban Institutions in the Low Countries, 1200–2010
Leo Lucassen and Wim Willems

15 **Historical Disasters in Context**
Science, Religion, and Politics
Edited by Andrea Janku, Gerrit J. Schenk, and Franz Mauelshagen

16 Migration, Ethnicity, and Mental Health
International Perspectives, 1840–2010
Edited by Angela McCarthy and Catharine Coleborne

17 Politics of Memory
Making Slavery Visible in the Public Space
Edited by Ana Lucia Araujo

18 Neutrality in Twentieth-Century Europe
Intersections of Science, Culture, and Politics after the First World War
Edited by Rebecka Lettevall, Geert Somsen, and Sven Widmalm

19 Americans Experience Russia
Encountering the Enigma, 1917 to the Present
Edited by Choi Chatterjee and Beth Holmgren

20 A Social History of Disability in the Middle Ages
Cultural Considerations of Physical Impairment
Irina Metzler

21 Race, Science, and the Nation
Reconstructing the Ancient Past in Britain, France and Germany
Chris Manias

22 Identity, Aesthetics, and Sound in the Fin de Siècle
Redesigning Perception
Dariusz Gafijczuk

23 Disease and Crime
A History of Social Pathologies and the New Politics of Health
Edited by Robert Peckham

24 Critical Perspectives on Colonialism
Writing the Empire from Below
Edited by Fiona Paisley and Kirsty Reid

25 Old World Empires
Cultures of Power and Governance in Eurasia
Ilhan Niaz

26 The Afterlife of Used Things
Recycling in the Long Eighteenth Century
Edited by Ariane Fennetaux, Amélie Junqua, and Sophie Vasset

27 Holocaust Consciousness in Contemporary Britain
Andy Pearce

28 The Invention of Race
Scientific and Popular Representations
Edited by Nicolas Bancel, Thomas David, and Dominic Thomas

29 Indigenous Networks
Mobility, Connections and Exchange
Edited by Jane Carey and Jane Lydon

30 Shadows of the Slave Past
Memory, Heritage, and Slavery
Ana Lucia Araujo

31 Expedition into Empire
Exploratory Journeys and the Making of the Modern World
Edited by Martin Thomas

32 Luxury and Gender in European Towns, 1700–1914
Edited by Deborah Simonton, Marjo Kaartinen, and Anne Montenach

The Afterlife of Used Things

Recycling in the Long Eighteenth Century

Edited by Ariane Fennetaux, Amélie Junqua, and Sophie Vasset

Routledge
Taylor & Francis Group
LONDON AND NEW YORK

First published 2015 by Routledge

2 Park Square, Milton Park, Abingdon, Oxfordshire OX14 4RN
52 Vanderbilt Avenue, New York, NY 10017

Routledge is an imprint of the Taylor & Francis Group, an informa business

First issued in paperback 2018

Library of Congress Cataloging-in-Publication Data

The afterlife of used things : recycling in the long eighteenth century / edited by Ariane Fennetaux, Amélie Junqua, and Sophie Vasset.
pages cm — (Routledge studies in cultural history ; 26)
1. Recycling (Waste, etc.)—History—18th century. 2. Material culture—History—18th century. 3. Secondhand trade—History—18th century. 4. Social history—18th century. 5. Economic history—1600–1750. 6. Economic history—1750–1918. 7. Literature—18th century—History and criticism. I. Fennetaux, Ariane. II. Junqua, Amélie. III. Vasset, Sophie.
TD794.5.A415 2014
363.72′8209033—dc23
2014019501

ISBN: 978-0-415-72630-6 (hbk)
ISBN: 978-0-367-20885-1 (pbk)

Typeset in Sabon
by Apex CoVantage, LLC

Contents

Figures

Introduction
The Many Lives of Recycling

Ariane Fennetaux, Amélie Junqua, and Sophie Vasset

The notion of novelty has often been called upon when discussing the eighteenth century. Historians have insisted on the economic transformations that characterised the period, leading to an "industrial revolution" and its companion, "consumer revolution," while historians of ideas have shown the impact of "the new science" on a specific Enlightenment culture, and literary critics have hailed the birth of a new print culture or tracked the rise of the novel. More recently, though, scholars have started to question the primacy of the new in their particular fields. Economic historians, for instance, have refined our vision of consumption by showing an interest in practices of second-hand retail and pawning. Beverly Lemire was first in drawing attention to the widespread importance of the second-hand trade in clothing in eighteenth-century England.[1] She showed how the availability of second-hand clothing was key to understanding the rise of mass consumption by allowing the less wealthy to form regular purchasing habits that would turn them into consumers, linking "the consumer revolution" to the old and the used rather than the new. Following in her footsteps, work has been carried out on other types of second-hand circulations—textile and nontextile—in the rest of Europe.[2] In a similar way literature specialists have added to our understanding of the novel by tracking its origins in seventeenth-century biographies, romances, and conversion narratives.[3] Departing from the idea that the novel was an invention that arose *ex nihilo*, scholars have confronted literary and nonliterary texts to map out the evolutions and transformations of genres.

These studies have allowed a more complex image of the period to emerge, but the corrective they bring to our reading of the century remains all too often piecemeal, focused as it is on one of its facets. The present collection brings together under the term recycling several of these questions whereas they are often viewed in isolation from one another. Let it be understood that recycling will here be distinguished from the question of the environment, which was yet to be constructed as a fully fledged category in the eighteenth century.[4] The book proposes to view recycling, and the related practices of reuse, salvaging, or transformation, not as a series of marginal, disconnected phenomena but as a fundamentally relevant operative process to understand the period, a *modus operandi* that ran through the whole fabric of eighteenth-century society and characterised several of its key developments. Recycling was thus central to consumption envisioned in its entirety—from the moment of purchase, with second-hand retail being widespread, to the everyday use of objects, which were often repaired, refashioned, and remodelled. In *The Social Life of Things*, anthropologist Igor Kopytoff argued that we should, when discussing consumption, look beyond purchase to embrace the whole biography of things.[5] Looking at recycling in terms of what Susan Strasser has termed the "stewardship of objects,"[6] that is the daily care and management of objects along the span of their long lives, enables us to heed the anthropologist's call. Eighteenth-century objects had complex, eventful biographies: they went through wear, tear, and repair, they moved from the hands of one owner to another through gift, theft, selling, or pawning, and they changed appearance and shape through alterations, transformations, and mending. For all that has been written about the gradual replacement of long-lasting materials such as pewter or silk by increasingly short-lived ones such as ceramics and cotton and the ensuing shortening of the lifecycle of objects, eighteenth-century things actually had very long afterlives.[7] Poised between the early modern economic model of scarcity and want and the modern world of consumerism and waste, the eighteenth century was marked by a specific relationship to the material where objects went through not one but several lifecycles. Caught between urbanisation, industrialisation, and rising consumption on the one hand and, on the other, by the enduring prevalence of traditional economic models, in which nothing went to waste, it was a world in which the logic of the *bricoleur*, who has "to make do with 'whatever is at hand,'" prevailed:[8] food scraps were made into meals, grease was turned into tallow candles and soap, wood ash served to make lye, human and animal excrement found a useful role as manure. In the labour-intensive reality that continued to characterise production, there was a regard for the labour involved in creating objects, which meant that they were not discarded easily. Donald Woodward, who first used the notion of recycling in relation to the early modern period, paid some attention to the complex afterlives of objects.[9] He pointed out how, in preindustrial England, "Few goods were lightly abandoned, fewer still were left to rot by the roadside. Nearly all items discarded by one person could be used by another in an unaltered form, in a repaired or partially reconstructed state, or in a totally new guise via the process of recycling."[10] These various processes that objects were subjected to—recirculation, reuse, repair, refashioning, transformation—he pointed out, affected clothing, building materials, metal, and paper alike. Woodward's recycling was thus very much the result of a situation of overall poverty and scarcity of goods. We would like to expand on Woodward's argument first by seeing recycling not only as driven by an avoidance of waste or a pursuit of thrift, although these will still provide an entry into the notion.[11] But recycling will be seen as part of transformative cycles that affected the whole of society—from the very poor to the very rich—with practices as varied as mundane second-hand clothes trading to elitist collecting, and actors ranging from the poor trying to eke out a living from the collection and inventive transformation of discarded materials, to monarchs whose display of magnificence rested on careful resource management and regular repairs. The old will thus be shown to have had several values. Not merely second best to the new, in some contexts the old acquired a value of its own, whether it be as a prized collectible or as a sentimental memento of the past. Another way in which the present collection will expand on Woodward's argument is that reuse, repurposing, and transformation together with the issues of subversion and recreation will also be seen in relation to texts and ideas, rather than just goods and objects. If Woodward did look at how the recycling of linen underpinned the papermaking industry, he failed to explore paper itself as a material that travelled across different states and different disciplines in the process of its recycling. Paper is viewed here at the intersection of texts and textiles, as a multivalent medium related to both literature and material culture. Reconnecting text and paper, the collection proposes to use recycling as a strong interdisciplinary tool with which to revisit textual creation from novels to medical treatises in an age when invention was not necessarily equated with innovation and originality. If texts could be reused, and recycled into different forms, so could the book, made as it was of ink and paper that could be torn, cut into, or made into curling papers or library storage boxes.

Recycling thus provides a converging lens through which to envision at one and the same time fields that are too often kept separate by artificial categorisation. Beneath this rigid taxonomy lies an incredibly flexible world of practices in which things, materials, and ideas circulated. Such constituted categories as literature, history, or science and such dichotomy as new/old, or valuable/waste, may provide scholars with seemingly useful tools to analyse the period but they are not necessarily those that best convey the constantly adaptive processes that characterised a period when a patient's private letter became the stuff of medical treatises, scientific breakthroughs were made using old kitchen pans, and men and women's garments were remade into children's clothing, pincushions, or patchwork quilts. The collection thus aims to restore some fluidity to a period when techniques, cultural practices and artefacts were not rigidly fixed but part of complex, often paradoxical cycles that constantly redefined their statuses and values.

Indeed, the question of value will be central to our understanding of recycling. Whereas the category of waste has attracted much critical debate,[12] the notion of recycling, when it has been used in a historical context, is often simply understood as a matter-of-fact equivalent of reuse.[13] The essays in the collection envision recycling as an operative, cyclical process of valuation, devaluation, and re-evaluation. In this context, the types of recycling discussed in the essays all entail the loss of value of a given object—be it real or imagined—which leads it to be discarded, seen as waste or obsolete matter, before conscious alteration requalifies its value, reintroducing it into a new cycle of consumption, whether it be the same circuit of wear and tear, that a mended ceramic or altered piece of clothing undergoes for instance, or a different one when the object/material/text is no longer considered, understood, or used in its first capacity but undergoes a transformation that changes its nature. Thus understood as a dynamic process of re-valuation, recycling not only asks economic questions but opens up social, aesthetic, political, and moral interrogations.

The first section, "The Circulation of Goods," charts the various trade networks that allowed eighteenth-century objects to go through several cycles of consumption. It focuses on the buoyant trade of second-hand goods—be it through everyday objects that were routinely pawned or sold off, or through the more elite auctions of luxury goods or the practices of collecting which turned the past and its patina into a valuable commodity. Natacha Coquery's analysis of the accounts of several eighteenth-century Parisian jewellers and upholsterers shows that second-hand trading was not part of a parallel, invisible economy but actually thrived at the very heart of the elite luxury market. Shopkeepers dealing in luxury and semi-luxury goods also bought and sold second-hand goods, repaired objects, and even routinely accepted barter as a form of payment. Recycling was not marginal but central to consumption, characterised as it was at the time by "overlapping practices that lent it a peculiar flexibility and adaptability." Jon Stobart's study of country house sales between 1750 and 1830 further explores the interconnectedness between luxury and second-hand trading, showing how the contents of country houses were often sold in public auctions either to meet financial pressure or when the owner of the house died. A wide variety of goods were then made available second-hand from rare books and paintings to looking glasses or curtains. Whether the motivation of those who bought them was to "capture value" by making a bargain or to "capture difference" by displaying taste in their selection of goods, country house sales provided the wealthy and the middling sort alike with an opportunity to furnish their own homes at a reduced price. The circulation of goods in and out of the houses of the elite shows the market for second-hand items to have thrived well into the nineteenth century. For some wealthy consumers, second-hand goods even became part of a specific market in which "the past itself became commodified," as Ilja Van Damme explains in his chapter on antiquarianism among the bourgeois elite of the Southern Netherlands. That is, the history and age of some objects actually added to rather than diminished their value. Taken out of the realm of usefulness to be integrated into collections, objects were turned into antiques. On the one hand this development went against the age-old tradition of recycling broken down objects to prolong their usefulness, but in the process another type of cycle was initiated, one that requalified the past as a valuable commodity with powerful political implications. In the context of the unstable politics of the Southern Netherlands, salvaging the "wreckage of history" participated in the collective writing of history and the building of a national identity. Similar added value can be found in William Beckford's collections of oriental objects and manuscripts. Laurent Châtel interprets Beckford's transformation and display of oriental objects as a translation for the Western culture of foreign art and design. Beckford's aesthetics of "reappropriation," the frames, mountings, and stands he had made for his exhibits, acted as a "material encounter between West and the East," one whose status may be seen by some as colonial but which, according to Châtel, had aesthetic, rather than political, ramifications. From the politics of patina to the translation of oriental aesthetics in the context of a collection, recycling was thus central to various aspects of eighteenth-century consumption.

Our second section deals with the material practices of recycling. The authors study the various processes of what Strasser has termed "the stewardship of objects,"[14] that is the different strategies at work to adapt, repair, or transform everyday objects in order to lengthen their lifecycles. In a world governed by scarcity rather than plenty, this economy of means—which applied to public buildings, royal furniture, ceramics, scientific instruments, or votive objects alike—was not merely a negative response to pressing economic circumstances but was also creative in its own right, leading to invention and novelty. In some cases, recycling was integrated to an overall system of management of resources, such as with the *Conseil des bâtiments civils* in postrevolutionary France. Allan Potofsky explains how the Revolution "created a dynamic of reselling, restoring, refitting, and reusing buildings." Under the aegis of the *Conseil*, the recycling of buildings, in the form of *biens nationaux*, became part of a public service of urban planning. And if initially this pragmatic policy responded to financial pressure, what the *Conseil* achieved was truly a modern, integrated approach to urban planning in which the city and its polluted atmosphere were recognised as a matter of public concern, a move that had significant political implications. The interconnectedness between recycling and politics is also illustrated by post–Glorious Revolution Britain. A close examination of the papers of the Great Wardrobe during the reign of William of Orange and Mary II shows recurring evidence of the furniture of Kensington palace being regularly mended and refashioned. Olivia Fryman's analysis of the archival material shows that the display of monarchical magnificence did not solely depend on conspicuous consumption but also on careful mending and frequent repair. In the context of the Glorious Revolution, such rational management of royal pomp had profound political implications: it displayed financial prudence at a time when the new monarchy was intent on distancing itself from their profligate predecessors by setting an example of virtue. Practices of mending and transforming objects were thus not restricted to the poor and needy. They were so widespread across society that they actually fuelled a whole sector of activity with highly-specialised jobs dedicated to the repair of broken objects. Sara Pennell explains how the mending of ceramics was "an opportunity for new occupations to develop," "an arena for exploring mankind's potential for mastering new materials." Specialised techniques such as rimming, riveting, and cramping had long existed while new ones, like china burning, appeared. Pennell shows that somebody like Josiah Wedgwood, who is traditionally presented by historians as one of the figureheads of the "consumer revolution" because of his keen sense of enterprise and innovative retail techniques,[15] was quick to realise the commercial potential of the technique of china burning in an age when the spread of ceramics also had the unavoidable consequence of increased chances of broken and chipped vessels. Securing the services of a worker who mastered the alchemical art of repairing china was part and parcel of his celebrated business sense. Partly based on extant repaired ceramics, Pennell's chapter also highlights the shift in museum practices, which of late have started to showcase rather than erase traces of repair and alteration in objects of their collections. Similarly based on surviving altered artefacts, Ariane Fennetaux's contribution surveys the professional avenues of textile recycling while also drawing attention to the pendant domestic industry that went into keeping clothes in good repair. From a consideration of the centrality of recycling to Britain's macro-economic development in the century, she moves on to an analysis of the minute techniques deployed by women to prolong the useful life of clothing. The variety of dress alterations she studies gives us material evidence of the complex relationship of the eighteenth century to the world of goods, since mending was driven, she shows, by a combination of fashion consciousness, prudent domestic economy, and sentimentality. Textile recycling thus leads Fennetaux to re-evaluate some traditional categories attributed to clothes and textile, such as old and new, class, gender, or even the object-subject divide. The new and the old also coexisted in the eighteenth-century laboratory—a place traditionally associated with innovation and invention. Simon Werrett's insight into the objects and tools of early scientists, their reuse and repair, and their transfer from the kitchen or the garden to the lab, opens up a vivid and refreshing view of their everyday work. He shows how the material context shaped the process and outcomes of the experiments, and informed the scientists, who also spent time reflecting on their tools. The stewardship of objects thus took part in the making of Enlightened scientific knowledge, though we tend to imagine the lab and even represent it—like Lavoisier's spotless laboratory in *Le Musée des Arts et Métiers de Paris*—as a sacred space devoid of mending, transfer, and transformation. Forcing us to rethink our categories further, Elizabeth Kowaleski Wallace ponders on the exceptional status of a wax votive doll later recycled as a play doll, found in the collections of the Bethnal Green Museum of Childhood. From this case study, she builds a twofold argument, exploring recycling through the key concepts of permanence and plasticity. Wax, she argues, is eminently malleable and morphs into almost anything, a fact that fascinated natural philosophers and doll makers alike. The appearance of mimetic wax baby dolls in the eighteenth century, instead of the stylised wooden adult dolls that had prevailed thus far, is interpreted by the author as a secular recycling of the sacred practice of the wax ex-voto. At the same time, she argues that some kind of "otherworldly intensity," inherited from its former religious association, is retained in the wax doll. Such a philosophical and material study brings to the fore a specificity of recycling that teleological approaches focusing on the "results" of recycling might have missed—it draws our attention to the traces of the original object underneath the transformations it underwent.

Our last section deals with "textual recyclings" both within and outside the literary sphere. It addresses questions of intertextuality, rewriting, and transformative strategies at work in texts, and confronts them to their material existence—as type, paper, or library books. Notions of waste, reclaim, and re-creation are thus made central to an understanding of Enlightenment print culture. In keeping with the previous section, the first chapter explores the material history of books, and invites the reader for a stroll in Winchester College Fellows' Library. Using first-hand research into the material makeup of eighteenth-century books kept in the library, Geoffrey Day scrutinises the different types of paper recycling that took place in the library providing original insights into the practices of the various actors of the book trade from authors and printers, to librarians and readers. The presentation bindings of some works reveal book printers' and authors' marketing techniques, while the recycled material used in the making of archival boxes provide a vivid picture of the constant cycle of destruction and reuse that texts went through when outmoded books were turned into bookbinding material. The same cycle of destruction is illustrated by some items in the collection which were dismembered in the eighteenth century when visiting libraries became a fashionable activity and porters offered tourists a souvenir of their visits in the shape of a fragment of one of the library's works. The many types of recycling evidenced in the collection of the library show how conservation in a library relies on a series of destructions, testifying to an altogether different relationship to the book and its materiality. The close connection between texts and their materiality is further explored by the following chapter, in which Amélie Junqua explains that both readers and writers of the eighteenth century were keenly aware that paper was not-too-distantly related to dirt, waste, and discarded linen. Based on an essay published by Addison in the *Spectator*, Junqua's analysis describes the full circle of metamorphoses from textile to paper and plays with the notion of waste and the various values it conferred on periodical prose. The aesthetics of recycling was thus at the heart of literary cultures, practices, and habits. They drew a playful parallel between the emergence of ideas and the base origins of books. Drawing a similar link between abjection and literature, Rebecca Anne Barr minutely dissects Clarissa's "mad papers" in Richardson's eponymous novel. This passage of the novel, which is a series of rough notes scrambled by the heroine after her rape, is visually laid out on the page to reproduce her confusion and trauma. This abject textual matter is thus made by Richardson-as-printer-of-his-own-works to break down the categories of what is considered "junk" and what is proper literature. The interplay of the mundane and the lofty within a literary work provides an unlimited area of investigation, as Brigitte Friant-Kessler demonstrates by offering a typology of recycled objects in Sterne's *Tristram Shandy* and *A Sentimental Journey* as well as a study of their narrative impact. Although Sterne's literary plagiarisms have been submitted to intense scholarly scrutiny, his representation of material practices of recycling has not been the subject of any sustained analysis. Friant-Kessler proposes looking at the "transformative craze" at work in the novels as "inseparable from the plasticity of the text" itself. As boots are turned into mortars, a piece of whalebone from a maid's stays is made into a makeshift splint for a broken nose, and loose sheets of manuscript notes are turned into curling papers, she shows how "Words and things at once collide and coalesce" bringing together "material transformation and Sterne's aesthetics in general." Textual recycling was not restricted to literary creation. The rewriting of medical cases in the eighteenth century further illustrates the practice, thus blurring the frontiers between scientific and literary texts, as Sophie Vasset points out. She shows how a public figure's account of his stone and gravel acquired a series of values and statuses as it moved from private letter to medical treatise. The painful testimony of a patient was in turn the narration of a life experience and a matter of scientific debate, one to be shared, quoted, and reused. Case studies were a crucial tool for the advancement of knowledge in an age when observation-based medicine was becoming increasingly important. By following the transformations and successive uses of one particular such case study, Vasset proposes to show that recycling was "part of medical knowledge in the making."

From pawning and papermaking to repaired ceramic punchbowls and self-plagiarizing scientific treatises, the collection thus uses the thematic and notional flexibility of recycling to offer a wide trans-disciplinary foray into a range of sources and topics without attempting to draw a projected synthesis on the subject. Such synthesis would not only be impossible in the space of this volume; it would also defeat its very purpose, which is to open up new research rather than bring definitive answers on a subject whose exploration has only just started. As Susan Strasser invites us to do in the preface to her book, the historian is to be considered as a rag picker trawling the archives and "recycling the figurative and literal rags he turns up to give them new meaning."[16] Necessarily partial and incomplete, our collection will hopefully nonetheless, like that of the *chiffonnier*, offer our readers some interesting pickings.[17]

NOTES

1. See in particular her "Peddling Fashion: Salesmen, Pawn-Brokers, Taylors, Thieves and the Second-Hand Clothes Trade in England, c.1700–1800," *Textile History* 22, no. 1 (1991): 67–82; "Second-Hand Beaux and 'Red-Armed

Belles': Conflict and the Creation of Fashions in England, c.1660–1800," *Continuity and Change* 15 (2000): 391–417.

2. Laurence Fontaine, ed., *Alternative Exchanges: Second-Hand Circulations from the Sixteenth Century to The Present* (New York and Oxford: Berghahn, 2008); Bruno Blondé, Natacha Coquery, Jon Stobart and Ilja Van Damme, eds., *Fashioning Old and New: Changing Consumer Patterns in Western Europe (1650–1900)* (Turnhout: Brepols, 2009); Jon Stobart and Ilja Van Damme, eds., *Modernity and the Second-Hand Trade: European Consumption Cultures and Practices, 1700–1900* (Basingstoke: Palgrave, 2010).
3. See in particular Michael McKeon, *The Origins of the English Novel 1600–1740* (Baltimore: Johns Hopkins University Press, 1987); J. Paul Hunter, *Before Novels, The Cultural Contexts of Eighteenth-Century English Fiction* (New York: Norton, 1990).
4. While environmental history has mainly focused on the nineteenth century, some scholars have shown an interest in the late eighteenth century, a key period for the rise of something like an environment-consciousness. See for instance Sabines Barles, *La ville délétère: médecins et ingénieurs dans l'espace urbain: XVIII–XIXe siècle* (Paris: Champ Vallon, 1999) and Barles, *L'Invention des déchets urbains, France: 1790–1970* (Paris: Champ Vallon, 2005). See also Thomas Le Roux, *Le laboratoire des pollutions industrielles, Paris 1770–1830.* (Paris: Albin Michel, 2011). Yet as the previous works or indeed chapter 5 in the present volume illustrate, if perceptions of deteriorating living conditions and anxieties over poor air quality in cities did start to come about at the end of the century, these concerns were not necessarily linked to a fully fledged notion of the environment as we understand it today.
5. See in particular Igor Kopytoff, "The Cultural Biography of Things: Commoditization as Process," in *The Social Life of Things. Commodities in Cultural Perspective*, ed. Arjun Appadurai (Cambridge: Cambridge University Press, 1986), 64–91.
6. Susan Strasser, *Waste and Want: A Social History of Trash* (New York: Metropolitan Books, 1999), 21–67.
7. Carole Shammas, "Changes in English and Anglo-American Consumption from 1550 to 1800," in *Consumption and the World of Goods*, ed. John Brewer and Roy Porter (Routledge: London and New York, 1993), 177–205.
8. French anthropologist Claude Lévi-Strauss opposed the mindset of the engineer who works with "tools conceived and procured for the purpose of the project" to that of the *bricoleur* who works with odds and ends. Claude Lévi-Strauss, *The Savage Mind* (Chicago: University of Chicago Press, 1966), 17–18.
9. Donald Woodward, "Swords into Ploughshares: Recycling in Pre-Industrial England," *Economic History Review* 38 (1985): 175–91.
10. Woodward, "Swords into Ploughshares," 176.
11. The "waste not, want not" imperative was part of a larger Protestant ethos of thrift; on that question see Joshua J. Yates and James Davison Hunter, eds., *Thrift and Thriving in America: Capitalism and Moral Order from the Puritans to the Present* (Oxford: Oxford University Press, 2011).
12. Philosophers such as François Dagognet first paid attention to such notions as waste; see for instance François Dagognet, *Des détritus, des déchets, de l'abject: une philosophie écologique* (Paris: Empêcheurs de Penser en Rond, 1997). Sociologists have also contributed to our understanding of waste, or the related categories of rubbish or garbage. See in particular John Scanlan, *On Garbage* (London: Reaktion Books, 2005). Historians too, beside Susan Strasser herself, have become interested in waste as a notion; see for instance

Tim Cooper, "Modernity and the Politics of Waste in Britain," in *Nature's End: History and the Environment*, ed. Sverker Sörlin and Paul Warde (Basingstoke: Palgrave Macmillan, 2009), 247–72; "Recycling Modernity: Waste and Environmental History," *History Compass* 8, no. 9 (2010): 1114–24. "Waste studies" has even appeared as a specific field of academic enquiry to which various disciplines contribute, including literature specialists; see in particular Susan Signe Morrison, *Excrement in the Late Middle Ages: Sacred Filth and Chaucer's Fecopoetics* (New York: Palgrave MacMillan, 2008). More recently the trope of waste and leftovers in eighteenth-century literature has been studied in Sophie Gee, *Making Waste. Leftovers in the Eighteenth-Century Imagination* (Princeton and Oxford: Princeton University Press, 2010).

13. This is how Woodward understands and uses the term "recycling" in his article. The same goes for Margaret Ponsonby in her chapter "Recycled Homes"; see Margaret Ponsonby, *Stories from Home: English Domestic Interiors 1750–1850* (Farnham: Ashgate, 2007), 79–102.
14. Strasser, *Waste and Want*, 21.
15. See in particular the work of Neil McKendrick on Wedgwood: Neil McKendrick, "Josiah Wedgwood: An Eighteenth-Century Entrepreneur in Salesmanship and Marketing Techniques," *The Economic History Review* 12, no. 3 (April 1960): 408–33; "Josiah Wedgwood and Thomas Bentley: An Inventor-Entrepreneur Partnership in the Industrial Revolution," *Transactions of the Royal Historical Society*, fifth series, 14 (1964): 1–33; or "Josiah Wedgwood and the Commercialisation of the Potteries," in Neil McKendrick, John Brewer, and J.H. Plumb, *The Birth of a Consumer Society*, 100–45. More recently see also Maxine Berg, *Luxury and Pleasure in Eighteenth-Century Britain* (Oxford: Oxford University Press, 2005), 117–53.
16. Strasser, *Waste and Want*, 18; she quotes Irving Wohlfarth, "Et Cetera? The Historian as *Chiffonnier*," *New German Critique* 39 (1986): 151.
17. The editors would like to thank their research centres at the Université Paris-Diderot (LARCA) and Université de Picardie (CORPUS) for their support for this project.

Part I

The Circulation of Goods

1 The Social Circulation of Luxury and Second-Hand Goods in Eighteenth-Century Parisian Shops

Natacha Coquery

In this chapter, I will attempt to define the extent to which shopkeepers in eighteenth-century Parisian shops played an essential role in the flourishing second-hand and antique markets within the luxury and semi-luxury sectors. Paris was distinguished by the market in luxury goods and, more widely, by a new consumer culture characterized by the sale of semi-luxury goods. Indeed, selling both old and new goods, shopkeepers were key in influencing spending patterns in the eighteenth century. Bold expressions such as "consumer revolution," "consumer society," or even "mass production"[1] have sometimes been used to describe the changes that took place in the eighteenth century. Central to such changes was redistribution. Shops are therefore a good starting point from which to observe the social circulation of goods and to demonstrate the relationship between the circulation of goods, selling practices, and consumer culture. The aggressive strategies of manufacturers and shopkeepers brought about the birth of the semi-luxury market and ensured its success. They encouraged constant change through technical innovation, mechanisation, and the lowering of quality to allow for lower prices. The goods that resulted from this production—with silk blends instead of pure silk fabrics, earthenware instead of china, metal plating, and wood veneers—are described today as semi-luxury. Eagerness to follow fashion fuelled a culture of imitation, a central element in any attempt to define and explain the sale of luxury items to a mass market.[2] Thanks to their lower prices and varying styles, as was the case for printed calico, semi-luxury goods could fulfil the dreams of more and more consumers.[3]

In the eighteenth century, the French capital, like its British counterpart, experienced a surge in retail trade. This was brought about by several factors: the dominant position of home markets; an increase in international trade and preindustrial development; the drive for profit; the increases in demand due to demographic changes, and the increased wealth of a significant part of the population. The cultural prestige of French fashions—the famous "articles de Paris"—as well as innovations in marketing also played their part. A specific factor was the strong influence of the French royal court. The demand from the elite was highly influential. The excessive consumption of aristocratic households was wide-ranging—covering food, clothing, architecture and interior design, and equestrianism—thus illustrating the courtiers' need for luxury, which was in turn closely imitated by the wealthiest members of society.[4]

Directly linked to these trends was the increase in the number of specialised shops and the growing popularity of the commercial press. An analysis of probate inventories shows that an increasing number of products had become social necessities:[5] ceramics, tables and chests of drawers, combs and razors, Indian and Chinese clothes and wallpapers, and printed calicos. Objects that had previously been uncommon were now widespread: books, mirrors, pottery, watches, and in particular new utensils such as china dinner sets, snuffboxes, and boxes. These were intended for previously unknown usages related to the consumption of goods imported from the colonies: tea, coffee, chocolate, sugar, or tobacco. The urban middle classes increasingly contributed to the demand for Asian or American goods. Although they were still less numerous than traditional goods, luxury items like Flemish or Levantine tapestries, Venetian mirrors, glass from Bohemia, or Chinese silks were remarkably successful not only among the elite—their primary target market—but also among the middle class. Even the lower class began to take part in the market for colonial goods, as is the case with cotton, for instance.

The main agents of the transformation of consumer behaviour were the consumers themselves, the manufacturers, and urban shopkeepers. Alongside Wedgwood, who now appears as a case in point in the manipulation of demand,[6] a great variety of ordinary or unknown people—small retailers, peddlers, resellers, and stallholders—took part in spreading consumption whilst working within the traditional world of corporations. The works of Maxine Berg on metalworkers in Birmingham or of William Reddy on the French textile industry in Rouen, Lille, and Mulhouse, have convincingly downplayed the image of the heroic entrepreneur,[7] with Maxine Berg in particular detailing a "workshop-dominated economy." Moreover, as the retail sector toiled to achieve prosperity, it benefited from an added incentive—advertisement. Quality, variety, and novelty became the magic words of a budding advertising press at the turn of the seventeenth century. Its discourse played on the social and cultural significance of objects, specific manufacturers, and status.[8]

The jewellers and upholsterers epitomised both the semi-luxury and luxury markets, and were the symbol of a thriving Parisian commerce. Just as jewellers adorned bodies, upholsterers adorned houses. The Paris archives (*Archives de Paris*) contain a number of eighteenth-century account books from companies that had filed for bankruptcy. These account books reveal the crucial role that shopkeepers played in the circulation of goods.[9] They offer a glimpse into a lively market where new and fashionable, outmoded and second-hand goods found their way to an equally mixed clientele. Jewellers and upholsterers thrived on two complementary activities: they supplied new products to wealthy, demanding patrons while at the same time maintaining, repairing, and supplying second-hand and used goods at moderate costs to a larger and more common clientele. This twofold activity accounts for the main features of the retail sector: a wide choice of objects of varying qualities, a broad spectrum of prices, and a variety of customer types. By focusing on the trade practices of several Parisian luxury and semi-luxury shopkeepers, and in particular their use of second-hand retail and barter, the chapter will study the importance of recycling in the development of consumption in the eighteenth century and show the way the latter was characterized by overlapping practices that lent it a peculiar flexibility and adaptability.

SECOND-HAND GOODS AND THE CULTURE OF REPAIR

The second-hand market of the seventeenth and eighteenth centuries has already been well documented, notably through the activities of peddlers and the clothing trade.[10] Even though some early modern historians have used contemporary words such as "consumer society," "consumer boom," or "mass production" to describe eighteenth-century consumption culture, manufacturing remained mainly bespoke and showed few signs of real standardisation.[11] Admittedly fashion, embodied by its novelties, was a desirably visible characteristic; cheaper objects were more readily available, as were breakable ones, like china. However, there still existed precious, often unique, items that were not thrown away but kept, maintained, and exchanged. Different forms of ownership coexisted as well as multiple ways of buying and selling goods. Almanacs, and even more so account books, throw light on the reuse of objects and the versatility of commerce, which was simultaneously innovative and conservative. Like peddlers, second-hand dealers, and retailers, shopkeepers were involved in the vast second-hand market. They supplied the latest novelties, but at the same time they repaired, reprocessed, and recycled to lengthen the serviceable life of an item, to refresh an old-fashioned article, or to bring it back to current tastes.

A large part of the activities of Mathurin Law, a tapestry-maker in Saint-Honoré street, near Saint-Germain-l'Auxerrois (faubourg Saint-Honoré),[12] were dedicated to mending furniture, maintaining, reorganising, or renewing interiors, his accounts evidencing many such interventions with descriptions such as: "have repaired," "redone," "made solid," "polished anew," "plated anew," "brightened," "coloured," "whitened," "sawn again," "covered," "trimmed anew," "replaced," "undone," "removed the gilt," "dismantled," "loosened."[13] Law also rented out beds, sitting-room furniture, folding screens, chandeliers by the month, the year, or for a single evening. As for the jeweller Nicolas Aubourg,[14] in Mazarine street, at the crossing of Guénégaud street (faubourg Saint-Germain), he "repaired"[15] or "had [someone] repair watches, boxes, rings, swords" and his accounts demonstrate that he routinely "reassembles,"[16] "has reassembled," "has remade," "puts together," "cleans," "redoes," "changes," "puts back to new" the objects he was entrusted with. Shopkeepers sold articles from "previous seasons" or "second-hand"[17] as well as brand-new objects—meeting the needs of two very different types of customers was quite common.

Advertisements in almanacs confirm the importance of the repair work of shopkeepers, particularly in the clothing sector:

The purse-maker Néant "makes and sells all kinds of new purses, exchanges and mends old ones."[18] The haberdasher Bonnein "sells, buys and barters all sorts of goods [. . .]. He takes back old Braids, Pearls and Diamonds, and undertakes any sort of such mending."[19] But not all transactions were conducted by the means of financial tokens. In the world of second-hand trade, objects could be bartered and exchanged.

BARTER, OR THE ORIGIN OF THE SECOND-HAND MARKET

In the sixteenth century as well as at the end of the eighteenth, as Jean Meuvret has shown in his studies on monetary circulation,[20] goods could be used as means of payment or as a pledge for credit. The shopkeeper agreed to receive part of the payment through barter. Let us, for example, examine Aubourg's accounts: which objects did he buy? The usual goods a jeweller would acquire included chains, watches, canes, rings, bracelets, buttons, buckles, cases, boxes, and strings. Yet, the frequency of depreciating qualifiers such as "old," "worn," "second-hand," "bad," and "weak"[21] is striking. Aubourg, for instance, bought a ring with a "poor diamond," a "poor chain," a "poor yellow diamond," "rings of little value," a "broken agate ring and golden box," "very low quality canes and watches," an "old keepsake trimmed with gold," an "old key," an "old clock," "old silverware," "bracelet charms in poor condition or of low quality," "bracelet charms of poor gold," a "green ring circled with poor stones," or a "bad sapphire."[22] The shopkeeper bought many worn-out or even damaged objects. The people who sold him such low-quality wares have remained anonymous for lack of information, but we know, thanks to the registers, that they were largely professionals, mostly courtiers, or private individuals in need of cash (a marchioness, a knight, an abbot, an officer in the musketeers, a furrier, two haberdashers, a surgeon-obstetrician). However, the need for cash did not explain it all. In fact, most payments comprised a mixture of money, bills, and barter.

Aubourg thus kept in a memorandum book of what was owed to him:

> downpayment 144 and a big plain watch in Geneva gold 96;
>
> taken back in barter a watch in Geneva gold 120;
>
> having received 9 in money and 9 in old buckle;
>
> taken in barter a ring of rose; a pair of golden bracelets 192, I took back the old ones 62;

took back for 55 of old amber; pair of silver buckles 28, took back his 9; I took a pair of needles for 50 livres.[23]

Law similarly resorted to barter according to his account book:

money 288 and a chest of drawers for the value of 192;

on account of stationery 60, a piece of mirror 10;

settled by 78 pounds the surplus with an old toilet case;

entry on account two new style fireplace implements [. . .] 21;

credit [. . .] in five old armchairs covered with poor tapestry;

on account cash 96, a mahogany music stand 24;

entry on account 2718 pounds [. . .] three money orders to my order [. . .], in cash 21, ten new pieces of tapestry and 11 off-cuts 259, deduction on the total supplied 38.[24]

This practice generally endured; the dictionaries of the time did define the word "barter" as "an exchange without money."[25] This contains no deprecatory innuendo, but rather a faithful description of the varieties of practices meant by the word. This custom notably involved the aristocracy, who were major consumers and hence suppliers of luxury objects. Several aristocrats could be found among the jeweller's customers who practised bartering, such as Sir Dorat, Count Strogonoff, the marquis de Tonnerre; and several knights, countesses, and marchionesses were numbered among Law's customers.[26] Noblemen, always looking for the latest goods, considered barter as a payment method and also as a way of getting rid of an old, outdated, or mediocre item—one which was simply not wanted anymore. It was an easy way to exchange old for new without spending any money.[27] For shopkeepers, it was a handy way of renewing stock and widening clientele. Hence bartering led to a wide-scale redistribution of items, which the almanac advertisements confirm: according to his ad, the tapestry-maker Languineux "makes, sells, rents, barters, buys and runs a shop which supplies all kinds of furniture, new as well as second-hand";[28] while the bookseller Gibert says he "keeps a store of second-hand books."[29] An almanac for 1776 similarly lists the widow Caudron, a hatter, who "keeps a store of second-hand hats, plain and trimmed"[30] and the haberdasher Biberon who "sells, barters, buys all kinds of jewels, china."[31]

Yet the term "second-hand" did not mean that the objects sold were of low quality or without worth, but that they were bought by less wealthy people, especially for tapestry and jewellery. Aubourg for instance sold earrings of "poor rose" (rose-cut diamonds) for 450 pounds. Conversely, novelty did not necessarily imply scarcity, high prices, and social elites. Old and new goods were mixed: dealers in luxury goods associated second-hand goods with the attractive characteristics of curiosity, quality, and fashion as well. And, as Ilja Van Damme shows in chapter 3 of this volume, the antique began to acquire value in the eighteenth century.

An advertisement for Dessenis, a fashion accessory dealer, claimed that the latter "stocks the most fashionable laces, muslins and second-hand goods at the right price"[32] while the shop of M. Delpeche, a Parisian earthenware dealer, was presented as "a shop with a large assortment of dishes, plates and vases of old china from Saxony and Japan, and other items in ormolu gilt-bronze, rare, valuable and varied kinds of second-hand goods, at Mr. Delpeche's."[33]

The aristocracy did not look down on expensive curiosities supplied by second-hand dealers: the duke of La Trémouille bought an ormolu gilt clock for 396 livres from Cresson, who "runs a shop selling second-hand goods."[34] Blurring the boundary between new and old, between second-hand and luxury, the trade of curiosities became a market where collectors, among other middlemen, acted as suppliers to second-hand dealers but also to art dealers such as Gersaint, Lazare Duvaux, Poirier, and Daguerre.[35] Between collectors and shopkeepers, barter remained the usual means of conducting business. Furetière writes: "The *connoisseurs* sell their jewels and paintings less often with money than with barter."[36] Savary des Bruslons uses the verb *brocanter* (to deal in second-hand goods) for the exchange of curios between Parisian collectors, painters, and haberdashers: "This word, almost only used in Paris, and mainly with amateurs and painters or among a few haberdashers, means to buy, to sell on or to barter paintings, cabinets, desks, bronze, marble table and figures, earthenware, clocks, tapestries, folding screens and other such goods, furniture or curios."[37] At the end of the eighteenth century, the development of the market for curios impacted on the prices in two ways. The "old" was "now worthless"[38] but the "antique" "which has been around for a long time or which dates from long ago,"[39] whether fake or real, gained in value.[40] The variety in quality affected all objects, all materials. Prices alone could not be relied on to know whether the goods were new or second-hand, since older goods could turn out to be more expensive than new ones, as the following examples illustrate:

> Dressing-table mirror 3, second-hand dressing-table mirror 21;
>
> Walnut dressing table 22, second-hand walnut dressing table 28;
>
> Pair of two-pointed coloured bronze candelabra 23, pair of second-hand two-pointed gilt-bronze ormolu 54.[41]

Therefore barter was a specific form of redistribution based on aristocratic over-consumption, which fuelled the market for luxury and semi-luxury goods. In Paris it allowed the less wealthy to follow fashion trends. As a consequence new styles started to spread, and soon become outdated.

BLURRING MARKETS, BLURRING CATEGORIES

As Fernand Braudel reminds us, "there is no simple linear history of the development of markets. In this area, the traditional, the archaic and the modern or ultra-modern exist side by side, even today."[42] These practices emphasised the flexibility of the market and stressed the attention paid to consumers by entrepreneurs.[43] The exchange of new and old goods stimulated production and distribution thanks to shopkeepers and craftsmen who agreed to receive payment in the form of used goods. The process combined an old tradition with a new practice: payment in kind widened the choice and selection of goods while allowing a larger number of people to participate in the market. Bartering developed new ways of acquiring goods and supported the spread of popular fashions, so much so that, as will be shown in detail by the third chapter of the present volume, the demand for second-hand products became as important a market as that for the latest goods.[44] The phenomenon of the growth of the second-hand market was also linked to the widespread theft of clothes and subsequent resale of stolen property.[45] However, the coexistence of new and old goods caused tensions in the marketplace. If one considers the existing networks and methods of supply among corporations, the frontier between "second-hand" or "used" and "old" goods was far from easy to define. On one side stood the seven hundred Parisian second-hand dealers (*fripiers*) who owned the right to trade second-hand and used goods and were allowed only a small part of the new goods market; on the other, a much larger number of shopkeepers and craftsmen, tailors, haberdashers, tapestry-makers, and cabinet makers who competed with the first group of dealers by supplying both new and old merchandise. The tensions between *fripiers* and shopkeepers give rise to several questions: the part played by each side in sales and auctions, and the confrontation between these two kinds of dealers as they both compete to conquer the essentially ambivalent market of second-hand goods.

Fusing second-hand clothes dealers and tailors into a single community in 1776 seemed to solve part of the problem. It brought a century-long rivalry to an end and abolished the legal boundary between new and used goods. From then on, second-hand dealers and resellers were banned from selling new goods.[46] But within the shop itself, there was an intricate balance between various qualities and categories of goods, especially when there was a tendency for the old to quickly lose its value, linked as it was to the swift changes in fashion and the accelerated obsolescence of objects.

The active presence of shopkeepers in the second-hand market and in the recycling of luxury goods relied on the long-established and widely shared practices of resale and barter. However, these practices had unforeseen consequences. They concerned a leading market sector, characterized by an aristocratic clientele and objects of high material and/or symbolic value—jewels, silverware, furniture, trinkets. Therefore, ancient and even archaic practices contributed to the expansion of a new market, that of semi-luxury goods, without which one cannot understand the birth of consumption. With "refined" and "fake," "new" and "old," traders could offer goods of various qualities to attract customers. This large offer was matched by varied and flexible commercial practices—refashioning, bartering, reselling, offering credit—thus merging the marks of archaism, tradition, and modernity. Thanks to the great diversity of their products, shopkeepers were ready for an unprecedented expansion of their market. This evolution contributed to a blurring of economic boundaries, between new and second-hand markets, as well as social boundaries, between the wealthy and the more modest. As Daniel Roche observed in his study of the clothing sector, flexibility was a constant feature of markets and practices, from shops to street peddling.[47] The account books of a tapestry-maker and a fashion jeweller illustrate this very feature. Thanks to Aubourg and to Law, pieces of furniture, jewels, and charms passed from hand to hand, and contributed as much as the clothing industry to the changes in consumer behaviour. The Parisian stars of luxury and semi-luxury markets such as Gersaint, Lazare Duvaux, Hébert, Poirier et Daguerre, Granchez, Julliet, or Hennebert have been swiftly replaced by numerous shopkeepers. Although less well known, less powerful and less talented, these shopkeepers have largely contributed to the development of new consumption patterns and networks. These account books perfectly reflect the interaction between the offer of quality goods and the demand of consumers and show how the old equation linking novelty and upper class, second-hand and lower class was abolished in eighteenth-century Parisian shops.

NOTES

1. The author would like to thank Marie-Agnes Dequidt and Helena Taylor for the translation.
   Joan Thirsk, *Economic Policy and Projects. The Development of a Consumer Society in Early Modern England* (Oxford: Oxford University Press, 1978); Neil McKendrick, John Brewer, and J.H. Plumb, *The Birth of a Consumer Society. The Commercialization of Eighteenth-Century England* (London: Europa Publications Limited, 1982).
2. John Styles, "Clothing the North: The Supply of Non-élite Clothing in the Eighteenth-Century North of England," *Textile History* 25, no. 2 (1994): 139–66; John Styles, "Custom or Consumption? Plebeian Fashion in Eighteenth-Century England," in *Luxury in the Eighteenth Century. Debates, Desires and Delectable Goods*, ed. Maxine Berg and Elizabeth Eger (Basingstoke: Palgrave Macmillan, 2003), 103–15; Cissie Fairchilds, "The Production and Marketing of Popular Goods in Eighteenth-Century Paris," in *Consumption and the World of Goods*, ed. John Brewer and Roy Porter (London & New York: Routledge, 1993), 228–48.
3. Ben Fine and Ellen Leopol, "Consumerism and the Industrial Revolution," *Social History* 15, no. 2 (May 1990): 155. According to Maxine Berg, the middle classes did not buy semi-luxury items because of their lesser price but because they were "fashion leaders," see Maxine Berg, *Luxury and Pleasure in Eighteenth-Century Britain.* (Oxford: Oxford University Press, 2005), 6.

4. Natacha Coquery, *L'Hôtel aristocratique. Le marché du luxe à Paris au XVIIIe siècle* (Paris: Publications de la Sorbonne, 1998).
5. Daniel Roche, *The People of Paris. An Essay in Popular Culture in the Eighteenth Century* (Berkeley and Los Angeles: University of California Press, 1987); Annie Pardailhé-Galabrun, *La naissance de l'intime* (Paris: Presses Universitaires de France, 1988).
6. The manufacturer has been celebrated by Neil McKendrick in "Josiah Wedgwood: An Eighteenth-Century Entrepreneur in Salesmanship and Marketing Techniques," *The Economic History Review* XII, no. 3 (April 1960): 408–33, and "Josiah Wedgwood and the Commercialisation of the Potteries," in Neil McKendrick, John Brewer & J. H. Plumb, *The Birth of a Consumer Society*, 100–45.
7. William M. Reddy, *The Rise of Market Culture. The Textile Trade and the French Society, 1750–1900* (Cambridge: Cambridge University Press, 1984), 20. See part one: "A World Without Entrepreneurs, 1750–1815." Maxine Berg, *The Age of Manufactures, 1700–1820. Industry, Innovation and Work in Britain* (London: Routledge, 1994), particularly chapter 12: "The Metal and Hardware Trades," 253–79. See also, by the same author, "New Commodities, Luxuries and their Consumers in Eighteenth-Century England," in *Consumers and Luxury. Consumer Culture in Europe 1650–1850*, ed. Maxine Berg and Helen Clifford (Manchester: Manchester University Press, 1999), 63–85.
8. Robin B. Walker, "Advertising in London Newspapers, 1650-–1750," *Business History* 15, no. 1 (January 1973): 112–30; Clement Wischermann and Shore Elliott, eds., *Advertising and the European City. Historical Perspectives* (Aldershot: Ashgate, 2000).
9. The upholsterer Law and the jeweller Aubourg went bankrupt in the 1780s. Aubourg's account books deal with the years 1773 to 1783 (Paris Archives, D5B6 1290, D5B6 1669, D5B6 1760, D5B6 2151) whereas Law's cover the years 1782 to 1787 (D5B6 1024, 3066, 3451, 3209).
10. Beverly Lemire, "Developing Consumerism and the Ready-Made Clothing Trade in Britain, 1750–1800," *Textile History* 15, no. 1 (1984): 21–44; Lemire, *Fashion's Favourite: The Cotton Trade and the Consumer in Britain 1660–1800* (Oxford: Oxford University Press, 1991); Lemire, "Peddling Fashion: Salesmen, Pawnbrokers, Taylors, Thieves and the Second-Hand Clothes Trade in England, c.1700–1800," *Textile History* 22, no. 1 (1991): 67–82; Lemire, "Consumerism in Pre-Industrial and Early Industrial England: The Trade in Second-Hand Clothes," *Journal of British Studies* 27 (January 1988): 1–24; Lemire, "Second-Hand Beaux and 'Red-armed Belles:' Conflict and the Creation of Fashions in England, c.1660–1800," *Continuity and Change* 15 (2000): 391–417; Laurence Fontaine, "Le colportage et la diffusion des 'galanteries' et 'nouveautés,"' in *Échanges et cultures textiles dans l'Europe pré-industrielle. Actes du colloque de Rouen, 17–19 mai 1993*, ed. Jacques Bottin and Nicole Pellegrin, special issue, *Revue du Nord* 12 (1996): 91–109; Laurence Fontaine, ed., *Alternative Exchanges: Second-Hand Circulations from the Sixteenth Century to the Present* (Oxford: Longham, 2008); Patricia Allerston, "The Market in Second-Hand Clothes and Furnishings in Venice, c.1500–c.1650," PhD diss. (Florence: European University Institute, 1996); Patricia Allerston, "Reconstructing the Second-Hand Clothes Trade in Sixteenth- and Seventeenth-Century Venice," *Costume* 33 (1999): 4–56; Patricia Allerston, "Clothing and Early Modern Venetian Society," *Continuity and Change* 15, no. 3 (2000): 367–90.
11. Patrick Verley, *L'Echelle du monde. Essai sur l'industrialisation de l'Occident* (Paris: Gallimard, 1997).

12. Mathurin Law was declared bankrupt in 1788. His sales books and bankruptcy petition are kept at the Paris Archives. The sales books run from 1782 to 1787 (D5B6 1024, 3066, 3451, 3209). This shopkeeper enjoyed a rather comfortable situation: his revenue comes close to 100,000 livres. When he went bankrupt, he had a credit of 22,000 livres and a debit of 74,393 livres.
13. "Avoir réparé," "raccommodé," "refait," "rendu solide," "repoli," "replaqué à neuf," "avivé," "mis en couleur," "blanchi," "recousu," "recouvert," "regarni," "remplacé," "défait," "dédoré," "démonté," "détendu" (Law, Paris Archives, D5B6 1024, 3066, 3451, 3209). See Natacha Coquery, "Fashion, Business, Diffusion: An Upholsterer's Shop in Eighteenth-Century Paris," in *Furnishing the Eighteenth Century: What Furniture Can Tell Us about the European and American Past,* ed. Dena Goodman and Kathryn Norberg (London and New York: Routledge, 2006), 63–77.
14. Aubourg's ledgers run from 1773 to 1783 (Paris Archives, D5B6 1290, D5B6 1669, D5B6 1760, D5B6 2151).
15. "Raccommode," "fait accommoder" (Aubourg, Paris Archives, D5B6 1290, 1669).
16. "Remonte," "fait remonter," "fait refaire," "fait mettre," "nettoie," "refait," "change," "remet à neuf," idem.
17. "À la dernière mode" or "de hazard."
18. Néant "fait et vend toutes sortes de bourses neuves, échange et raccommode les vieilles" (*Almanach du Dauphin, ou Tableau du vrai mérite des artistes célebres, et d'indication générale des principaux Marchands Négocians, Artistes et Fabricans des Six Corps Arts et Métiers de la Ville et Fauxbourgs de Paris et autres Villes du Royaume* [Paris: Dumas, 1776]).
19. "Vend, achete et troque toutes sortes de Marchandises [. . .]. Il reprend les vieux Galons, Perles et Diamants, et entreprend toutes sortes de raccommodages en ce genre" (M. Thomas, *Almanach des marchands, négocians et commerçans de la France et du reste de l'Europe* [Paris: Valade, 1770]).
20. Jean Meuvret, "Circulation monétaire et utilisation économique de la monnaie dans la France du XVIe et du XVIIe siècles," *Études d'histoire économique. Recueil d'articles, Cahier des Annales* 32 (Paris: Armand Colin, 1971): 127–38.
21. "Vieux," "usé," "hasard," "mauvais," "faible" (Paris Archives, Aubourg's ledgers).
22. "Bague de mauvais brillant," "chaîne mauvaise," "mauvais brillants jaunes," "bagues de peu de valeur," "bague d'agathe et boîte d'or cassées," "cannes et montres très faibles," "vieux souvenir garni en or," "vieille clé," "vieille pendule," "vieille argenterie," "breloques en mauvais état" or "mauvaises," "breloques de mauvais or," "bague verte entourée de pierres faibles," "mauvais saphir" (Paris Archives, Aubourg's ledgers).
23. Acompte 144 et une grosse montre d'or de Genève unie 96; repris en troc une montre d'or de Genève 120; ayant reçu 9 d'argent et 9 en vieille boucle; pris en trocq une bague de rose; une paire de bracelet d'or 192, jai repris les vieux 62; j'ai repris pour 55 de vieux ambre; paire de boucles d'argent 28, repris les siennes 9; j'ai pris une paire d'aiguilles pour 50 livres.

    (Extract from Aubourg's account book "livre de ce qu'on nous doit" [D5B6 2151])

    The currency is the livre.
24. En argent 288 et une commode [. . .] pour la valeur de 192; en à compte sur les fournitures 60, un morceau de glace 10; soldé par 78 livres en argent le surplus par un vieux nécessaire; avoir en à compte deux feux à la moderne

[. . .] 21; avoir [. . .] en cinq anciens fauteuils couverts de mauvaise tapisserie; avoir [. . .] par argent 96, un pupitre en musique de bois d'acajou 24; avoir de 2 718 livres [. . .] trois mandats à mon ordre [. . .], en espèces 21, dix neuf pièces de tapisserie et onze morceaux 259, déduction sur la totalité de fourniture 38.

(Law's sales book [D5B6 3066 et 3451])

The currency is the livre.

25. Exchange of one thing for another. A shopkeeper says that he bartered a good for another to mean that he did not give money, that only goods were exchanged to and fro. (Echange d'une chose contre une autre. Un Marchand dit qu'il a troqué une marchandise contre une autre, pour dire qu'il n'a point déboursé d'argent, qu'il ne s'est donné que des marchandises de part et d'autre.)

(Jacques Savary des Bruslons, *Dictionnaire universel de commerce* [Paris: Veuve Estienne, 1741], art. "Troc," vol. 3, col. 513–14)

26. Extract from Aubourg's account book "livre de ce qu'on nous doit" (D5B6 2151).
27. Barthouilh pays part of his purchases in goods:

inkwells and copper hourglasses 12, rosewood backgammon, with price of 21, old three-arms fireplace implements with shovel and tongs valued 12, desk 48; tow golden pairs of chandelier 150 each, both 300. (encriés et sabliés de cuivre 12, trictrac en bois de palisante, du prix de 21, vieux feu à trois branches en fer, estimé avec pelle et pincette [. . .] 12, un bureau 48, deux paires de flambeaux tige à poire surdorés à 150, la paire 300.)

So does the comte de Coucy:

cane commode with its earthenware pot 18, writing desk marble set in cupboard [. . .] with a trestle bed [. . .] 14, plated cupboard valued 120, little rocaille fireplace implement and golden copper 24, walnut chest of drawers and plated chiffonier valued 105. (chaise percée garnie en canne et de son pot-à-œil de fayence 18, marbre de secrétaire en armoire [. . .], avec un lit de sangle [. . .] 14, armoire [. . .] de bois de plaquage, estimée 120, petit feu à rocailles et chevaux de cuivre doré d'or de feuille 24, commode en noyer et une chiffonnière de plaquage, estimées 105.)

(Extracts form Law's account books)

The currency is the livre. The jeweller's customers perform similar exchanges.

28. "Fait, vend, loue, troque, achete et tient Magasin de toutes sortes de Meubles, tant neufs que de rencontre" (M. Thomas, *Almanach des marchands* [Paris: Valade, 1770]).
29. "Tient Magasin de Livres de hazard" (*Essai sur l'Almanach général d'indication d'adresse personnelle et fixe, des Six Corps, Arts et Métiers* [Paris: Veuve Duchesne, 1769]).
30. "Tient magazin de chapeaux d'hazard, unis et bordés" (*Almanach du Dauphin* [Paris, 1776]).
31. "Vend, troque, achete toutes sortes de bijoux, porcelaine" (*Almanach du Dauphin* [Paris, 1776]).
32. "Tient Dentelles, Mousselines et Marchandises d'occasion des plus à la mode, et à juste prix" (Paris Archives, "fonds privés départementaux" D 43 Z/1, "Publicité commerciale, 1680–1822," vol. 1).
33. "Magasin et assortiment considérable de plats, assiettes et vases d'ancienne porcelaine de Saxe, du Japon et autres effets en bronze dorés d'or moulu,

rares, curieux et précieux en différens genres de hazard, chez le sieur Delpeche [faïencier]" (*Almanach du Dauphin* [Paris, 1777]).

34. The shop is located on rue de Viarmes, "the new market" ("à la nouvelle halle") (French National Archives T 1051/42).
35. Guillaume Glorieux, *À l'Enseigne de Gersaint. Edme-François Gersaint, marchand d'art sur le pont Notre-Dame (1694–1750)* (Paris, Seyssel: Champ Vallon, 2002), 299–300. About the art market, together with the work of Glorieux and of Carolyn Sargentson's *Merchants and Luxury Markets: The Marchands Merciers of Eighteenth-Century Paris* (London: V&A Museum, 1996), see Pierre Verlet, "Le commerce des objets d'arts et les marchands-merciers à Paris au XVIIIe siècle," *Annales ESC* 1 (January–March 1958): 10–29; Krystof Pomian, *Collectionneurs, amateurs et curieux. Paris, Venise: XVIe–XVIIIe siècle* (Paris: Gallimard, 1987); Antoine Schnapper, *Le géant, la licorne, la tulipe. Collections françaises au XVIIe siècle* (Paris: Flammarion, 1988); Charlotte Guichard, *Les amateurs d'art à Paris au XVIIIe siècle* (Paris, Seyssel: Champ Vallon, 2008); Ann Bermingham and John Brewer, eds., *The Consumption of Culture 1600–1800* (London: Routledge, 1995); Michael North and David Ormrod, eds., *Art Markets in Europe, 1400–1800* (Aldershot: Ashgate, 1998).
36. "Les curieux font le commerce de leurs bijoux et tableaux moins en argent, qu'en troc" (A. Furetière, *Dictionnaire universel contenant tous les mots français tant vieux que modernes et les termes de toutes les sciences et des arts* [1690] [Paris: SNL-Le Robert, 1978]).
37. Ce terme, qui n'est gueres en usage que dans Paris, et particulièrement chez les Curieux et les Peintres, ou parmi quelques Marchands Merciers, signifie, acheter, revendre, ou troquer des tableaux, des cabinets, des bureaux, des bronzes, des tables et figures de marbre, des porcelaines, des pendules, des tapisseries, des paravens, et autres semblables marchandises, meubles, ou curiosités.

    (Savary des Bruslons, *Dictionnaire universel de commerce*, art. "brocanter," vol. 1, col. 1118)

38. "Ne vaut plus rien" (Furetière, *Dictionnaire universel*).
39. "Qui est depuis long-temps, ou qui a été autrefois" (Furetière, *Dictionnaire universel*).
40. Michael Vickers, "Value and Simplicity: Eighteenth-Century Taste and the Study of Greek Vases," *Past & Present* 116 (August 1987): 98–137.
41. "Miroir de toilette 3, miroir de toilette d'hasard 21," "toilette de bois de noyer 22, toilette d'hazard en bois de noyer 28," "paire de bras à deux branches cuivre en couleur 23, paire de bras d'hazard à deux branches de cuivre d'orrés d'or moulüe 54" (Extracts from the account books of Law and Aubourg).
42. Fernand Braudel, *Civilisation and Capitalism 15th–18th Century, Vol. II: The Wheels of Fortune*, trans. S. Reynolds (London: Fontana, 1982), 26.
43. Lemire, "Peddling Fashion," 67–68.
44. Lemire, "Peddling Fashion," 67–76; "countless numbers of British men and women usually quenched their needs and desires by buying worn goods" (Lemire, "Consumerism in Preindustrial and Early Industrial England," 2).
45. Daniel Roche, *The Culture of Clothing, Dress and Fashion in the 'Ancien Régime'* (Cambridge: Cambridge University Press, 1994), 330–63; Lemire, "Peddling Fashion," 78–79 and "The Theft of Clothes and Popular Consumerism in Early Modern England," *Journal of Social History* 24 (Winter 1990): 255–76.
46. Roche, *The Culture of Clothing*, 349, sqq.
47. Roche, *The Culture of Clothing*, 332.

2 Luxury and Country House Sales in England, c. 1760–1830

Jon Stobart

The English country house is often seen as a key site for the consumption of luxury goods: a place where no expense was spared to make a very public statement of the wealth, taste, and connoisseurship of the owner.[1] Today, the resulting material culture of the country house often seems permanent—a priceless collection uniquely associated with a particular place; yet the eighteenth-century reality of country houses was very different, with the nature and arrangement of furniture, paintings, books, tableware, and so on being in constant flux. New goods came into the house as fashion or fortune dictated, whilst others were removed to less public rooms, put into storage, or disposed of altogether. One key mechanism by which luxury goods, amongst others, left the country house was via public auctions, which normally took place at the house itself.[2] This draws the country house firmly into wider processes and debates concerning the recycling of goods and the second-hand trade. These are often seen as being associated with poverty and supply-side inadequacies: goods were recycled amongst needy citizens or down-cycled from wealthier to poorer sections of society.[3] However, there is plenty of evidence that recycling formed an important activity within prosperous and even elite households: clothes were mended, curtains were adjusted for hanging in other rooms, and garments were taken apart to make bags or line drawers. Indeed, such practices were seen as central to thrifty housewifery and "good Christian stewardship" which had long been central to notions of good housekeeping.[4] Other items were bequeathed or gifted to friends or family members and were thus recycled between generations and households. Many wealthier households also engaged in commercial recycling, actively seeking out second-hand goods, especially at the house sales of their departed neighbours and peers. At these events, they bought a wide range of useful and durable goods with which to furnish their own homes and, in the process, enjoyed the occasion and drama of the auction itself.[5]

The country house sale brought together buyer, seller, and a wide variety of goods. For the seller, the contents of their house were an important asset which could be realised to meet debts or finance redevelopment or refurbishment of the property.[6] For the buyer, they represented an opportunity to acquire a range of luxury goods. The motivations underpinning such processes of acquisition were complex.[7] The widening attraction and accessibility of luxury consumption was already a social phenomenon in the sixteenth century when Harrison noted that it had spread "even unto the inferior artificers and many farmers" who had "learnt also to garnish their cupboards with plate, their joint beds with tapestry and silk hangings, and their tables with carpets and fine napery."[8] Acquiring such goods second-hand opened up the world of luxury consumption to a section of the population unable to afford them new; but it also gave other, wealthier consumers the chance to "capture value" by buying luxury goods at a discounted price; to "capture difference" through the ownership of unusual items, or more arguably to "share in another's 'genuine' world" by buying personal or unusual items.[9]

In this chapter, I will explore the recycling of luxury goods through sales at a range of country houses in the English county of Northamptonshire. These include the residences of fourteen gentlemen or esquires, three titled aristocrats (including a notable local magnate: the Earl of Halifax), and two women and five other men whom we only know by name. The sales were therefore predominantly of goods from substantial country houses, rather than aristocratic palaces. They were not national events of the kind that took place in 1801 and 1822 when the fabulously wealthy William Beckford sold off a huge variety of luxury goods to fund the construction of Fonthill Abbey and subsequently to help clear some of his debts.[10] Beyond advertisements, there was little interest in the local or national press and they were usually organised by local auctioneers, rather than notable London figures such as Christie or Phillips. As a consequence, the material at our disposal is primarily comprised of the sale catalogues, produced and distributed by the auctioneers in advance of the sale. These include long lists and sometimes detailed descriptions of the items being offered for sale, but of course tell us nothing about the people who purchased these goods or the uses to which they subsequently put them. My analysis therefore centres on the nature of the luxury goods being offered for sale and the ways in which these fitted into broader frameworks of (second-hand) consumption. In particular, I want to explore the underpinning attraction of buying luxury goods second-hand and ultimately to assess the extent to which we can see luxury as a category which transcends distinctions between new and used.

LUXURY GOODS: CAPTURING VALUE

Even a cursory glance through the catalogues shows that these sales offered a wide variety of luxury goods. These ranged from the turret clock listed in the 1772 sale at Kirby Hall, the harpsichords by Tabal and Goodfellow being sold at Rolleston Hall in 1801, to the high-quality furniture and wines which could be bid for at Wollaston Hall in 1805.[11] Alongside such luxuries were myriad mundane items, including deal furniture, cooking pots and saucepans, carpenters' benches, and chicken coops. In between were objects that might be termed decencies: tea urns and coffee pots, wainscot furniture, feather beds, and carpets. Drawing a line between luxury, decency, and necessity is highly problematic, not least since the quality as well as the type of goods was important. However, to make some sense of the huge variety of items appearing in the catalogues, some kind of classification is needed. An indication of the types of things that might be thought of as luxury can be drawn from contemporary commentators whose accounts suggest both continuity and change. In 1587, Harrison identified tapestries, silverware, fine linen, and Turkey work as elite luxuries; a hundred and forty years later, Lady Strafford, writing to her husband about the aristocratic houses she visited as part of the social round, made particular mention the sconces, pier glasses, and silver tableware; whilst Vickery suggests that many of her male contemporaries focused their spending on coaches, horses, and wine cellars.[12] More generally, there was a transition from pewter to porcelain, turkey work to mahogany, and (to an extent) tapestry to damask wall hangings.[13] Something of this increasing diversity is captured in an incident in Burney's *Cecilia*. When Miss Larolles plans to go to the sale at Lord Belgrade's house, Cecilia asks her what will be sold there. Her reply tells us much about the nature of desirable luxuries: "O every thing you can conceive; house, stables, china, laces, horses, caps, every thing in the world."[14]

Taking these as starting points, it is possible to identify a wide variety of luxury goods in the catalogues, although the range and type available at particular auctions varied considerably. The sales at Brixworth Hall, Wollaston Hall, and Welton Place offered consumers the opportunity to acquire fourteen kinds of luxury goods, whilst those visiting the auctions at Pychley Hall, Kirby Hall, and Rushton Hall would have found only two or three types of luxuries were available. This kind of variation is not very surprising since country houses differed considerably in their size and character, and sales varied from complete house clearances (as appears to have been the case at Stanford Hall) to selective sales of high-quality goods (Barton Hall) or everyday items from bed chambers and service wings (Kirby Hall). Especially prominent were goods which could be everyday household items, but were defined as luxuries by their price or the complexity of their acquisition.[15] They included furniture, glass and chinaware, mirrors, curtains, and clocks, and were distinguished in one of three ways. First were goods differentiated by the richness of their raw materials. For example, the drawing room curtains sold on the second day of the Barton Hall sale were made of "rich crimson silk damask [. . .] lined, with tassels and fringe," whilst the three-by-five-foot pier glass from the dining room in Rolleston Hall was set in "strong frame, richly carved with elegant top ornaments gilt in burnished gold."[16] Here it was the cost of the materials that came to the fore: the silk, gold leaf, and silver burnishing. A second set of luxury goods stood out because of their exotic or cosmopolitan nature—the cultural capital represented in such goods being heightened by a layering of their costliness, the contacts required to obtain them, and their cultural associations.[17] The Sevres porcelain dessert service and "tea and coffee equipage" offered on day two of the Stanford Hall sale would only have been available through a handful of London tradesmen or, more likely, via contacts in France. Equally, the Indian china vases, scent jars, and glass cases sold at Sudborough House in 1836 were clearly seen as rare pieces, to be valued for their provenance—a quality which distinguished them from locally produced and more readily available pieces.[18] A third set of goods were luxurious because of the intricate nature of their manufacture. Design and craftsmanship was becoming increasingly important through the eighteenth century, particularly in items such as furniture, silverware, and porcelain.[19] The intricacy of design and manufacture was communicated through detailed descriptions of the goods. At the Rolleston Hall sale, for example, Lot 252 in the Best Chamber was a "mahogany case of four large, and two small compress drawers; the upper part, with folding doors, encloses a valuable ebony cabinet, *the fronts of the drawers of which are* most delicately pencilled *with the history of the journeying the Israelites in the Wilderness, and a great number of exquisite miniature figures.*"[20] Whilst extreme, this level of detail was by no means unusual, especially for elaborate furniture or when a complex design was coupled with exotic materials—effectively rolling into one all three of these dimensions of luxury. Several marble tables—luxury goods by any standard—were offered for sale in 1772 following the death of the Earl of Halifax. The stone itself was invariably described rather nonchalantly as a "marble slab," but its dimensions were precisely noted and the "frame" carefully described, one typical example in the drawing room being set on a "rich carv'd frame, gilt and burnished."[21]

Such luxuries were not, of course, being bought second-hand from financial necessity, but it is apparent that cost and practicality were important considerations. It is difficult to compare prices exactly, but what appear to be reserve prices marked in the catalogue of the 1761 Cottingham sale suggest that curtains and upholstered items were perhaps one fifth the price they would be new. Two pairs of damask window curtains and rods had a reserve of just £1 and ten walnut chairs, upholstered in "rich brocade," were £2 15s. Around the same time, Lord Leigh of Stoneleigh Abbey in Warwickshire spent £5 2s. 6d. on "23 yards of red check with binding, laths &c." for making curtains, and £8 8s. on twelve "fine walnut chairs."[22] Elsewhere, the emphasis on the size of curtains suggests perhaps a concern with their possible adaptation to the differently sized windows of another house, but also the volume of cloth contained in them and thus the "bargain" they comprised. There were, however, other motivations at play. With luxuries defined by the complexity of their acquisition,[23] the virtue of buying second-hand was that the consumer could short-circuit the complex systems of manufacture and supply—they could take advantage of the cultural and logistical "reach" of the primary consumer. Rather than having to source Italian marble, organise its shipping to England, and commission the carving and gilding of an appropriate frame, a consumer visiting the Earl of Halifax's sale could simply buy the piece complete. Country house sales thus formed a convenient way of furnishing a house with high-quality goods or adding choice pieces to an existing scheme.[24] Indeed, second-hand was the only way in which some items could be acquired. This is clearly true of paintings and unique pieces of furniture such as the mahogany cabinet sold at Rolleston Hall, but also books and prints. There is not space here to discuss the second-hand book trade in detail, but a few examples serve to illustrate the point. The 1836 sale of the effects of W. Lucas, Esq., of Hollowell included at least five volumes published in the seventeenth century, and at Wollaston Hall in 1805 there were fourteen seventeenth-century and three sixteenth-century volumes, including Baker's *Bible* of 1599 and Stephano's *Thesaurus Graecae* in four volumes, published in 1577.[25] Such volumes were impossible to buy new and bibliophiles were dependent upon good contacts in London and elsewhere to secure sought-after books.[26] Country house sales thus afforded an invaluable opportunity to raid the libraries of other gentlemen for choice volumes without recourse to the labyrinthine book trade.[27] Their significance is made tangible by the handwritten notes added to some of the catalogues. For the Hollowell sale, eighteen volumes are marked, presumably to denote an interest in buying these; but it is the catalogue for the Earl of Halifax's sale that is most revealing. Here, there are names written against some books (Afflick, Lacy, Dash, Burnham), indicating the identity of the successful bidder. There are also notes on the binding ("bad," "gilt," "elegant morocco," "neat") suggesting that the appearance of the books was important; but there are others marked "wants 1 vol" which indicates an equal interest in the integrity and content of the edition.[28] Most significantly, perhaps, the purchase price has been noted for every book.

Cost was clearly important to those buying at country house sales; not because of financial impecunity, but because these sales offered the chance to acquire luxury goods at much reduced prices. This was a major attraction at the Fonthill sales, where the prices paid were clearly some way below what was anticipated as the sale failed to produce the returns that had been hoped for.[29] The Earl of Halifax's books included many commonplace volumes, which fetched only a few shillings; but also some that were clearly much sought after. At one extreme, we have Lot 61, "Locke on Education and Arlington's letters," which sold for 1s. 6d., and Lot 20, "Votes of the House of Commons," which failed to sell and had to be rolled into the next lot. In contrast, "Campbell's Vitruvius Britannicus" fetched £3 18s. and "Montfaucon's antiquities" made £5 15s. 6d.[30] Yet even these more costly items represented something of a bargain: the Earl's *Vitruvius Britannicus* comprised all three volumes and a total of around one hundred copperplate engravings. The notion that buying at country house sales often focused on "capturing value" becomes still more apparent from the catalogue for the 1761 sale at Thomas Medleycot's house in Cottingham. Unique amongst this sample, this contained reserve prices for many of the lots (though not, significantly, for some of the more obviously luxury items, including silver plate and paintings). These prices suggest that bargains were to be had. For about £35 a parlour could be fitted out in reasonable luxury with, amongst other things: three large pier glasses, a walnut writing table, an elm sideboard, a mahogany card table, curtains, walnut sofas upholstered in brocade, six velvet seated chairs, a mahogany fire screen, and an eight-day clock.[31] Buying more selectively, anyone visiting this sale could have secured high-quality or rare pieces for very modest sums: an India japanned cabinet for £6 or a set of nine large engravings of classical scenes by Rubens for £2 10s. Careful bidders could thus hope to "capture value."[32]

LUXURY AND INDIVIDUALITY: CAPTURING DIFFERENCE?

Luxury was more than simply a reflection of cost; buying goods recycled through country house sales involved other motivations. Some goods were attractive because they provided the opportunity to mark the distinctive taste of the individual. Antiques were important in this regard because of their "long association with times, events, and names that have an historical interest and that move our feelings deeply by means of such powerful associations."[33] However, this sentiment only grew to prominence at the very end of the period covered here: the catalogues contain just twenty-one references to antiques, mostly describing china. Whilst country house sales were an obvious and important source of such items, this potential had not yet been realised: auctioneers were keen to stress many qualities, but not often or in any sustained manner the "antique" nature of the goods being sold.[34]

Collecting was more firmly established in eighteenth-century elite culture: coins, scientific instruments, and paintings by old masters or fashionable modern artists were luxury goods of the highest order, differentiated in terms of their economic as well as their cultural value. Acquiring such goods required and reinforced specialist knowledge and thus helped to mark out the cognoscenti from mere consumers.[35] Purchasing these things second-hand was little different from acquiring them new: a set of coins or medals, for example, could be absorbed into one's own collection—indeed, filling the different categories to ensure a full set is one of the key attractions of collecting. Again, though, whilst paintings were fairly widespread, featuring in over half the sales sampled, other forms of collection were comparatively rare—especially if we look for something more serious than the six glass cases of stuffed birds (including a curlieu, goshawk, and ptarmigan) at Welton Place or the model of a church, assortment of china eggs and shells, and stuffed pheasant sold at Hollowell.[36] In many ways, these fall into the category of decorative items, of which there was no shortage: the sale at Sudborough House included "four very handsome Dresden china ornaments," "a pair of Ormolu chimney candlesticks," and a "pair of Indian glasscases and flowers"; that at Barton Hall included decorative china such as: "a slipper [. . .] Harlequin and Columbine, old man and harvest girl, pair eggs, pair dogs, pair rabbits, and a nurse."[37] These might best be viewed as semi-luxury items, produced in quantity by manufacturers in England and Europe, and carrying little cultural capital. Serious collections usually required deeper pockets and greater knowledge of the scientific or artistic world—both of which are often associated with the Grand Tour.[38] This makes the "11 antique casts in lead" sold at the Kirby Hall in 1772 and the coin collection belonging to J. P. Clarke, Esq., of Welton Place important because of their rarity.[39] That the sales only occasionally included such collections suggests that they afforded few opportunities for marking distinction in this way.

Social and cultural difference could, of course, be communicated in ways other than displays of taste and learning. Cynthia Wall has argued that recycled goods offered an entrée into other people's lives and worlds.[40] "Capturing difference" in this way could feed into what Susan Stewart sees as a wider eighteenth-century desire for objects which conferred human interest.[41] Items which allowed this kind of transfer of personal association might include family portraits, engraved silverware, or jewellery. Paintings were regularly sold from country houses, but most were landscapes, classical scenes, allegorical pieces, or still lifes rather than portraits. When they did appear, most portraits showed public figures. At Kirby Hall in 1772, we find: "Lord Longer-ville, 3 qrs," "Queen of Hungary, half-length," "the Countess of Pembroke, whole length," and "Lord Strafford, 3 qrs"; and at Rolleston Hall, there were paintings of "K. Charles II, 3 quarters," "Oliver Cromwell, Protector," and "Lancelot Andrews, Bishop of Chichester."[42] Whilst these figures carried cultural and political associations, they lacked the intimacy of connection that might be accorded by less easily recognisable figures. In this light, the two paintings of "a lady" sold at Rolleston may have held certain attractions, as might the "Four family pictures" listed in the Chapel Room at Kirby Hall. It is notable, however, that the Finch-Hattons chose to retain most of their family portraits. This makes the long list of family portraits sold after the death of the Earl of Halifax all the more striking. There were twenty-seven pictures in all, including paintings of his parents and grandparents, as well as himself and his wife.[43] Clearly, bidding for such pictures did not make the buyer part of the Earl's family, but it did provide a rare chance to acquire a very personal part of his property and thus in some sense facilitated association with this branch of the aristocracy.

Much the same might be said about silverware, which could be highly personal and was often personalised. The Leigh family in Warwickshire, for example, invariably paid for newly acquired silverware to be engraved with the family crest.[44] Again, however, there is little sign of personal items in the sales catalogues. Silverware and plate mostly comprised cutlery and other tableware, with more personal items appearing but rarely, the "larger two-handled cup and cover" at the Wollaston Hall of 1805 being exceptional.[45] Perhaps most telling, however, is the fact that those items most linked to the person and the body—clothing and jewellery—were totally absent from these sales. They were generally dispersed through personal or postmortem gifts, sometimes taken apart and refashioned for use by the new owner, and sometimes recycled via the second-hand market. If Cynthia Wall is right, and buyers at auctions really did want to buy into another's world, they clearly needed to do it through far more mundane items, such as curtains, tables, and beds. More likely, such concerns were not at the forefront of the minds of those visiting the auctions. Indeed, the importance of the country house sale as a venue for acquiring the kind of luxury goods that might distinguish the consumer as a person of refined taste or particular cultural qualities seems to have diminished over the period covered here. Between the late eighteenth and early nineteenth centuries, there were few profound changes in the nature of luxury goods offered for sale: furniture, glass and chinaware, and mirrors remained the most common items, and the overall range of luxuries declined only slightly, from around nine to about eight types per sale. However, certain categories of goods appeared far less frequently after about 1815 than they had done before. The most marked decline was seen in firearms, perhaps a reflection of the changing military situation, but more likely an indication of the changing cultural character of the elite.[46] More telling, perhaps, was the drop, by over one half, in the number of sales that included paintings or prints—a trend broadly followed by scientific instruments and clocks. The implication of this is that the country house was declining in importance as a means of recycling those luxuries that might be defined in terms of their cultural associations (their meanings, links to specialist knowledge systems or personality) rather than simply their price or the complexity of acquisition.

There are two possible explanations for this. The first is that it was linked to the growth of more specialised dealers or auctions. This might be seen in the growing reach of London auction houses such as Christie's and Phillips's, although both of these sold quite a wide range of goods. Probably more significant were the growing number of art dealers in the streets around the Royal Society of Arts and, to a lesser extent, the emergence of specialist antique dealers, initially in Soho and later around Bond Street and Jermyn Street.[47] Given the lack of specialist knowledge amongst provincial auctioneers in particular, it would make sense for sellers to look to specialist and knowledgeable dealers, who had good contacts amongst potential buyers, in order to get the best possible price for the goods being sold.[48] The second is that there was a more general decline in demand for recycled luxury goods. This might be seen as part of a broader shift in consumer preferences from second-hand to new goods that is often seen as taking place through the nineteenth century. Linked to this was the growing provision of luxury and semi-luxury goods by manufacturers such as Wedgwood and Boulton, who aimed their production, if not their rhetoric, firmly at middle-class consumers who might previously have sought luxury goods at country house sales.[49] However, recent work challenges this secular trend, arguing that second-hand goods retained an important role in meeting consumer demand throughout the nineteenth and into the twentieth century.[50] Any decline in the availability of certain luxury goods appears to have been more closely linked to the changing character of the country house sales sampled. Clearances were less common and more selective sales appear to have grown in number, especially those involving the remnants from earlier sales, for example when a family shifted their main residence elsewhere, as was the case with Kirby Hall and Geddington House for instance. Sales at the former became progressively less wide-ranging in the goods on offer, with luxury items in particular diminishing in both quantity and quality. The house itself followed a parallel decline, gradually slipping from eighteenth-century splendour to a decaying ruin by the turn of the twentieth century.[51] Whatever the cause, the early nineteenth century may have formed something of a hiatus in the ability of the country house sale to offer buyers real opportunities to mark difference.

CONCLUSIONS

Country house sales were thus an important mechanism for the recycling of luxury goods. This was true of grand and well-known events such as the Fonthill sales of the early nineteenth century, but also of the more modest events that have been the subject of this paper. Significantly, these sales continued well into the nineteenth century and beyond, further questioning the supposed decline in the demand for second-hand goods over this period. The underlying reasons for holding sales did not go away; indeed, as the agricultural economy declined in the later decades of the nineteenth century and the costs of maintaining large country houses escalated in the early twentieth century, the need to sell up or sell off significant amounts of high-value goods became more acute. The supply of used luxury goods was therefore at least maintained. Whilst the emergence and growth of specialist art auctions and antique dealers might have taken the cream of the luxury goods, a sizeable amount of high-quality items remained to be sold from the property itself. Indeed, the country house sale remains, to this day, an important mechanism whereby luxury goods re-enter circulation. For example, the 2005 sale of art and furniture held on the premises at Easton Neston in Northamptonshire included old masters, chairs by Thomas Chippendale, seventeenth-century plaster busts of Sir William and Lady Fermor (ancestors of the current owners), and a 1690 scale model of the house itself. The quality of the items being sold generated national interest in the press and around seven thousand people attended over the three days of the sale—some to bid, but many simply to witness the proceedings and be part of the occasion.[52] The parallels between past and present are clear and close: the Easton Neston sale, like that of many of the eighteenth- and nineteenth-century auctions studied here, offered a rare chance to buy luxury goods and to glimpse something of the life of the elite. There is a risk in pressing the evidence too far, especially when the catalogues tell us little about those who bought at the sales. However, country house sales seem to have appealed to those seeking to buy quality goods at reduced prices or secure items that could not easily be obtained through other means. Only in exceptional cases did they afford clear opportunities to buy into another's authentic world. Personal goods were rarely sold at these sales and, whilst it is possible that something of that world might rub off through owning a grand bed or handsome dinner service, relatively little of the previous owner accompanied curtains, chairs, or mirrors. These were luxury goods because of their material qualities and, as such, were situated in the same value systems as new goods. In this sense, at least, new and used goods were part of the same consumer world.

NOTES

1. See, for example, Christopher Christie, *The British Country House in the Eighteenth Century* (Manchester: Manchester University Press, 2000), 179–273.
2. Anne Nellis Richter, "Spectacle, Exoticism, and Display in the Gentleman's House: The Fonthill Auction of 1822," in *Eighteenth-Century Studies* 41 (2008), 643–64; Rosie MacArthur and Jon Stobart, "Going for a Song? Country House Sales in Georgian England," in *Modernity and the Second-Hand Trade. European Consumption Cultures and Practices, 1700–1900,* ed. Jon Stobart and Ilja Van Damme (Basingstoke: Palgrave, 2010), 175–95.
3. See the discussions in Ilja Van Damme, "Second-Hand Dealing in Bruges and the Rise of an Antiquarian Culture, c.1750–1870," in *Modernity and the Second-Hand Trade,* ed. Stobart and Van Damme, 74–77; Donald Woodward, "'Swords into Ploughshares': Recycling in Pre-industrial England," in *Economic History Review* 38 (1985): 175–91; Laurence Fontaine, "The Exchange of Second-Hand Goods Between Survival Strategies and 'Business' in Eighteenth-Century Paris," in *Alternative Exchanges. Second-Hand Circulations form the Sixteenth Century to the Present*, ed. Laurence Fontaine (New York and Oxford: Berghahn, 2008), 97–114.
4. Amanda Vickery, *Behind Closed Doors. At Home in Georgian England* (London and New Haven: Yale University Press, 2009), 164.
5. Amanda Vickery, *The Gentleman's Daughter. Women's Lives in Georgian England* (London and New Haven: Yale University Press, 1998), 150–58; see also Vickery, *Behind Closed Doors*, 164; Valérie Pietri, "Uses and the Used. The Conventions of Renewing and Exchanging Goods in French Provincial Aristocracy," in *Alternative Exchanges*, ed. Laurence Fontaine, 115–26; Margaret Ponsonby, *Stories from Home. English Domestic Interiors, 1750–1850* (Aldershot: Ashgate, 2007), 79–102; Stana Nenadic, "Middle-Rank Consumers and Domestic Culture in Edinburgh and Glasgow 1720–1840," *Past and Present* 145 (1994): 122–56.
6. The far larger asset of the land itself was sometimes covered by strict settlement that limited the ability to sell estates in whole or part. Even where this was not in place, there was a strong presumption against selling land. The literature on this is vast, but see Eileen Spring, "The Strict Settlement: Its Role in History," in *The Economic History Review* 41 (1988): 454–60.
7. For a summary of the various motivations behind second-Hand consumption, see: Jon Stobart, "Clothes, Cabinets and Carriages: Second-Hand Dealing in Eighteenth-Century England," in *Buyers and Sellers. Retail Circuits and Practices in Medieval and Early-Modern Europe,* ed. Bruno Blondé Peter Stabel, Jon Stobart and I. Van Damme (Tournhout: Brepols, 2006), 225–44.
8. William Harrison, *The Description of England* (London, 1587), 197.

9. Nicky Gregson and Louise Crewe, *Second-Hand Cultures* (London: Berg, 2003), 11–12; Cynthia Wall, "The English Auction: Narratives of Dismantlings," *Eighteenth-Century Studies* 31 (1997): 20.
10. See Richter, "Spectacle, Exoticism, and Display"; R. J. Gemmett, "'The Tinsel of Fashion and the Gewgaws of Luxury': The Fonthill Sale of 1801," in *The Burlington Magazine*, 40 (2008): 381–88.
11. Northampton Central Library, hereafter NCL, M0005646NL/3, Kirby Hall, 1772, 18; M0005647NL/2, Rolleston Hall, 1801, 21; M0005644NL/5, Wollaston Hall, 1805, passim.
12. Harrison, *Description of England*, 197; Hannah Grieg, "Leading the Fashion: The Material Culture of London's *Beau Monde*," in *Gender, Taste and Material Culture in Britain and North America 1700–1830*, ed. John Styles and Amanda Vickery (London and New Haven: Yale University Press, 2006), 293–313; Vickery, *Behind Closed Doors*, 124–25.
13. Jan De Vries, *The Industrious Revolution. Consumer Behaviour and the Household Economy, 1650 to the Present* (Cambridge: Cambridge University Press, 2008), 122–85.
14. Fanny Burney, *Cecilia. Memoirs of an Heiress* [1782] (London: Virago, 1986), 28.
15. Price is the first criterion for luxury noted by Arjun Appadurai, "Introduction: Commodities and the Politics of Value," in The *Social Life of Things: Commodities in Cultural Perspective* (Cambridge: Cambridge University Press, 1986), 3–63.
16. NCL, M0005646NL/5, Barton Hall, 1784, 13; M0005647NL/2, Rolleston Hall, 1801, 20.
17. Linda Levy Peck, *Consuming Splendor. Society and Culture in Seventeenth-Century England* (Cambridge: Cambridge University Press, 2005), 113–51; Maxine Berg, *Luxury and Pleasure in Eighteenth-Century England* (Oxford: Oxford University Press, 2005), 46–84.
18. NCL, M0005646NL/11 Stanford Hall, 1792, 12; M0005645NL/22, Sudborough House, 1836, 7–8.
19. See, for example: Geoffrey Beard, *Upholsterers and Interior Furnishing in England, 1530–1840* (London and New Haven: Yale University Press, 1997); Helen Clifford, "A Commerce with Things: The Value of Precious Metalwork in Early Modern England," in *Consumers and Luxury. Consumer Culture in Europe, 1650–1850*, ed. Maxine Berg and Helen Clifford (Manchester: Manchester University Press, 1999), 147–68.
20. NCL, M0005647NL/2, Rolleston Hall, 1801, 10.
21. NCL, M0005647NL/6, Earl of Halifax, 1772, 19.
22. NCL, M0005644NL/2, Cottingham, 1761, 9; Shakespeare Central Library and Archives, DR18/5/4408.
23. See Appadurai, "Introduction."
24. This appears to have been important to some of the buyers at the Fonthill sales and at the public auctions held in some Swedish towns. See Gemmett, "The Tinsel of Fashion"; Sofia Murhem, Göran Ulväng, and Christina Lilja, "Tables and Chairs under the Hammer: Second-Hand Consumption of Furniture in the Eighteenth and Nineteenth Centuries in Sweden," in *Modernity and the Second-Hand Trade*, ed. Stobart and Van Damme, 211–12.
25. NCL, M0005644NL/20, Hollowell, 1836, 10–14; M0005644NL/5, Wollaston Hall, 1805, 30–45.
26. John Raven, *The Business of Books. Booksellers and the English Book Trade, 1450–1850* (Cambridge: Cambridge University Press, 2007).
27. Such was the importance of the sales of gentlemen's or clergymen's libraries that they were sometimes sold at auctions separately from the household

goods. The collection of catalogues in Northampton Central Library contains several catalogues for such sales.
28. NCL, M0005647NL/6, Earl of Halifax, 1772, 29–32.
29. Gemmett, "The Tinsel of Fashion," 388.
30. NCL, M0005647NL/6, Earl of Halifax, 1772, 29–31.
31. NCL, M0005644NL/2, Cottingham, 1761, 8.
32. See Gregson and Crewe, *Second-Hand Cultures*, 11–12.
33. Andrew Jackson Downing, *The Architecture of Country Houses* (London: D. Appleton, 1850), 450.
34. For a fuller discussion of the language deployed in the catalogues, see Jon Stobart, "The Language of Luxury Goods: Consumption and the English Country House, c.1760–1830," *Virtus* 18 (2011): 89–104.
35. See John Brewer, *Pleasures of the Imagination: English Culture in the Eighteenth Century* (Chicago: Chicago University Press, 1997), 201–87, 427–92; John Elsner and Roger Cardinal, eds., *The Cultures of Collecting* (London: Reaktion Books, 1997)
36. NCL, M0005644NL/13, Welton Place, 1830, 24; M0005644NL/20, Hollowell, 1836, 18, 24.
37. NCL, M0005645NL/22, Sudborough House, 1836, 8; M0005646NL/5, Barton Hall, 1784, 15.
38. See Christie, *British Country Houses*, 179–88.
39. NCL, M0005646NL/3, Kirby Hall, 1772, 11; M0005644NL/13, Welton Place, 1830, 17–18.
40. Wall, "English Auction," 14–15, 20.
41. Gregson and Crewe, *Second-Hand Cultures*, 12; Susan Stewart, *On Longing: Narratives of the Miniature, the Gigantic, the Souvenir, the Collection* (Baltimore: Johns Hopkins University Press, 1984), 133.
42. NCL, M0005646NL/3, Kirby Hall, 1772, 10, 12; M0005647NL/2, Rolleston Hall, 1801, 4.
43. NCL, M0005647NL/6, Earl of Halifax, 1772, 38.
44. Jon Stobart, "Gentlemen and Shopkeepers: Supplying the Country House in Eighteenth-Century England," *Economic History Review* 64 (2011): 885–904.
45. NCL, M0005644NL/13, Welton Place, 1830, 29–31. See also M0005646NL/9, Stanwick Hall, 1788, 11; M0005644NL/2, Cottingham, 1761, 13; NCL, M0005644NL/5, Wollaston Hall, 1805, 7.
46. See Norbert Elias, *The Civilizing Process, Volume I. The History of Manners* (Oxford: Blackwell, 1969).
47. Clive Wainwright, *The Romantic Interior* (London and New Haven: Yale University Press, 1984), 35.
48. This echoes changes taking place in eighteenth-century Antwerp: see Dries Lyna, "Power to the Broker: Shifting Authorities over Public Sales in Eighteenth-Century Antwerp," in *Modernity and the Second-Hand Trade*, ed. Stobart and Van Damme, 158–74.
49. See Nenadic, "Middle-Rank consumers," and Berg, *Luxury and Pleasure*, 117–92.
50. For example: Deborah Cohen, *Household Gods. The British and their Possessions* (London and New Haven: Yale University Press, 2006); Ponsonby, *Stories from Home*, 79–102. See also the various contributions to *Alternative Exchanges*, ed. Fontaine and to *Modernity and the Second-Hand Trade*, ed. Stobart and Van Damme.
51. MacArthur and Stobart, "Going for a Song."
52. *Country Life*, 25 February 2005; *The Daily Telegraph*, 21 May 2005.

3 Recycling the Wreckage of History

On the Rise of an "Antiquarian Consumer Culture" in the Southern Netherlands

Ilja Van Damme

In 1804, Martinus De Bast (1753–1825), priest of the Saint-Nicolas Church in Ghent, published a curious overview of Roman and Gallic antiquities found in Flanders.[1] The goal of his *Recueil* served to synthesise and more widely distribute existing information about old monuments and antiquarian objects. As such, he was a precursor of systematic archaeological research, a rapidly expanding historical discipline he introduced in the Napoleonic Netherlands.[2]According to De Bast, the study of such things as potsherds, urns, and old coins was not to be taken lightly, "despite the fact that certain persons, enlightened to be sure, regard it as tedious."[3] From an intellectual perspective, objects of the past provided the sort of knowledge that was lacking in written records: antiquities were complementary to these written accounts, touched on untold aspects of daily life, and, for prehistory, were often the only sources available.

Indeed, in the course of the "long" eighteenth century—comprising, in this chapter, the period that gave rise to modern day Belgium (c. 1760–c. 1830)—historians in the Southern Netherlands began to gain a broader awareness and recognition of the value of material objects and debris of the past.[4] However, for most people living in the eighteenth-century Southern Netherlands, such public discourse and appreciation of old objects for the sake of oldness certainly seemed new and novel. Evolving historical consciousness regarding used goods was in a sense counterintuitive for a society that still embraced the salvaging and recycling of objects and materials.[5] The surrounding material culture was essentially an inconspicuous "fellow traveller" in a person's life, with goods being repaired and reused as effectively as possible, albeit with little respect for or knowledge of an object's historical significance.[6] The familiarity with the reuse and recycling of old objects for all sorts of utilitarian purposes—such as rebuilding a house, mending worn-out garments, and melting down precious metals—did not necessarily lead to growing awareness of the "age value" of things.[7] On the contrary: just as consumers normally tried to remove from objects any material scratches, stains, or marks made by previous usage and owners, so too did second-hand dealers of all sorts try to sell their wares as "nearly new" or, owing to various repair and refashioning processes, as not "visibly old."[8]

The point resided precisely in removing the age value or patina of material remains: not so much the veneer of the past, but being *à la mode* was what counted in the households of elite and middle-class stations. Paradoxically, Antwerp newspapers, for instance, frequently advertised the postmortem sales of household belongings as featuring items that were new or according to the latest French fashion. Especially from the 1750s onwards, adjectives like "new" or "modern" were increasingly employed to sell what were clearly already used belongings.[9]

As is evident from another antiquarian enthusiast, Adriaan Heylen (1745–1802), the "careless" (in his opinion) reuse of old remains was nothing short of dramatic. General negligence and ignorance regarding the historical value of old things threatened existing antiquities, and even increased the likelihood of loss or mishandling of accidental findings in the future. Heylen was prepared to pay Flemish farmers and field labourers handsomely even for old jars of little value that they dug up, if only "to prevent the further destruction of antiquities which can be discovered."[10] By so doing, he hoped to motivate the country folk to carefully handle and preserve all future findings. However, in retrospect the transition from the eighteenth to the nineteenth century can clearly be pinpointed as the period when a public consumer culture of antique objects began to emerge.[11] Excited collectors from different social stations sought old coins, potsherds, urns, jewellery, sculptures, engravings, weapons, or architectural debris. These goods were recycled from the material surroundings not for reuse or repair, but more and more for collecting and preserving. Their supposedly unaltered age, historicity, and reference to a national past or shared heritage made them precious collectibles. As I will show in this chapter, increasing scholarly interest in the material remains of the national past was in fact only the tip of the iceberg: in the late eighteenth- and early nineteenth-century society at large, the past itself became, for various reasons, commodified.

HUMANIST ORIGINS

To be sure, specialised interest in the study, preservation, and collecting of old materials had existed before the eighteenth century in the Southern Netherlands. Many a Catholic abbey, monastery, or local church functioned as repositories for old relics and precious trophies of the past. These goods, sometimes as common as a piece of wood or rock from the Holy Land, were highly valued and drew authority from the particular biblical stories or ancient saints and martyrs to which they referred. The consent of the Church to open tombs and transfer relics from one institution to another even led, from the middle ages onwards, to the *de facto* commercialisation of such objects.[12] Both the Church and the retailers along the pilgrimage routes of the Low Countries realised the potential of these devotional objects to mobilise faithful masses. However, the motivations behind these sporadically assembled "treasures" were on a religious level that lacked any genuine interest for the past as such.

It was not until the rise of Renaissance humanist activities, such as the translation and study of classical texts, that interest in goods with historical significance began to increase, primarily with strong focus on the Roman heritage.[13] It was within those socially narrow humanist circles that genuine antiquarian re-evaluation of old objects was growing; this was the sort of scholarship whose practitioners, according to the famous Italian historiographer Momigliano, subordinated "literary texts to coins, statues, vases and inscriptions."[14] Sixteenth-century Antwerp, being in the centre of world trade and luxury consumption, rapidly pooled precisely these sorts of erudite, humanist intellectuals. One of the central figures of emerging antiquarian research within the Low Countries was the famous Antwerp-born cartographer and humanist Abraham Ortelius (1527–1598).[15] He was among the first to publish about antiquarian objects and the (scarce) Gallo-Romain remains in the Netherlands, and pioneered a method of empirical research and *in situ* investigation that directly influenced, among others, William Camden (1551–1623), dubbed one of the "godfathers" of archaeological research in England.[16] In fact, through intense scholarly conversation and travel Ortelius formed part of a select international nucleus of intellectuals from within the wider Netherlands (North and South), France, Germany, England, and, of course, Italy: scholars who were keen on unveiling, preserving and assembling the material culture of the ancient world.[17]

More important, however, for the further dissemination of an antiquarian consumer culture within the Southern Netherlands were Ortelius's affiliations with the world of artists and their affluent patrons. Being born in a merchant family, and a member of the Antwerp artist guild of Saint Luke, Ortelius dealt in prints and maps, and functioned as both supplier and keeper in the emerging trade of artful luxuries and antiquarian objects. Having befriended many Antwerp artists, including Joris Hoefnagel (1542–1601), Lucas d'Heere (1534–1584), and important patrons and connoisseurs of the arts, such as Nicolaas Rockox (1560–1640), Ortelius directly influenced broader social circles by passing on and amplifying the rather narrow antiquarian discourse of intellectuals and scholars. Already from the beginning of the sixteenth century, artists from within the Low Countries were eager to travel to Rome to perfect their skills by making drawings and etchings of antique sculptures and monuments.[18] The most learned and versatile of them, such as Lambert Lombard (1505/6–1566), became antique collectors in their own right. It was through the example of these humanist scholars and artists that many powerful noblemen within the Southern Netherlands began collecting old objects laden with historical value and meaning. At the end of the sixteenth century, the influential Dutch numismatic Hubertus Goltzius (1526–1583) counted more than a hundred such cabinets in the Southern Netherlands alone.[19] Among these were important statesmen of the Habsburg dynasty, such as cardinal Granvelle

(1517–1586), the count of Egmond (1522–1568), Philips of Marnix de Saint Aldegonde (1540–1598), and many lesser noblemen. Artists and scholars, such as the Antwerp-born Abraham Gorlaeus (1549–1608), a specialist of engraved gems, figured prominently in this group as well.

However, the connection between antiquarianism and the world of artists and their patrons also demonstrates that many an emerging collector of antiques was not primarily motivated by narrow scholarly concerns for the past as such.[20] Essentially, the consumption of antiques became intertwined with the activities of *liefhebbers van de kunst*, "art lovers," who were enthusiastically searching, conserving, and cherishing old objects primarily for their unique, curious, and, above all, aesthetic qualities.[21] Old coins and medals, for instance, became highly popular within the Low Countries, not so much because they were relatively easily available and transportable, but mainly because they often included graceful visualisations of old emperors and the like. Similarly, old "cameos" or engraved gems and stones were cherished for their skilful artistry and refinement in technique.[22] The first decades of the seventeenth century saw a proliferation of private art collections, now often belonging to wealthy merchant families who compiled their own take on the *Kunst* and *Wunderkammer* models of mighty rulers and aristocrats. This is evidenced by the emergence of a new genre of paintings in Antwerp, mainly displaying bourgeois collectors and their cabinets on display.[23] Flemish Baroque painters, especially Frans Francken the Younger (1581–1642), specialised in such depictions, indicating the degree to which private collecting had become a popular activity among the well-to-do citizens in the Southern Netherlands, particularly in Antwerp. Recent probate inventory research confirms that, despite the decrease of its inhabitants' fortunes, the quantity of artistic goods in Antwerp, especially paintings, rose markedly between 1630 and 1680, both for the higher and the lower urban middle classes.[24]

Nevertheless, it is also evident from these cabinet paintings that antiquarian objects formed a recurrent albeit minor part of collections. Antique coins and engravings, and a few sculptures and vases, figured especially prominently. While some people, no doubt, still collected these goods for "scientific" purposes, many others now used antiques as one of many emblems of accepted taste and social standing. In the seventeenth century, for a wealthy citizen as well as for aspiring noblemen, maintaining a collection was first and foremost a way to signal the owner's status and taste. Above all it signalled upward social mobility: it was the mark of a gentleman in the aristocratically inclined society of the Spanish Netherlands.[25] For such persons, the acquisition of antiquities was essentially a new, tasteful, and polite form of consumption, one laden with the sort of intellectual satisfaction and aesthetic pleasures for which paintings, rare gems, and natural and man-made "curiosities" could be equally mobilised.

In such a context, excessive interest in past objects was even ridiculed as suspect or socially inappropriate.[26] Especially for those "art lovers" who considered themselves representatives of the continental *connoisseurs* and the English *virtuosi*, scholarly respect for the past, and valuation of objects for the sake of antiquity, in the end had to be subordinated to a pleasing display of aesthetics and taste.[27] Yet, intellectuals and *erudites* too—who, in the seventeenth-century Southern Netherlands, were often people belonging to the order of the Jesuits—were keen not to be ridiculed as peculiar scrutinisers of the dead and bygone or as mindless compilers of the past who, without any higher intellectual purpose or model, were merely salvaging the "wreckage of history."[28] In the correspondence of the Utrecht-born antiquarian and humanist Arnoldus Buchelius (1565–1641), for example, antiquarianism is described in precisely such terms: "beachcombing the flotsam and jetsam of history."[29] In the end, the study and collecting of old objects had to serve and assist the higher, literary goals of writing history—a concern that became especially apparent in the discourse of the enlightened eighteenth-century *philosophes*.[30] By that time, however, antiquarian collecting had spread beyond the confines of scholars, noblemen and wealthy bourgeois art lovers, spurring new evolutions and criticism in its wake.

THE COMMODIFICATION OF THE PAST

Despite a growing number of participants, trade in antiques remained a haphazard and incidental affair before the eighteenth century, and was generally a matter of chance and good connections.[31] Ploughboys and farmers often dug up objects like old pottery, coins, and weapons and were usually willing to give, exchange, or sell their finds to interested scholars and collectors.[32] Letters of introduction and lively correspondence brought together likeminded antiquarian enthusiasts. Wealthy collectors, of course, could travel to Italy where a full-scale—and sometimes counterfeit—antique business had long been established and where merchants were eager to accommodate travellers and artists with souvenirs from their Grand Tour or artistic voyage to Italy.[33] Rare and precious pieces, however, were costly, and required precisely the professional assistance that specialist dealers could provide. For example, the brothers Jan (1601–1646) and Gerard (1599–1658) Reynst, who came from a prosperous shipping family involved in the East India trade, acquired the largest antiquarian collection of their day in the Northern Netherlands, by using their business contacts in Italy, Turkey, and Greece to export specific antiques on commission.[34] From the eighteenth century onwards, however, acquiring old art and antiques became intrinsically linked to the rapidly professionalizing European art markets.[35] With the spread and expansion of antiquarian interest—and collecting culture in general—the resale of possessions and collections of private estates through auctions became paramount for the circulation of art and antiques. In an early preserved auction catalogue from 1739, for instance, mention is made of "antiques, rings [. . .] & and several other curiosities" that will be sold in

Brussels. The catalogue also refers to “a complete cabinet of antiques medallions in gold, silver or bronze [. . .] which is one of the most perfect [cabinets] to be found in this country.”[36]

The appearance and growth of auction catalogues in vernacular—in Dutch and mostly French—language in the eighteenth-century Southern Netherlands marks the arrival of more continuous sale and resale mechanisms; such mechanisms catered to a growing audience for whom attendance at auctions provided the principal means of forming and expanding collections. Especially from 1760s onwards, growing numbers of sale advertisements and auction catalogues indicate an increasingly commercialised resale market for art and antiquarian objects in large metropolitan centres like Brussels and Antwerp.[37] Adhering both to specific social conventions and usage of aesthetic language, the emerging *connoisseur-marchands* created a popular and specialised environment for the public sales of artistic goods.[38] Art and antique auctions were often held in auction rooms specifically designed for such purposes, and, eventually, in auction houses, thereby spatially segregating the commerce in antiques away from the broader market of second-hand commodities.[39] Thus, the idea gained prominence that ancient art and antiques were special commodities, not to be recycled or casually reused but rather treated with appropriate respect and knowledge. The inflated prices of these goods reflected their rising cultural prestige and served to distinguish and legitimise respectable old goods from the junk of second-hand commerce.[40] By organising open viewing days and allowing buyers to observe, discuss, and comment on biddings, auctioneers succeeded in broadening the interest in art and antiques. A central idea was the anti-authoritarian notion that anyone could become a passionate collector of old art, and judge according to his or her individual taste and values, without necessarily having much time, money, or intellect to become a true *connoisseur*.[41]

Naturally, such democratizing tendencies towards antiquarian consumption triggered debates about defining the difference between old “rubbish” and “polite” antiquarian collectables.[42] The persistence, and even intensification, of the antiquarian ridicule in the latter half of the eighteenth century hints at the fact that antique collecting had gained an established place amongst the fashionable leisure pursuits and hobbies of upper-class—if not snobbish—gentlemen who sought after old and vulgar objects, without allegedly much taste, forethought, or intellect.[43] The rise of a wider consumer culture of antiques, however, cannot be explained only by referring to the increasing professionalisation of art and antique dealing. Between c. 1760 and c. 1830 mounting public interest in the (initially classical) past as such was growing in the Southern Netherlands. As happened more or less simultaneously in the surrounding European countries, the past became fashionable in itself and, in a sense, ever more commodified.[44]

In the Southern Netherlands, broadening historical consciousness became intrinsically entangled with touring and travelling, with the formation of intellectual clubs and societies, and an increasing literature on the subject. Newspapers began to report on excavations in Italy (for example, the findings of Pompeii in 1709 and Herculaneum in 1738, both of which created quite a stir throughout Europe), and antiquarian collectors used the medium to establish and maintain contact with each other. The numismatic Pieter Willem Van Muysen (1737–1788), for example, published precisely such "notice for antiquaries" in the newspaper *L'esprit des Journaux, François et Etrangers* to complete his "assembly" of coins.[45] Dutch and Brabantine travel guides with references to historical dates and places thrived from the beginning of the eighteenth century onwards, although, in general, interest in the predominant gothic cities and significant "places of remembrance" in the Netherlands was limited. Adriana de la Court (1696–1740), a member of a wealthy Dutch textile family, while en route to France described Bruges as a dead and ugly place with limited tourist appeal.[46] Lingering nationalist sentiments for the specific medieval and renaissance heritage of the Southern Netherlands only began to blossom later—for now the historical fascination of the wider eighteenth-century audience was still very much focused on finding Roman remains in the country. In this sense, eighteenth-century city descriptions and almanacs could also be of use to passing visitors with antiquarian interests, since such works made reference to art and antique cabinets that were open to the public. Théodore-Augustin Mann (1735–1809), himself a historian and antiques collector, noted in 1785 at least four such "cabinets of antiquities & medallions" in Brussels, although he added that "others, without a doubt, own such similar Cabinets."[47] An Antwerp almanac from 1806 mentions thirteen "cabinets of paintings" and four "cabinets specialised in natural history, physics, antiquities, etc."[48] Finally, as the nineteenth century progressed, collectors and antiquarian and historical societies found each other in a specialised Belgium periodical on the subject, the *Messager des sciences historiques*.[49]

The broader material culture also became influenced by the growing fascination for historical heritage. From the 1760s onwards, neo-classical art inspired a new aesthetics in building, decoration, furnishing, and clothing in the Southern Netherlands.[50] Pushing aside the important traditions of Flemish Renaissance and Baroque art, the Antwerp-born Andreas Cornelis Lens (1739–1822), then considered as the principal "restorer" of the art of painting in Flanders, proclaimed in 1776 that "the principal object of painting, sculpture and other similar arts, is to represent memorable events from Antiquity."[51] His book on the clothing, manners, and customs of people in antiquity became an instant success at home and abroad. It provided the sort of descriptions of ancient costumes, weapons, jewellery, household goods, and even hairstyles that could be used as templates in high culture as well as applied arts. Borrowing neo-classical imagery for decorative purposes became widely popular after, most famously, the internationally acclaimed Wedgwood potteries brought the classical heritage to noble and wealthy bourgeois homes alike.[52] But the commercialisation of neo-classical taste was only the first of numerous subsequent historical styles within the Netherlands: Napoleon's endeavours in Egypt (1798–1801) would soon spur a craze for Egyptian antiques and decorative motifs; English visitors and artists discovering picturesque Bruges after the Battle of Waterloo (1815) would popularise the Gothic revival within Belgium; and, finally, the once-despised Flemish renaissance style became *en vogue* again due to its significance for the national past.[53]

Broadly speaking, the nineteenth century saw a clear breakthrough in antiquarian collecting—and furnishing homes with—historical materials.[54] Although in most collections and art auctions in the Southern Netherlands old master paintings remained the predominant items, the circulation and consumption of antique objects were clearly on the rise. This is evidenced by a growing number of auction catalogue pages and lots dedicated to such goods, and, most importantly, by the steady rise of specialised antique dealers (*brocanteurs*) and antique shops.[55] Interest in the historical past began to broaden, with a shift away from classical antiquity and towards the rediscovery of the "national" medieval and early modern history. These changes in historical consciousness were not accidental. Throughout Western Europe the seeds of political and socio-economic change were beginning to flower, giving way to profound material alterations and destructions. Within the Southern Netherlands, for instance, many a gothic church or cloister fell under the zeal of enlightened Austrian politicians and, later to the institutional and economic turmoil following the 1795 French annexation and rapid industrialisation.[56]

Due to the unstable political nature of the Southern Netherlands, collecting historical artefacts and restoring national monuments even became a matter of urgent public concern.[57] This became especially apparent after the formation of the new nation-state of Belgium in 1830 and the conversion of private cabinets into public museums of antiquities.[58] Thus, by the end of the "long" eighteenth century, antiquarian consumption in the Southern Netherlands was no longer a social elitist matter of intellectual and aesthetic concerns. For a widening segment of society, antiquarian objects became important signifiers of "national identity." Therefore the widening scope and scale of antiquarian consumerism was certainly connected to an emerging "modernity."[59] Antique objects became meaningful and exciting novelties for a much broader public since they simultaneously and paradoxically succeeded in representing attachment to the past and present. Such items manifested the progress that had been achieved while fulfilling a romantic yearning and desire for a bygone world.[60]

NOTES

1. Martin-Jean De Bast, *Recueil d'antiquités romaines et gauloises, trouvées dans la Flandre proprement dite, avec désignation des lieux où elles ont été découvertes* (Ghent: Steven 1804, second edition 1808). On De Bast, read Tom

Verschaffel, *Historici in de Oostenrijkse Nederlanden (1715–1794). Proeve van repertorium* (Brussels: Facultés Universitaires Saint-Louis, 1996), 29.
2. See Tom Verschaffel, *De hoed en de hond. Geschiedschrijving in de Zuidelijke Nederlanden* (Hilversum: Verloren, 1998), 196–212.
3. De Bast, *Recueil d'antiquités*, xix: "néanmoins certaines personnes, éclairées d'ailleurs, la regardent comme fastidieuse."
4. This is, for instance, further evidenced by intensified activity on the subject by the official *Académie Impériale et Royale des Sciences et Belles-Lettres* of Brussels. Read Edouard Mailly, *Histoire de l'Académie Impériale et Royale des Sciences et Belles-Lettres de Bruxelles* (Brussels: Hayez, 1883).
5. Read, for the Southern Netherlands, for instance Harald Deceulaer, "Second-Hand Dealers in the Early-Modern Low Countries: Institutions, Markets, and Practices," in *Alternative Exchanges. Second-Hand Circulations from the Sixteenth Century to the Present*, ed. Laurence Fontaine (New York and Oxford: Berghahn, 2008), 13–42.
6. As is, for instance, testified in Ilja Van Damme and Reinoud Vermoesen, "Second-Hand Consumption as a Way of Life: Public Auctions in the Surroundings of Alost in the Late Eighteenth Century," *Continuity & Change* 24 (2009): 275–305. The expression "fellow traveler" is from Daniel Woolf, *The Social Circulation of the Past. English Historical Culture 1500–1730* (Oxford: Oxford University Press, 2003), 141.
7. A remark by Stephen Bann, *The Inventions of History: Essays on the Representation of the Past* (Manchester: Manchester University Press, 1990), 125.
8. Ilja Van Damme, "Changing consumer preferences and evolutions in retailing. Buying and selling consumer durables in Antwerp (c. 1648–1748)," in *Buyers and Sellers. Retail Circuits and Practices in Medieval and Early Modern Europe*, ed. Bruno Blondé, Peter Stabel, Jon Stobart and Ilja Van Damme (Turnhout: Brepols, 2006), 199–223.
9. Dries Lyna and Ilja Van Damme, "A Strategy of Seduction? The Role of Commercial Advertisements in the Eighteenth-Century Retailing Business of Antwerp," *Business History* 51 (2009): 100–21.
10. Cited in Verschaffel, *De hoed en de hond*, 203. On Adriaan, brother of Pieter Jozef Heylen, read Verschaffel, *Historici in de Oostenrijkse Nederlanden*, 59.
11. For a similar argument read Ilja Van Damme, "Second-Hand Dealing in Bruges and the Rise of an Antiquarian Culture," in *Modernity and the Second-Hand Trade. European Consumption Cultures and Practices, 1700–1900*, ed. Jon Stobart and Ilja Van Damme (Basingtoke: Palgrave, 2010), 73–92; and Mark Westgarth, *The Emergence of the Antique and Curiosity Dealer 1815–1850: The Commodification of Historical Objects* (Aldershot: Ashgate, 2011).
12. Hubert Silvestre, "Commerce et vol de reliques au moyen âge," *Revue Belge de Philologie et d'Histoire* 30 (1952): 721–39.
13. For more references, see Paula Findlan, "Possessing the Past: The Material World of the Italian Renaissance," *The American Historical Review* 103 (1998): 83–114.
14. Arnoldo Momigliano, "Ancient History and the Antiquarian," *Journal of the Warburg and Courtauld Institutes* 13 (1950): 285.
15. Nils Büttner, "De verzamelaar Abraham Ortelius," in *Abraham Ortelius (1527–1598): cartograaf en humanist*, ed. Dirk Imhof (Turnhout: Brepols, 1998), 169–180.
16. On the early English antiquarian milieu, read Graham Perry, *The Trophies of Time: English Antiquarians of the Seventeenth Century* (Oxford: Oxford University Press, 1995).
17. This network of Ortelius is expertly analysed by Tine L. Meganck, *Erudite Eyes: Artists and Antiquarians in the Circle of Abraham Ortelius (1527–1598)*, PhD diss. (University of Princeton, 2003).

18. Frederic L. Bastet, "Reizigers en oudheden," in *Herinneringen aan Italië. Kunst en toerisme in de 18de eeuw*, ed. Ronald De Leeuw (Zwolle: Waanders, 1984), 35–41.
19. As mentioned in Jean De Mot, "Collectionneurs et collections d'antiques en Belgique," *La Belgique Artistique et Littéraire* 4 (1906): 530–31.
20. For the international context of collecting, read the influential work of Krzysztof Pomian, *Collectionneurs, Amateurs et Curieux. Paris, Venise: XVIe–XVIIIe siècle* (Paris: Gallimard, 1987).
21. On collecting in the Netherlands, read Jaap van der Veen, "Vorstelijke en burgerlijke verzamelingen in de Nederlanden vanaf het einde van de zestiende eeuw tot omstreeks 1700," in *Kabinetten, galerijen en musea. Het verzamelen en presenteren van naturalia en kunst van 1500 tot heden*, ed. Ellinoor Bergvelt, Debora J. Meijers, and Mieke Rijnders (Zwolle: Waanders, 2005), 101–28.
22. Pieter Paul Rubens, for instance, was an avid collector of old, engraved gems. On the antique collection of Rubens, read Jeffrey M. Muller, *Rubens, The Artist as a Collector* (Princeton: Princeton University Press, 1989).
23. See Zirka Z. Filipczak, *Picturing Art in Antwerp 1550–1700* (Princeton: Princeton University Press 1987), 47–72.
24. Bruno Blondé, "Art and Economy in Seventeenth- and Eighteenth-Century Antwerp: A View from the Demand Side," in *Economia e arte secc. XIII-XVIII*, ed. Simonetta Cavaciocchi (Florence: Monnier, 2002), 379–91.
25. On this aspect also, read Bert Timmermans, "Networkers and Mediators in the 17th-Century Antwerp Art World: The Impact of Collectors-Connoisseurs on Artistic Processes of Transmission and Selection," in *Luxury in the Low Countries*, ed. Rengenier C. Rittersma (Brussels: Pharo Publishing, 2010), 109–34.
26. In England, for instance, the emerging genre of caricature was evidence of this. See Daniel Woolf, "Images of the Antiquary in Seventeenth-Century England," in *Visions of Antiquity: The Society of Antiquaries of London 1707–2007*, ed. Susan Pearce (London: Society of Antiquaries of London, 2007), 11–43.
27. Daniel Woolf, *The Social circulation of the Past*, 173–77; and Brian Cowan, "An Open Elite: The Peculiarities of Connoisseurship in Early Modern England," *Modern Intellectual History* 1 (2004): 151–83.
28. Sandra Langereis, *Geschiedenis als ambacht: oudheidkunde in de Gouden Eeuw: Arnoldus Buchelius en Petrus Scriverius* (Hilversum: Verloren 2001), 53.
29. Langereis, *Geschiedenis als ambacht*, 53. The same metaphor was used by Francis Bacon in *The Advancement of Learning* published in 1605, and became a mainstay in historical discourse until the nineteenth century.
30. Read also Thomas Dacosta Kaufmann, "Antiquarianism, the History of Objects, and the History of Art before Winckelmann," *Journal of the History of Ideas* 62 (2001): 523–41.
31. For an excellent overview, read Arthur MacGregor, *Curiosity and Enlightenment. Collectors and Collections from the Sixteenth to the Nineteenth Century* (New Haven: Yale University Press 2007), 179–212; and Woolf, *The Social Circulation of the Past*, 141–82.
32. Sandra Langereis, "*Antiquitates*: voorvaderlijke oudheden," in *Erfgoed. De geschiedenis van een begrip*, ed. Frans Grijzenhout (Amsterdam: Amsterdam University Press, 2007), 74.
33. Bastet, "Reizigers en oudheden," 35–41.
34. See Anne-Marie S. Logan, *The 'Cabinet' of the Brothers Gerard and Jan Reynst* (Amsterdam: North-Holland Publishing Company, 1979).

35. Literature on the evolution of European art markets has grown exponentially in the last few years. For a recent overview (with many more references), read Neil De Marchi and Hans J. Van Miegroet, eds., *Mapping Markets for Paintings in Europe 1450–1750* (Turnhout: Brepols 2006), 3–13.
36. All quotations are from *Auction Catalogue of Joseph Sansot* (Brussels: Poppens, 1739): "Antiques, bagues [. . .] & plusieurs autres curiositez"; "un cabinet complet de medailles antiques tant en or, argent, qu'en bronze [. . .] qui est un des plus parfaits, qui se trouve en ce pays." A copy of this catalogue can be found in the Rijksbureau voor Kunsthistorische documentatie, The Hague. I wish to thank Dries Lyna (University of Antwerp) for bringing this to my attention.
37. Dries Lyna, "Power to the Broker. Shifting Authorities over Public Sales in Eighteenth-Century Antwerp," in *Modernity and the Second-Hand Trade*, ed. Stobart and Van Damme, 158–74.
38. Historical interest in art connoisseurship connected to the process of auction is growing; read, for instance, Charlotte Guichard, "From Social Event to Urban Spectacle: Art Auctions in late Eighteenth-Century Paris," in *Fashioning Old and New: Changing Consumer Patterns in Western Europe (1650–1900)*, Bruno Blondé, Natacha Coquery, Jon Stobart and Ilja Van Damme(Turnhout: Brepols 2009), 203–16; and Dries Lyna, Filip Vermeylen and Hans Vlieghe, eds., *Art Auctions and Dealers: The Dissemination of Netherlandish Art during the Ancien Régime* (Turnhout: Brepols 2009).
39. Dries Lyna, "Changing Geographies and the Rise of the Modern Auction. Transformations on the Second-Hand Markets of Eighteenth-Century Antwerp," in *Fashioning Old and New*, ed. Blondé, Coquery, and Stobart, 169–84.
40. Jon Stobart and Ilja Van Damme, "Modernity and the Second-Hand Trade: Themes, Topics and Debates," in *Modernity and the Second-Hand Trade*, eds. Stobart and Van Damme, 6–7.
41. This point is made evident in Neil De Marchi and Hans J. Van Miegroet, "Transforming the Paris Art Market, 1718–1750," in *Mapping Markets for Painting*, eds. De Marchi and Van Miegroet, 383–402.
42. Stephen Bending, "Every Man Is Naturally an Antiquarian: Francis Grose and Polite Antiquities," *Art History* 25 (2002): 520–30.
43. Stephen Bending, "'The True Rust of the Barons' Wars: Gardens, Ruins and the National Landscape," in *Producing the Past. Aspects of Antiquarian Culture and Practice 1700–1850*, ed. Martin Myrone and Lucy Peltz (Aldershot: Ashgate, 1999), 83–93.
44. Read, for instance, Chantal Grell, *Le dix-huitième siècle et l'antiquité en France, 1680–1789* (Oxford: Voltaire Foundation, 1995); Rosamary Sweet, *Antiquaries: The Discovery of the Past in Eighteenth-Century Britain* (London: Hambledon and London, 2004) and Athena Tsingarida and Donna Kurtz, eds., *Appropriating Antiquity. Saisir l'antique. Collections et collectionneurs d'antiques en Belgique et en Grande-Bretagne au XIXe siècle* (Brussels: Le Livre Timperman, 2002).
45. Verschaffel, *De hoed en de hond*, 206.
46. Gerrit Verhoeven, *Anders reizen? Evoluties in vroegmoderne reiservaringen van Hollandse en Brabantse elites (1600–1750)* (Hilversum: Verloren, 2009), 207.
47. Theodore-Augustin Mann, *Description de la ville de Bruxelles ou etat présent tant ecclésiastique que civil de cette ville* (Brussels: Chez Lemaire, 1785), vol. 2, 53: "cabinets d'antiquités & de médailles'; and "d'autres, sans doute, possèdent des Cabinets en ce genre." On Theodore-Augustin Mann, read Verschaffel, *Historici in de Oostenrijkse Nederlanden*, 69–70.

48. *Almanach d'Anvers et du département des deux-nethes* (Antwerp: Chez Allebé, 1806), 218: "cabinets de tableaux" and "cabinets particuliers d'histoire naturelle, physique, antiquité, etc."
49. Jo Tollebeek, "Geschiedenis en oudheidkunde in de negentiende eeuw. De *Messager des sciences historiques* 1823–1896," *Bijdragen en Mededelingen betreffende de Geschiedenis der Nederlanden* 113 (1998): 23–55.
50. Dennis Coekelberghs and Pierre Loze, *Om en rond het neo-classicisme in België, 1770–1830* (Brussels: Gemeentekrediet, 1986).
51. Andreas Cornelis Lens, *Le costume ou essai sur les habillements et les usages de plusieurs peuples de l'antiquité prouvé par les monuments* (Luik: Chez J.F. Bassompierre, 1776), vii: "Le principal objet de la peinture, de la sculpture et d'autres arts semblables est de représenter les faits mémorables de l'Antiquité."
52. MacGregor, *Curiosity and Enlightenment*, 196.
53. Read Eric Gubel ed., *Egypte onomwonden: Egyptische oudheden van het museum Vleeshuis* (Antwerp: Pandora, 1995); Jean van Cleven, *Neogotiek in België* (Tielt: Lannoo, 1994); and Alfred Willis, "Flemish Renaissance Revival in Belgian Architecture (1830–1930)," PhD diss. (Ann Arbor University, 1984).
54. See also this aspect in Jo Tollebeek, "Het verleden in de negentiende eeuw. Arthur Merghelynck en het kasteel van Beauvoorde," *Verslagen en mededelingen van de Koninklijke Academie voor Nederlandse Taal- en Letterkunde* 109 (1999): 108–16.
55. Anneleen Arnout, "Het adres van de kunst of de kunst van het adres. Locatiepatronen en de verschuivingen op de scène van de Brusselse kunst- en antiekhandel, 1830–1914," *The Low Countries Journal of Social and Economic History* 9 (2012): 30–56. For the context in France, read Manuel Charpy "The Auction House and its Surroundings: The Trade of Antiques and Second-Hand Items in Paris during the Nineteenth century," in *Fashioning Old and New*, ed. Blondé, Coquery, Stobart and Van Damme, 217–33. For England, see especially Mark Westgarth, *A Biographical Dictionary of Nineteenth-Century Antique & Curiosity Dealers* (Glasgow: Regional Furniture Society, 2009).
56. On the changing historical consciousness in this period, read Brecht Deseure, "Ouvrez l'Histoire. Revolutionary Historical Politics in the Southern Netherlands (1792–1799)," *Low Countries Historical Review* 125 (2010): 25–47.
57. Herman Stynen, *De onvoltooid verleden tijd. Een geschiedenis van de monumenten- en landschapszorg in België 1835–1940* (Brussels: Stichting Vlaams Erfgoed, 1998).
58. For a broader overview, read Daniela Gallo, "Verzamelingen van oudheden van 1750 tot heden," in *Verzamelen. Van rariteitenkabinet tot kunstmuseum*, ed. Ellinoor Bergvelt, Debora J. Meijers, and Mieke Rijnders (Heerlen: Open Universiteit, 1993), 279–316.
59. This tension is analyzed in Belgium and the Netherlands by Jo Tollebeek, *De ijkmeesters. Opstellen over de geschiedschrijving in Nederland en België* (Amsterdam: Bakker, 1994).
60. A similar argument, but curiously enough not related to antiquarianism, is made by Stena Nenadic, "Romanticism and the Urge to Consume in the First half of the Nineteenth Century," in *Consumers and Luxury. Consumer Culture in Europe 1650–1850*, ed. Maxine Berg and Helen Clifford (Manchester: Manchester University Press, 1999), 208–27.

4 Recycling Orientalia
William Beckford's Aesthetics of Appropriation

Laurent Châtel

> [. . .] as if I were the Grand Turk.
>
> (William Beckford to Franchi, Paris, 31 October 1814[1])

Postmodern critical theory argues that since the 1960s art has been based on distance, pastiche, juxtaposition, and playful cut-and-paste with a view to recombining items into an eclectic whole without aiming at coherence or closure.[2] Pastiche, rewriting, and revisiting point to a strategy of recycling whereby authors and artists are subsumed or masked behind their eclectic renegotiation rather than foregrounded as they used to be in so-called romantic or modernist productions. But from a historical perspective what goes by the name of postmodernism could well be seen as an age-old artistic moment that crops up at regular intervals in time. However apt recycling may be to define the postmodernist approach, the concept proves equally operative to describe earlier artistic rhetoric characterised by nonlinearity, historical reference, ironic self-awareness, and witty ornament. The late eighteenth-century aesthete William Beckford of Fonthill (1760–1844) is a case in point to illustrate a Georgian manifestation of protean deconstruction, appropriation, incorporation, and reassembling with a view to reclaiming a forgotten past. The attempts by Alessandro Mendini's *Studio Alchymia* (1970s) to transform an existing object into a surprising, alluring thing are not so alien to Beckford's ventures that, in reinterpreting a given item, aimed at bewildering in a new, unexpected way.

Beckford was drawn to the East from a very early age: he was a distinguished collector who bought objects that came from Venice (often thought to be halfway from Mecca at the time), China, Japan, India, Persia, Turkey, and Syria. Throughout his life he acquired exceptional oriental pieces that had once belonged to aristocratic courts either in France or in the East: oriental drawings (Chinese, rare Indian miniatures) as well as artefacts and manuscripts in Arabic (notably a transcription of the *Arabian Nights* imported from Egypt by Edward Wortley Montagu). These items had been set in a prestigious context but had come to the end of their life cycle, such as the dismantling of aristocratic collections in Paris as well as the monarch's own collection, the sale of objects from Indian courts, and the circulation of written transcriptions of oral traditions. By integrating these items within a new location, literally by translating them, Beckford conferred upon them a new lease of life and thus qualifies as a "recycler." Admittedly, recycling does not come to mind when thinking of Beckford. The idea of waste—precisely its opposite—comes more naturally since he wasted away his fortune. As a collector with a taste for the extraordinary, he frittered away his inheritance and even pulled down his father's house, Fonthill "Splendens"—he hardly reclaimed anything from waste. However, there are ways of seeing recycling as a paradigm that is actually relevant for Beckford's achievements. Leaving aside the idea of reclaiming waste, I will focus on other definitions, such as "returning to a previous stage of a cyclic process," "rejuvenating," and "giving a new lease of life," which are the ingredients of Beckford's attitudes to oriental material and collecting.

LOCATING BECKFORD'S AESTHETICS AND RECYCLING

Beckford needs to be relocated on the eighteenth-century social and cultural map. Standard presentations tend to say that he was the "author" of *Vathek*, a patron of British architecture and a collector of exceptional standing. But the use of such terms as author, patron, and collector somehow do not pin down his creative talent.[3] Greater understanding of Beckford can be achieved when one is willing to reconsider him not as self-proclaimed author, or failed artist, but as an impersonator or interpreter. In the history of art, Beckford could hardly be called an antiquarian—a word he disapproved of since it was synonymous with inventory, catalogue, and factual data for him.[4] Antiquarianism in the 1780s under the auspices of the Society of Antiquarians was increasingly associated with the interest in so-called low and vulgar items, fragments of national heritage.[5] He was not a Grangerizer either, like Richard Gough, cutting and pasting bits and pieces here and there to create a *collage* of recycled items.[6] From a literary point of view, Beckford never positioned himself as an author, unlike his oft-mentioned Gothic *alter ego*, Horace Walpole, or for that matter, his orientalist contemporary and admirer, Lord Byron. Publication, diffusion, and promotion of his prose were never a priority; he would rather have read out a story with a view to impressing an audience, visually and orally, than be concerned with the laying out of a text. He ought to be seen as a fabulist, interested in impersonating a tale, making it alive, acting it out, without necessarily ascertaining its authorship. Throughout his life he was fascinated with hiding the source or origin of most of his creations, whether it be music emanating at Fonthill behind curtains, or Fonthill itself, bursting forth over the Wiltshire plains;[7] just as the ball in *Vathek* seems to roll on and on, without any visible agent, Beckford's writings were committed to the world of print without the author being directly involved.

Beckford's aesthetics lies in following up a lead: he enjoyed slipping into a narrative, integrating a given material, or seizing on an item and transforming it by giving it an idiosyncratic twist. Most of his artistic and literary "interventions" lay in lodging himself within a preexisting object or text, surreptitiously adding on to what had already been created or written. In other words, Beckford was less concerned with creating a new structure *ex nihilo* than in interpreting an item/event/story otherwise and providing it with a sequel. He had a profoundly cyclical sensibility that explains his taste for "enfilade," whether it be his patronage of an ever-growing architecture or the predominance of letters, sequels ("suite"), episodes, and "thoughts" in his scriptural production.[8] His interpretation can be understood as a form of horticultural grafting, or linguistic translation, or even in dramatic terms as an impersonation. Therefore, I argue that the old model of writer-turned-dilettante should give way to a new model—an overall aesthetics characterised by supplementing.[9] It is in the light of such a redefined perspective that the nature and extent of Beckford's recycling makes sense, as can be evidenced from his handling of oriental objects as well as manuscripts—a twofold illustration of his talent.

Reverting to a previous stage of a cyclic process and reactivating the lifespan of an object constituted the spirit of Beckford's creative energy. Indeed his flair for interpolating, interpreting, and grafting amounts to a denial of the dead letter. Once an item was perceived as losing value or becoming ineffective, he gave it a new lease of life through wit, satire, or sublimity—from dead letter to "second" life. Thus he (re)used items from Egypt, China, Japan, and India in order to produce an idiosyncratic *objet d'art* for use and/or contemplation, which he displayed in an individualised, Western context. I am not arguing that he considered an oriental piece to be wasted unless/until he metamorphosed it into a luxurious one by changing its format or setting. Recycling is to be understood as re-activating a cycle, namely rejuvenating an object, interpreting it, and conferring new meaning onto it: translating manuscripts or mounting precious stones anew forces admiration on the viewer, whose eyes open up and become alive to the object. Beckford thus revived the antique and medieval practice of *spolia*, whereby parts of building material were reused for new architecture, generating different economic, ideological, and aesthetic values. Considering the objects were subjected to a use for which they were not initially destined, the ideological valence of Beckford's recycling cannot be overlooked and will be examined in the last part of this study.

BECKFORD'S RECYCLING OF "CHINA," "OLD JAPAN," AND INDIAN JADE

Beckford's appreciation of Japanese lacquer led him to commission furniture specifically designed to insert disassembled pieces of lacquer. In its life cycle the "old Japan" thus shifted from being used for a box to being used for a cabinet. Three cabinets are considered exceptional in this respect, the two "Buys" *secrétaires* and the "Elephant" cabinet.[10] The design of new furniture with incorporated lacquer necessitated an adequate supply of lacquer, but the best specimens of export lacquer were by then few and far between. Beckford left the celebrated Van Diemen lacquer box[11] and the Mazarin chest[12] untouched—considered to be the most refined export lacquers produced on Japanese order as gifts to Europeans—but he had the "Buys" box dismembered.[13] In a note dated "1803," the clockmakers Benjamin and Lewis Vulliamy had however informed Beckford of the possible damage incurred:

> Cutting into several pieces (at a very great risque) a very fine Old Japan box and tray and making the design for two Cabinets in which the different parts of the box and tray are introduced the cover of the box and bottom of the tray form the two pannels of the doors & the sides of the box make the front of the drawers the Cabinet is made of purple wood and black ebony.[14]

The highly distinctive decoration of the box was made of gold and silver *hiromakie* and *takamakie*, with scenes inspired from the *Tales of the Genji*: reuse of the panels constituted a visual recycling of stories and as such the first form of reception of Japanese literature in Britain. Although Beckford must have gathered that the cut-out episodes came from a Japanese poetic cycle, it is not known whether he realised how pioneering he was. In the words of James Storer (no doubt picked up from Beckford himself), the end result was "two inestimable cabinets of the rarest old japan enriched with bronzes by Vulliamy" (Figure 4.1).[15]

More cabinets were ordered in Paris from the goldsmith Henri Auguste, one of which, bearing the *ébéniste* Adam Weisweiller's stamp, has been identified as the "elephant cabinet" and was described as such in 1822: "A Superb Cabinet of Gold Japan and Various Foreign Woods, on a stand ornamented with ormoulu, the frieze most exquisitely chased and gilt, surmounted by an Egyptian granite slab, made by Auguste."[16]

Beckford's reuse of lacquer points to several aspects of recycling. First, the reinterpretation of the material lies in inserting it into a new setting and thus prolonging its lifespan; it is a kind of naturalisation or acclimatisation. Second, delicate mounting was a tradition of French aristocratic patronage on the wane that Beckford perpetuated. In placing himself on a par with a few select collectors such as Madame de Pompadour, Empress Marie Thérèse in Vienna, or her daughter Queen Marie Antoinette in Paris, he therefore resumed a prestigious line and reassumed a discarded practice. Third, the element of risk-taking casts an interesting, if controversial light, on this type of recycling. According to Hugh Roberts, "the decision to sacrifice one of his two best boxes seems all the more difficult to explain [. . .] it is not inconceivable that he felt the existence of the second box in some way diminished the importance of the Van Diemen box."

Figure 4.1 Design for a *secrétaire*, c.1803, pen and watercolour. Attributed to Benjamin and Benjamin Louis Vulliamy. MS. Beckford c.84, fol.113r, The Bodleian Libraries, The University of Oxford.

Such a sacrifice reveals interconnected, somewhat paradoxical, elements within the recycling process. Collecting is not a passive activity of purchase and display of objects: the collector needs to "interpret" them and leave his mark. But since there is something hazardous about endangering lacquer, the collector, perversely enough, willingly runs the risk of being deprived of his object—an elaborate negotiation between life and death. What may strike as perverse or objectionable is that Beckford was dissatisfied with the object as it stood (the box could very happily have remained a box). In reverting to a previous stage of lacquer and in carrying its mounting one stage further, luxury is outdone by even greater luxury; "high" recycling, one might be tempted to call it, as opposed to "low" recycling which processes waste. Such "Solomonian richness,"[17] folly, and caprice could attract condemnation, as in fact it did in 1822–1823 when Fonthill Abbey was sold and opened to the public. In William Hazlitt's newspaper articles lashing out at Fonthill, the quibs about Beckford being a "jewel-maker" still reflect today negatively on the reuse and appropriation of luxurious items: "a desart of magnificence, a glittering waste of laborious idleness, a cathedral turned into a toy-shop and immense Museum of all that is most curious and costly [. . .] Mr Beckford has undoubtedly shown himself an industrious *bijoutier.*"[18] Yet instead of castigating Beckford outright for running the risk of jeopardizing an object for the sake of self-empowerment, it would be fairer to give a balanced picture based on the realisation that recycling was *one* aspect of his collecting. His taste for lacquer was dually manifested: on the one hand, a collection of "ready-made," as it were (untouched boxes and chests) and on the other hand, adventurous and playful recasting (recycled lacquer).

Beckford's commissions to silversmiths in the 1810s also partake of a creative pattern of recycling. Mounting precious stones or Chinese porcelain was naturally not new; in fact, in Beckford's psyche, it was very much associated with prerevolutionary French aristocratic circles and so here again some of his motivations (apart from aesthetic ones) may be put down to cultural and ideological reasons since in resuming such a practice he was recycling distinguished collectors' habits. What is striking about the way Beckford mounted creamware is that the inspiration for the silver came from the original itself, thus signalling a great degree of attention and respect for the taste and creativity of the culture from where the object originated. Indeed a number of "mountings" echo the very object that they enclose in such an elaborate and refined fashion as to make the Western interpolation discreet. I would like to suggest that such mounting is not an aggressive hold over the object but a delicate compromise or alliance between the object "extracted" and the "displaying" mode. It is highly relevant here that the objects created with Asian porcelain were not just for luxurious, top-of-the-range display cases but useful ware such as sugar basins and bowls; in fact, the ceramic wares were sometimes modest pieces or fragments recycled into utensils for everyday use. Were it not for the silver mounting which was an expensive item, these creations would qualify for Lévi-Strauss's "bricolage"[19]—a do-it-yourself activity which the anthropologist had theorised in relation to the simple, useful wares fabricated by the "savage mind" with very modest financial means and which is now applied to postmodern jumbling up of materials. Allowing for the difference in means, one cannot but be struck by the almost shocking proximity between the aesthete's mind and the "savage mind."

Several pieces created with the help of his friend Gregorio Franchi and the professional expertise of James Aldridge and John Harris testify to a flair for dressing oriental *exotica* in Western garb and to a dialogue between East and West. A cream jug dated 1820–1821, bearing the Aldridge hallmark,[20] is a typical case of cross-feeding as the oriental pattern of the chrysanthemum drawn on the porcelain is delicately echoed in the engraving patterns of the silver foot base, which, in turn, also echo Beckford's heraldic cinquefoils. In several areas, the shapes of the jug take their inspiration from the Chinese vases drawn on the octagonal sides. For instance, one vase has two handles with a complex, convoluted pattern, which find themselves echoed on the jug in the ornate curving of the gilded handle as well as in the forms engraved around the cinquefoils on the upper lid.[21] The very texture of the lower branch of the handle is reminiscent of the convoluted intricacy of the forms of the vases drawn on the Chinese porcelain (in one case, trellis-like and in the other, crenelated). The delicacy of such interpolation is all the more noticeable when seen next to the heavier rococo mounting of the celadon vases[22] which in comparison seem more pompous, or as Beckford termed it, "Pompadourised."[23] Another stupendous example is an *Imari* cup mounted in the form of a loop-handled jug: the handle echoes the feet of the stool as well as the curvilinear shape of the lady's back, which creates a wonderful *mise en abyme* effect, whereby the mounting unobtrusively frames the mounted (Figure 4.2).[24]

In the 1810s and 1820s in England other silversmiths such as Frederick Crace were also engaged in a type of "chinoiserie" mounting that enhanced

Figure 4.2 Mounted *Imari* cup in the form of a loop-handled cream jug. West Dean College, UK (Edward James Foundation-1163 OPT 75).

Chinese porcelain, but Beckford's idiosyncrasy is to have mixed references, at once Chinese, Mughal, and European heraldic motifs. The intricacy, precision, and beauty of the *objets d'art* that came into being as a result of such syncretic processing are clearly exemplified by a number of Beckford pieces now in the collections at Charlecote Park (National Trust), Brodick Castle (NT for Scotland[25]), and at West Dean (Edward James Foundation), notably a flask glass with red and black mottling, and a number of bowls and cream jugs (Figure 4.3).

The conceit of imitating one material with another is taken a step further with the glass flask: the fluted shape is turned into a sardonyx-like jar with Islamic elegance thanks to the addition of extremely refined, delicate twisted handles.[26] As for the *famille noire* bowl,[27] it has an unusual decoration with silver-gilt lining bearing Beckford's coat of arms surrounded by a flurry of martlets all rushing up to the rim before cascading over it in a way that revives a style seen on Japanese lacquer. Two traditions are thus being recycled—a medieval one, with the heraldic dimension and a Japanese one, with the decorative inventiveness typical of lacquer.

One last illustration of the diversity of his recycling is his reuse of precious stones. Jade was reused to produce bowls, cups, and ladles or, in one

Figure 4.3 Silver mounted *Imari* sugar bowl. Mounts by James Aldridge, c. 1817–1818; Japan porcelain, 13.5 cm. West Dean College, UK (Edward James Foundation-1163 OPT 78).

specific and rare case, a tobacco pipe. Most often the stone was acquired on the continent (lapis lazuli or agate), but in order to evoke the distant lands they originate from, Beckford, Franchi, and James Aldridge designed the metalwork in 1815–1816 with an oriental feel. The lapis lazuli cup[28] and the "Persian" cup[29] are for instance stupendous examples of an encounter between East and West, not just because the "West" has reused an Eastern matter, but because "Western" craft took its cue from the East for the design of the mounting: the trumpet-like fluted base of the cup and the decorative details have a distinct oriental flavour. Finally, if one looks at the jade tobacco pipe (Figure 4.4)[30] the alliance between varied elements is refined and complex: the recycled object is a Mughal ewer or water vase made of nephrite. It is a rare object as most other extant water pipes are either in base or precious metal with only six items in jade traced.

Beckford's hookah had a distinguished provenance if one is to believe the 1823 Fonthill sale catalogue, that of Tippoo Sahib (1750–1799), known as Tipu Sultan, the ruler of Mysore, who was killed by the British in the Fourth

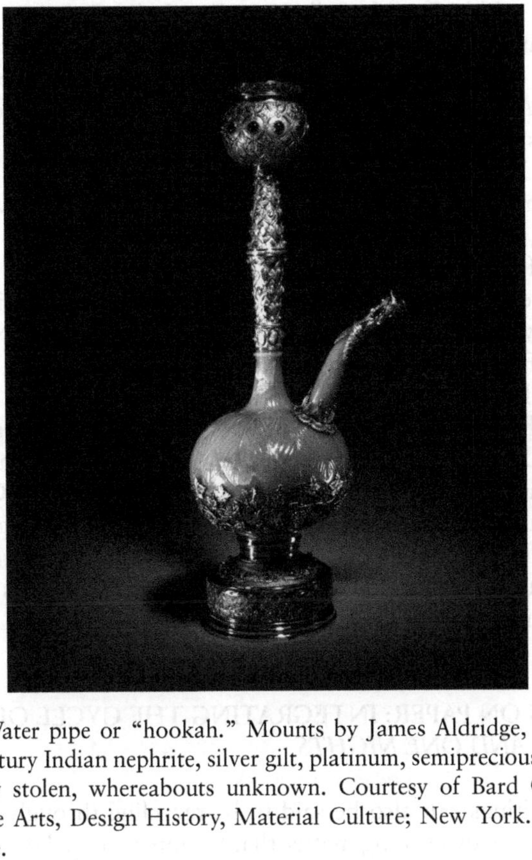

Figure 4.4 Water pipe or "hookah." Mounts by James Aldridge, c. 1814–1822; eighteenth-century Indian nephrite, silver gilt, platinum, semiprecious stones, 57.2 × 21.6 cm; now stolen, whereabouts unknown. Courtesy of Bard Graduate Center: Decorative Arts, Design History, Material Culture; New York. Photographer: Antonia Reeve.

Anglo-Mysore War. The sack of the fort at Seringapatam in 1799 generated a British rage over Tippoo Sahib's possessions that became trophies of the British victory and were displayed proudly in a gesture that some deem typical of "cultural colonizing."[31]

In view of a certain parallelism between Beckford and royal patronage—with the employment of Wyatt at Windsor or the orientalising taste of the Prince Regent—some have connected Beckford's "hookah" to the royal family's nationalist enthusiasm for the Duke of Wellington and their "nationalist" detestation of Tipu's sultanic rule.[32] Indeed the resonance that Tipu's memorabilia had for members of the royal family merged with that of the population at large into a wider consensus of British hatred for "despotism." However it is more likely that Beckford saw it otherwise: he who named Europeans "Firenguis" and entertained no warmth towards his own compatriots enjoyed his "hookah" as a reminder *not* of British power but rather of Indian intensity. The recycling of Tipu's nephrite within Fonthill Abbey cannot be compared to the reuse of Tipu's tiger—the automaton that attracted droves in Regency London.[33] For one thing, the "hookah" was exhibited privately and could not have been instrumentalised for a national cause. The public exhibition of the "tiger" within English walls in an East India Company house shifted the meaning and vocation of the roaring automaton: although fear and shock could still be managed by the tiger on display—and still does today in its Victoria and Albert glass case—what immediately followed were feelings of comfort, reassurance, and pride at seeing the tiger captured and made inoffensive. While in India the viewer's excitement would have been directed against the Englishman, in Britain it was redirected against the one who unleashed such violence, the tiger's owner, Tipu himself. One might argue that the reappropriation of the tiger killed off its original vocation, intensity, and meaning. Conversely, Beckford's reappropriation of the Tipu's nephrite in the privacy of Fonthill revived the power and aura of the Indian sultan. Newly set and translated at Fonthill, the "hookah" connected its owner to an exotic imaginary, princely lifestyle and endowed him with a usurped identity and "kudos." Thanks and through the "hookah" Beckford could enjoy a vicarious experience of the luxury of a South Indian court—which points to a playful, if at times immature, self-empowering dimension of "recycling." Consequently, relocation, transplantation, and resetting are not univocally negative or positive, "political" or "aesthetic:" Tipu's recycled nephrite illustrates the rich overlay of values—at times conflicting ones—which individuals or communities may read into another cultural object.

RECYCLING ON PAPER: INTEGRATING THE CYCLE OF THE *THOUSAND AND ONE NIGHTS*

Beckford's writings can also be said to be recycling through and through. He reused an already existing matter that he impersonated or enacted anew. Some might be tempted to connect this practice to age-old rewriting, which, in part it is, but the paradigm of recycling fits more accurately. For instance, his first publication, *Biographical Memoirs of Extraordinary Painters* (1780), is made up of recycled "real" lives of artists mixed with invention: entire passages were lifted out of Decamps's *Vie des peintres flamands* (1753–1763) or are references to recent prints by Volpato of *Raphael Loggia* (1777); Beckford's hallmark lies in the wit and irony of his adaptation. His so-called "travel diary," *Dreams, Waking Thoughts and Incidents* (1783) is in fact composed of letters which are reworked and recycled into a travel tale; his so-called "satiric novels," *Azemia* and *Modern Novel Writing*, are mostly bits and pieces culled from contemporary women's novels plagiarised and cobbled-up together into an eclectic whole, with interpolated passages in Beckford's hand. To indulge in recycling partakes of the joke, the send-up, the farce, but also mischief as a good dose of impertinence is needed to outdo what is given and surpass it. When dealing with the Arabic manuscripts of the *Arabian Nights*, the subversive dimension inherent in interjecting and interpolating was enhanced since the "source" material already contained subversive subjects (luxury, lust, homosexuality, unaccountable despotism, vice, etc.). Assuming the oriental gaze and guise suited Beckford particularly well.

Until recently Beckford was ranked as a pseudo-orientalist alongside other British or European contemporaries engaged in translating or supplementing Galland's *Mille et une nuits* (1704–1717) for the English market.[34] In fact, Beckford should by now have earned a different place in the history of orientalist tale-telling not only because he orchestrated a new translation of the *Arabian Nights* conceived as a follow-up to Galland but also because he himself composed a new cycle of "nights" with *Vathek and Its Episodes*.[35] Beckford did not use one of the early archetypal "mother" sources that Galland had—a three- or four-volume medieval manuscript of *Alf Layla wa-Layla* imported from Syria—but he came close to the Frenchman's authentic, scholarly perusal of genuine manuscripts. In the early 1780s, Lady Elizabeth Craven (1750–1828), his "dear Arabian,"[36] later Margravine of Anspach, provided Beckford with a once-in-a-lifetime opportunity to have a first-hand access to Arabic manuscripts dated 1764—now known as the Edward Wortley Montagu or Bodleian "Arabian Nights." Sometime between 1780 and 1786 he commissioned a Turk born in Mecca ("Zemir, the old Mahometan who assisted me in translating W.Montague's M.S"[37]), and with the help of Lady Craven and Marianne-Agnès de Fauques de Vaucluse, transcriptions and translations were made. In October 1782 he announced that the Christmas festivities would include "a right old Mussulman to serve up tales hot & hot."[38] In January 1783, he wrote from Fonthill: "We [. . .] translate Arabic every Night."[39]

Such orientalist work generated various forms of recycling. Beckford resumed the cycle of the "Thousand and One Nights" where Antoine Galland had left it and instilled extra life into it by providing fresh stories and adding his own personal twist to them. He thus gave a new lease of life to a material that might have fallen on deaf ears or remained invisible to

Europeans; until Galland translated the *Nights*, Europe had been deprived of this abundant wealth of stories. In the 1780s, Beckford belonged to the "second generation" of the *Nights*' discoverers and was intent not only to live up to Galland but also pursue his task by providing readers with more.[40] The appetite for further tales had been growing in Europe. In the 1780s, recycling the *Nights* thus meant keeping the interest going. The Earl of Caylus and Cazotte in France did just that, the latter publishing a *Suite des Contes arabes* in 1788. Note the title both Beckford and Cazotte chose—"Suite des . . . "—which is literally a follow-up to Galland's work, itself subtitled "Contes arabes." If Beckford's own *Suite* had been published at that time, he could have been credited with keeping the English interest in the *Nights*. Yet Beckford's translations were into French and he never published them.[41] The most obvious or expected form of recycling would have been to supervise a translation into English for his fellow countrymen. Indeed, part of the motivation of orientalists was patriotic as their concern for translating the "Arabian Nights" was contiguous with the concern for English letters, or what they would have called the "rise of poesy." By turning the stories into English the translator paid homage to a foreign material but was also appropriating it as part of "English fiction." None of this "service for the nation" in Beckford's case: he would not have seen himself as "ambassador of the *Nights*" in England. Just as he cared little to exhibit objects to public view, he was not concerned with rejuvenating English letters or publishing the material. This is confirmed by his choice of language, French, rather than English, because French was the natural language of oriental scholarship—a hallmark of authenticity, historicism, and purification away from the fake and fraudulent "pseudo-orientalist" ventures. He wanted to locate his self in the wake of prestigious predecessors like Galland, connect with this tradition, and pursue the cyclical process of the nights, guaranteeing their afterlife. Above all, what mattered to him was to integrate and infiltrate the cycle so as to be part of an embedded structure, a nonlinear "progress" without beginning or end; voicing, prompting, interpreting tales and impersonating a crafty fabulist. By reading stories aloud to a "happy few," he somehow refused to close his "cycle" into a book, letting it spiral away, left to its own devices. Finally, writing new tales or supplements such as *Vathek and the Episodes* should not be seen in relation to the context of the rise of the novel in British literature, but rather as a movement backwards, looking back to previous literary models. Beckford's tales recycled already published historical data, visual items, and cultural accounts of the East pieced together from Carsten Nieburh's *Description de l'Arabie* (1774), D'Herbelot's *Bibliothèque orientale* (1776), Richardson's *Dissertation* (1778), the Koran, and notably the plates found in Chardin's *Journal du Voyage . . . en Perse* (1686), such as the "View of Persepolis Ruins."[42] The choice of assuming a persona that voices constructs of the past partakes of a larger reactionary posture against England and repressive forces generally. As Ros Ballaster put it, the trope of the Orient is "backwardness."

"To travel to oriental territories [. . .] is to travel 'backward' in time (to retrace ancient history), in space (from the 'new' to the 'old' world) and in identity (from contract and civility to despotism)."[43] In recycling Orientalia, Beckford found a repression-free terrain and identified with figures invested with strong despotic authority such as the powerful Caliph "Wathek" with his petrifying gaze. Although "Wathek" may have been a figure compensating for his own helplessness, it was not necessarily a model. Beckford's self-identification with the "contes arabes" and the figure of "Wathek" is a playful, self-derisive embodiment of power and the sublime. Just as the country expected someone like Beckford to take up the cudgels for antislavery and lower his gaze, he went right the other way—reactionary, rearguard, *Ancien Régime*—to free his self and buttress up his identity through Eastern tropes. Egotist recycling, some might say? Let me now turn to an interpretative overview of the ideological implications of recycling.

THE AESTHETICS AND POLITICS OF RECYCLING: "WASTING" IT ON EUROPEAN EYES?

In his aesthetic and literary productions alike, whether these productions are words, "china" or jade, common patterns of recycling emerge: designing and writing both engage in the same structural process of grafting, interpolation and *collage*. Equally, similar questions have been raised about controversial or ambivalent implications: recycling of rare and luxury items is not univocally "correct" or "incorrect." I would like to recapitulate the above arguments. Looking at the various ways recycling is processed, several paradigms have been identified: horticultural (grafting), linguistic (translating, interpreting), and dramatic (impersonating). The spatial dimension of "translation" proves to be an essential component of all three: lacquer, ceramics, or manuscripts were transported and relocated. However, can the purchase and use of a foreign item not be perceived as forced transportation or deportation? Admittedly, an interest in incorporating oriental *exotica* on English soil and in English letters is not without connotations. Moving an object, or piece of an object, is not harmless. The history of Western art is based on the uprooting of objects with (in)famous cases such the Elgin Marbles or the French sack in 1861 of Beckford's cherished Chinese Summer Palace and the Yuan Ming-Yan Gardens. Seizing on a piece of china or precious stone and mounting it with a European-made silver or gold mount is literally an "encounter" between East and West, but to what extent does such hybridizing generate a travesty? One may readily see that the mounting or resetting of an Eastern object can be perceived as a patriarchal and domineering strategy. One may claim, with Edward Said's *Orientalism* in mind, that it is a hegemonic appropriation typical of colonizing, imperialist countries. Said's argument was that English orientalists "are primarily to be understood as prisoners of an institutionalised system of discourse which makes it impossible for them to regard Orientals as human beings like themselves."[44] Beckford's Jamaican roots make his uprooting of Oriental items, if not suspect, highly politically and ethically incorrect. Son of a West Indian planter, an arrogant exploiter (since he never committed anything in writing against slavery)—some would rank him as a nonabolitionist, "selfish giant"—Beckford fits the description of the hegemonic Westerner appropriating and uprooting the Orient for his personal consumption and use.

Can the reuse of ceramics or stones and its novel appearance in gilded bronze be considered as highlighting the country, art, and craft from which they originate? Historians of taste often say that the bronze "enriches" or "improves" the item—which it does literally, if only in terms of costliness—but they underestimate the condescending undertone of such "added value." Others argue that it pays homage to it: "a wide variety of ceramic wares [. . .] have been enriched with metal mounts in the course of European history [. . .]. These mounts were a tribute not so much to the beauty of the porcelains as to the extreme rarity of the material."[45] When the mounting aims at tempering or toning down the exoticism of the object itself, such taming amounts to naturalisation or acclimatisation. Inevitably the ultimate reaction against such usurpation might be, is it not wasting the oriental other upon unappreciative European eyes?

There is room for a more positive interpretation of relocation, though. One's perception of transfer actually depends on the (re)use of the material, thus precisely on the ways and means in which it is subjected to recycling. Another aspect of translation here appears—an adaptation and re-presentation of the Orient: an object, like a word, may be "borrowed" from its source culture and translated into a target culture; the means by which this "cultural transfer" is done (whether it be understood as borrowing, *calque*, adaptation, compensation) are indicators that help assess the manner in and extent to which an object has been "recycled." In Beckford's case, the recycling process takes its cue from the recycled item; in other words, the piece is inserted in a recipient that is not only adequate but shaped, moulded, inspired from the object itself. This kind of recycling respects the otherness of the foreign item by making it the standard or reference of its displaying dress. The result is idiosyncratic novelty: each item keeps its own autonomous, self-reflexive value while producing new effect by its recombination. Most objects studied above are eclectic but are mounted in such a way as to stand for themselves with a wonderful unity of purpose and design that makes them autonomous. Far from grotesque hybridity so typical of mongrel *chinoiseries*, this type of object is singular: the recycling process has not detracted from the intrinsic value of the item, nor from the quality of inserted motifs.

Finally, looking at the motivations behind recycling, several reasons may be found: astonishment, self-empowerment, and estrangement. The oriental ingredient served less an authoritarian ideology than an aesthetics of "surprise" and novelty; to capture the Western senses and guarantee astonishment Beckford felt the need to recast his oriental items, provide a shrine for them and give them a new shine. Cleanliness and lustre mattered. Recycling is a negotiation between a revivalist, historicist streak turned backwards and a cult of freshness, newness and youth turned forward. Such an aesthetics drawn to revival, novelty, and youth places Beckford between Joseph Addison's discussions of "novelty" and "strange," William Chambers's principles of sublimity in his *Dissertation on Oriental Gardening* (1772), and Oscar Wilde's cult of beauty and youth. But behind the need to be "refreshed" and "astonished" lies a search for new authority and sovereignty. Rather than assert a colonizing posture in the Orient, Beckford collected oriental items to displace his self and find a new locus of power. Sourcing power in the East was familiar to eighteenth-century figures such as Madame de Pompadour, Stalisnaus Leszynski, Empress Maria Theresa, and Marie Antoinette. In fact, I would argue that Beckford's fascination for lacquer, Persian drawings, and Indian miniatures which art historians tend to connect with France (or to ascribe to a specific French taste and tradition) was a wider phenomenon in Europe.[46] The deposed Stalisnaus of Poland legitimised and reinforced the sovereignty of his peripheral court in Lunéville through the oriental trope by reusing Turkish models, as Nebahat Avcioglu brilliantly contends.[47] As for Marie Antoinette, she inherited the extraordinary lacquer pieces now exhibited at Versailles from her mother, Habsbourg Empress Marie Thérèse, who taught her children how to recycle "old Japan" and Mughal miniatures.[48] Schönbrunn Palace boasted some of the most stupendous instances of oriental recycling in Europe: the "Vieux-Laque" Zimmer, with its large panels of lacquer embedding family portraits, and the "Millionenzimmer," with its cut-out Deccan miniatures incorporated within rococo gilded cartouches and a ceiling with imitations of Persian drawings painted by a European artist.[49] Ebba Koch and Michael Yonan have investigated the complexity as well as playfulness involved in the *collages* orchestrated by Marie Thérèse, while Natasha Eaton has pointed out the positive, enlightening value of oriental cosmopolitanism adopted by Western rulers.[50]

Therefore, Beckford's collection was instrumental in taking him a stage backwards in the cyclical process of time, both in his "recycling" of aristocratic lacquer and in his use and display of pieces from eastern royal courts. He did not revive the French *Ancien Régime* or *Empire* (for that would imply a political project he did not entertain), but he wished to recycle some of the aura attached to their courts. Recycling conferred some of the glow and magnificence of the places where the objects came from and caused astonishment cause astonishment. The strategy of recycling is less imitation or mimicry than reenactment—embedding the Orient in his private spaces and in turn embedding himself within an orientalised dress. While the collector recycles a piece for a new life, he is also recycled and bewildered, becoming a stranger to himself and others. "[A]s if I were the grand Turk," Beckford wrote in 1782, showing "the respect which [he] had always conceived for the Sublime Porte."[51] Such egotist delusions of grandeur entailed loss and alienation not simply for the recycled object, but also for the recycling subject.

NOTES

1. Letter from Beckford to Franchi, Paris, 31 October 1814, William Beckford, *Life at Fonthill, 1807–1822: From the Correspondence of William Beckford*, trans. and ed. Boyd Alexander, (Stroud: Nonsuch, 2006), 142.
2. The various definitions here are based on Frederic Jameson, Postmodernism: The Cultural Logic of Late Capitalism (Durham, NC: Duke University Press, 1991); Charles Jencks, *What is Post-Modernism?* (London: Academy, 1986) and Glenn Adamson Paola Antonelli Jane Pavitt Glenn Adamson, Paola Antonelli and Jane Pavitt, eds., *Postmodernism—Style and Subversion, 1970–1990* (London: Victoria and Albert Museum Publications, 2011).
3. Although Beckford's collection has long been examined closely, art historians interested in the study of taste have looked at Beckford as a collector and patron, not as a creator. However, the work of Clive Wainwright, Malcolm Baker, Michael Snodin, and Bet Mcleod sheds extensive light on Beckford's participation and collaboration with his friend Gregorio Franchi, touching on issues of "authorship" and "creativity." I therefore acknowledge the work that has gone into the study of taste but choose to redirect attention onto Beckford himself, rather than his objects; I locate my research within cultural studies, keeping an eye on "production" and creation. See Malcolm Baker, Michael Snodin, and Tim Shroder, *Beckford and Hamilton Silver from Brodick Castle* (London: Spink & Son, 1980); Michael Snodin and Malcolm Baker, "Beckford's Silver I & II," *The Burlington Magazine* 122, no. 932 (November 1980): 734–48, 820–34 (updated in Derek E. Ostergard, ed., *William Beckford-An Eye for the Magnificent* [New Haven: Yale University Press, 2001], chapter 11); Clive Wainwright, *The Romantic Interior* (New Haven: Yale University Press, 1984); Bet McLeod, "A Celebrated Collector," in *An Eye for the Magnificent*, ed. Derek E. Ostergard, chapter 9, 155–75; Laurent Châtel, "'One Must Become Half-Catholic.' William Beckford (1760–1844) as 'Impolite and Uncommercial' Aesthete" in *Marketing Art in the British Isles, 1700 to the Present. A Cultural History*, ed. Charlotte Gould and Sophie Mesplède (Aldershot: Ashgate, 2012), 195–211.
4. "The people of the house [. . .] officiously delivered me up to a professed antiquary, one of those diligent, plausible young men, to whom, God help me! I have so capital an aversion." *Dreams, Waking Thoughts and Incidents* (1783), letter XIII (10 September), ed. Robert J. Gemmett (Stroud: Nonsuch, 2006), 121.
5. Rosemary Sweet, *Antiquaries: The Discovery of the Past in Eighteenth-Century Britain* (Hambledon: Continuum Press, 2004).
6. See Lucy Peltz's work and especially Lucy Peltz and Martin Myrone, eds., *Producing the Past: Aspects of Antiquarian Culture and Practice* (Aldershot: Ashgate, 1999).
7. When he staged an opera with Lady Craven in April 1782, he wrote: "The efficient chorus is behind the scenes, enveloped in mystery." Quoted in John W. Oliver, *The Life of William Beckford* (London: Oxford University Press, 1932), 110.
8. See Laurent Châtel, "Utopies paysagères: Les sublimes 'progrès' de William Beckford," *RSEAA* 51 (2000): 281–322; http://www.persee.fr/web/revues/

home/prescript/article/xvii_0291-3798_2000_num_51_1_1529 (accessed 8 July 2014).

9. I argued against a separation of literary and artistic achievements and a remapping of Beckford in my doctoral dissertation, "Utopies paysagères: vues et visions dans les écrits et dans les jardins de William Beckford" (PhD Diss., Université Paris III, 2000).
10. The documentation about Beckford's lacquer is listed below chronologically: Francis Watson, "Beckford, Mme de Pompadour, the Duc de Bouillon and the Taste for Japanese Lacquer in the Eighteenth Century," *Gazette des Beaux-Arts* 61 (1963): 101–27; John Earle, "Genji meets Yang Guifei: A Group of Japanese Export Lacquers," *Transactions of the Oriental Ceramic Society* 47 (1984): 45–76; Hugh Roberts, "Beckford, Vulliamy and Old Japan," *Apollo* 124, no. 296 (October 1986): 338–41; Alexandre Pradère, *Les ébénistes français de Louis XIV à la Révolution* (Paris: Chêne, 1989), 40–45; Thibaut Wolvesperges, *Le Meuble français en laque au XVIIIe siècle* (Paris: L'Amateur, 2000), fig. 3; Oliver Impey and John Whitehead, "Observations on Japanese Lacquer in the Collection of William Beckford," in *An Eye for the Magnificent*, ed. Ostergard, 217–27; Adriana Turpin, "'Filling the Void': The Development of Beckford's Taste and the Market in Furniture," in *An Eye for the Magnificent*, ed. Ostergard, 177–202.
11. V&A, London; W.49:1–1916; see http://collections.vam.ac.uk/item/O18899/document-box-the-van-diemen-box/ (accessed 8 July 2014).
12. V&A, London 412:1–1882; see http://collections.vam.ac.uk/item/O18900/chest-the-mazarin-chest/ (accessed 8 July 2014).
13. Its date is c. 1635 and its provenance is the Dutch couple Philips and Pieternellae Buys; see Roberts, "Beckford, Vulliamy," 341.
14. Public Record Office, C 104/58/1: bill written out for Beckford in the Vulliamy firm papers.
15. James Storer, *A Description of Fonthill Abbey, Wilts.* (London, 1812) 11–12. The cabinets now stand at Elton Hall, UK.
16. Catalogue of the aborted Fonthill Sale, Christie's, 18 October 1822, lot 96. The cabinet is now in a private collection; see Wolvesperges, *Le Meuble français*, 3.
17. Letter from Beckford to Franchi, 4 July 1814; *Life at Fonthill*, translated and edited by Boyd Alexander (Stroud: Nonsuch, 2006), 136.
18. *The London Magazine*, November 1822.
19. Claude Lévi-Strauss, *The Savage Mind* (Chicago: University of Chicago Press, 1966).
20. National Trust for Scotland, Brodick Castle (58.534); reproduced in Ostergard, *An Eye for the Magnificent*, 209.
21. Previous commentators have argued that the decoration of the upper lid owes more to Renaissance patterns than to the actual details on the Chinese ceramic, but I would like to argue for an even greater affinity between the mounted object and the mounting than has been credited before.
22. Metropolitan Museum, New York; 49.7.80–81; reproduced in Ostergard, *An Eye for the Magnificent*, 328.
23. Letter from Beckford to Franchi, 30 June 1814, *Life at Fonthill*, translated and edited by Alexander Boyd, 136: "other pieces of seagreen and seacoal, cleverly made [?] if you like and fine, but Pompadourised enough to make one vomit." Bet Mcleod discusses the use of this term in Ostergard, *An Eye for the Magnificent*, chapter 9.
24. The jug is in the Edward James Foundation collection, West Dean 1163 OPT 75.
25. See for instance the bowl reproduced in Ostergard, *An Eye for the Magnificent*, 324.

26. The flask was reproduced in Ostergard, *An Eye for the Magnificent*, 387.
27. The bowl, no longer in the Collection of the Trustees of Edward James Foundation (1163 OPT 97), was reproduced in Ostergard, *An Eye for the Magnificent*, 323.
28. Fitzwilliam Museum, Camb., M.I & A-1990.
29. V&A 428: 1–1882.
30. The "hookah" is now missing and its whereabouts unknown.
31. Layla S. Diba, Notice 55 in Ostergard, *An Eye for the Magnificent*, 339.
32. Natasha Eaton discusses the ambivalent reading of despotism in the eighteenth century: according to her, "Montesquieu admits to a threshold of ambiguity separating the structures of monarchical government from despotism: both have real and symbolic power concentrated in the hands of a single ruler" (66) in Natasha Eaton, "The Art of Colonial Despotism. Portraits, Politics and Empire in South India, 1750–1795," *Cultural Critique* 70 (Fall 2008): 363–92.
33. See Richard H. Davis, *Lives of Indian Images* (Princeton: Princeton University Press, 1997), chapter 5; and Susan Stronge, *Tipu's Tigers* (London: V&A Publishing, 2009); see also the notice on the V&A website: http://www.vam.ac.uk/content/articles/t/tippoos-tiger/ (accessed 8 July 2014).
34. Mahmoud Manzalaoui, "Pseudo-Orientalism in Transition: The Age of Vathek," in *William Beckford of Fonthill 1760–1844: Bicentenary Essays*, ed. Moussa-Mahmoud (Port Washington: Kennikot, 1964), 123–50.
35. See my "Les sources des contes orientaux de William Beckford (*Vathek* et la "Suite des contes arabes"): bilan de recherches sur les écrits et l'esthétique de Beckford," *Etudes Epistémé* 7 (2005): 93–106, http://revue.etudes-episteme.org/?les-sources-des-contes-orientaux (accessed 8 July 2014); "Orientalist Translations, Grafts and Outgrowths: New Perspectives on the *Complete Works* of William Beckford," *The Beckford Journal* (2005) 39–49; "The Lures of Eastern Lore: William Beckford's Oriental Dangerous Supplements," *RSEAA* 67 (2011) 127–44; "Re-Orienting William Beckford: Translating and Adapting the *Thousand and one Nights*," in *The Arabian Nights: Encounters and Translations in Literature and the Arts*, ed. Philip Kennedy and Marina Warner (New York: New York University Press, forthcoming).
36. Letter to Lady Craven, 29 June 1782, Red Copy Book (MS Beckford e.1).
37. Letter to S. Henley, dated from Vevey, 9 February 1786 in Alfred Morrison, ed., *Collection of Autograph Letters and Historical Documents*, second series, privately printed (1893), I, 196.
38. Letter to S. Henley, dated 28 October 1782 in Morrison, I, 187.
39. Letter to Mr. Hamilton, dated "Fonthill, Jan. 4th 1783" in Bodleian, MS Beckford e.1 (RCB) fol.6–9.
40. That later generations felt entitled to add to Galland's work can be gauged from a note by Jonathan Scott: "From what Dr Russell has said of his manuscript, the contents of Wortley Montague's and the above fragment [. . .] I conjecture that no two copies will be found to accord in arrangement, or Tales, but that each will vary according to the Place or Country in which it was procured, as the popular Stories of this or that have been added in continuation of the original work. All that the intelligent Orientalist of Europe requires, is to prevent European fabrication being foisted upon him for Oriental composition." (Bodleian Library, Orient. 557, fols 50–52)
41. Eventually it behoved Jonathan Scott and Richard Burton to rekindle the flame and produce a translation of new "Arabian Nights."
42. For a study of the recycling of "real" views and data into "visions," see my PhD diss., "Utopies paysagères," 149–216.

43. Ros Ballaster, *Fables of the East-Selected Tales from the East* (Oxford: Oxford University Press, 2005), 1.
44. Kathryn Tidrick, *Heart-Beguiling Araby* (Cambridge: Cambridge University Press, 1981), 2.
45. Francis Watson and Gillian Wilson, *Oriental Mounted Porcelain* (Los Angeles: The J. Paul Getty Trust, 1999), introduction.
46. I do not question Beckford's francophile taste (Ostergard, *An Eye for the Magnificent*, 159) but I wish to suggest that Beckford was not just being "French" in collecting and reusing lacquer since after all the English had early on taken to inserting lacquer in furniture; see Wolvesperges, *Le meuble français*, 70–74.
47. Nebahat Avcioglu, "A Palace of One's Own: Stanislaus I's Kiosks and the Idea of Self-Representation," *Art Bulletin* 85, no. 4 (December 2003): 662–84; see also her *'Turquerie' and the Politics of Representation, 1728–1876* (Farnham: Ashgate, 2011).
48. See Michael A. Yonan, "'Veneers' of Authority: Chinese Lacquers in Maria Theresa's Vienna," *Eighteenth-Century Studies* 37, no. 4 (2004): 652–72; and his *Empress Maria Theresa and the Politics of Habsburg Imperial Art* (Philadelphia: Penn State University Press, 2011), especially chapters 3, 4, and 5 and "Découpage and the Other," 137–40.
49. Following a restoration in the 1980s, Maria Theresa's genuine miniatures have been stored for conservation and replaced with photocopies. For a 360-degree tour of the rooms, consult the Schönbrunn website: http://www.schoenbrunn.at/fileadmin/content/schoenbrunn/panoramas/29_vieux_laque_zimmer.swf (accessed 8 July 2014); http://www.schoenbrunn.at/en/things-to-know/tour-of-the-palace/millions-room.html (accessed 9 July 2014).
50. Ebba Koch, "The Moghuleries of the Millionenzimmer, Schönbrunn Palace, Vienna" in Rosemary Crill, Susan Stronge, and Andrew Topsfield, eds., *Arts of Mughal India: Studies in Honour of Robert Skelton* (London: V&A Publications, 2004), 153–67; and Eaton, "The Art of Colonial Despotism," 68; for Yonan, see above.
51. *The Journal of Beckford in Portugal and Spain, 1787–1788*, ed. Boyd Alexander (London: Rupert Hart-Davis, 1954), 291. He enjoyed being surrounded with Turks, as evidenced in his "Spanish Journal" and in his Fonthill correspondence with the presence of a Turkish "friend" in residence in 1817.

Part II

The Stewardship of Objects and the Material Practices of Recycling

5 Recycling the City

Paris, 1760s–1800

Allan Potofsky

Recycling the city—refurbishing, reusing, and redeploying buildings—is a practice as old as the first primitive hut redesigned for fresh purpose. Even caves were repeatedly reclaimed for animal husbandry, shelter from predators, and human dwellings. Pagan religious structures were also commonly remade to suit secular purposes or new forms of worship. But in urban France during the *Ancien Régime* recycling in general and recycled buildings in particular suffered from a bad press. The timeless practice was condemned by an Enlightenment discourse that was deeply critical of urban life, and, in particular, of the poor quality of city air, water, and spaces.[1] Enlightened commentators saw a particular danger in dilapidated buildings and crumbling infrastructure, propped up and patched up beyond their useful lives by dangerously precarious means. While the urban production of hazardous materials could be moved beyond a city's walls, the stone, brick, and mortar needed for new urban structures were, of course, less mobile. Older edifices with few windows or doors, as in converted farm buildings or poorly adapted ecclesiastic constructions turned into hospitals, spread disease by trapping and recirculating dangerously corrupted air, often called "miasma." Porous and poorly designed city roads and sewers made of recycled construction detritus, according to the celebrated physicist Pierre Bertholon de Saint-Lazare, in 1786, trapped fouled water during rainstorms and forced people to wade through raw sewage.[2] Overused and overextended urban structures were increasingly the favoured target of scorn by enlightened hygienic specialists.

Indeed, eighteenth-century Paris was perhaps the most congested and polluted city of Europe. The capital city, whose population in 1789 is estimated at between seven hundred thousand and eight hundred thousand souls in a nation of twenty-seven million people, was teeming with an impoverished population eking out a precarious existence in often cramped housing. Although no statistics can measure the quality of life in preindustrial urban centres, the environment of many Parisians was clearly far from idyllic. Large swaths of Paris on the eve of Revolution had become foul and insalubrious receptacles of new forms of mineral, animal, and human waste. Despite a certain image of *Ancien-Régime* Paris as a tidily ordered and well-policed city peopled with skilled artisans of the luxury trades, in fact the city was rapidly becoming a rough-and-tumble manufacturing centre. Many commentators, most prominently Louis-Sebastien Mercier, Réstif de la Bretonne, and Siméon-Prosper Hardy, underscored how Paris' formal administrative existence and its messier, gritty realities were often deeply at odds with one another. The perception was widespread that the average Parisians' quality of life declined precipitously in the century of the Enlightenment.[3]

Paradoxically, however, while older construction was condemned as unbefitting the capital of the empire—too cramped, too closed, in sum, too confining of inhabitants and their exhalations and excretions—it was precisely newer construction that contributed greatly to the capital's miseries.[4] With its steadily growing population, Paris was clearly in need of more inexpensive housing; but the very fabrication of low-cost building materials only added to the polluted urban environment of the capital. From start to finish, a given structure demanded the production of a wide range of chemical derivatives. As all construction begins with destruction, a range of concoctions were required to make explosive black powder, including charcoal, sulphur, and saltpetre, to pulverise boulders and to raze older structures. Once a given lot was emptied of debris, other materials, such as brick, mortar, and plaster, were increasingly made on a large scale and with new methods of production, which in turn generated waste products and much detritus, as well as presenting an ever-growing challenge to the health and safety of inhabitants.[5]

Along with the hygienic advocates of the Enlightenment, the policing and guild authorities overseeing Parisian construction during the *Ancien Régime*'s boom years also rejected the reuse of materials and buildings. Obsessive newness in construction paradoxically added to unhygienic conditions in the capital. A post-1763 construction boom—encouraged by the easing of fiscal pressures in the period after the Seven Year's War—greatly expanded the market for inexpensive construction. Money flowing to stones increased dramatically after the August 1766 ordinance permitting investors in a project to claim all property on a construction site if their building contractors went bankrupt. This ordinance virtually eliminated risk for speculation, while increasing the financial burden of credit-worthy guilds.[6] Guild masters, who would lose their total outlay in cases of the bankruptcy of a collaborating building contractor, came to rely increasingly upon their guilds as credit unions. The resulting financial and housing bubble for investors had spectacular consequences. Between 1770 and 1789 Parisians accumulated debts averaging 28 million livres per year; almost half, 12 million livres, of these debts were invested annually in apartments, houses, and land, with the vast majority of this real estate located in Paris.[7]

But the credit crunch amidst the economic downturn of 1787 initiated the very fiscal crisis that helped topple the *Ancien Régime*, leading to a sudden collapse of the housing market. During a fragile recovery, beginning in the spring of 1791, administrators of the Revolution shifted priorities from wholesale new construction to the large-scale recycling and conversion of nationalised buildings in the form of *biens nationaux*. The mission of a pragmatic, cost-efficient, revolutionary architecture in the capital was later to be defined as the guiding principle in the period of the Directory (1795–1799), which created a national policy of public construction under the centralised and powerful *Conseil des bâtiments civils*. Under the guidance of the *Conseil*, an often-haphazard and improvised system of refitting older structures was transformed into a public service of construction. Accountability to public finances, access to any and all public structures to all citizens, and transparency in the way older structures were transformed, imposed a powerful logic of revolutionary-era urban development. Finally, in the articulation of a national policy of public construction based on recycling older structures, the French Revolution's administrators sketched out the vital elements of what future generations would call modern urban planning, in the sense of the concerted search for the greater integration, harmony, and coherence of an entire city.[8]

If seen through the anachronistic perspective of Haussmannisation, urban planning or revitalisation, rehabilitation, reform, and other ways to designate *embellissement* in the aestheticizing vocabulary of the eighteenth century, meant the wholesale razing and rebuilding of large parts of the city. Yet, the preindustrial search for orderly and aligned streets; homogenous construction styles and materials; "rational" use of buildings and public space; and generalised systems of sanitation and hygiene throughout the city, certainly did not have to wait for the second half of the nineteenth century.[9] Without the financial means to realise these objectives, administrators of the Directory also sought to assure the health, well-being, and comfort of urban dwellers, particularly in the capital city. A durable achievement of the *Conseil des bâtiments civils* was to inscribe ambitions of *Ancien-Régime embellissement* within a new political order, in which republican administration took responsibility for making the city functional as a public service and later as an integral right of citizenship. At the core of the Directory's *embellissement* project for the capital city was a policy to recycle nationalised buildings, in particular, former ecclesiastical structures, to create a civic architecture whose primary quality, as we will see, was attention to a strict economy of means.

THE PARISIAN ENVIRONMENT ON THE EVE OF THE FRENCH REVOLUTION

Eyewitness accounts at the end of the *Ancien Régime* converge on the quality of air, water, and soil in Paris of many quarters: they were characterised as a "miasma" of nasty chemicals, detritus, and industrial waste.[10] To the north and east, beginning in the 1770s, chemical laboratories, primitive manufactures, breweries, and distilleries germinated. The putrid smell of sulphuric acid, nitric acid, hydrochloric acid, as well as vinegars, salts, and metallic chalks, choked inhabitants of entire quarters. To the south, sewage and polluted waters led to stench-filled summers in swaths of the capital city, such as the quarters where the Bièvre tributary trickled through the capital city. Used as a depository of by-products derived from horse urine by over thirty officially registered tanners, and as an open sewer by much of the Left Bank, the Bièvre caused people to faint from its devastating fumes.[11] Even to the wealthier northern and western areas, a construction boom kicked up irritating clouds of vapour riddled with dust, dirt, plaster, and hazardous chemicals used in explosions to clear away older structures. Almost everywhere, in a capital lacking the most basic sanitation facilities, and with very few sewers, human, horse, and other animal excrement added to the stench of decaying meat, fish, and vegetables, often leftover spoilage from the many markets.[12] Near the quarter of the central market, *les Halles*, Parisians living around the *Cimetière des innocents* were regaled with the smell of decomposing corpses when the shallow level of the graves proved insufficiently deep, with the quarter invaded by foul exhalations, leading to the cemetery's hasty closure and evacuation of remains to the former quarries of the *Tombe-Issoire* in 1785.[13]

Nor was there easy escape for most Parisians. Green patches were increasingly rare in a cramped capital city. Nature paid the heaviest price where rental prices exploded and labour migration from the provinces continued unabated, estimated at about seven to fourteen thousand arrivals per year in the second half of the eighteenth century. The population explosion in Paris fed a burgeoning market in sordid lodging homes (*chambres garnies*) for migrant Creusois, Normands, Auvergnats, and other "*étrangers*." In the outlying areas, particularly to the west where monasteries and convents once thrived amidst agricultural terrain interspersed with a few *hôtels particuliers*, vast expanses of farmland and pasture were snatched up and developed by speculators. The purchase and development of the immense property of the ruined Mathurins order, for example by the wealthy property developer and *fermier général* Jacques-Louis-Guillaume Bouret de Vézelay in the 1770s, led to the hasty construction of several new neighbourhoods out of once-bucolic areas. The Chaussée d'Antin area, in the vicinity of the Faubourg Montmartre, Saint-Lazare, and the Buttes Saint-Roche, was transformed from a sparsely built pastoral into a bustling neighbourhood in the space of one generation.[14]

The Parisian eighteenth-century economy was fast becoming a hybrid economy of scale where old and new coexisted in perfect symbiosis. For example, in the outlying Faubourg Saint-Marcel the labour-intensive activity of textile and leather production, with its timeless artisanal organisation of work, grew side-by-side with novel and fast-developing sectors such as the extraction of saltpetre for explosives, needed for land-clearing, demolition, and military purposes. (Saltpetre collection by ordinary citizens was later promoted by revolutionaries as a patriotic contribution to the war effort.)[15]

But what tied together both old and new was the propensity to pollute—this ensured that Paris was a hazardous environment for many inhabitants. The lucky few who could flee avoided even the prestigious neighbourhood of the Marais, stigmatised with the stamp of aristocratic old money, and where the foul atmosphere was hardly purer. As a partial result of pollution in the city centre, the quarter close to the Invalides, in the far-western parts of the Left Bank, was chosen for elite *hôtels particuliers*. The area enjoyed a more wholesome atmosphere, at least in the minds of contemporaries, for it was widely believed that purer air was assured to blow directly from the plains to the west of the capital.

Of all the sectors of the Parisian economy, moreover, the "carbon footprint" was perhaps the widest and deepest in construction because of its sheer scale. The building industry was the second most important economic sector of the French economy—a runner-up to agriculture—until the end of the nineteenth century. Yet, most building methods scarcely changed since the abolition of wood construction during the reign of Henry IV, when combustible timber frames were banned in Paris by a 1604 ordinance.[16] Even after this formal eradication within the city walls of Paris, the conversion of the primary material of buildings from wood to minerals was a slow process. The greatest challenge was the prohibitive cost of producing, assembling, and shipping most building materials to a capital which imposed an onerous merchandise tax, the *octroi*, on material passing through the city walls. This added significant cost to erecting buildings in the capital. Despite the expense of keeping manufactures of explosives, plaster, brick, and mortar away from population centres, hazardous production methods incited authorities to ban their manufacture within cities.[17]

The sheer quantity of construction in the Parisian building boom between the 1760s and 1780s led to growing recourse to illegal methods of preparing building materials. The history of the clandestine production of construction supplies begins with coal. As deforestation drove up the price of wood, ruining many urban lumberyards, coal became the alternative fuel of choice in the late eighteenth century. The intense heat generated by newly designed kilns emboldened building contractors to design ever-larger ovens to prepare plaster.[18] As Thomas Le Roux convincingly shows, these industrial ovens were frequently confiscated by the Paris police within the city walls as clandestine coal-burning ovens circumvented the *octroi* tax. The size of one industrial oven, seized in 1765, measured an intimidating three metres in diameter and six metres in height. Bricks, mortar, limestone, and chalk were hence rendered less expensive but were more dangerous to greater numbers of inhabitants to produce. No fewer than thirty-four illegal industrial-sized coal-burning chalk ovens were counted by the police in northeast Paris in 1789.[19] These merely added another layer to the stench of new plaster manufactures, as well as the clouds of dust emitted from massive quarries scattered throughout the city, in particular, in Montmartre, Saint-Victor, Saint-Marcel, Vaugirard, the Buttes-Chaumont, Pantin, Belleville, and Ménilmontant. Explosives used to raze older structures and to clear the ground, gypsum plaster and limestone plaster for the construction of walls, highly corrosive metal forges for ironworks, as well as the increasing demand for large-scale brickworks and noxious glassworks, led to the accumulation of bad air, water, detritus, and foul waste products in the capital city.[20]

The political implications of a heavily polluted capital city for the tottering *Ancien Régime* should not be underestimated. The accretion of bad air and water that sickened Parisians also inspired demands for expanding civic rights and responsibilities. The public sphere was also a space to demand the right to breathe and to have access to clean water. Earlier, Louis XIV had understood this in a vast campaign to build fountains to bring water to increasingly thirsty Parisians in the seventeenth century.[21] His Bourbon successors, more conscious of emptied royal coffers, were less capable and inclined to invest public finances in an extravagant manner. In reaction, an Enlightenment urban discourse insisted on the necessity to remake urban centres with greater attention to the health and well-being of their inhabitants. Perhaps the first writer to use *embellissement* to mean the "rational" organisation of Parisian streets and places for the population was the architect and entrepreneur Pierre-Alexis Delamair (1676–1745). In two noted publications of 1737 and 1738, Delamair denounced the declining quality of life in the capital city as linked to its environment. While he employed a familiar hygienic discourse to question whether Paris was a new Rome or new Babylon, Delamair also helped transform the larger debate over possible solutions. Rather than promote the physical enlargement of Paris' size, as was then a commonplace, he focused on transforming the inner city by razing unhealthy quarters to allow for the free circulation of fresh air.[22]

The great debate elaborated by those later called "urbanists" centred upon the aerian discourse sketched out by Delamair. Free circulation was a central metaphor for the movement of not just air, but traffic, people, light, water, goods, and ultimately even capital. Architects who contributed to public debates on urban revitalisation, such as Pierre-Louis Moreau, Pierre Patte, and Charles Wailly, had frequent recourse to the terms of aerian discourse. The dismal, cramped housing in the city centre should give way to spacious squares and large streets. Contributing to this refrain, the architectural theorist Marc-Antoine Laugier and architect Nicolas Le Camus de Mézières sought the cause of the declining quality of life in the capital in the actions of profiteers who preyed on the misery of the labouring poor by piling up unworthy and crowded housing—perhaps the first denunciation of what the future would call slumlords.[23] Another adherent to the aerian discourse was no less a figure than Voltaire. In 1749, Voltaire noted the brutal contrast between wealthy, airy and spacious neighbourhoods of the outskirts and the city centre of Paris:

> Oversized neighbourhoods demand public places; and whereas the Arc de Triomphe of the porte Saint-Denis and the equestrian statue of

> Henri le Grand, the two bridges, these two superb quais, that of the Louvre, the Tuileries, the Champs-Élysées, equal or surpass the beauties of ancient Rome, the city centre, obscure, packed, hideous, represents the most shameful barbarism of the past. We say it without end: but how long can we say it without fixing it?[24]

Voltaire's conclusion, never heeded, was that the Crown needed to focus more on *embellissement* of the quotidian life of Parisians—in particular, by creating more open spaces—rather than on wasteful monuments to imperial grandeur.

CONSTRUCTION IN THE *ANCIEN RÉGIME*

Ancien Régime public construction imposed newness over reuse; expansion over rehabilitation; and wastefulness over recycling. Then, as now, not only the fabrication of building materials, but the very act of construction produced much pollution. Moreover, the ravages of building the city were made worse by the lack of comprehensive urban planning. Controls over private building in Paris were largely fragmented within a dense web of *Ancien-Régime* corporate institutions which jealously assured the quality control of construction. In Paris, the *Chambre des bâtiments* was a particularly efficient corporate body that resembled a housing authority of more contemporary times. The *Chambre* comprised inspectors, architects, master artisans, and magistrates who carefully policed over the contractual relationship between builders and proprietors.[25] No private construction in Paris took place without plans previously approved by this housing authority—and the soundness of materials, scrupulously inspected before and after construction, formed the bulk of the corporation's affairs.[26]

Protectionism was enforced by the *Chambre* upon the labour force above all. Guild statutes were applied to the letter in seeing to it that all journeymen were properly working for a master, and "masterless men" in incorporated trades, called *chambrelains*, were banned from the profession by blacklisting and the confiscation of their tools. Towards the end of the *Ancien Régime*, corporations increasingly cracked down on recycled building materials, based on the fear that used materials were compromised and would quickly disintegrate, causing structures to collapse.[27] While an oft-exaggerated threat, the use of recovered supplies was a condemnable form of cheating, *malfaçon*, in the terminology of the epoch. Entrepreneurs and masters accused of *malfaçon* risked lawsuits and banishment from the annual trade almanac, the *Almanach des bâtiments*, a listing of the names and addresses of qualified Parisian builders with the technical expertise for each task on the building site.[28] Also, the guilds routinely exercised their privilege to raid construction sites to inspect materials. The powerful carpentry guild, one of the most restrictive of construction guilds, was fiercely protective of the quality of materials. Carpentry guild syndics and other officers concentrated on seizing recycled wood—which they claimed might have been fished out of the Seine—used in scaffolding, or roof beams, window frames, or stairs, a most dangerous form of deceit for masters, workers, and passers-by alike. Clearly, the increasingly high price of lumber, which surged dramatically in the freezing winter of 1788–1789, made the use of mouldering or humid materials a real danger for the carpentry trades. In collaboration with the police commissioner Allix, the syndics and *adjoints* of the carpentry guild engaged in at least eighty-one raids in the years between 1784 and 1790. Predictably, the raids provoked much rancour between journeymen and masters in the waning years of the *Ancien Régime*.[29]

The profligate material culture of *Ancien Régime* construction was aggravated by haphazard development. Public construction was guided more by royal magnificence to celebrate the power of the Bourbon state than by urban planning. It was also informed by financially driven principles. Sparkling new structures in neglected parts of the city were intended to encourage urban revitalisation. Monuments and royal places were thus purposefully planned for peripheral areas. Marginal neighbourhoods were subsequently developed by speculators and developers around these projects. On the Right Bank, the aristocratic Marais quarter was one of the most famous examples, having received a boost with the Place Royale—today's Place des Vosges—completed after 1612. The Place Dauphine, near the newly constructed Pont Neuf in the early seventeenth century as well the innovative Halle au Blé, designed by Nicolas le Camus de Mézières and completed in 1782, were other examples of this earlier aspiration to stimulate private development in neglected areas of the capital city by the erection of major public structures. Urban rehabilitation, in other words, was a mere corollary to royal monumentalism.

TWO PATHS TO URBAN *EMBELLISSEMENT*: PARIS' FAUBOURG SAINT-MARCEL AND LYON'S BROTTEAUX, 1764–1789

What difference, if any, did the French Revolution make in matters concerning *embellissement*? On the periphery of Paris, a prominent example of renewal through grandiose projects, first royal then revolutionary, was the Left Bank Church of Sainte Geneviève near the Faubourg Saint-Marcel. It was a magnet for new commerce after ground was broken in 1764. The diverse social profile of Faubourg Saint-Marcel, populated by about ten percent of the Parisian population, belied its reputation as a poor, marginal, and even dangerous zone. During the quarter century of its construction, many small enterprises, grocers, and larger workshops owed their prosperity by furnishing the site's building materials, the food, water, and wine, and even by coordinating specialised labour—especially the skilled workmen such as sculptors, carpenters, and metalworkers. A conveniently located limestone quarry was heavily exploited by contractors with ties to the site. By the time of the Revolution, the neighbourhood earned a reputation as a vital industrial engine for the capital city. Here again, Paris was rapidly transformed into a manufacturing centre well before the age of industrialisation.[30]

Aided in particular by the infusion of four million *livres tournois* in borrowed credit for the completion of the Church of Sainte-Geneviève in June 1784, the neighbourhood was steadily benefiting from the massive *chantier* on its outskirts. For example, a multitude of stores as well as indoor and open-air workshops were frequented by more than five-hundred-and-fifty building tradesmen of the construction site.[31] The Revolution's transformation of the Sainte-Geneviève Church into the Panthéon in April 1791 also served the dynamism of the quarter. In June 1791 the National Assembly voted a million *livres tournois* in credits transferred directly to public workshops where the indigent poor was engaged in menial tasks, particularly, clearing brush and preparing grounds for road construction. The Revolution's major recycled monument, logically enough, called for recycled funds. Such infusion of public monies in the neighbourhood launched anew a virtuous commercial cycle. Numerous bonnet makers and blanket weavers were clustered around the Gobelins sector; a host of shoe smiths thrived near the site of the Panthéon; and several breweries were installed on the rue de Mouffetard.[32] The formerly marginal neighbourhood was fast becoming an economically flourishing quarter.

The worksite of the Pantheon also gave greater visibility to the Revolution's public employment efforts, to the exasperation of its newly nominated supervisor, Quatremère de Quincy. In the summer of 1791, Quatremère denounced the autonomy of the site's labourers who "look upon their work as their property, and the building as a republic where they are co-citizens and believe as a consequence that it is their right to name their chiefs, their inspectors and to distribute the tasks arbitrarily."[33] He was reacting to the deluge of petition literature threatening strikes and challenging the site's direction in labour issues, for the *Panthéon* had a difficult but avowed social function to assure jobs. As certain tasks of refurbishing were brought to completion, such as carpentry work for scaffolding, labourers resisted being laid off. Amidst a strike of carpenters on the site, the chief engineer of the site Rondelet, wrote: "We might say that in dedicating this Temple to Glory, we were building a charity workshop."[34] Following its economic fortunes, the political integration of the contentious Faubourg Saint-Marcel within revolutionary Paris was well underway.

While public investment in the Panthéon advanced the fuller social, economic, and political incorporation of the Faubourg Saint-Marcel, however, efforts in provincial cities to develop outlying neighbourhoods were far less successful during the end of the *Ancien Régime* and Revolution. In contrast to some quarters of Paris, for example, was the second city of France, Lyon. At the start of the same post–Seven Year's War building boom that transformed Paris, a private real-estate scheme in Lyon was crafted by architect, speculator, promoter, and developer Jean-Antoine Morand. His trusted collaborator in this venture was none other than Sainte-Geneviève's chief architect, Jacques-Germain Soufflot. Together, they created a company to project Lyon's densely crowded and insalubrious residential areas towards the east starting in the 1760s. In Lyon, the particular challenge to develop the city's suburbs was not only incarnated by city walls but imposed by its second river, the Rhône. Despite demographic and economic pressures to expand, to breach not only the city walls but to cross the Rhône itself, the weight of tradition embodied by many local interests repeatedly blocked the development of Lyon.[35]

Morand's celebrated *Plan circulaire* for Lyon, first sketched out in 1764 but republished as a lavishly engraved map in 1775, incorporated manufactures and warehouses, residential quarters, parks, promenades, and squares. Creating a model of integrated urban planning for future centuries, Morand had cleverly conceived of what future generations would call zoning. His plan neatly separated habitations and areas where manufacturing created hazards to the Lyonnais population. The *Plan circulaire* also reimagined the city of Lyon as an orderly and coherent whole. It sought, above all, to rehabilitate a neglected outlying suburb, which became a century later the Brotteaux, also called the Quartier Morand. Morand's agenda was, in fact, that of many a future urban planner: the annexation and development of a city's suburbs to alleviate congestion, limit manufactures to outlying areas, enlarge the tax base, and generally renovate by allowing freer circulation of people and goods. It represented, in theory at least, the triumph of aerian discourse in urban matters. But the end of the *Ancien Régime* was not propitious to such "rational" urban development. Opposition from individual proprietors as well as foot-dragging by traditionalists in Lyon's *Hôtel de ville*, led to fruitless years of litigation.[36]

The cumulative pressures brought by intransigent municipal officers, proprietors demanding feudal dues, and ecclesiastical institutions asserting fiscal privileges, kept Lyon enclosed within a constricted geographic compass for over a century. Morand wasted much time lobbying the Crown's ministers at Versailles for dispensation against this slew of powerful local interests. He found welcome support with those connected to the brave new world of engineering at the *Ecole national des ponts et chaussées*, which opened in 1747. But even as he triumphantly returned to Lyon with a royal decree authorising the beginning of construction in 1771, Morand became ever more a threat as an outsider to Lyon's conservative elite. Morand's positioning in the Revolution, however, paradoxically left him exposed to the charge of complicity with the very elite he had detested; he was condemned and executed during the Terror. The guillotine that took Morand's life in January 1794 was situated next to an innovative wooden bridge he had designed, built, and that would carry his name.[37]

The revitalisation of the Parisian Faubourg Saint-Marcel and Morand's unsuccessful plan to remake Lyon provide a contrasting, but deeply telling, narrative about the erecting, expansion, and *embellissement* of cities at the end of the *Ancien Régime*. Along with the diminishing capacities of the bankrupt monarchy to build monumental structures, urban development was chaotic and arbitrary. Business ventures and commercial opportunities borne of profitable developmental schemes were determinant in building schemes—but they were in turn entirely dependent on arbitrary factors, particularly, those of entrenched local interests, that at times assured their failure. *Ancien Régime* municipalities, every bit as much as the Crown, often lost control of the administration in favour of "feudal" factionalism.

The French Revolution's attention to urban matters flowed directly from the frustrating experiences of a multitude of failed efforts to transform cities. Small wonder that the National Assembly received and published many projects for reconstructing Paris from prominent architects, critics, and even amateur connoisseurs, underscoring a conviction that vast opportunities existed for remaking the capital. Notable plans to remake Paris were submitted by the architects De Wailly, Brogniart, Poyet, Ledoux, Boullée, Lequeu, Gisors, Rousseau, Legrand and Molinos, Percier, and Fontaine, with little success for their authors.[38] While these ambitious plans were not feasible in the midst of an economic crisis, they point to an ambition among architects to put their art to use in the new order. In theory, the regeneration of the French nation would follow a symbolic appropriation of the public space of the capital by architects. In practice, however, it was not the science of architecture but political solutions to urban breakdown that were prominently featured on the revolutionary agenda of 1789. Reforms directly dismantled the entrenched, arbitrary, and corrupt world of France's municipal elites. Also, starting in late 1789, the decree of the seizure and sale of ecclesiastic *biens nationaux* opened fresh economic opportunities for investment in land and stones. Confiscations were later extended to the émigrés and former nobility. The creation of a new currency, the *assignats*, and above all the refounding of municipal institutions, were intended to make sure that future entrepreneurs would not be blocked—as happened in Lyon—by "feudal" interests again.[39]

REVOLUTION, CONSTRUCTION, AND RECYCLING

The French Revolution is associated not with construction, and with cranes, stones, mortar, and scaffolding, but their precise opposite—vandalism, demolition, and the obliteration of the past with the project to annihilate the *Ancien Régime*. The Revolution evokes, in sum, deconstruction and violence, the ground-clearing to prepare the way for an uncontested capital city. Its history, in fact, is far more complex, and was intimately tied to the rise of the secularisation, safeguarding, and redeployment of older structures. At the same time, the institutions of the French Revolution did not have the financial means to alleviate what Voltaire called the "shameful barbarism" of Parisian neighbourhoods by remaking urban centres.[40] Nevertheless, the revolutionary period created the opportunity for bourgeois urban dwellers to articulate the right to a "hygienic" protection from the pollution entailed by the rapid economic and urban development of the capital.

The Parisians' lists of grievances, the *cahiers de doléances*, submitted early in 1789, were attentive to the environmental problems of the capital created by unnecessary construction. Many *doléances* denounced the fervour for new development by relating them to symptoms of monarchical megalomania. The case of the recently completed *Mur des fermiers-généraux* surrounding Paris exposed inhabitants on the outskirts to the dust, noise, and contamination of futile monumentality between 1785 and 1788.[41] As the wall could be breached only by Claude-Nicolas Ledoux's *barriéres*, thirty planned tollhouses, they were the first targets of the revolutionary crowd, which vented their fury in destroying many of them in the days before the taking and dismantling of the Bastille. Apparently, with the Revolution, the occasion to rein in the excessive zeal of speculators, promoters, builders, and even visionary architects had finally arrived.[42]

The Revolution, in sum, was a propitious political moment to halt haphazard construction and provide an interlude to the dangers and inconvenience of long-term *chantiers*. For the decade of the 1790s was among the most outstanding moments of architectural recycling in the history of modern Europe. In Paris alone, at least a thousand noble and ecclesiastical structures—nearly one in ten of Parisian properties and twelve percent of all land in the capital—were nationalised and auctioned as *biens nationaux* starting in the fall of 1790. This transfer of land and buildings to the state, and then to new private owners (thirteen percent of investors in *biens nationaux* were building contractors), created a dynamic of reselling, restoring, refitting, and reusing buildings.[43]

During the Revolution, however, financial pressures to maintain, alter, or repair dictated a policy of fresh stewardship and reuse. But in contrast to the modern idea of patrimony or historical monuments, central to contemporary urban planning, there was no corollary claim for conserving original structures in their original state. The Revolution's architectural recycling was the fruit of circumstance not connoisseurship or ideology. The need to stave off the ravages, first of sovereign debt and then of war, starting in the summer of 1792, imposed the logic of giving new proprietors free hand to do as they wished with the confiscated buildings. From the distant Abbey of Fontenay, reused as a paper mill, to the Parisian church-run chapter houses on the rue de Charonne, transformed by the entrepreneur François Richard (later known as Richard-Lenoir) into spinning establishments, the Revolution shaped a vibrant dynamic for the profitable refitting of existing constructions.[44]

Perhaps no single individual understood the metaphoric and commercial importance of revolutionary recycling more than self-described "architect, entrepreneur, former master mason, former journeyman," Pierre-François

Palloy (1754–1835), the building contractor engaged to dismantle the *Bastille*. Starting on the evening of 14 July 1789, without authority from national or municipal officials, Palloy mobilised a massive labour force of four-hundred building tradesmen to dismantle the fortress while turning its debris into souvenirs. Iron shackles were melted into medals and the stones were carved into souvenir likenesses of the fortress, and were then sold to commemorate the cult of the *Vainqueurs de la Bastille*. Palloy thus contributed a "patriotic cult of relics" to festive celebrations of the taking of the Bastille.[45]

In sharp contrast to *Ancien Régime* corporations Palloy made recycling central to his particular "brand" as contractor. As a prolific entrepreneur, seeking fame and fortune, he sent to municipalities throughout France the Bastille's carved souvenir stones. He was a shrewdly ambitious and dynamic representative of new man at the pinnacle of the building trades. Having started as a bricklayer, Palloy's autobiography, repeated incessantly in pamphlets, was a classic example of social ascension helped, he stressed, by the Revolution's meritocratic inspiration.[46] His tireless self-promotion led to the publication of two hundred distinct publications of political brochures, maps, songs, and assorted construction proposals, many under assorted pseudonyms, and nearly all self-financed. Palloy's prodigious wealth flourished in the construction business during the Revolution, but was ultimately squandered in massive printing bills for publications.[47]

Palloy and the Panthéon were the private and public antipodes of revolutionary-era recycling. They also embody the haphazard and disordered nature of building in the period when the corporate universe of the *Ancien Régime* was dismantled but the institutions of the new regime were not yet in place. The administrative vacuum no doubt boosted Palloy in his ambition to appropriate and transform the Bastille's debris into a lucrative commerce in souvenirs. Also, as witnessed in the labour strife at the *Panthéon's* site, the lack of a clear political and managerial hierarchy emboldened the contentious labour force to make greater demands for employment opportunities and higher salaries.

As nature hates a vacuum, so does civilisation. The impulse to centralise authority over construction led to the foundation of the *Conseil des bâtiments civils* to oversee the recycling and reconversion of nationalised religious buildings and the confiscated property of *émigrés*. This unique administration survived all phases of the Revolution. Starting in late 1795, the Directory gave this bureaucratic organ a broad mandate over public structures, distinguishing thereafter between infrastructure and buildings. Its directive was to centralise all public investment construction in the hands of the three celebrated public architects. The Panthéon's Chief Inspector Rondelet, the prodigious civic architect, Alexandre-Théodore Brogniart, and the future architect of the Arc de Triomphe, Jean-François Chalgrin, three advocates of a classical and practical civic architecture, oversaw a team of official inspectors. In a finely defined schema, each inspector had complete responsibility over one of six "classes" of structures, in which the function of a given building—hospitals, barracks, prisons—dictated its place in a hierarchy of investment priorities. In the new order, the administration of public edifices made steep demands on the time, labour, and even equipment of construction entrepreneurs to engage in the renovation of nationalised buildings: a form of requisition by another name. Finally, the mission of a pragmatic, cost-efficient, revolutionary architecture was defined and made the core of official building policy.[48]

The council's charge was formulated in a circular issued by Rondelet in the spring of 1796. Rondelet called for assurances that "no work relating to civic buildings be undertaken at national expense without its utility, necessity, or other possible advantages having been established beforehand." He demanded scrupulous "perfection, solidity, and economy" as well as methodological verification of all payments.[49] These directives were scrupulously applied. In pursuit of economy, half of the numerous detention centres, prisons, courthouses, and police stations were located in recycled former religious structures, in particular, churches, monasteries, convents, and former dependencies such as stables. These were systematically recalibrated and refurbished to suit their new function. However, a focus on perfection at times led inspectors to excess zeal. They rejected for payment the slightest negligence to detailed proposals. Hospitals designed with beds less than sixty centimetres apart—considered the minimum space to avoid the spread of disease—were ordered to be completely overhauled. Legal tribunals that did not allow for theatrical courtroom entries were condemned to be redone. In sum, the *Conseil des bâtiments civils* created an architecture of design tightly defined by a written program, a series of serviceable demands entirely suited to their function rather than to aesthetic form.[50]

As Dominique Margairaz argues, the origin of public service in the modern sense of the term began in the Directory period of the Revolution as the state assumed responsibility to assure equal access to a service and the continuity of its exploitation.[51] A national policy of recycling nationalised structures in accordance with a strictly functional architecture represented the origin of a public service of construction. It also scrupulously respected the economy of public finances. Unlike the random and wasteful urban development of the *Ancien Régime*, the Revolution henceforth promised strict financial and functional accountancy to the nation. And while the notion of national patrimony would await the July Monarchy, and the founding of the office of an *Inspecteur général des monuments historiques*, the Revolution also created a movement for the systematic cataloguing and assessment of important historical structures for their functional value to the capital and nation. Revolutionary institutions thus adopted a centralised method of reconceiving the use of old buildings and redeploying structures within their urban context—a first step towards what the future would loosely call urban planning. Whether by rebuilding (as on the site of the Panthéon), refitting (as with numerous hospitals and prisons), or even remaking into artefacts (as Palloy did to the Bastille), the logic of recycling prevailed. The slower but steadier development of urban France during the Revolution permitted, in accordance with Rondelet's promise cited above, the beginning of planned construction guided by the public's demand for of "perfection, solidity, and economy."

NOTES

1. Sabine Barles, *La ville délétère: médecins et ingénieurs dans l'espace urbain, XVIIIe–XIXe siècles* (Seyssel: Champs Vallon, 1999), 19.
2. Pierre Bertholon de Saint-Lazare, *De la salubrité de l'air des villes et en particulier des moyens de la procurer par M. l'abbé Bertholon* (Montpellier, 1786), 58.
3. Vincent Milliot, *Un policier des Lumières, suivi de Mémoires de J.C.P. Lenoir, ancien lieutenant de police de Paris, écrits en pays étrangers dans les années 1790 et suivantes* (Seyssel: Champ Vallon, 2011). Allan Potofsky, *Constructing Paris in the Age of Revolution* (Basingstoke and New York: Palgrave Macmillan, 2009), 22–24.
4. Barles, *La ville délétère*, 77.
5. André Guillerme, *La naissance de l'industrie à Paris. Entre sueurs et vapeurs: 1780–1830* (Seyssel: Champ Vallon, 2007), 66–76, 183–84.
6. "Délibérations des maçons," Paris, Bibliothèque de l'Assemblée Nationale, MS 1229. Jean-François Cabestan, *La conquête du plain-pied. L'immeuble à Paris au XVIIIe siècle* (Paris: Picard, 2004), 28.
7. Philip T. Hoffman, Gilles Postel-Vinay, and Jean-Laurent Rosenthal, *Des marchés sans prix: une économie politique du crédit à Paris, 1660–1870* (Paris: EHESS, 2001), 204–05.
8. Michel Gallet, *Demeures parisiennes* (Paris: Editions du Temps, 1964). Potofsky, *Constructing Paris*.
9. Jean-Louis Harouel, *L'Embellissement des villes. L'urbanisme français au XVIIIe siècle* (Paris: Picard, 1993). On "Haussmanisation before Haussmann," see Karen Bowie, ed., *La modernité avant Haussmann: Formes de l'espace urbain à Paris, 1801–1853* (Paris: Éditions Recherches, 2001), and Nicholas Papayanis, *Planning Paris Before Haussmann* (Baltimore and London: Johns Hopkins University Press, 2004).
10. Alain Corbin, *Le miasme et la jonquille : L'odorat et l'imaginaire social aux XVIIIe et XIXe siècles* (Paris: Flammarion, 1982).
11. John Graham Smith, *The Origins and Early Development of the Heavy Chemical Industry in France* (Oxford: Clarendon Press, 1979). André Guillerme, Anne-Cécile Lefort, and Gérard Jigaudon, *Dangereux, insalubres et incommodes: paysages industriels en banlieue parisienne (XIXe–XXe siècles)* (Seyssel: Champ Vallon, 2005).
12. On sanitation: Antoine Tournon, *Moyens de rendre parfaitement propres les rues de Paris, ainsi que les quais, places, culs de sacs, atteliers, cours, allées, manufactures, halles & boucheries . . . dans toutes les villes, bourgs & autres lieux du royaume* (Paris, 1789). On the evolution of the Parisian sewage system: Barles, *La ville délétère*, 213–14.
13. David Garrioch, *The Making of Revolutionary Paris* (Berkeley: University of California Press, 2002), 213–16.
14. Allan Potofsky, "Paris-on-the-Atlantic, from the Old Regime to the Revolution," *French History* 25, no. 1 (March 2011): 89–107. Sabine Juratic,

"Mobilités et populations hébergées en garni," in *La Ville Promise. Mobilité et accueil à Paris (fin XVIIe—début XIXe siècle)*, ed. Daniel Roche (Paris: Fayard, 2000), 187. Louis-Sébastien Mercier, *Tableau de Paris*, ed. Jean-Claude Bonnet (Paris: Mercure de France, 1994), 129–31 (chapter 47, "Chambres garnies").

15. Camille Richard, *Le Comité de Salut Public et les fabrications de guerre sous la Terreur* (Paris: Rieder,1921). Ken Alder, *Engineering the Revolution. Arms and Enlightenment in France, 1763–1815* (Princeton: Princeton University Press, 1997). Guillerme, *La naissance de l'industrie*, 70–74.
16. Potofsky, *Constructing Paris*, 8.
17. Haim Burstin, *Une révolution à l'œuvre. Le faubourg Saint Marcel (1789–1794)* (Seyssel: Champ Vallon, 2005), 175–76.
18. Denis Woronoff, "Le charbon épuré vers 1780: un essai manqué," in *La houille avant le coke*, eds. Paul Benoit and Catherine Verna (Liège: Université de Liège, 1999), 169–75.
19. Thomas Le Roux, *Le laboratoire des pollutions industrielles. Paris, 1770–1830* (Paris: Albin Michel, 2011), 156–57, 159.
20. André Guillerme, *Bâtir la ville: révolutions industrielles dans les matériaux de construction. France-Grande-Bretagne, 1760–1840* (Seyssel: Champ Vallon, 1995).
21. Isabelle Backouche, *La trace du fleuve. La Seine et Paris (1750–1850)* (Paris: EHESS, 2000), 22–25.
22. Pierre-Alexis Delamair, *La pure vérité, ouvrage d'architecture . . . pour faire graver et imprimer son livre des Embellissements de Paris*, 1737, Bibliothèque de l'Arsenal, MSS 3054. Delamair, *Plan pour démontrer la meilleure situation du nouvel hôtel de ville, par Delamair en 1738*, Bibliothèque de l'Arsenal, MSS 2912.
23. Marc-Antoine Laugier, *Essai sur l'Architecture* (Paris, 1755). Nicolas Le Camus de Mézières, *Le guide de ceux qui veulent bâtir*, 2 vols. (Paris, 1781). For an overview: Richard Wittman, *Architecture, Print Culture, and the Public Sphere in Eighteenth-Century France* (New York and London: Routledge, 2007).
24. Voltaire, *Des embellissements de Paris. Œuvres complètes de Voltaire / Complete works of Voltaire*, ed. Theodore Besterman (Genève, Banbury, Oxford: Voltaire Foundation, 1968), 199–233, vol. 31B.
25. Robert Carvais, "La force du droit: Contribution à la définition de l'entrepreneur parisien du bâtiment au XVIIIe siècle," *Histoire, économie et société* 2 (1995): 163–89; and Carvais, "Le statut juridique de l'entrepreneur du bâtiment dans la France moderne," *Revue historique de droit français et étranger* 74 (1996): 221–52.
26. Potofsky, *Constructing Paris*, 43–47. At the beginning of the eighteenth-century (1718–1722) forty-four building projects out of the forty-seven projects (94%) that received authorisation from the Parisian Chambre des bâtiments were constructed; by 1788 until 1792 that figure fell to 104 out of 122 (85%). Daniel Roche, *The People of Paris. An Essay in Popular Culture in the Eighteenth Century* (Berkeley and Los Angeles: University of California Press, 1987), 100.
27. Steven Kaplan, "Les corporations, les faux ouvriers et le faubourg Saint-Antoine," *Annales: ESC 40* (March–April 1988): 253–78.
28. Potofsky, *Constructing Paris*, 44–47.
29. A series of raids by commissaire Allix on behalf of "La communauté de Maîtres Charpentiers," 1785–89, Archives Nationales, MSS Y 10806-Y 10810.
30. Burstin, *Une Révolution à l'œuvre*, 18–23.

31. Potofsky, *Constructing Paris*, 105, 112.
32. Ibid., 106, 119–20.
33. Antoine Quatremère de Quincy, *Rapport sur l'édifice de Sainte-Geneviève* (29 July 1791), Bibliothèque Nationale de France (hereafter, BNF), MSS Lb 40, 165, 169.
34. Ibid., quoted in Mark Deming, "Le Panthéon révolutionnaire," in *Le Panthéon: symbole des revolutions: de l'Eglise de la Nation au Temple des grands hommes* (Paris: Picard, 1989), 114. Jean-Claude Bonnet, *Naissance du Panthéon: essai sur le culte des grands hommes* (Paris: Fayard, 1998).
35. Pierre Claude Reynard, *Ambitions Tamed: Urban Expansion in Prerevolutionary Lyon* (Montreal and Kingston: McGill–Queen's University Press, 2009).
36. Ibid., 80–84, 118–19. Jean-Antoine Morand, Projet d'un plan général de la ville de Lyon et de son agrandissement en forme circulaire dans les terrains des Brotteaux (Lyon, 1775).
37. Reynard, *Ambitions Tamed*, 152–54.
38. Werner Szambien, *Les projets de l'An II. Concours d'architecture de la période révolutionnaire* (Paris: Ecole nationale supérieure des beaux-arts, 1986), 12, 18. An example is Pierre Le Sueur, *Projet d'utilité et embellissement pour la Ville de Paris, adressé aux sections* (May 1790), B.N.F. MSS Le Senne 6410 C.
39. Ted W. Margadant, *Urban Rivalries in the French Revolution* (Princeton: Princeton University Press, 1992), 178–219 (especially chapter 5, "The Politics of Parochialism").
40. Voltaire, *Des embellissements*, 199–233.
41. Charles-Louis Chassin, ed., *Les élections et les cahiers de Paris en 1789* (Paris: Imprimerie nationale, 1888–89), 387–89, vol. 1.
42. Examples of complaints: Siméon-Prosper Hardy, Mes Loisirs, *ou Journal d'événemens tels qu'ils parviennent à ma connoissance* (1753–89), in "Mardi, 15 novembre, 1785, Etat actuel des travaux publics," BNF, MSS Fonds français 6685, fol. 227, vol. 6. Louis Sébastien Mercier, *Tableau de Paris* (Chapitre CCCXXX, "Les heures du Jour"), 873–81, 875.
43. Emile Ducoudray et al., *Atlas de la Révolution française,* no. 11 (Paris: EHESS, 2000), 11, 22–23, 33. Gérard Béaur, *L'Immobilier et la revolution: marché de la pierre et mutations urbaines, 1770–1810*, (Paris: Cahiers des Annales, 1994), 119–26. Georges Lefebvre, *Etudes sur la révolution française* (Paris: P.U.F., 1959), 336. Bernard Bodinier and Eric Teyssier, *L'Evénement le plus important de la Révolution. La vente des biens nationaux* (Paris: Société des Études Robespierristes, édit. du CTHS, 2000).
44. Lisa DiCaprio, *The Origins of the Welfare State. Women, Work and the French Revolution* (Urbana and Chicago: University of Illinois Press, 2007), 8–9.
45. James A. Leith, *Space and Revolution. Projects for Monuments, Squares, and Public Buildings in France, 1789–1799* (Montréal: McGill-Queen's University Press, 1991). On Jean-François Palloy: Hans-Jürgen Lüsebrink and Rolf Reichardt, *The Bastille: A History of a Symbol of Despotism and Freedom* (Durham, NC: Duke University Press, 1997), 81–82, 151.
46. Jean-François Palloy, *Adresse à l'Assemblée nationale législative. Discours prononcé à l'Assemblée nationale législative, le 7 octobre, 3e année de la liberté* (1791), BNF, MSS LB39-10260.
47. Jean-Francois Palloy, *Plan général des terrains de la Bastille . . . appartenant au domaine national (1790)*, Bibliothèque historique de la ville de Paris, MSS B-1234. Palloy, *Projet d'un monument à élever à la gloire de la Liberté* (1790),

BNF, MSS 4-LB39–10467 (BIS). Hans-Jürgen Lüsebrink and Rolf Reichardt, *The Bastille*, 118–23.

48. Charles Gourlier and Charles-Auguste Questel, *Notice historique sur le Service des Travaux et sur le Conseil Général des bâtiments civils à Paris et dans les départements, depuis l'an IV (1795) jusqu'en 1886* (Paris, 1886).
49. Cited in Lauren Marie O'Connell, "Redefining the Past: Revolutionary Architecture and the Conseil des Bâtiments Civils," *The Art Bulletin* no. 77–2 (June 1995): 207–24. For context: Georges Teyssot, "Planning and Building in Towns: The System of the Bâtiments Civils in France, 1795–1848," in *The Beaux-Arts and the Nineteenth-Century French architecture*, ed. Robin Middleton (Cambridge MA: MIT Press, 1982), 34–49.
50. Discussion by Rondelet on abuses of the *Conseil* and on the need for a *bureau de vérification* to check architectural plans and bills: "Notes sur l'état actuel du Conseil des bâtiments civils, 27 germinal an X," Archives Nationales, MSS F^{13} 201.
51. Dominique Margairaz, "L'Invention du 'Service Public': entre 'changement matériel' et 'contrainte de nommer,'" *Revue d'histoire moderne et contemporaine* 52–53 (July–September 2005): 10–32, on 31.

6 Renewing and Refashioning

Recycling Furniture at the Late Stuart Court (1689–1714)

Olivia Fryman

During the spring of 1699 the renowned cabinetmaker Gerrit Jensen (d.1715) made a series of visits to the royal palace of Kensington, where he and his assistants began work cleaning and repairing a variety of furnishings in William III's apartments.[1] Amongst other tasks, Jensen's work included "mending and cleaning seven large Oval Sconces and the Chimney Sconces in the council chamber," "cleaning and Polishing a Princeswood Table and Stands and Frame and cleaning the chimney glass in the little Bedchamber," and "mending ye Varnish and Polishing ye Marquettree Tables and Stands and Bookcase and varnishing the clockcase in the Gallery."[2] This account for Kensington is typical of many warrants and bills that record work on dirty, damaged and unwanted furnishings at English royal palaces during the period. These can be categorised in two ways: furniture renewal through cleaning and repairs, and furniture refashioning that involved either the partial alteration or whole scale transformation of objects. Both of these strategies were intended to maintain the worth, appearance, and usefulness of furnishings and materials that were exceptionally valuable and symbolically rich. Focusing on the period from the accession of William III and Mary II in 1689 to the death of Queen Anne in 1714, this chapter discusses the methods of renewing and refashioning royal furniture and contextualises these practices in relation to contemporary aesthetic taste and attitudes towards monarchical spending and magnificence.

Jensen's bill for his work at Kensington during the spring of 1699 survives today in the papers of the Great Wardrobe, the household department that was responsible for supplying furniture for the court. The majority of the Wardrobe papers are held within records of the Lord Chamberlain, the court official who managed the public and ceremonial life of the sovereign.[3] For court and furniture historians, these archives have provided a rich source of information. In particular, studies have focused on the celebrated craftsmen Gerrit Jensen (mentioned above), the French upholsterer Francis Lapiere (d.1714), the Huguenot carver and gilder Jean Pelletier (d.1704), and the identification of records relating to their extant works.[4] In addition, scholars have stressed the significance of taste, fashionability, and conspicuous consumption as key components of sovereignty during this period.[5] Although the courts of William and Mary and Queen Anne were less dazzling than those of their Stuart predecessors, the purchase and display of fine furnishings remained central within constructions of monarchy. As Simon Thurley and Adam Bowett have argued in regard to William III, the King's acquisition of rich furniture in the fashionable French style for his new suite of State Apartments at Hampton Court Palace was an important aspect of his self-fashioning as a powerful and magnificent monarch.[6] As Bowett states, for William the arts and politics "were indivisible"; architecture, painting, sculpture, and furnishings were all visible and outward manifestations of his authority.[7] At the same time, Mary II employed her patronage of leading designers and craftsmen, her taste for rare and exotic commodities, such as porcelain and lacquer, and her own domestic creativity, to construct her image as queen and exemplar of elite femininity.[8] Records of Queen Anne's commissions for furnishings also indicate that she strove to project a splendid public image, despite her natural shyness and frequent ill health.[9] The Wardrobe papers reveal that on one occasion the Queen spent the incredible sum of £1273 8s. 6d. on "gold flower'd Tissue Brocaded with flowers of silver and silk" to line the interior of her state bed and matching furniture at St James's Palace.[10] This appears to be one of the most expensive commissions for textiles during the period, especially given that a further £567 was spent on velvet to upholster the exterior of the bed and furniture.[11] Palace furnishings were thus costly and impressive symbols of royal power which were at their most potent when mobilised in court rituals and ceremonies that highlighted the special status of the sovereign. Nevertheless, the sheer volume of warrants and bills relating to the renewal or refashioning of preexisting furniture calls into question the extent to which monarchical magnificence was dependent on the acquisition and use of newly fabricated wares. As this essay aims to demonstrate, the strategies of recycling furniture were a key aspect of the work of the Great Wardrobe, and one that played a vital role in upholding the magnificence of the late Stuart court.

Evidence from the Wardrobe papers shows that considerable efforts were made to preserve royal furnishings from dirt, damage and wear. Nearly all items of furniture provided for the court were protected by some form of covering or curtain made from cheaper or hard-wearing materials such as taffeta or leather.[12] During periods of cold and damp, orders were given for the interiors of palaces to be aired with fires and charcoal braziers, to "preserve ye furniture from spoiling."[13] Inventories of furnishings were also regularly taken to monitor their condition. Nevertheless, entries in the Wardrobe accounts indicate that despite these efforts, numerous problems arose. In 1702–03, for example, it was recorded that "the old Crimson flowered Velvett state [canopy of estate]" and the matching chairs and stools in the king's state apartments at St James's Palace were "mighty foul and black," most probably due to the smoke and soot spread by wood and coal fires.[14] In a period when insulation was poor, damp was also a common cause of rot and infestations. The warrant book for 1699 reveals, for instance, that the stuffing of the velvet stools in the king's gallery and the couch in the great closet at Kensington required replacing, "the new stuffing that is in them being rotten, and turns to moths."[15] Vermin were also an occasional problem. In 1706 it was recorded that the Indian hangings in the privy chamber, also at Kensington, were in need of repair on account of them having been "eaten by a rat."[16] Additionally, light damage, a build up of dust, and dirt introduced by animals and insects were further concerns. In the long term, it was also unavoidable that some furnishings would become outmoded or unsuited to the particular preferences or needs of the monarch. This was especially the case at the beginning of a reign, when the newly crowned monarch inherited furniture that had been acquired by their predecessor. However, in such instances it was rare for furnishings to be discarded entirely. More often than not they were cleaned, repaired, altered, or remade.

One of the key motivations for maintaining palace furnishings in the best possible condition was the contemporary association between material magnificence and royal power. As previously suggested, the furnishings of palaces were an important symbol of the monarch's wealth and status, yet this was ultimately dependent on their dependent on their condition. While the negative signs of dirt, damage, and wear threatened to sully monarchical splendour, the positive actions of cleaning and repairing served to ensure against this by restoring furnishings to their original or desired state. In addition, renewing and refashioning existing furniture, rather than buying new, had significant financial benefits. These strategies improved the longevity of objects that were exceptionally valuable. They also allowed for the reuse of existing materials, and as such, the cost was considerably less than the production of new pieces. During this period, the labour of furniture makers was far cheaper than the velvets and silks, the gold and silver leaf, the exotic woods and lacquer that were used in the manufacture of fine furniture.

Although there was a long tradition of renewing and refashioning royal furniture at the English court, under the later Stuarts these recycling strategies unfolded within the context of financial strain and political compromise.[17] By William III's death in 1702, royal debt stood at £307,000, a sum accrued by a series of costly wars, the dramatic expansion of the royal household, and the ambitious building campaigns at Hampton Court and Kensigton Palace.[18] Despite retrenchment, much of this debt remained unpaid until the later 1710s. Further to this, any attempt to avoid undue waste and extravagant expense in the furnishing of palaces may have been regarded as politically advantageous, particularly in the decades following the Glorious Revolution of 1688. While magnificence undoubtedly remained central to notions of sovereignty, the removal of the Catholic King James II and the accession of William and Mary established a more politically limited and strictly Protestant monarchy in England. From this period onwards, monarchs were especially aware of the benefits of appearing financially prudent in order to avoid both public criticism of their spending, and any association with Catholicism and tyranny which were perceived as the profligate traits of the French.

On a fundamental level, the furnishings of royal palaces were subject to a continual process of renewal through the daily practices of cleaning that were undertaken by the domestic servants of the royal household. During a period of royal residence the interiors of the state apartments and the royal lodgings were cleaned and prepared each morning by servants known as Necessary Women. Evidence suggests that in the monarch's household alone there were up to four Necessary Women who, with the help of assistants, each cleaned a particular room or suite of rooms in the king's apartments for the duration of the court's stay.[19] Warrants for payment to these servants reveal that they were reimbursed for cleaning equipment including items that included mops, brooms, brushes, pails, polishing cloths, ash pans, chamber pots, and stool pans, indicating that their work was similar to that performed by housemaids and chambermaids in elite households.[20] On the removal of the court to another royal residence, the task of cleaning the furnishings passed to the resident Housekeeper or Wardrobe Keeper and their servants, who were responsible for the interiors during the monarch's absence.[21] Orders for supplies for these individuals include items such as whisks used for brushing textiles, goose wings for dusting delicate surfaces, braziers for airing the lodgings, and covers for protecting furnishings. Deliveries of sewing thread, tacks, and hammers suggest that they may also have undertaken, or overseen, some minor furniture repairs.[22]

However, the maintenance of royal furnishings often required expertise that was beyond the capabilities of the House and Wardrobe Keepers and Necessary Women. The royal palaces were furnished with objects that were representative of the highest standards in design, fashioned in the most costly materials using complex techniques and fine finishes. Cleaning and repairing such items was highly skilled work as it often required an understanding of the original materials and techniques used, and, in some cases, the ability to replicate them. This was also the case with altering existing furnishings or refashioning them into new pieces. Consequently, this work was most often undertaken by the craftsmen of the Great Wardrobe, the original designers and makers of royal furniture. Although during this period the distinctions between the furniture trades were not always clear-cut, it was usually the case that upholsterers and embroiderers were responsible for textiles, while joiners, carvers, and gilders worked on bedsteads, tables and stands and the frames of chairs and stools. The care of tapestries was carried out by arras-workers, while cabinets, mirrors and silver were maintained by cabinetmakers and the goldsmiths of the royal Jewel House.[23] The work of all of these craftsmen was usually timed in anticipation of the monarch's arrival at a royal residence, and carried out either on site or at the firm's workshop in London. In contrast to the Necessary Women and the House and Wardrobe Keepers, who received set yearly wages, the craftsmen employed by the Wardrobe were commissioned by warrant from the Lord Chamberlain and submitted bills for their work. These warrants and bills provide the most detailed evidence for the practices of renewing and refashioning royal furniture and, as such, will be the focus for the following discussion of recycling techniques.

RENEWING: CLEANING AND REPAIRING ROYAL FURNITURE

The renewal of furniture through cleaning and repairs is the most common type of recycling detailed in the Wardrobe accounts. Of this, a significant proportion of the records relate to work on textiles. During this period, textiles were some of the most costly and highly prized furnishings owned by the crown. Display pieces such as state beds, canopies of estate, and their suites of matching furniture were upholstered in the finest silks and velvets with braid, embroidery, fringes, and tassels (known today as passementerie) applied as decoration. The two canopies of estate (both of 1699) and state beds (c. 1699 and 1714) belonging to William III and Queen Anne that survive today at Hampton Court Palace showcase the richness and complexity of textile design and the skill of upholsterers (Figure 6.1 and 6.2).

Figure 6.1 The privy chamber at Hampton Court Palace furnished with the canopy of estate provided for William III in 1699. © Historic Royal Palaces.

Figure 6.2 Queen Anne's state bed (1714) originally purchased for Windsor Castle but now at Hampton Court Palace. The bed was upholstered by Hamden Reeve in cream, crimson, and yellow figured velvet. © Historic Royal Palaces.

Accounts for cleaning and repairing such textiles appear in the bills submitted by Richard Bealing and Hamden Reeve, who successively held the position of upholsterer to the crown from 1688 to 1714.[24] In 1702–03 for example, Bealing undertook work on the aforementioned blackened canopy of estate and matching furniture in the king's apartments at St James's Palace.[25] He charged £6 10s. for "repairing the old Crimson flowered Velvett state and Cleaning all the Velvett of the state Chairs and Stooles" and "making it up anew."[26] Although the techniques used to clean the velvet are not recorded in Bealing's bill, it is likely that this would have been done using the common methods of wiping with cloths, brushing using soft-haired brushes, and rubbing with bread and bran that acted to dislodge and soak up the dust and dirt. Later bills submitted by the royal upholsterers John and Sarah Gilbert provide some evidence for these techniques in charges for "wiping" and for cleaning with "bread and bran."[27] The same technique was also used by the arras-workers of the Great Wardrobe who were responsible for maintaining the crown's exceptionally valuable collection of tapestries. As the work of Wendy Hefford has shown, tapestries in regular use were thoroughly cleaned by the arras-workers once every twenty to thirty years using a combination of brushing and applying bread and bran.[28]

In some instances it was also necessary to remove more stubborn marks from textile furnishings. In November 1705 for example, a warrant was sent to the Great Wardrobe requesting that "the wax spots" be taken out of "two Crimson Velvet Chairs fourteen stooles and four long form cases suitable in her Majesties New Drawing Room at St James's."[29] Eighteenth-century recipe books suggest that this could be achieved by applying toasted bread or a hot coal wrapped in linen that acted to melt and absorb the spot.[30]

In the case of textiles that were more extensively worn or damaged, the Wardrobe accounts reveal that they were most often replaced in part or discreetly patched. An example of this type of work appears in the accounts of December 1690, when a warrant was issued for "the Queenes Bleu and White Damaske Bed [at Whitehall] to be repaired with a new inward Vallains [valance] suitable to the Bed."[31] Remarkably, this replacement was required on account of "the vallains which did belong to the bed being cut off and stolen."[32] To repair the bed twenty yards of three-coloured damask at £14 7s. were supplied by the mercer William Sherrard. This had to be specially made for which Sherrard charged an additional £13 10s. for "putting up a loom to make the said damask by her majesties particular command."[33] By far the most expensive element to replace, however, was the valance fringe described as fine gold and silver knotted and faggotted. Bought from the fringe maker John Stanton, this cost £296 12s. 6d.[34]

Replacement textiles were also provided in 1703–04 for repairing a bed belonging to Queen Anne that was described as "much out of order."[35] William Sherrard supplied twenty-one yards of white satin, costing £15 15s. for "two paire of sattin quilted Blanketts for her Majesties White Indian Embroidered Bed mended and set up at Hampton Court and for repairing one Sattin thick quilt for ye s[ai]d Bedd."[36] The work of cleaning, repairing and erecting the bed was undertaken by Richard Bealing, at a total cost of £3 13s.[37] In the case of embroidered textiles that had become worn or been damaged, they were reworked by the embroiderer to the crown, William West. In 1699–1700 West was sent to Kensington Palace to repair a set of embroideries in the queen's gallery that had been "spoilt by ye Moths."[38] In 1708–09 he was also employed at Windsor where he cleaned and repaired embroideries "wrought by Mary Queen of Scotts with a large addition of gold and silver wrought into ye defective places thereof," for which he charged £24.[39] Notably, as West's account indicates, even historic textiles were restored to the best possible condition, without much concern for preserving the original materials or workmanship.[40]

Similar work was also undertaken on passementerie. The decorative braid, fringing, tassels, and embroideries on upholstered furnishings were often the most expensive component and, as such, maintaining their condition and ensuring their longevity was exceptionally important. References to work on passementerie in the Wardrobe papers indicate that upholsterers were usually employed to clean and tidy up silk tassels, tufts and fringing. In 1703–04 for example, Hamden Reeve charged £3 10s. for "cleaning the fringe & new Clipping and Combing all the Tuffts" on Prince George of Denmark's state bed at St James's Palace.[41] Alternatively, for more complex work on gold and silver decoration William West was commissioned to undertake cleaning and repairs. His bill, of the same year, includes a charge of £66 10s. for "cleaning and gilding all the Gold Lace [i.e. braid] and embroidery" on Queen Anne's crimson velvet state bed, window curtains, and matching chairs and stools at St James's. At the same time he also cleaned and gilded a gold embroidered satin headboard and counterpoint belonging to Prince George's bed, mentioned above, for which he charged £18 15s.[42] The reference to re-gilding passementerie here is unusual and no further accounts for this can be traced in the Wardrobe papers of the period. Judging by the large sums expended on this work, West applied new gold leaf to the surface of the threads, although this would not have been permanent as the movement of the textiles would have caused the gold to flake over time.[43] This may therefore have been an expedient, if ephemeral, way of renewing the splendour of the state beds at St James's in time for a special occasion. While cleaning and re-gilding was costly, this was still cheaper and quicker than sourcing new passementerie and would have had the same magnificent effect.

In addition to textiles, the craftsmen employed by the Great Wardrobe also undertook work on wooden, gilt and inlaid furniture. These types of furnishings were costly and prized for the splendid effects of their surfaces that enhanced the magnificence of palace interiors; carved and gilt work, polished woods, and decorative inlays contributed colour, glow and shine. Accordingly, much of the work on these furnishings was focused on renewing surfaces that had become degraded or damaged in order to restore their splendid appearance. Gilt furniture in particular was especially fragile and prone to chip and scratch, necessitating that new gold leaf was applied in areas of loss. This was usually undertaken by Thomas Roberts, the joiner to the crown from 1685–1714, or by a member of his firm. In 1702–03 for example, a gilder from Roberts's workshop was employed at Hampton Court "to mend the guilt Chaires and Sopheas [sofas] in the Long Gallery."[44] For labour, travelling expenses and for "gold used" Roberts charged £3.[45] In 1705–06 his firm also undertook similar work at Kensington that included "mending six rich carv'd stooles and two arm'd Chaires and repairing the guilding of them being much Damaged in her Majesty's Bedchamber" at a cost of £8 15s.[46] In cases where furniture with veneers of wood or inlay required cleaning or repairs, this work was most often undertaken by Gerrit Jensen. His bill for work at Kensington in 1699–1700 includes numerous charges for "Scraping off," "Varnishing," and "Pollishing" wooden and inlaid pieces.[47] Judging by the advice given in contemporary guides to craftsmen, these tasks involved removing the old layer of varnish with a metal scraper and the application of a new lac-based varnish, which, when dry, was polished with powdered Tripoly (a fine earth or powdered stone) lubricated with water or a paste of oil and brick dust.[48] As research by Adam Bowett has shown, varnishing and polishing in this way acted to enhance the brilliancy and luminosity of woods in particular, giving furniture a remarkable visual impact.[49]

Silver and glass were a further category of furnishings that were cleaned and repaired by the craftsmen of the Great Wardrobe. Like gilt, wooden, and inlaid furniture, mirrors, sconces and chandeliers were valued especially for the lustre of their surfaces that added to the splendour of palace interiors and also enhanced the light. It was therefore essential that they were maintained in pristine condition. During the period, a large proportion of the work on silver items was carried out by the royal Jewel House, which was based at the Tower of London. Warrants sent by the Lord Chamberlain to the Master of the Jewel House include numerous requests for candlesticks, chandeliers and sconces to be immersed in boiling water, the most efficacious method of removing tarnishing and drips of wax.[50] In 1702 for example, prior to the funeral of William III, an order was given for "the Silver Branches that were in the Privy Chamber, Drawing Room and Bedchamber [at Kensington to] be all new boyld for that occasion."[51] Larger sets of silver furniture were similarly cleaned in this way. In December 1696 the Jewel House received a warrant for "ye boiling and burnishing of Two large tables two looking Glasses Stands and Branch &c which were in ye withdrawing roome on ye Queens side being for his Majesties service at Kensington."[52]

In 1707-08 Gerrit Jensen was employed at Hampton Court for "cleaning all the glasses and sconces" in the royal apartments and adding "a new border about the great glass in the Presence Chamber and several Roses and Cleaning the glasses in our Privy Chamber."[53] The mirrors that still survive today in the king's privy chamber at Hampton Court had originally been supplied by Jensen for William III in 1699–1700. They feature small rose-shaped embellishments around the mirror borders and it is therefore likely that Jensen's work involved replacing several of these that had broken off. On other occasions, Jensen renewed the silvering of mirrors. The silver layer of tin and mercury that was applied to the back of glasses was prone to degrade over time, especially if damp penetrated any faults in the foil. This caused small circular grey "blooms" on the face of the mirror, or even caused the foil to fall off altogether.[54] In cases where such damage had occurred, a new layer of foil was applied. In 1700–01 for example, Jensen's bill included a charge for "new silvering the chimney glass" in William III's private closet at Kensington.[55] Similarly, in 1694–95 a craftsmen by the name of Nicholas Pic was employed at the palace for "covering the glasses with quicksilver where they wanted repairing."[56]

REFASHIONING: ALTERING AND TRANSFORMING ROYAL FURNITURE

In addition to the many accounts relating to the renewal of furnishings, the Wardrobe papers also shed light on the practices of altering and transforming royal furniture. In this second type of recycling, the furnishings chosen were normally in good condition, but considered out of date or unsuited to the monarch's needs or tastes. As can be expected, they were also usually those furnishings wrought in the most valuable and rare materials that were simply too precious to be discarded. In regard to textile furnishings, the accounts reveal that they were frequently selected for alteration, largely due to the fact they could be unpicked and the fabric reused relatively easily. In 1702–03, for example, work was undertaken on a canopy of estate from Kensington Palace that Queen Anne had recently inherited following the death of William III. Like many items of royal furniture, the canopy was embroidered with the King's arms and cipher, and accordingly these were removed from the textile ground and replaced by the Queen's. The embroiderer William West was employed to take out "the Escutcheon of the Pretence in the Middle of his late Majesties armes [and] [. . .] his Majesties Letters and Cyphers round the Vallance &c." He then embroidered "her Majesties Letters and Cyphers in their Places."[57] The canopy was then moved to St James's Palace, where it was set up in Queen Anne's state apartments.

In other cases, the alterations made to textile furnishings were considerably more extensive. In the same year, the Queen selected a velvet bed from her rooms at Hampton Court to be remade for her apartments at Kensington. While the reasons for this are not known, it is likely that a lack of time and funds precluded the Queen from commissioning a new suite of bedchamber furnishings, while at Hampton Court, which was infrequently occupied in the early years of Anne's reign, there was a bed surplus to requirements. In August 1703 an order was issued by the Lord Chamberlain for "the Party coloured [multicoloured] velvet bed and hangings in the little Bedchamber at Hampton Court to be made into a great Bed, to be set up at Kensington."[58] Designed for a little bedchamber this would have been a relatively small bed in which the monarch actually slept, while larger great or state beds were intended for state bedchambers and used only for show. The transformation of this bed therefore involved the royal joiner providing a new bed frame (or bedstock) and the upholsterer, Richard Bealing, making up and applying new textiles to match the existing ones.[59] Bealing's bill for "taking to pieces the Velvett Bedd [. . .] making the Bed larger and altering and new doing up the same," altering four window curtains, making up new bedding, four additional curtains and cornices, and upholstering a new elbow chair and two stools to match, amounted to £73 8s. 6d.[60] A further £105 11s. 6d. was expended on braid, fringes and tassels from the fringe maker Thomas Carr and additional fabrics supplied by the mercers Jacob Davidson and William Sherrard.[61] In total, the amount expended on remaking this bed came to £215 6d. While a large sum, this allowed for the reuse of textiles that were evidently in good condition and, above all, cost significantly less than the commission of an entirely new state bed.[62]

In addition to textiles, silver furnishings were also especially suitable for refashioning as they could be easily melted down and cast into new pieces. One key example of work on silver furniture appears in the accounts of the Jewel House for the year 1698–99. In July 1698 William III commissioned a set of silver furnishings for his apartments at Kensington, including a "large Enchased and Engraved table," a looking-glass frame "curiously wrought and enriched," a pair of candle stands "curiously enchased and engraved on the tops," a pair of large andirons (firedogs), and a chandelier.[63] However, rather than being newly made, these pieces were refashioned from an earlier set of silver furniture that was deemed outmoded. The Master of the Jewel House received orders for "making the Silver Table Stands and Frame of Glass in the Drawing room at Kensington of a newer fashion and that the frame of the Glass be made fit to contain a larger glass."[64] A further warrant requested that he "give orders for the making of the silver Branch in the Privy Chamber and the andirons in the Bedchamber att Kensington of a new fashion and very strong."[65] Of this magnificent set of furnishings, the table and mirror both survive in the Royal Collection today. They bear the maker's mark of the silver chaser Andrew Moore, while the engraved table-top is signed by the unidentified engraver R. H.[66] While the making of these furnishings involved the reuse of existing silver objects, it was nevertheless an exceptionally expensive commission, costing nearly £3,600. The new furniture was heavier than the set it replaced, indicating that some additional silver was used. This, together with the workmanship involved in refashioning the set into such splendid and highly decorative pieces, meant that even recycling was an extremely costly process.

The final example of furniture refashioning discussed in this essay highlights the value of the lacquer furniture owned by the crown during this period. By the late seventeenth century, lacquer wares imported from Japan were an essential component of the fashionable interior. They were prized for their rarity and were acquired at great cost. It is therefore not surprising that one of the most dramatic incidences of furniture refashioning detailed in the Wardrobe accounts involved the transformation of two lacquer cabinets from St James's Palace. In 1703–04, Gerrit Jensen was commissioned to dismantle the cabinets and reuse their component parts to make new pieces of furniture. His bill reveals that he removed the lacquer panels on the tops, backs, and sides of the cabinets, and the interior drawers. He then replaced the drawers with shelves and quilted the interior of the cabinets with silk, suggesting that their new function may have been for storing the Queen's clothes or linen. The leftover pieces of lacquer from the drawers were added to another pair of cabinets that were sent to Kensington, while the tops were made into tables fixed onto carved and gilt frames.[67] Remarkably, both of these tables survive, having being acquired in the nineteenth century by the Earl of Warwick, in whose possession they remained until their sale at Sotheby's in 1998.[68] As this example demonstrates, in some instances the refashioning of royal furniture could result in the creation of new objects with a function entirely divorced from that of the original piece.

"UNFIT FOR THEIR MAJESTIES SERVICE": DISCARDING AND RE-HOMING ROYAL FURNITURE

As the examples of renewal and refashioning discussed in this essay clearly demonstrate, all manner of royal furnishings were recycled by the Great Wardrobe. These practices were intended to maintain the worth, appearance, and usefulness of furnishings, and ensure against waste and undue expense. However, there were some instances where royal furnishings were in too poor a condition to be reused. In 1692 for example, James Marriott, the Wardrobe Keeper at Hampton Court, was requested to make an inventory of the goods that had been put into store at the palace.[69] He recorded that many of the furnishings were old and in a state of disrepair; amongst other items there was a "Cloth of State of Crimson & purple Cloath of Gold Embroidered with ye arms of England with a Chaire Two Stooles & one foote stoole all very old," a standing bedstead "not worth anything," "six old downe pillows foure old downe Quilts Two paire of old fustian blankets," as well as tapestries and carpets, looking glasses, tables, and chairs, many of which were "much broke."[70] The inventory and the furnishings were then inspected by the Lord Chamberlain who subsequently reported back:

> Upon Observing ye Goods above written they appeare to be very old rotten & full of Moths, & altogether unfit for their Majesties service, & also of ill Consequence to be kept in their Majesties wardrobe where rich & good goods are to be kept lest they should infect ye other Goods with moths & rottenness I do therefore hereby Authorise & require you to remove and take away ye afore written Goods of their Majesties Wardrobe And dispose of them as you shall think fit for y^{r} owne use.[71]

Judging by the poor condition of these goods, it is likely that their monetary value was negligible. On the other hand, the phrase "fit for y^{r} owne use" suggests that Marriott may have reaped some benefit from this collection of unwanted furniture, perhaps by selling it or keeping some pieces for use in his own household.[72] At the English court it was established custom that furnishings no longer fit for royal use were given away to courtiers as gifts or perquisites. This could be lucrative for high-ranking servants such as the Lord Chamberlain and the Groom of the Stole who had rights to claim especially choice items such as the royal death-bed.[73] It is for this reason that there are many royal objects surviving today in the collections at courtiers' houses. Two notable examples are the royal state beds at Knole in Kent, that were acquired by the Lord Chamberlain, Charles Sackville, 6th Earl of Dorset, in the early years of William and Mary's reign. These two beds, known as "the king's bed" (c. 1673) and "the Venetian ambassador's bed" (1688), belonged to James II but remained in the royal wardrobe after he fled to France in 1688.[74] As Lord Chamberlain, Dorset was entitled to claim old or unwanted palace furnishings as his perquisite of office. As both beds were closely associated with the disgraced King they would not have been considered fit for use by William and Mary, who fervently sought to distance themselves from James. This may have been especially the case in regard to the "Venetian ambassador's bed," which was emblazoned with James's ciphers, carved into the gilt wood cornice of the bed. Over the course of the eighteenth century these beds became star attractions in the show rooms at Knole.[75] In 1696 William III also gave a "black table, stands and looking glasse [. . .] garnished with silver with the Duke of Yorks [James Stuart, later James II] Cypher" as a gift to Simon de Brienne, the House and Wardrobe Keeper at Kensington Palace.[76] If Brienne appreciated this valuable piece it must have been merely for its intrinsic value as his papers reveal that, less than a year later, he took these pieces to the London silversmith David Willaume, who removed all the silver, for which he paid Brienne the handsome sum of £230 19s.[77] In the hands of a Jacobite, such a piece might well have become a revered relic. Brienne, however, was a loyal servant to William III and evidently felt no attachment to this object or its previous owner. Nevertheless, as the re-homing of James II's furnishings highlights, even where furnishings were deemed no longer suitable for use by the monarch, they enjoyed a second life as tokens of court patronage and gift giving.

As this chapter has shown, the papers of the royal Wardrobe provide considerable evidence for the important role that recycling played in maintaining the magnificence of the late Stuart court. The numerous accounts for cleaning and repairs shed light on the methods and techniques used to restore the splendour of palace furnishings. Furthermore, the evidence for the refashioning of furniture highlights the extent to which objects were altered and remade to allow for their reuse and to ensure their longevity. Even in the case of furnishings that were no longer fit for royal use, some found a secondary function in networks of patronage that were integral to the functioning of the court. The recycling of furnishings was a key aspect of the work undertaken by the craftsmen of the Great Wardrobe, and as such, deserves consideration alongside the more celebrated practices of design, production and the acquisition of new goods.

NOTES

1. Bill of Gerrit Jensen, The National Archives (hereafter TNA) LC5/44, fol.104. For the corresponding warrant issued by the Lord Chamberlain on 20 April 1699 see LC5/152, fol.185. The research for this article is derived from the author's unpublished PhD thesis, "Making the Bed: The Practice, Role and Significance of Housekeeping in the Royal Bedchambers at Hampton Court Palace, 1689–1737" (PhD diss., Kingston University, 2011).
2. TNA LC5/44, fol.104.
3. On the role of the Lord Chamberlain see Robert Bucholz and John Sainty, *Officials of the Royal Household 1660–1837, Part One: Department of the Lord Chamberlain and Associated Offices* (London: Institute of Historical Research, 1997), 1. The Wardrobe accounts and bills for this period can be found at TNA LC5/42–45 and LC9/279–285. In addition to the records of the Wardrobe, the Lord Chamberlain's papers also include warrants many of which relate to the commission of new furnishings. See TNA LC5/149–155 and LC5/115–126.
4. See for example Tessa Murdoch, "Jean René and Thomas Pelletier, a Huguenot Family of Carvers and Gilders in England 1682–1726, Part 1," *The Burlington Magazine* 139, no. 1136 (November 1997): 732–42; and also Part 2, *The Burlington Magazine* 140, no. 1143 (June 1998): 363–74; Annabel Westman and Geoffrey Beard, "A French Upholsterer in England: Francis Lapiere 1653–1714," *The Burlington Magazine* 135, no. 1085 (August 1993): 515–24; Geoffrey Beard, "Thomas and Richard Roberts: Royal Chair-Makers," *Apollo* 148 (1998): 46–48; R. W. Symonds, "Gerrit Jensen, Cabinet Maker to the Royal Household," *Connoisseur* 95 (1935): 268–74; Adam Bowett, *English Furniture 1660–1714, from Charles II to Queen Anne* (Woodbridge: Antique Collectors Club, 2002).
5. The relationship between the material culture of courts and the construction of the royal image has been the subject of a number of important studies from within the fields of court and furniture history. See for example Gervase Jackson-Stops, "The Court Style in Britain," in *Courts and Colonies: The William and Mary Style in Holland, England, and America*, ed. Renier Baarsen et al. (New York: Cooper Hewitt Museum, distributed by the University of Washington Press, 1988), 36–61; Robert Malcolm Smuts, "Art and the Material Culture of Majesty in Early Stuart England," in *The Stuart Court and Europe: Essays in Politics and Political Culture,* ed. Robert Malcolm Smuts (Cambridge: Cambridge University Press, 1996), 86–112; Jane Roberts, *George III and Queen Charlotte: Patronage, Collecting and Court Taste* (The Royal Collection, 2004); and Michael Snodin, "The Palace," in *Baroque. Style in the Age of Magnificence 1620–1800*, ed. Michael Snodin and Nigel Llewellyn (London: V&A Publications, 2009), 298–324.
6. Gervase Jackson-Stops, "William III and French Furniture," *Furniture History* 7 (1971): 121–26; Simon Thurley, *Hampton Court Palace, A Social and Architectural History* (New Haven and London: Yale University Press, 2003); Adam Bowett, *English Furniture*, 170–95.
7. Adam Bowett, *English Furniture*, 176.
8. On Mary II's patronage and her public image see Joanna Marschner, "Mary II: Her Clothes and Textiles," *Costume* 34 (2000): 44–50; and Lois G. Schwoerer, "Images of Queen Mary, 1689–1695," *Renaissance Quarterly* 42 (1989): 717–48. For a discussion of her furnishings at Kensington and Hampton Court see T.H. Lunsingh Scheurleer, "Documents on the Furnishing of Kensington House," *The Walpole Society* 38 (1960–62): 15–58; and Thurley, *Hampton Court*, 172–76.

9. Queen Anne's taste and cultural patronage has yet to be fully addressed by historians. To date the most comprehensive biography is Edward Gregg, Queen Anne (London: Routledge and Kegan and Paul, 1980) and Anne Somerset, *Queen Anne: The Politics of Passion* (London: Harper Collins, 2012).
10. TNA LC9/284, fol.42.
11. TNA LC9/284, fol.40.
12. For references to cases, curtains, and covers see for example, TNA LC9/279, fol.101; LC9/280, fol.358; LC9/281, fols.20 and 79. For a discussion of the design and use of case covers see Margaret Swain, "Loose Covers, or Cases," *Furniture History* 33 (1997): 128–33; Lucy Wood, *The Upholstered Furniture in the Lady Lever Art Gallery* (New Haven and London: Yale University Press, 2008), 84–88.
13. TNA LC5/154, fol.305.
14. TNA LC9/281, fol.206.
15. TNA LC5/152, fol.206.
16. LC5/89, fol.37, British Library, (hereafter BL) MSS. Add. 20101, fol.8.
17. For earlier examples of furniture recycling within the royal wardrobe see for example, TNA LC9/91–102 (1600–1638). Maria Hayward has highlighted the extent to which Henry VIII's furnishings were cleaned and repaired by the Wardrobes of the Robes and Beds in order that they remained in the best possible condition. See Maria Hayward, "Repositories of Splendour: Henry VIII's wardrobes of the Robes and Beds," *Textile History* 29 (1998): 134–56.
18. Robert Bucholz and John Sainty, *Officials of the Royal Household 1660–1837, Part One: Department of the Lord Chamberlain and associated offices*, lxiii.
19. This arrangement was replicated in the other households of the court, those of the consort, princes and princesses. See the Lord Chamberlain's establishment books, TNA LC3/3–6. The fullest account of the division of labour between Necessary Woman can be found in a petition submitted by Henry Lowman, the House and Wardrobe Keeper at Kensington Palace, during the reign of Queen Anne. See British Library, BL, MSS. Add. 20101, fol.15.
20. TNA T53/21, fol.434; LC5/158, fol.65, LC9/279, fols.17, 28, 94, 116, 151; LC9/280, fols. 28, 52, 59, 98, 134, 182. BL MSS. Add. 5751, fol.179.
21. On the role of the Under-Housekeepers and Wardrobe Keepers at royal residences see R.O. Bucholz, "Office Holders in Modern Britain: Volume 11: Court Offices, 1660–1837."
22. TNA LC5/154, fol.365; LC5/155, fol.210; LC5/42, fol.308; LC5/44, fol.241; LC9/282, fol.51.
23. On the distinctions and crossovers between the furniture trades during this period see Pat Kirkham, *The London Furniture Trade 1700–1870* (London: Furniture History Society, 1988).
24. On the careers of Bealing (1688–c. 1714) and Reeve (1704–1714) that ran concurrently during the reign of Queen Anne see Geoffrey Beard, *Upholsterers and Interior Furnishing in England 1530—1840* (New Haven and London: Yale University Press, 1997), 99–145.
25. TNA LC9/281, fol.206.
26. TNA LC9/281, fol.206.
27. See for example, TNA LC9/287, fol.157; LC5/75, fol.10. Alternatively, in some instances, royal textiles were dry scoured, a technique that involved rubbing the fabric on both sides with turpentine and an absorbent powder such as fuller's earth, and then wiping with a clean cloth. See LC5/47, fol.124. For contemporary advice on the use of fuller's earth see Hannah Glasse, *The Servant's Directory or the Housekeeper's Companion: Wherein the Duties of the Chambermaid, Nursery Maid, Housemaid, Laundry-Maid, Scullion, or Under-Cook are Fully and Distinctly Explained* (London, 1760), 35–36.

28. Wendy Hefford, "'Bread Brushes and Bran,' aspects of tapestry restoration in England, 1660–1760," in *Acts of the Tapestry Symposium*, ed. A. Bennett, (San Francisco: Fine Arts Museum of San Francisco, 1979), 66.
29. TNA LC5/154, fol.125. Notably, the work of removing the wax was undertaken by the embroiderer to the crown, William West, rather than Bealing or Reeve. Why this was the case is unclear, yet it may have been for the simple reason that West was already employed at the palace at that time to undertake work on two state beds. For his bill for this work see TNA LC5/44, fol.234.
30. *Valuable Secrets Concerning Arts and Trades or approved directions from the best artists* (London, 1775), 299.
31. TNA LC5/123, no.99.
32. TNA LC5/123, no.99.
33. TNA LC9/280, fol.48.
34. TNA LC9/280, fol.54.
35. TNA LC9/282, fol.29.
36. TNA LC9/282, fol.19.
37. TNA LC9/282, fol.29.
38. TNA LC5/131, no.90.
39. TNA LC5/45, fol.50.
40. This was also the case when pieces from the crown's collection historic tapestries (many of which has been acquired by Henry VIII) were repaired. They were occasionally rewoven in places that were found to be weak or broken with new silk, gold, and silver wefts. See for example TNA LC9/279, fol.140.
41. TNA LC9/282, fol.71. See also LC9/281, fol.206; LC5/47 fol.124; LC5/44, fol.197.
42. TNA LC9/282, fol.76.
43. I am grateful to Sebastian Edwards and Annabel Westman for their advice on this reference to regilding passementerie.
44. TNA LC9/281, fol.91.
45. TNA LC9/281, fol.91.
46. TNA LC9/282, fol.112.
47. TNA LC5/44, fols.36 and 104. See also TNA LC9/281, fols.172–73.
48. Alternatively, fuller's earth, pipe clay, whitening, alum, and wood ash could be mixed with sweet oil (olive oil) or other oils to make less abrasive polishing pastes. The London cabinetmaker Samuel Norman's inventory of 1760 included forty-one fish skins and five-dozen fins that were also used for polishing woods. European craftsmen also used shark skins that were considered especially good polishing agents as they had large numbers of small sharp "teeth" (dermal dentils) which gently rubbed the fibres of the wood. See Edwards, *Encyclopaedia of Furniture Materials, Trades and Techniques* (Aldershot: Ashgate, 2000), 1, 171.
49. Bowett, *English Furniture*, 168–69.
50. For the Jewel House warrant books for this period see TNA LC5/108–09 and 112. For the bill books LC9/46–47.
51. TNA LC5/108, fol.333.
52. TNA LC5/151, fol.350. Given that the table and candle stands were boiled it is probable that they had silver surfaces. They most likely resembled a table, stands, and looking glass of sheet silver on a wooden core, made for the Countess of Dorset at Knole, Kent, by Gerrit Jensen (between 1676 and 80). See Adam Bowett, *English Furniture*, 126–27.
53. TNA LC9/282, fol.198.
54. Bowett, *English Furniture*, 130.

55. TNA LC5/44, fol. 36. See also LC9/281, fol.193; LC9/285, fol.56.
56. TNA LC5/43, fol.143.
57. TNA LC9/281, fol.196. This may have been the same canopy of estate that was cleaned and repaired in the same year at St James's by Richard Bealing.
58. TNA LC5/153, fol.397.
59. The joinery work on the bed was carried out by Thomas Roberts. In addition to providing a new bedstead he also altered the carved tester from the old bed and added a new piece of cornice, altered four window cornices, made two new portieres, an easy elbow chair, and two square stools carved and gilt. His bill amounted to £36, 12d. See TNA LC9/281, fols.201–02
60. TNA LC9/281, fols. 206–07
61. TNA LC9/281, fols.104, 203, 211. Interestingly, the amount of new fabric purchased for the alterations was small. This suggests that Bealing may have used a stock supply of the velvet that had been bought for the original bed and had remained in store in the Great Wardrobe.
62. This bed was in fact one of two beds at Hampton Court that Anne chose to have refurbished. The other was a bed of green velvet that was almost completely remade for her apartments at Windsor. Remarkably, recent research by Lucy Wood has shown that the multicoloured bed and its furnishings survive today at Warwick Castle and at the Victoria & Albert Museum, having been gifted to the Earl of Warwick by George III. All the pieces reflect later restorations including the addition of new covers that entirely obscures the original velvet. see Lucy Wood, "A Royal Relic: The State Bedroom Suite at Warwick Castle," *Furniture History* 67 (2012): 45–103. I would like to thank Lucy Wood for generously allowing me to cite her research prior to publication.
63. TNA LC9/46, 3 October and 23 November.
64. TNA LC5/109, fol.279. This may have been one of the two sets of silver furniture that were boiled and burnished in 1696 for William III's use at Kensington that are mentioned earlier in this essay.
65. TNA LC5/109, fol.279.
66. Jane Roberts, ed., *Royal Treasures, A Golden Jubilee Celebration* (London: Royal Academy, 2002), 151.
67. TNA LC5/44, fol.242.
68. Adam Bowett, *English Furniture*, 149.
69. This store was known as the "standing wardrobe."
70. TNA LC5/151, fols.277–78.
71. TNA LC5/151, fols.279.
72. The Marriott family who held the office of Wardrobe Keeper at Hampton Court from 1689–1710 were of gentry status. It therefore seems unlikely that they themselves would have used the furnishings mentioned, given that they were in such poor condition. They may however have been useful for their own servants or those who were employed as domestics at Hampton Court.
73. The Lord Chamberlain had rights to claim furnishings following the death of a monarch, although the death bed itself and its matching furniture was the perquisite of the Groom of the Stole. Following the death of William III at Kensington in March 1702, his Groom of the Stole, the Earl of Romney, was given "ye Crimson Damask Bed with Gold lace [braid] which stands in ye little Bedchamber at Kensington where ye King dy'd, with ye Bedding, Hangings, Chairs, Stools, Window Curtains Portier Curtains & Clock all ye furniture belonging to that Room." See TNA LC5/153, fol.261. For the gift of Queen Anne's death bed and furniture see TNA LC5/156, fol.37. However, this was bought back by the crown. In February 1715 a warrant for £3,000

was issued for the Duchess of Somerset, "for goods of the late Queen claimed by the said Duchess as Groom of the Stole as by the sign manual of Dec. 24 last." see William A. Shaw, ed., *Calendar of Treasury Books*, Vol. 29, Part 2 (London, 1957), 237, 375, 671. This bed and furniture that was later given to the Earl of Warwick, see note 62. For a full discussion of perquisites at the 17th and 18th century English court see Olivia Fryman, "Rich Pickings: The Royal Bed as a Perquisite, 1660–1760", *Furniture History* 68 (2014, forthcoming).

74. Christopher Rowell, "the King's bed and its Furniture at Knole," *Apollo* 160, no. 513 (2004): 58–65; Margaret Jourdain, *Stuart Furniture at Knole* (London: Country Life, 1952). Elizabeth Jamieson and Peter Kidd, "Report on the James II bed," unpublished document, The National Trust, July 2009. I would like to thank Elizabeth and Peter for allowing me to read and cite their report. In addition to the Knole beds, there is an important royal bed at Chatsworth. This belonged to George II and was acquired by the 4th Duke of Devonshire, who served as Lord Chamberlain from 1757 to 1762. See Annabel Westman, "A Royal Bed at Chatsworth, The Puzzle of the 4th Duke's Perquisite," *Apollo* 75 (2008): 68–75.
75. Christopher Rowell, "the King's bed and its Furniture at Knole," 65.
76. TNA LC5/108, fol.254.
77. Lunsingh Scheurleer, "Documents on the Furnishing of Kensington House," 16.

7 Invisible Mending?

Ceramic Repair in Eighteenth-Century England

Sara Pennell

"He that teacheth a fool is like one that glueth potsherds together."

(Sirach, 22:7)[1]

In the 27 January 1776 probate inventory of Samuel and Mary Smith of Bristol, the following list of china was appended to the details of chattels in their "best room," the "fore parlour" of their property:

One burnt China Bowl cracked 9s

One small [China Bowl] 3s one Enamelled China Bowl 3/-

Three enamelled Dishes 14s

Two fruit Dishes 6/- six enamelled Plates one X 10/-

One blue and white Turene 10/6

Three blue & white Dishes X 6/-

Ten blue and white Plates six of them damaged 8s

Twelve blue & white Soup Plates 18s

Twelve common Plates five broke ditto 12s

Three odd blue and white plates 12s

Six butter plates X five ditto sound 2s 6d

Thirteen Worcester blue & white Plates 4s

One blue & white Bowl one cracked Bowl 5/-

Six different basons some X 5/-

Seven small Basons some X 2s 6d

One burnt China bason one half Pint ditto

Six cups six saucers 6s

One Pint one half pint Basons

Seven Cups five Saucers damaged 3s

One blue and white Bason one sugar dish

Six cups and six saucers 5s 6d

Six chocolate cups six saucers X 3s/9

Five cups five saucers 5/9

Two cups two saucers 1/ four saucers one cup 1s/6

Three Cups five Saucers damaged 1s/6

Two foreign China tea Potts 1/- three English Tea Potts 3/-

Three coffee Cups one Spoon Boat two stands 1s

Eleven coffee Cups 2s

Fourteen different kinds of Basons 7s

Three sauce boats 2 ditto 2s 6d

Six different Kinds of Drinking cups 4/6d

Five odd Pieces of China 1s 6d[2]

This listing of the couple's display china (other ceramics, more mundane blue-and-white delftware and stonewares, including yet more broken items, are listed in the kitchen), demonstrates that, across a lifetime of ownership, things do often fall apart. The descriptors used—"cracked" bowls, "damaged," and even "broken" plates—suggest a fine attention to the degrees of damage the goods have sustained. The appraiser also uses an "X," perhaps as shorthand to indicate those items which were beyond use (notably used within a set or group of goods). The listing gives a very good glimpse into a mid-Georgian, middling-sort English china closet: it is definitely not the stuff of future museum displays, but rather the stuff of lived materiality.[3]

In this chapter, the choices and techniques for material curation will be explored for ceramics in circulation in eighteenth-century England, in particular porcelains and porcelain substitutes, in order to understand better the ways in which the difficulties of owning and keeping ceramic goods were negotiated. Ceramic repair was certainly not new in the eighteenth century; nor were all the techniques deployed for mending likewise novel. Yet new techniques, and indeed new trades focused on ceramic repair, came into being in eighteenth-century England, at the very time that ownership of decorative yet functional ceramics was widening, across the socio-economic spectrum.[4]

Elsewhere I have argued that anxieties about the fragility of decorative ceramics, and consequent attention to the mending of "china" (both porcelains and finer earthenware), became more visible from the late seventeenth century in England. As more people owned such goods, or encountered them during their work as domestic servants, so recipes for mending ceramics began to appear in printed and manuscript recipe books used in domestic surroundings. At the same time and into the eighteenth century, discourses about the multiple values of ceramics both sound and broken, and about the possible afterlife of broken ceramics, so as to avoid unnecessary waste, speak of a society increasingly concerned with the consequences of material superfluity.[5] This chapter builds on that account, by looking more closely at the materials and methods adopted and developed for mending ceramics in the period. Was the gluing of potsherds a pointless (and indeed foolish) task, as the Apocrypha intoned? Or was it in fact an arena for exploring mankind's potential for mastering new materials, and an opportunity for new occupations to develop?

To mend china does seem a pointless business in the twenty-first century. If a plate chips, we can buy a matching one to "re-complete" our sets. Actually, the process of replacing broken objects in modern society is less straightforward than one might expect: the rapid turnover of goods whether through technological or aesthetic change, and the disappearance of the very companies that might have made one's good in the first place, may make replacement difficult.[6] But mending isn't just about avoiding expenditure on the new: what about the teapot lid (which breaks but doesn't mean the teapot cannot be used), the much-loved teacup, the irreplaceable Chinese garniture knocked off a windowsill at a major museum by a freak accident?[7] We mend because we wish to retain the object in question, for some end. That end may be economic, or because the object itself is scarce and difficult to replace. It may also be because the object, once mended, still has a function that mending will not impair; in turn, that purpose may be practical, decorative, or a combination of the two. We might also mend out of curiosity and for the challenge: does this glue do what it says it does; and can we make whole again this infinitely shattered vessel?

Given these various motivations, it follows that the form of mending used might be influenced by the reasons for mending. Yet the processes of engaging with what Susan Strasser has called the "stewardship of objects" in domestic life has not attracted many historians, beyond those (like Strasser herself) concerned with housework as a historical activity, or who are involved in technical conservation of such objects in the present.[8] In particular, practices of material/object use and conservation during the long eighteenth century—a period now so seamlessly identified with the so-called "consumer revolution" in England and elsewhere in continental Europe and America—have been until recently overshadowed by a preoccupation with identifying novelty and innovation in materials, object production, retailing and consumer taste.[9] Yet, until the last quarter of the eighteenth century England was still not industrialised to such a degree as to be able to sustain truly mass production of all such new goods, with a very few exceptions that by no stretch of the imagination fall into the category of "luxury" objects (pins and tobacco pipes, for example).[10] Wasting materials and goods was difficult to conceive of, let alone countenance, and strategies of reuse, refashioning, and recycling were commonplace in households across the social scale, and across Europe.[11]

PURSUING DURABILITY: DEVELOPING NEW CERAMIC BODIES IN THE EIGHTEENTH CENTURY

Understanding the appeal to the Georgian consumer of imported Far Eastern porcelains, one of the luxury goods frequently identified at the vanguard of changing consumption practices in England, has preoccupied many a scholar.[12] The story of the European race for a substitute for imported Asian porcelains in the late seventeenth and early eighteenth centuries is well known, stressing the proto-scientific and geopolitical agendas at stake.[13] The search to provide European "white gold" was of course economically motivated too, given the widespread alarm at the seemingly vast sums of money flooding towards the Far East, and, by the 1730s, towards the German manufactories, in exchange for such "gaudy furniture."[14]

Yet this does not wholly explain why Far Eastern porcelains were considered without equal. Their functional qualities were highly regarded by contemporaries, even if historians tend to sideline such concerns.[15] Imported porcelains were more resistant to thermal shock, as well as being less subject to surface losses than British or continental glazed earthenwares (the bond between body and glaze in porcelains being stronger). Porcelain's durability, combined with the exceptional translucence and lightness of the body material, was what made it seem alchemical in contemporaries' eyes.[16] We need only look at the ways in which English pioneers of porcelain substitutes in the middle of the eighteenth century claimed their wares were comparable to Far Eastern products to see the prominence of concerns with durability. As Hilary Young notes of Worcester soft-paste porcelain in the 1760s, "most of the newspaper articles that mention the qualities of Worcester porcelain stress the practical nature of its soap rock body and its ability to withstand thermal shock."[17]

Yet even once the English "white gold" had been discovered and developed in the 1760s and 1770s, concerns about the inherent fragility of such ceramics, against their cost, remained.[18] To prevent these "semi-durables," to use Carole Shammas's term, from becoming expensive potsherds, one could protect them by putting them on display in china closets. But much of what was produced from the Far East, and latterly in England was intended as "useful" ware. These were not the lions and dogs of the Hogarthian mantelpiece, but objects of utility *and* adornment.[19] As such, there had to be viable strategies for dealing with the moment when the servant might trip, and as one early eighteenth-century plate ventriloquized, "break me with a fall."[20]

MATERIALISING MENDING

At the time of their deaths, the Smiths had not seemingly mended or had repaired any of their china (although as we shall see, they lived in a city where such services were certainly on offer). Usually, it is almost impossible to recover expressed motivations for mending from the sources at our disposal. What we have is either the economic register of the process (as payments out of accounts for mending, or more rarely, the repairers' records of dealing with repairs); or the material evidence of it. To make use of the economic data on repairing, long-run household accounts that detail payments for (and, better still, types of) repair require analysis, to explore differentiation in frequency of repair between categories of object, as well as shifts in the cost of repair. In the current absence of this sort of research,[21] it is nevertheless possible to look at the range of mending techniques on offer to householders in the eighteenth century in terms of their efficacy and aesthetic impact, and to look at surviving repairs, to speculate why such a repair was effected in the way that it was. I want now to turn to three key items in the panoply of eighteenth-century porcelains and fine earthenware—the teapot, the punchbowl, and the teacup and saucer—to consider what type of repairs could and were effected upon them; and for what possible reasons surviving examples were mended in the way that they were.

TEAPOTS

In pure design terms, ceramic teapots are surely destined to be semi-durable: not only are they intended to hold hot liquids, but they also have a variety of protuberances, including handle, spout, and lid knop, vulnerable to chipping and breaking off entirely. Yet the ceramic, and ideally, imported porcelain teapot, was a much-aspired to and desirable object for the genteel household by the early eighteenth century in London, and the 1740s in provincial centres.[22] Fortunately for the teapot owner, damage to its extremities (a broken handle, a chipped lid or spout) did not impair its main function of holding hot tea, so techniques focused on those broken elements alone could be deployed.

Searches of the Burney Newspaper collection, held at the British Library and now available digitally,[23] reveal that repairing of ceramic vessel rims, spouts, and handles was a distinctive trade by the 1720s, although advertisements for such services did not appear until the 1740s.[24] One of the earliest advertisements, in *The Penny London Post* for 27 February–1 March 1745, for the services of Richard Wright, of Moorfields, London, puts teapot mending at the head of his specific services, saying the craftsman:

> MENDS broken China, and makes the same durable, and capable of containing Liquids; and mathes [sic] pieces lost, in the most exact and

> nice Manner. He fixes Handles, and Spouts to Tea-Pots; rivets and Cramps all sorts of China. He has an Art, practised by no other Peson [sic], of fixing grates in Tea-pots, which prevents all Obstructions from the leaves in pouring. He also has a new and peculiar Method of Sewing and rimming China.[25]

Advertising in September 1743, Daniel Jones offered to fix "Silver Spouts to China Tea-Pots, at 2s. 6d. each; Brass wicker'd Handles for Tea-Pots at 1s. ea[ch]," as well as more general "rivets and Cramps [to] all sorts of China."[26]

By specifying both prices and materials for his work, Jones's advertisement provides an insight into the practicalities, aesthetics, and perhaps even the pedigree of teapot repair. In the fifteenth and sixteenth centuries, highly valued imported and continental ceramics were often enriched with gold and silver-gilt mounts, including rims, handles, and lids. This is conventionally read as a process of value-adding to already prized (if not actually costly) goods; but, in some cases, it was also a means to conceal and prevent further deterioration of cracks, chips, and flaws on the base object. Jones's silver spouts for teapots and Wright's "rimming" (that is refinishing a rim with a metal trim) are clearly direct descendants of such mounting techniques. The "brass wicker'd Handles" reveal another strategy: that of using more durable substitutes, fixed to the ceramic with rivets, to provide a long-lasting repair. Of course, brass was not the ideal material for mending a teapot handle, because of its conductivity, hence its wicker covering (and other repairers using wood, ivory, and bone). All these materials would take drilling (although at the risk of shattering the ceramic itself), so that they could be securely attached to the ceramic body. At 2s. for a new spout, Jones offered a service that just about put off buying a new teapot; in a 1706 inventory of the stock of a London china shop, the cheapest teapot is listed at 2s. 6d., the most expensive at 6s. 6d., although Wedgwood pots could go for as much as 18s.[27]

That such repairs were used is visually and materially evident. Several of William Hogarth's 1730s paintings include a blue-and-white teapot with a visibly darker, probably repaired handle and a replacement spout.[28] A 1740–1760 Staffordshire red stoneware teapot in the National Conservation Centre, Liverpool, has been repaired with a pewter spout and metal lid rimming, while in the Victoria and Albert Museum collection, an imported Yixing (c. 1700–1750) redware teapot has elaborate repairs including a silver-plated copper spout, a bone and metal-mounted handle, and a metal knop to the lid, itself attached to the handle with a chain (Figure 7.1).[29]

These survivals point to the fact that good quality mending did not devalue the objects in question, or render them so visually unacceptable, so that new purchase was preferable. Mending teapots in the eighteenth century was, it seems, not an act of economic necessity, but rather more tied up with enduring practices of adding value, preserving utility, and acknowledging the design flaws inherent in the object itself.[30]

Figure 7.1 V&A Museum, Yixing (China), brown stoneware teapot with metal mounts and bone handle, eighteenth century (museum no. FE3–2003). ©Victoria and Albert Museum, London.

PUNCHBOWLS

In the 1772 inventory of the Bristol mariner George Walker is listed a "beaufet" [buffet] full of china and glass. Most of Walker's household goods are described by his administratrix, his widow Mary, as old, "worm eaten," even "much abused." The china is no different, including "one cream jug (broke)" valued at 6d, one "odd [decanter] broke" (6s.), and one small punchbowl "mended" (1s.).[31] The punchbowl was a key artefact of Georgian sociability, particularly homosocial gatherings.[32] The combination of alcohol, toasting, and testosterone which often accompanied the use of punchbowls—Hogarth's *A Modern Midnight Conversation* (c. 1732) satirises just such a heady brew—did mean that they were often damaged. The cracked and unmended punchbowl sitting on the shelf in the Countess's squalid lodgings as she expires, in another Hogarth image, the last of the *Marriage A-La-Mode* series (1745), is of symbolic value in Hogarth's moral shorthand, a signifier that virtue cannot been repaired once squandered; in reality, however, the unsound bowl could well have been mended.

Surviving repairs to punchbowls show both the ingenuity of the repairer and the possible reasons that lay behind the choice of mending. Chips to rims may not have been repaired at all, since (unlike the chip in a teapot spout which would impair pouring), the punch ladle did the work of transferring punch from bowl to cup. More major losses from the rim could be repaired using a long-established patching technique, where material from another (presumably irrecoverable) ceramic piece was shaped to fit the void, and attached with either staples or glue to the larger body. Depending on the extent of the loss into the bowl, this mend could still mean the bowl was usable, especially when done, as Richard Wright advertised in 1745, "in the most exact and nice Manner."[33]

But catastrophic breakage or substantial cracks would surely only have been repaired if the punchbowl was seen to have a value and a life beyond holding punch. Before the middle of the eighteenth century, it was very difficult to effect a watertight (let alone a discreet) repair using mechanical or gluing techniques, so surviving bowls with clamped or riveted repairs were almost certainly intended for display purposes only. Returning to George Walker's cracked and mended punchbowl, and given his trade, it may have been one decorated with an appropriate maritime theme, marking the launch of a ship or the success of a naval victory that Walker himself had been involved in. For all its evident flaws, its signification to him and his wife afforded it a place in the Walker "beaufet."[34]

TEACUPS AND SAUCERS

Substantially damaged punchbowls could, through repair, become decorative items, while teapots might have their functional lives extended by mending using mechanical methods. Their companions on the mid-Georgian tea board, teacups and saucers, were more difficult to repair or salvage in these ways. As Jonathan Swift, in his 1745 mocking guide for the anti-servant, had it, china teacups were meant for handling—how else would one use one?—but "the thing is possible that it might break in your hand."[35]

This tension between fragility and utility was complicated further by the fact that teacups and saucers were increasingly purchased and owned in sets. By the mid-eighteenth century, the idea of the *en suite* ceramic set—the tea set, coffee and tea cups, dessert and dinner services—was firmly ensconced in the minds of potential purchasers by manufacturers and retailers alike; surviving billheads from this period show purchases of "tea sets," and of matching cups and saucers in sixes, eights, and even twelves.[36] Damage to such sets would undoubtedly diminish their value and their appearance; certainly, those who advertised their skills in mending china were keen to point out the value of their art in this respect. A. Crookshanks, advertising in the *Dublin Mercury* in 1769, suggested to potential clients that "the want of this art [china burning, of which more below] has rendered great quantities of valuable china useless, when broke belonging to sets and otherwise."[37]

The late eighteenth-century account book for the Yorkshire household of gentleman William Danby records on 6 May 1776 payment for "a china saucer mending 2d."[38] Tuppence is no great sum, especially in this well-appointed household, but it had to be weighed against the cost of whether the saucer would break again, once mended; and whether a new saucer could be bought to replace the broken one. Danby—or rather his steward, Anthony Cundall—clearly felt the need to have the china saucer mended, but the work the saucer had to do might have made some of the available repair options unfeasible. Riveting or cramping, although long-lasting, was probably unsuitable since these might interfere with the "sit" of the cup on the saucer; for teacups to be reused, they were simply impracticable. Yet gluing would also have been unsatisfactory and only a short-term solution, in the first half of the eighteenth century. For all the claims by artisans like Edmund Morris (whose trade card advertised that broken articles, once mended, would do "as much Service as when new" and last for thirty years), the fact that these repair media were based on water-soluble organic materials such as isinglass, lime, egg, and cheese made this unlikely.[39]

In the middle of the century however, there is a discernable shift in the terminology used by china menders to describe the techniques deployed for mending objects other than teapots and handled goods. In the 1740s, a new technique was advertised in the *Daily Advertiser*, by one Aaron Moore, "From the East Indies," who "MENDS China Bowls or Dishes, or any other sorts of China Ware, in a neat and sound Manner, and in a Method entirely new. He also mends Flint-Glass, so that it shall hold Liquors as well as if it had not been broke, at very reasonable Rates."[40] Although Moore's advertisements never stated his technique, it was almost certainly the process that became known as "china burning" or "enamelling," but which is today known as glass-bonding.[41] This involved applying a high-lead-content ground glass (frit) blended with animal-derived glue, in a paste to join the fractured pieces; the mend was then fused by kiln heating (hence "burning"). This technique produced a join, which, as Tomoko Suda's modern experiments have shown, was durable and reasonably imperceptible.[42] It was particularly suited to hard-paste porcelains (much of which was imported, Far Eastern wares), with overglaze or enamelled decoration, which were harder to drill for mechanical repairs; and which could withstand secondary firing. A fine surviving example of such a repair is to be seen on a c. 1760–1770 Jingdezhen slop bowl decorated (and perhaps also repaired) in the style of the workshop of the ceramic painter-enameller James Giles: the repair itself is concealed beneath the overpainted decoration on the inside of the bowl (Figure 7.2).

The secrecy surrounding Aaron Moore's declaration of "a Method entirely new" was not just the stuff of advertising puffery. Moore, about whom I have managed to discover very little,[43] does not sound "Indian," but later newspaper references to him, make much of his Far Eastern connections (possibly because this is where the technique may have originated). They also make much of his "art" in china mending, which Moore himself fought to protect and promote as his own monopoly. In an advertisement appearing just before his death in February 1756, Moore declared himself still to be in the "sole business" of china mending, railing against "the many

Figure 7.2 V&A Museum, Jingdezhen (China), slop bowl decorated and possibly repaired in the style of the workshop of the ceramic painter-enameller James Giles, c. 1760–1770 (museum no. C.13–2008). ©Victoria and Albert Museum, London.

Tricks imposed on the Public by Pretenders to the Art, which is known to no one in England but himself." His declaration that "Several Imposters and Pretenders to the said Method [. . .] having of late taken away divers Pieces of China, &c. and not returned the same, under the Assertion that they were the Servants, or had served their Time to the said Aaron Moore" suggests that the "secret" was of some value, as does his concluding warning: "Any Person for the future that shall take in my name or work in my Name, shall be prosecuted as the Law directs."[44] Further evidence that there was a tussle for the sole rights to Moore's "secret" is given in a series of advertisements placed by Samuel Vanhagen, appearing in the spring and early summer of 1765, following the death of John Downes, Moore's successor.[45] Vanhagen disappears from the advertising columns of the London press at the end of 1765, to be supplanted by one William Fleming. Fleming advertised his skills as a "China-Rivetter, at the China Jar" in Honey-Lane market, London from November 1765; but in April 1768, he announced he had

> found out that invaluable and long wanted art of mending China, without riveting, by burning it in, so that the pieces unite together, and certainly is as strong as whole China, and rings as well, almost

> imperceptible to the eye, and we make no doubt but this much wanted art, will be of infinite service to the public, as it can be done much cheaper than rivetting.[46]

Fleming's endorsement of china burning as providing durability and soundness (even restoring the much-vaunted "ring" that sound china gave when struck), as well as virtual invisibility and cheapness, has once again the hallmarks of advertising hyperbole. Yet the potential of glass-bonding was not lost on Josiah Wedgwood. His securing of David Rhodes, "master Enameller and China-piecer," as a tenant in his London warehouse-cum-studio in 1768, becomes more interesting in the light of what glass-bonding could effect. Suda notes Wedgwood's enthusiastic letter to Thomas Bentley describing Rhodes's skill in joining "old valuable pieces of China not with Rivits, but a white glass, & burns them till the glass vitrifys, & they are as sound as they ever were." However, the letter goes further than Suda's extract, with Wedgwood concluding, "The having such a man as this under the same roof with the Warehouse [. . .] is the most convenient thing imaginable, & *nobody but ourselves will know what he is doing*."[47] Evidently Wedgwood was very happy to enlist the services of an artisan who could, with such expertise, make the imperfect and less than saleable, perfect and perfectly saleable.[48]

CONCLUSION: INVISIBLE MENDING?

Wedgwood was clearly not concerned about the ethics of presale repairing: this was mending as commercial opportunism.[49] But not all glass-bonded mending was intended to be entirely invisible, and this leads us finally to a modern display of mended ceramics, viewable at the Bristol City Museum. Misleadingly labelled as a case telling the story of "Chinese Export Porcelain in Bristol," it in fact tells us much more about the relative visibility of mending in late eighteenth-century Bristol, and the sense of value invested in the art of mending itself.[50]

The case contains several examples of the work of two "china burners" (as glass-bonders were often called) working in Bristol in the last quarter of the eighteenth century: Edward Combes (fl. 1785–1820) and Philip Daniel (fl. 1793–1806).[51] Both men used glass-bonding technology in their repairs although Combes also clearly undertook riveting, as a surviving October 1797 bill shows.[52] But both men also left further marks on their mended pieces, by signing them on the base: thus, a c. 1780s Chinese export saucer is signed "Combes China Burner Queen Street Bristol 1790."[53] By marking up their repair work in this style, presumably with the approval of the items' owners, Combes and Daniel were advertising their skills as much as any newspaper advert could; and undermining the notion that all mending, historically, aspired to be invisible.[54]

The ethics of modern ceramic conservation—championing reversibility, noninvasive techniques, and transparency of process—have complicated the visibility of historic repairs, just as long-standing museological unease about displaying the cracked, flawed, and repaired made imperfection and approaches to it mostly invisible in public.[55] This unease has relaxed somewhat, with the work of the National Centre for Conservation and the small display of repaired ceramics within the award-winning Ceramics galleries at the V&A.[56] By displaying and discussing less than perfect ceramics, these institutions have taken a step along the path towards making visible what the National Centre for Conservation calls the "universal problem" of ceramic impermanence; and towards historicising that problem. Wedgwood might not have wished for his clientele (or us) to see the join, but in bringing such cultures of repair to public view, we are better able to encounter and understand how Georgian ceramic owners faced up to and dealt with their things falling apart, and to know more about those who tried to put them back together again.

NOTES

1. From the Apocrypha cited in Stephen Koob, "Obsolete Fill Materials Found on Ceramics," *Journal of the American Institute for Conservation* 37, no. 1 (1998): 49.
2. Inventory and administrative papers for Samuel and Mary Smith, 27 January 1776, in *Bristol Probate Inventories, part III: 1690–1804*, ed. Edwin and Stella George, with the assistance of Peter Fleming, Bristol Record Society vol. 60 (Bristol: Bristol Record Society, 2008), 227–28.
3. Frank Trentmann, "Materiality in the Future of History: Things, Practices and Politics," *Journal of British Studies* 48, 2 (2009): 283–307.
4. Koob, "Obsolete Fill Materials," 52, table 1; Sara Pennell, "For a Crack or Flaw Despis'd: Thinking About Ceramic Durability and the 'Everyday' in Late Seventeenth and Early Eighteenth-Century England," in *Everyday Objects: Medieval and Early Modern Material Culture and Its Meanings*, ed. Tara Hamling and Catherine Richardson (Farnham: Ashgate, 2010), 27–40. See also Lorna Weatherill, *Consumer Behaviour and Material Culture in Britain, 1660–1760* (London: Routledge, 1988), 26 table 2.1, 49 table 3.3, 88 table 4.4, and 108 table 5.2.
5. Pennell, "For a Crack or Flaw"; Sophie Gee, *Making Waste: Leftovers and the Eighteenth-Century Imagination* (Princeton: Princeton University Press, 2010), 4–5.
6. At the time of writing, Habitat, a British furnishing store, has closed all but three of its UK stores; all my domestic china came from Habitat, so if the company was to stop altogether I would no longer be able to replace broken items.
7. In January 2006, three Qing Dynasty vases on open display at the Fitzwilliam Museum, Cambridge were broken by a visitor falling down stairs. See http://www.fitzmuseum.cam.ac.uk/gallery/chinesevases/faq.html (accessed 1 November 2012).
8. Susan Strasser, *Waste and Want: A Social History of Trash* (New York: Henry Holt and Co., 1999), 21–67 and her *Never Done: A History of American*

Housework (New York: Pantheon Books, 1982); Nigel Williams, "Ancient Methods of Repairing Pottery and Porcelain" in *British Museum Occasional Paper 65: Early Advances in Conservation*, ed. V. Daniels (London: British Museum, 1988), 147–50; Susan Buys and Victoria Oakley, *The Conservation and Restoration of Ceramics* (Oxford: Butterworth-Heinemann, 1993); Koob, "Obsolete Fill Materials."

9. John Styles and Amanda Vickery, "Introduction," in *Gender, Taste and Material Culture in Britain and North America 1700–1830* (London: Yale University Press, 2006), 6; Maxine Berg, *Luxury and Pleasure in Eighteenth-Century Britain* (Oxford: Oxford University Press, 2005), 85–278.
10. Joel Mokyr, *The Enlightened Economy: An Economic History of Britain 1700–1859* (London: Yale University Press, 2009); Sara Pennell, "Material Culture in Seventeenth Century 'Britain': The Matter of Domestic Consumption," in *The Oxford Handbook of the History of Consumption,* ed. Frank Trentmann (Oxford: Oxford University Press, 2012), 64–84; c.f. Carole Shammas, *The Pre-Industrial Consumer in England and America* (Oxford: Clarendon Press, 1990),181–86.
11. Strasser, *Waste and Want*, 12–15 and 22–23; and Jon Stobart and Ilja van Damme, "Introduction," in *Modernity and the Second-Hand Trade: European Consumption Cultures and Practices, 1700–1900* (London: Palgrave, 2010), 2–3.
12. For example, Sarah Richards, *Eighteenth-Century Ceramics: Products for a Civilised Age* (Manchester: Manchester University Press, 1999); Hilary Young, *English Porcelain 1745–1795: Its Makers, Design, Marketing & Consumption* (London: V&A Publications, 1999), 15–16; Robert Batchelor, "On the Movement of Porcelains: Rethinking the Birth of Consumer Society as Interactions of Exchange Networks, 1600–1750" in *Consuming Cultures, Global Perspectives: Historical Trajectories, Transnational Exchanges*, ed. John Brewer and Frank Trentmann (Oxford: Berg, 2006), 95–122; Berg, *Luxury and Pleasure*, 46–84.
13. Janet Gleeson, *The Arcanum: The Extraordinary True Story of the Invention of European Porcelain* (London: Bantam Press, 1998).
14. Gleeson, *The Arcanum*, 85–96; Richards, *Eighteenth-Century Ceramics*, 93; Young, citing Josiah Wedgwood in February 1769 in *English Porcelain*, 192; Berg, *Luxury and Pleasure*, 56–57.
15. E.g. Richards, *Eighteenth-Century Ceramics*, 94; Berg, *Luxury and Pleasure*, 131–33.
16. For contemporary views of the merits of Chinese porcelain see Mr Sanders's advertisement in the *Public Advertiser*, Monday 21 May 1753, issue 5791, 3.
17. Young, *English Porcelain*, 172; Pennell, "For a Crack or Flaw," 35.
18. Young, *English Porcelain*, 178.
19. Ibid., 180–81.
20. The plate in question is a survival from a 1712 Brislington (Bristol), set of six inscribed with verses describing the very fragility of china, now in the Ashmolean Museum: see Richards, *Eighteenth-Century Ceramics*, 108; and a full set with a slightly differing set of verses, illustrated in Louis Lipski and Michael Archer, *Dated English Delftware* (Woodbridge: Antique Collectors' Club, 1984), 71, nos 262A-E.
21. The author is currently undertaking such a study for the period c. 1600–1800.
22. Young, *English Porcelain*, 180–81; Weatherill, *Consumer Behaviour*, 32.
23. The online collection was searched using the following terms: "china burner/burning," "china enameller/enamelling," "china riveter/riveting," "china tipper/tipping," "china rimming/rimmer," "mends china," "china mending," "china mended," "broken china." This produced the materials cited

throughout this chapter, but it should be acknowledged that these searches resulted in a minimum return, and brief sampling of specific issues and runs of issues produced further data (as well as repeated advertisements).

24. There are references to china riveters, tippers, and rimmers amongst the declarations of bankrupts in the 1720s, for example Henry Ward, "China-Tipper," *London Gazette*, 1–5 November 1720, no. 5900, 2.
25. *Penny London Post: Or the Morning Advertiser*, 27 February–1 March 1745, issue 288, 4.
26. *Daily Advertiser*, Thursday 29 September 1743, no. 3962, 3.
27. London Guildhall Library, MS 3041/9 (v): miscellaneous papers of Thomas Bowrey, "Valuation of Goods at the China shop, Oct 20th 1706"; Berg, *Luxury and Pleasure*, 150.
28. Image II of *The Harlot's Progress* (1732 and subsequent versions), *The Strode Family* (Tate Britain: c. 1738), and *The Western Family* (National Gallery of Ireland: 1738). Lars Tharp, *Hogarth's China: Hogarth's Paintings and Eighteenth-Century Ceramics* (London: Merrell Holberton, 1997), 32 and 37.
29. National Conservation Centre, Liverpool, accession number M1036: http://www.liverpoolmuseums.org.uk/conservation/objects/gallery/Ceramicsandglass/stoneware_teapot.aspx (accessed 1 November 2012)
30. In a recent (2011) episode of the BBC television show *Antiques Roadshow* a c. 1748–1749 Limehouse pottery teapot with a very visible thermal shock crack was discussed and its value (about £20,000) based in part on the fact that it is one of the very few to survive the inherent weakness of the body material: http://www.bbc.co.uk/programmes/b015sgjw (accessed 6 January 2012).
31. Inventory and administrative papers for George Walker, taken 29 May 1772, in George and George, ed., *Bristol Probate Inventories*, 195.
32. Karen Harvey, "Barbarity in a Teacup? Punch, Domesticity and Gender in the Eighteenth Century," *Journal of Design History* 21, no. 3 (2008): 205–21.
33. See for example, National Conservation Centre, accession number 54.171.617: http://www.liverpoolmuseums.org.uk/conservation/objects/gallery/Ceramicsandglass/patch_repaired_bowl.aspx (accessed 1 November 2012); *Penny London Post: Or the Morning Advertiser*, 27 February–1 March 1745, issue 288, 4.
34. E.g. a Lowestoft porcelain punchbowl, dated to c. 1765–1770, decorated with maritime imagery, and the text "Success to the Frances" and "Captain Osborn from Colchester," V&A Museum, Museum No. C. 72–1938: http://collections.vam.ac.uk/item/O279025/punch-bowl/ (accessed 1 November 2012).
35. Jonathan Swift, *Directions to Servants* (1745) (London: Hesperus Press, 2003), 58.
36. See for example the billhead for a "a teaset of Nankeen China" (£4 4s.) and "six large cups and sau[cers]" (6s.) sold to a Mrs Dennis, by Todd and Lambden, china dealers, August 1767: British Museum, Prints & Drawings, Heal Trade Cards 37.50. See also Mimi Hellman, "The Joy of Sets: The Uses of Seriality in the French Interior," in *Furnishing the Eighteenth Century: What Furniture Can Tell Us About the European and American Past,* ed. Dena Goodman and Kathryn Norberg (London: Routledge, 2007), 129–54.
37. *Dublin Mercury*, 16–18 February 1769, issue 362, 2.
38. Yale University, Beinecke Rare Book and Manuscript Library, James Marshall and Marie-Louise Osborn Collection, Osborn MS c537, Anthony Cundall housekeeping book.
39. Pennell, "For a Crack or Flaw," 36–37; Koob, "Obsolete Fill Materials," esp. 53, 58. For Morris' tradecard (British Museum, Prints & Drawings,

Heal 37, 37), see http://www.britishmuseum.org/research/collection_online/collection_object_details/collection_image_gallery.aspx?assetId=52127&objectId=1527037&partId=1 (accessed 24 February 2014).
40. *Daily Advertiser*, Wednesday 2 November 1743, issue 3991, 2.
41. Koob suggests this technique was in existence from at least the sixteenth century but provides no support for his claim: "Obsolete Fill Materials," 59.
42. Tomoko Suda, "Eighteenth-Century Glass Bonding Repairs to Porcelain," *Transactions of the English Ceramic Circle* 19, no. 3 (2007): 424–27.
43. An Aaron Moore, pawnbroker was declared bankrupt the *Daily Courant*, Saturday 20 November 1725, issue 7519, 2.
44. *Gazetteer and London Daily Advertiser*, Wednesday 7 January 1756, 3; c.f. Koob, "Obsolete Fill Materials," 49.
45. See for example, *Gazetteer and New Daily Advertiser*, Saturday 13 April 1765, issue 11258, 3; repeated in the same paper on 30 April 1765, issue 11272; 30 May 1765, issue 11298; 22 June 1765, issue 11319; 6 July 1765, issue 11330.
46. *Gazetteer and New Daily Advertiser*, Tuesday 12 November 1765, issue 11441, 1; Ibid., Thursday 28 April 1768, issue 12216, 2.
47. My emphasis: Josiah Wedgwood to Thomas Bentley, from Charles Street, London, 24 March 1768: printed in Katherine Euphemia, Lady Farrar (ed.), *Letters of Josiah Wedgwood*, 3 vols (1903–06) (Manchester: E.J. Morten Ltd & Wedgwood Museum, 1973), vol. I, 210–11; cf. Suda, "Eighteenth-Century Glass-Bonding Repairs," 419.
48. See also Wedgwood to Thomas Bentley, from Burslem, dated 23 March 1769; and idem to Bentley, from Etruria, 12 May 1770: both in Farrar (ed.), *Letters*, I, 253–54 and 345.
49. One aspect of Wedgwood's commercial genius not mentioned by Neil McKendrick, in his "Josiah Wedgwood and the Commercialisation of the Potteries," in *The Birth of a Consumer Society: The Commercialisation of Eighteenth-Century England*, Neil McKendrick, John Brewer, and J.H. Plumb (London: Europa Publications Limited, 1982), 100–45.
50. On the second floor of the museum in April 2011.
51. Further details of both men can be found at Rod Dowling, "Early China and Glass Repairers," at http://www.kalendar.demon.co.uk/repairers.htm (accessed 1 November 2012).
52. Gloucestershire Archives, Blaythwayt Papers, D1799/A390, advertisement/billhead for Edward Combes, with handwritten bill on reverse: cited by Dowling, "Early China and Glass Repairers."
53. Bristol City Museum, item no. N8222. See Dowling, "Early China and Glass Repairers" for examples of such signatures on items in private hands.
54. Such inscriptions may also have been intended to make clear to potential buyers of such pieces on the second-hand market that they had been repaired.
55. Koob, "Obsolete Fill Materials," 51; See for example the V&A Chinese export dish, c. 1735–45 recorded as *having had* a riveted repair, but the "rivets [were] removed [. . .] during conservation," see Museum no. 824–1882: http://collections.vam.ac.uk/item/O183706/dish/ (accessed 1 November 2012).
56. The National Centre for Conservation closed permanently to the public in December 2010, but its work can still be seen online at: http://www.liverpoolmuseums.org.uk/conservation/departments/ceramics/index.aspx (accessed 1 November 2012).

8 Sentimental Economics

Recycling Textiles in Eighteenth-Century Britain

Ariane Fennetaux

The Adventures of a Quire of Paper, one of the many eighteenth-century narratives in which an inanimate object tells its picaresque adventures, allows the reader to view the various lifecycles of its narrator, from the moment the threshers reaped the field in which "it" was growing, to its current state as printed material. First woven into a piece of fine cambrick, it is turned into a handkerchief, given, stolen, turned into a duster, diapers, and ends up in rags to be recycled into paper, which is itself put to many uses and undergoes more transformations.[1] The story unwittingly offers a narrative of the various types of textile recycling that routinely took place in the eighteenth century. That we need to read fiction to have our attention drawn to the long social and economic life of textiles is characteristic of the historiography on the period, which has tended to focus on novelty, consumption, industrialisation, and fashion. Although widespread at the time, practices of reuse, salvage, economy, or transformation have on the whole been neglected by dress and social historians alike.[2] Looking at the different forms of textile recycling that characterised the period—from pawning to rag collecting, and from refashioning to patchwork—this chapter aims at showing recycling to be central to understanding not only eighteenth-century dress and textiles but also more widely the relationship to the material world of the period, structured as it was by an economic system which rested as much on reuse and resale as it did on novelty and invention.

The prime economic function of recycling in the eighteenth century will be our first subject of analysis, paying particular attention to the second-hand market and the development of the paper industry. Recycling in this instance will be shown to be both at the centre of an age-old economy of survival and of the burgeoning industrialisation of the country.

Before they were sold off or fell into the ragman's bag to be made into paper in one of England's industrial papermills though, clothes were painstakingly cared for, darned, altered, or refashioned; either privately by women working in the confines of their homes or by professional dressmakers and tailors. Studying the industrious stewardship of textile possessions will enable us to redress the traditional perspective according to which the century witnessed the triumph of avid consumption and novelty.

Last, the chapter will look at the sentimental associations of textile reuse as evidenced by such practices of inheritance or patchwork which will be shown to bring into question the status of some of the very categories traditionally used to understand the period and its relationship to the material world.

THE ECONOMICS OF TEXTILE RECYCLING

As Beverly Lemire has shown, the trade in second-hand clothing was a crucial part of the burgeoning consumer culture of the eighteenth century.[3] The trade was widespread but particularly developed in urban centres with an overwhelming dominance of London over the rest of the country.[4] In the capital, the business of dealing in second-hand clothing was carried out by various professionals: street hawkers who peddled their ware to passers-by, tailors, linen drapers, and haberdashers who offered to buy off old clothes at the same time as they also made and sold new ones, whereas specialised shopkeepers only traded in old clothes. The specialists in second-hand clothing concentrated in Monmouth Street, Houndsditch, Rosemary Lane, and Rag Fair, which became real hubs of the recirculation of clothes. The insurance records of some of these salesmen give an insight into both the value of recycled clothing and the economic importance of the trade at the time. In 1786, Thomas and Edward Smith, in Houndsditch, thus appraised the value of their stock in used clothing at a staggering £2,820.[5]

Second-hand clothes salesmen fulfilled a double role. Their shops were places where old cast-offs could be sold and exchanged for money—performing thus a vital function in middle-class and lower-middle-class budget strategies by providing individuals with a place to trade possessions for cash. In this respect, second-hand clothes dealers had a rather similar economic function to pawnbrokers, from whom they sometimes became hard to tell apart. The activity of the latter often concentrated on textile goods. The ledger book of York pawnbroker George Fettes, which has survived for the years 1777–1778, shows that about 75 percent of the articles pledged in his shop were articles of clothing.[6] Pawning, like second-hand sale, was central to the economy and the survival strategies of many, offering people a quick means to get ready money when strapped for cash. They were even sometimes used as a deposit bank of sorts that enabled people to cash in on the potential resale value of their goods while affording them security for the actual items, in an age when personal possessions were hard to secure. By lending money on pledged possessions, pawnbrokers were actors of the recirculation of clothing since the goods that remained unredeemed would be sold on, either directly on the premises or to specialist second-hand dealers.

On the receiving end of the recycling process, those who purchased second-hand clothing were given access to possessions they could otherwise not have afforded. At a time when ready-made clothing remained limited, second-hand clothing filled a gap in the market by supplying the lower classes with a source of inexpensive—if worn—clothes. In his 1797 survey of the poor in Britain, Frederick Eden remarked that for their dress, the labouring classes hardly ever bought anything but second-hand, especially in London where used garments were readily available for sale: "In the vicinity of the metropolis, working people seldom buy new clothes; they content themselves with a cast off coat, which may be usually purchased for about 5s. and second-hand waistcoats and breeches. Their wives seldom make up any article of dress, except making and mending cloaths for the children."[7] But the second-hand market was not limited to the metropolis, nor was it the preserve of the poor.

Country Parson James Woodforde, always aware of a good bargain, noted in his diary in 1799: "Miss Woodforde bought a very handsome Scarf-Shawl of Aldridge, late Miss Stone's as good as New—3.yards-long and a Yard wide which cost at first three Guineas & which Miss W. bought of Aldridge for 1. 11.6."[8] Aldridge, a travelling salesman, effected the local recycling of clothing by buying from and selling to several people he visited with his pack. The activities of some second-hand clothes dealers ensured the recycling of clothes on a nationwide, and even an international scale. An ad published by a London Salesman in an Oxford newspaper in 1770 shows there were also middlemen who collected second-hand clothing nationwide with distribution networks that also went beyond the capital or even the country:

> John Matthews, Salesman from London, buys ladies and Gentlemans cast off cloaths, either laced, embroidered, or brocaded, full trimmed, or not, of every colour and sort, will give the most money for any: as I deal for London, the country and abroad, nothing can be out of my way, according to the price and if any person has any thing to dispose of and will favour me with the sight of it, they may depend on having the full value of their goods.[9]

The second main economic circuit of used clothing was the trade in scraps and rags. The salvaging and the professional transformation of textile scraps and rags offered networks of recycling that were integral to the eighteenth-century economy and its nascent industry. We know that both precious and base metals were routinely recycled in the early modern period.[10] Some textiles made use of metal thread, which consisted of metallic wire twirled around a silk thread that was then embroidered onto, or woven into, certain fabrics. Metal thread was also made into what was called silver lace or fringe that was used for trimmings and buttons. These decorations, when old and tarnished, could be cut off and sold by the weight to lacemen, silversmiths, or goldsmiths to be melted down. On their tradecards, Pitter & Fox, gold and silver lacemen in Covent Garden, thus promised "the utmost value given for old gold and silver lace etc." while Edward Dobson, a jeweller and goldsmith, offered "most money for [. . .] gold lace and burnt silver."[11] The other type of textile scrap that was professionally recycled was linen rags, which were used by the paper industry.[12]

In *The London Tradesman* (1747), which is a description of the various trades young men and women could get into, R. Campbell writes that ragmen made a living out of "picking up and selling rags"—woollen rags were sold to make mops, while ragmen also "[bought] up linen rags for the paper mills"—and according to Campbell made "a genteel living" out of it.[13] This was not new. Coming home late at night in March 1661 Samuel Pepys met a boy "picking up of rags [. . .] and had great discourse with him how he could get sometimes three or four bushels of rags in a day, and gat [sic] 3d a bushel for them."[14] The development of print culture, literacy but also consumption—since goods were wrapped in paper—in the course of the century meant that there was an increasing demand for rags and that they were an increasingly valued material. It is estimated that in the last two decades of the century, the price of rags went from 35s. per hundredweight in 1780 to 58s. in 1804.[15] Rag merchants sometimes doubled as papermakers or stationers and carried out large business. The high price of rags also meant that the bales of rags they stored in their warehouses were prized targets for thieves. In 1785, the papermakers Fourdrinier, Bloxam, and Walker had thus 200 pounds of rags valued at 30s. stolen from their warehouse in London.[16] The company, which was to become prominent in the British paper industry, is representative of the scale of the industry and the degree to which rags were part of an integrated industrial system itself linked to that of the textile industry, whose development provided increasing sources for rags.[17] From the rag picker, to the rag merchant, on to the papermaker/stationer, the recycling of textile was part and parcel of the development of Britain's industry.

The trade in second-hand clothing and rag collecting operated differently but both were central to the economic developments witnessed by the country in the eighteenth century. One was key to the emergence of a wider consumer public who contracted purchasing habits seen as formative in the advent of mass consumption.[18] The other depended on an integrated network of production that was linked to the burgeoning industrialisation of the country. The prevalence of these activities and their social, cultural, and economic import in the eighteenth-century landscape show recycling to be in no way marginal or peripheral but actually central to the century and its economy. Similarly central, but maybe less visible because of being carried out mostly at home by industrious women rather than in paper mills by budding industrialists, were a series of other recycling practices aiming at prolonging the useful lives of textiles, to which we will now turn.

THE STEWARDSHIP OF TEXTILE GOODS

Fabrics being more expensive than the labour that went into making garments, every care was taken to make textiles go as far as possible. Different techniques were used to that effect. In the most extreme cases, this could involve a complete overhaul of the piece, which was unpicked and redone into either a different version of the same garment or an altogether different one. This seems to have been a routine practice in institutions such as Saint Sepulchre's workhouse, whose clothing stock books show how garments for inmates were "made of old things."[19] On 21 October 1743 for instance, an entry for two gowns for girls "made of old linnen" was recorded,[20] whilst five undercoats were recorded as having been "made of old curtains" on 17 September 1745, on 4 October 1739, six infants' caps and shirts were made "of womens' shirts."[21] Sometimes several old garments were made into one good one as in March 1744 for instance when a woman's gown was "made of 2 old gowns."[22]

These transformations were not restricted to the poor and needy. Elite clothing was also frequently cut up and remade. Cleaning was an opportunity for repairs and alterations since garments often had to be taken to pieces when cleaned. In 1760 Martha Washington sent a dress to London for cleaning accompanied by a letter from her husband reading: "Mrs Washington sends home a green sack to get cleaned, or fresh dyed of the same colour; made up into a handsome sack again would be her choice but if the cloth wont afford that, then to be thrown into a genteel night Gown."[23] If fabrics were good, they would be transformed, refashioned into a new style. Parson Woodforde's niece, Nancy Woodforde, who was given several gowns which had belonged to her uncle's late aunt, Mrs Parr, had them refashioned to modern taste. In 1782, eleven years after the death of Aunt Parr, Parson Woodforde noted in his diary: "Gave Nancy this morning an old brown silk gown very good never the less, and was my late Aunt Parrs."[24] A month later, Nancy had it remade and new-trimmed: "Nancy had a brown silk gown trimmed with Furr brought home this evening [. . .] from her Mantua maker Miss Bell. It was good rich silk that I gave her which formerly belonged to my poor Aunt Parr, whose effects came to me."[25] The same happened on 11 December 1790, when he wrote "gave this morning a green silk damask gown that was formerly my poor aunt Parrs."[26] And only a fortnight later, on Christmas Day, he noted: "Nancy having herself new made the later green silk gown I gave her, wore it this day for the 1st time."[27] This happened close to twenty years after the death of the said Aunt Parr, which shows the length of time willed clothing could be stocked as an asset to be realised by refashioning when opportunity arose. In museum collections these alterations result in gowns in late eighteenth-century styles using fabric that date from the early eighteenth century, like a British blue damask gown in the Colonial Williamsburg whose style is typical of the 1790s fashions while the exotic, large-patterned, blue damask fabric is characteristic of the 1740s (Figure 8.1).

Figure 8.1 Colonial Williamsburg, blue damask gown, style 1780–1795, textile 1740–1750. Acc. No 1960–713. © The Colonial Williamsburg Foundation.

Some alterations were particularly complex. The makeup of a man's waistcoat in the same collection shows how the piece has been cut up and cleverly remounted to adapt to the changing styles of late eighteenth-century fashion. At a time when the long flared skirts and cut-away fronts of the waistcoat had fallen out of favour, the waistcoat was remade into the new slimmer, shorter shape of the 1800. The two front hems were turned inside out and sewn to the neckline to form the stand-up collar while the old pocket flaps were turned into the new-style pocket welts (Figure 8.2).[28]

Such a complex alteration was probably made professionally by a tailor. Dressmakers and tailors often combined services of making new garments and altering old ones. A 1772 bill kept in the Gallery of English Costume shows Robert Johnson charging a client for various services including "to a pair of scarlet foreparts / Lacing them with an old Gold lace, small trimmings & materials" or "to cleaning a stone colour suit and making new cuffs and collars."[29] Personal accounts testify to the frequency of such interventions. Martha Dodson's account book in the Museum of London has several entries: "March 24 1746/7—for mending a muslin apron, 0 1 0,"

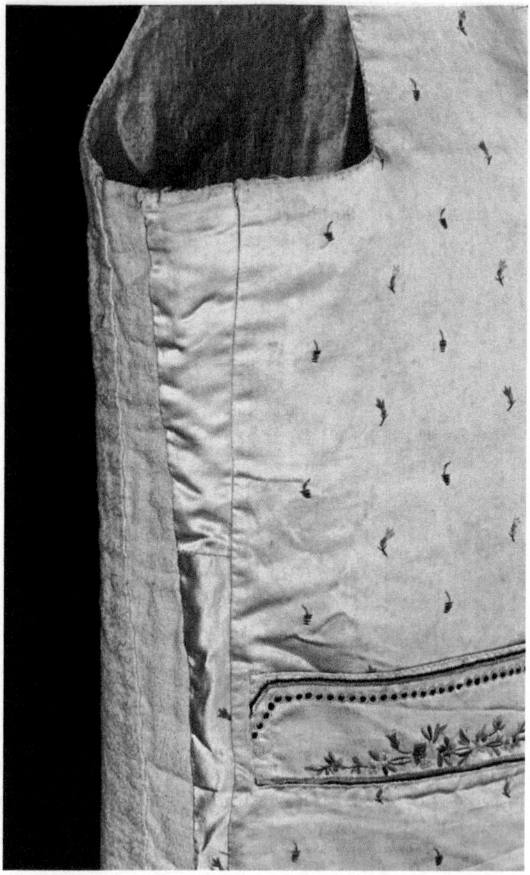

Figure 8.2 Colonial Williamsburg, man's white silk satin waistcoat, remodelled c. 1800, detail. Acc. No. 1971–1562. © The Colonial Williamsburg Foundation.

and a few days later on 10 April 1747, "Paid mending lace mob 0 1 6." She also has entries for alterations, such as on 30 October 1746: "paid Hannah Perry for altering Gown and petticoat 0 1 6," and on 24 February 1746: "Paid altering and binding white stomacher 0 1 0."[30] One distinctive eighteenth-century technique used to lengthen the lifecycle of garments included what was termed "turning." This consisted in disassembling a garment and turning the fabric inside out so that the faded or worn side would be against the lining and the unworn side would now be facing outside. This excluded some nonreversible fabrics such as brocaded damasks or velvets but was particularly used for wool. Henry Mayhew described the practice as characteristic of the eighteenth century in his 1851 survey of the London poor: "in the last century [. . .] when woollen cloth was much dearer, much more substantial, and therefore much more durable, it was common for economists to have a good coat 'turned.' It was taken to pieces by the tailor and remade, the inner part becoming the outer [. . .] this way of dealing with the second hand garment is not so general now."[31] The practice is evidenced by several eighteenth-century written and material sources. Among other similar notations along the years, the clothing account books of Elizabeth Jervis of Staffordshire have an entry in 1753 that reads: "turning Scarlet gown and Sleeve linings 4s. 6d." and in 1757 she noted: "turning my Lutestring negligee by Vernon 5s."[32]

Outside of these professionally sourced recycling services, the home was a central recycling unit.[33] Repairs and small alterations were daily carried out at home to lengthen the life of old clothing. Mending, patching, or darning were part of the crucial needlework skills that constituted good housewifery. Women running households and their servants were expected to be able not only to make but also to mend and keep in good repair household and body linen such as pillowcases, sheets, shirts, and shifts. Priscilla Wakefield in her *Reflections on the Present Condition of the Female Sex* (1798) insisted it be part of female education: "In addition to reading, they ought to be well instructed in plain work, knitting, marking, cutting out and mending linen."[34] Indeed these were tasks which occupied even women from the gentry. Lancashire-based Elizabeth Shackleton noted in her diary in 1777, "busy mending old shifts, shirts and sheets," and other mentions are made throughout her diary of mending gowns under the armholes, putting new binding to aprons or new sleeves to old shifts.[35] The needle-busy Gertrude Savile, a spinster from the Nottinghamshire gentry, regularly noted in her diary the mending she did as part of the rest of her needlework. On 14 August 1728 she wrote: "Mend lace a little" and in September of the same year: "Mended a hoop petticoat all day."[36] Women were not only expected to take care of their own clothes but of the linen and textile accessories of the whole household. Parson Woodforde thus noted on 19 September 1789, "gave Nancy this morning for well mending a pair of velveret breeches for me 0 1 0."[37] The occasional traces of mending, patching, and darning on museum objects show the time, care, and skill invested in repairs and the various techniques used to do so (Figure 8.3).

These marks of wear, tear, and repair used to be seen as blights on objects, making them less desirable for collectors and museums. Museum practices have gradually changed and more emphasis is now put on the testimony such marks afford by giving us concrete access to the everyday practices of housekeeping.

Thrift was of the essence of good household management and being economical in all things was one of the paramount virtues of women running efficient houses. This included mending, patching, and darning but also salvaging off-cuts and scraps and laying them by for future use. Elizabeth Shackleton was thus critical of her son Tom's household when she realised he was unable to give her a piece of cloth for her to make a pincushion with. "He told me he had none. I said he sho'd keep bits. If they had not done

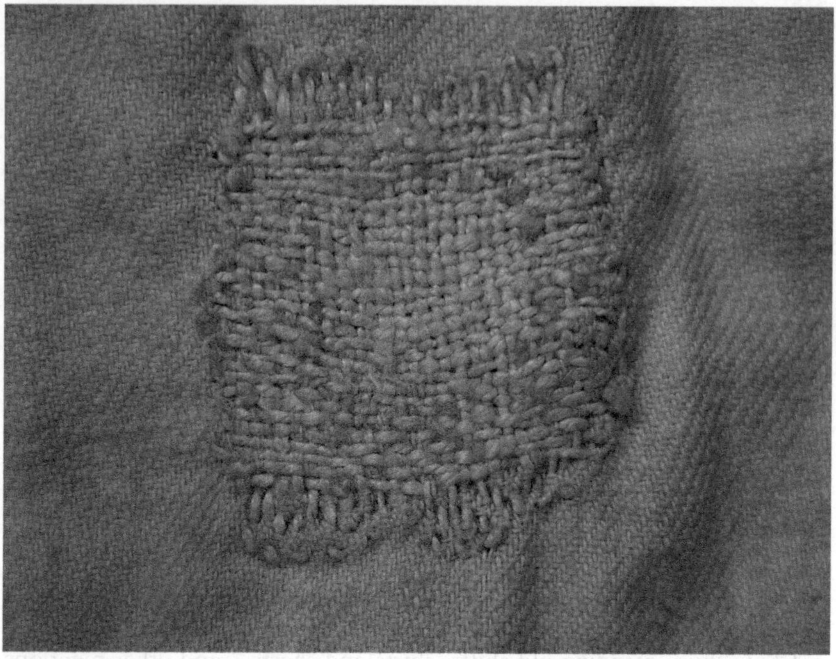

Figure 8.3 Museum of Scotland, pocket, detail of patching at the back. Acc. No. 1968.419. Reproduced with permission. © National Museums Scotland.

so at Newton, how co'd the old Lady have made my own dear nice little [grandson] a pair of shoes."[38] The same value bestowed onto laying bits aside is illustrated by a late eighteenth-century pedagogical children's book called *The Adventures of a Pincushion*. The story starts off by opposing two sisters, one thrifty, tidy, and obedient, the other improvident, slipshod, and wayward. Their opposed characterisation is neatly encapsulated by the way Martha makes a pincushion—which will be the narrator of the story—from "a square piece of pink satin" given by her mother, reusing the pins of an older, damaged pincushion which "she cut open on an old newspapers," whereas, her sister Charlotte "though her Mamma had given her as much silk as her sister had only cut it to waste" leaving "threads and slips littering the room."[39] The thrifty use of materials through the salvaging of off-cuts and remnants is here extolled as a model transmitted from mother to daughter, with the mother having several off-cuts at hand from which the girls can choose and the good daughter recycling what is left of the small piece of silk to make "a housewife for her doll."[40] The reuse of small pieces of dress fabrics for homemade accessories was not just the stuff of moralistic tales. Museum collections abound in pincushions, garters, housewives, or pockets that use recycled textiles.

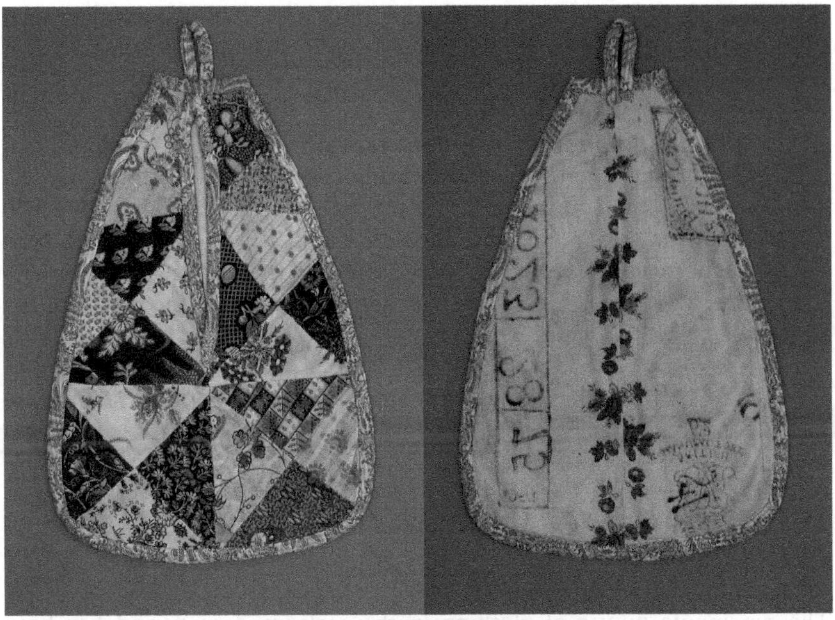

Figure 8.4 Museum of Scotland, patchwork pockets front and back, Acc. No. H. UF. 91. Reproduced with permission © National Museums Scotland.

An early nineteenth-century patchwork pocket in the Museum of Scotland is particularly interesting in this respect at it combines two types of recycling (Figure 8.4).

The back of the pocket has been made by using a piece of "waste fabric"—the selvage of a piece of Calico on which the customs mark has been stamped "British Calico" / "British Manufactory"—while the front of the pocket offers an example of decorative patchwork in which small scraps of differently patterned cottons are used to create colourful motifs. The maker of the pocket thus reclaimed from waste a piece of fabric that would otherwise be unusable, with the narrow band of the selvage being cut into two and assembled down the middle to make the back; while the front recycles twenty scraps of colourful dress fabric into a new object. Similarly inventive, a pocket in the Manchester Gallery of Costume is made of twenty-two pieces of printed and plain cottons dating from various periods in the eighteenth century: some fabrics are clearly late eighteenth-century cotton prints while the pocket also uses pieces of much older embroidery.[41] Decorative needlework was often kept across generations and sometimes rejuvenated by being inserted into new projects. In a letter to his brother-in-law dated 31 March 1656 Heneage Finch, 1st Earl of Nottingham, described his wife's endeavours decorating a bed, carpet, chairs, and stools in matching embroidered flower motifs. She was helped in her ambitious project by a man called John Best, probably a professional embroiderer, who suggested reusing some of her mother-in-law's old embroidery:

> [. . .] John [Best] takes those borders which my mother wrought, and cutts out every single flower and leafe, and when these are so voyded, He draws some Turning stalks for my wife to work, upon which he will so place the flowers and the leaves that it shall seem as if all had been wrought together, and be perfectly sutable to the pattern on the bed. So in time wee hope to erect an handsome furniture to the honor of my mother.[42]

The reuse of fabric thus did not only make economic good sense but also served practices of memory and love.

THE STEWARDSHIP OF MEMORY—THE ECONOMICS OF SENTIMENT

The mnemonic power of clothing in the early modern period has been explored by Peter Stallybrass'.[43] The recent work of John Styles on the fabric tokens left with babies who were abandoned to the care of the Foundling Hospital in London by mothers who had fallen on hard luck has shown that the power of fabric to transmit memory and feeling remained extremely strong in the eighteenth century.[44] Out of all the tokens left by mothers, swatches of textile were by far the most common and John Styles has shown how the choice in patterns and fabrics was endowed with strong sentimental meanings.[45] The piece left with foundling 16516 admitted in February 1767 combines several mnemonic strategies (Figure 8.5).[46]

The token is indeed half what looks like a patchwork needle case on which half a heart and initials have been embroidered in red silk. In the sentimental language conveyed by the tokens, leaving one part of an object with the baby while the mother kept the other half had wide currency, expressing the mother's hope to be reunited to her child.[47] In the case of foundling 16516, close analysis of the heart and initials shows they were embroidered on the piece as a whole which was then cut into two, the cut edge being then bordered in the same red thread to keep it from fraying. Further scrutiny reveals that despite what first appears, the token is not a needle case or a housewife, the back of the piece in thin blue-and-white silk being actually sewn to the front in several places across the width of the piece, which would have kept it from acting as an envelope, pocket, or sheath of any kind. It appears therefore that it was a piece of patchwork that was assembled purposefully by the mother from several scraps as the love token she wanted to leave with her child. We can only speculate as to the meanings embedded by the maker in the different fabrics and their assemblage but clearly this is an

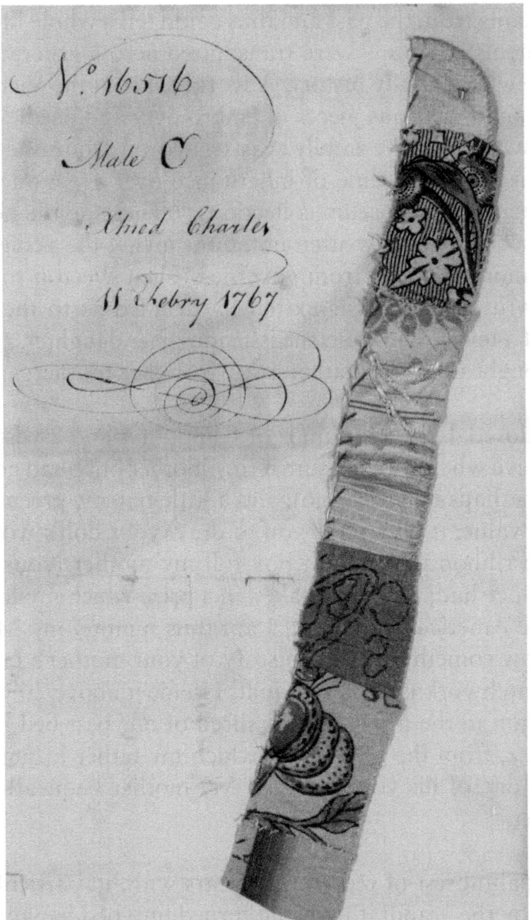

Figure 8.5 Foundling Hospital, admission records, detail of fabric token for Foundling 16516, London Metropolitan Archives. Reproduced with permission of the Thomas Coram Foundation for Children (Coram).

example of recycling in which thrift and good housewifery have little to do. In dire financial circumstances forcing her to abandon her child, the woman made up a memento out of shreds of silks and printed linen, which fulfilled a sentimental rather than an economic purpose.

As argued by Barbara Kirshenblatt-Gimblett, "The recycling of materials is a common method of embedding tangible fragments of the past in an object that reviews and recaptures the experiences associated with those fragments."[48] Quilting or patchwork was a way in which scraps could be recycled into a new object, assembled as they were in an artefact that pieced together remnants from the past and thus could tell a whole life-story. Sometimes textile items or scraps were transmitted across generations, carrying with them the whole family history. A workbasket in the Victoria & Albert Museum containing various pieces of embroidery and needlework made by the different women in the family was passed on from one generation to the next down the female line of inheritance over a period of two centuries before entering the museum collections.[49] These textile heirlooms were sometimes associated with written notations giving the pedigree of objects and their meaning. A letter from governess Ellen Weeton to her daughter Mary Stock written in 1824 is extremely detailed as to the contents and significance of a textile heirloom she is sending her daughter, aged nine, who was being brought up by her father away from her mother:

> I have inclosed 4 different kinds of Gimp, of 4 and 2 yds length as you may perceive when you measure it (my mother once had gowns trimmed with it—perhaps 60 years ago); and a little narrow green ribbon which is of little value; it may serve you to draw your doll's work bags. [. . .] The green ribbon is part of a box-full my mother (your grandmother Weeton) once had; they were taken in a prize which my father captured during the American war [. . .] I am thus minute, my Mary, that you might know something of the history of your mother's family [. . .] the piece of patchwork is of an old quilt, I made it above 20 years ago [. . .] the Hexagon in the middle was a shred of our best bed hangings, they were chintz, from the East Indies which my father brought home with him from one of his voyages [. . .] My mother bequeathed the bed to my brother.[50]

In this tale a palimpsest of recycling appears with, in particular, the chintz brought back by the grandfather being turned into bed hangings, the shreds of which were made into a quilt by the mother, from which a piece of patchwork has been cut out and is being willed to the grand-daughter. Not only do we see how objects could transmute along their lives but we also see how each cycle led the object to become replete with always more memories and thicker with meaning.

The numerous gifts of clothing in wills and the distribution of the linen and wearing apparel of the deceased to friends and family thus did not fulfil a purely economic function. They testify to the wide currency of the expressive value of textile. Private papers and the mere survival of some textile family heirlooms show how recipients treasured clothing items which had once belonged to people they loved.[51] The fabric recycled from the possessions of loved ones thus could take part in mnemonic practices that used the strong association of worn garments with bodily presence. The Manchester wigmaker Edmund Harrold recorded in his diary in 1712 after the death of his second wife Sarah: "I have given her workday cloths to Mother Broadman [his late wife's mother] and Betty Cook our servant [. . .] I am making me a black shute [suit] of her black mantue and petticoat I bought her on Edwards and if God gives me life and health I will wear them for her sake."[52] Less tragically because her son had not died, Elizabeth Shackleton similarly used the memorial power of recycled textiles on her son's birthday in 1778 to make up for his absence on the day. She wrote in her diary: "[I] put on in honour to this good day my quite new purple cotton night gown and a new light brown fine cloth pincushion [made of] a piece of coat belonging to my own Dear child, my own dear Tom, with a new blue string."[53] The quote exemplifies the power of recycled fabric to transmit memory. But it also shows how textile recycling blurred the distinction between animate and inanimate, between object and subject. The pincushion made from the son's coat is turned into a synecdoche for the absent son, and worn by his loving mother close to her side in a bid to avert physical distance and replace it by intimate proximity. Such recycled garments as Edmund Harrold's mourning suit made from his dead wife's gown or Elizabeth Shackleton's pincushion made from her son's coat—as well as many others whose stories have now been lost—materialised the bonds of love and care between individuals at the same time as they partook in processes that nurtured the self through ritual and imagination. [54] They make any strict frontier between object and subject almost impossible to tell.

To close this chapter, I would like to expand on the way textile recycling cuts across a series of categories and invites us to rethink some of the tools that are often used to view consumption and material culture in the eighteenth century. The idea of novelty and fashion as driving forces of the expanding eighteenth-century market is obviously called into question by practices of recycling. The recycling of clothing enabled by the thriving trade of pawnbrokers and second-hand dealers blurred clear distinctions between old and new. Not only did someone's cast-off become somebody else's new possession by going through their shops, but second-hand dealers also sold new objects alongside the second-hand ones that were their stock-in-trade. The reverse was equally true since many tradesmen dealing in new objects often offered to buy off old possessions or to exchange them. More often than not, in the reality of the eighteenth-century market, old and new were closely interconnected. Material objects themselves show the same blurring of old and new since old garments were routinely "new made," a practice which accounts for most museum artefacts today bearing signs of alterations and refashioning.

Such examples mitigate the vision of the eighteenth century as the period that witnessed the triumph of consumerism but also of the advent of anonymous or alienating commodities. Objects, textile and otherwise, were not all impersonal goods made in distant production centres by anonymous workers. If Adam Smith's description of a pin factory did reflect part of the economic reality of the eighteenth-century world of goods with its increasing industrialisation and the beginning of mass production, Smith's description tells only part of the story.[55] For a start, the pincushions that held the manufactured pins were sewn at home by women who were often recycling textiles they had been carefully salvaging over the years, relaying the stories that could be attached to them.

Another category which recycling leads us to interrogate is gender. Contemporary representations as well as historians have emphasised the role of women as avid consumers of fashion. But recycling, part of which was the result of the deft needlework skills of housewives, rather casts women as industrious producers who excelled at turning an adult woman's shirt into a child's linen shift or bringing a man's waistcoat up to fashion. Moreover, the material practices of recycling themselves did not always follow gender distinctions—a boy's coat could be turned into a woman's pincushion and women's gowns were often remade into men's garments. In 1661, Samuel Pepys had a waistcoat made from one of his wife's petticoats: "I went home and put on my gray clothe suit and faced white coate, made of one of my wife's pettycoates—the first time I have had it on."[56] An English brocaded nightgown and matching waistcoat in the Colonial Williamsburg collection were made from a woman's sack-back gown and petticoat as shown by the clear crease lines that run down the front and which used to be the pleated back of the woman's dress it was made with (Figure 8.6).

Just as the categories of novelty or gender are made somewhat ambiguous when looking at recycling practices, so is class to be interrogated. Indeed, socially, the circulation of objects should not be understood as strictly vertical with objects simply trickling down the different layers of a neat wedding-cake-style hierarchy of social orders. Sometimes objects went up rather than down the social ladder: the linen rags that barely dressed the beggar could be recycled into genteel writing paper.[57] And if the second-hand market did allow the garments discarded by ladies and gentlemen to be available to people lower down the social scale, the descent was not necessarily vertical and direct but rather windy and convoluted. It is impossible to track down precisely what course one particular object followed. Not only are records lacking in precision, but the many sorts of recycling available when it came to clothing meant that a garment could become divided into various recyclable elements: one could decide to sell only the lace trimming of a garment and keep the latter or sell the fabric and keep the trimming to use on a different garment, or even buy a garment second-hand and add a new trimming. All these possibilities show the eighteenth-century world of goods to be so extremely fluid that the very question of the identity of the object is raised here. When a woman's sack-back gown could be taken to bits, its gown transformed into a man's nightgown, its silver trimming melted down and made into buttons, its petticoat pawned and made into a little girl's outfit, its linen ruffles—reduced to rags—turned into paper, how may one say where the original object has gone?

In view of such epistemological instability, our own categorisation of the different types of recycling which we have adopted for the sake of this chapter need to be complexified in their turn.

Figure 8.6 Colonial Williamsburg, man's nightgown, detail. Acc. No. 1941–208, 1–2. © The Colonial Williamsburg Foundation.

The professional routes for recycling which integrated textile into an economic system with specific networks and intermediaries cannot be simplistically opposed to the domestic practices of recycling carried out by women at home. A good example of this is patchwork. The fragments of fabric used could originate from the bits and off-cuts that women conscientiously collected at home but could also be bought in large quantities from dealers who made a profit from reselling unusable remnants of fabric sold to them by dressmakers.[58]

Similarly, if recycling had an economic function in the household, that of prolonging the useful life of objects, we saw that it played a sentimental role as well. Economy and sentiment could dovetail, without the first precluding the other. And it is sometimes difficult to disentangle the two: although mending seems to perform a purely practical function, patching and darning was also a labour of love to some extent. Elizabeth Shackleton continued to lovingly repair her grown-up sons' linen when they came to visit. She wrote in 1778: "I am happy to have [John] here. Mended up slightly some shirts and night caps, all his things much out of repair."[59] Moreover, the stitches used in darning or repairing textile accessories were so intimately known to those who had made them that in cases of disputes over property, those practical repairs would turn into crucial marks of personal identification, irrefutable evidence of identity thus calling into question any strict opposition between economy and sentiment.[60] Cutting across social classes, professional activities, gender, or the object-subject traditional divide, thus recycling invites the eighteenth-century specialist to interrogate her own categories and restore its peculiar fluidity and complexity to a period poised between tradition and modernity.

NOTES

1. "Adventures of a Quire of Paper," in *The London Magazine or Gentleman's Monthly Intelligencer* (London, 1779).
2. Dress historian Madeleine Ginsburg was the first to draw attention to the importance of second-hand clothes in Britain, in her "Rags to Riches: The Second-Hand Clothes Trade 1700–1978," *Costume* 14 (1980), 121–35. The social historians who have shown an interest in pawning and second-hand are Berverly Lemire for Britain and Laurence Fontaine for France, more recently Jon Stobart and Ilja Van Damme have added their contribution to this scholarship. Linda Baumgarten's work on altered eighteenth-century clothing in the Colonial Williamsburg Collection stands out as a notable exception among dress historians. See her *What Clothes Reveal: The Language of Clothing in Colonial and Federal America, the Colonial Williamsburg Collection* (New Haven: Yale University Press, 2002), 182–207.
3. See in particular Beverly Lemire, "Consumerism in Preindustrial and Early Industrial England: The Trade in Second-Hand Clothes," *Journal of British Studies* 27, no. 1 (1988): 1–24, and "Peddling Fashion: Salesmen, Pawnbrokers, Taylors, Thieves and the Second-Hand Clothes Trade in England, c. 1700–1800," *Textile History* 22, no. 1 (1991): 67–82.
4. Lemire, "Consumerism," 12, table 1.
5. Cited in Lemire, "Peddling Fashion," 73.
6. Alison Backhouse, *The Worm Eaten Waistcoat* (York: Backhouse, 2003), 25.
7. Sir Frederick Morton Eden, *The State of the Poor or an History of the Labouring Classes in England*, 3 vols. (London, 1797), vol. 1, 554.
8. Entry for 15 January 1799. Parson Woodforde, *The Diary of a Country Parson, 1758–1802*, ed. John Beresford (Oxford: Oxford University Press, 1924), vol. 5, 161.
9. March 17 1770, *Jackson's Oxford Journal*, cited in Lemire, "Peddling Fashion," 72.
10. See Donald Woodward, "'Swords into Ploughshares': Recycling in Pre-industrial England," *The Economic History Review*, New Series 38, no. 2 (1985): 183–86.
11. Pitter and Fox, John Johnson collection of printed ephemera, 21(34); 21(35), see also British Museum, Banks 75.33 and 75.34. For Edward Dobson's card, see British Museum, Heal, 67.122.

12. On the fabrication of paper see chapter 12 by Amélie Junqua in this volume.
13. R. Campbell, *The London Tradesman* (London: T. Gardner, 1747), 258.
14. 25 March 1661, Samuel Pepys, *The Diary of Samuel Pepys*, ed. Robert Latham and William Matthews (London: Bell, 1970–87), vol. 2, 60.
15. See Donald Cuthbert Coleman, *The British Paper Industry, 1495–1860* (Oxford: Clarendon Press, 1958), 173.
16. Old Bailey proceedings, hereafter Old Bailey, t17850629–28
17. They developed the Fourdrinier machine in particular. On Fourdrinier, or Bloxam and Fourdrinier as they would be later known, see Coleman, *The British Paper Industry*, passim.; see also the company's papers in the John Johnson Collection in Oxford.
18. On this topic see for instance Lemire, "Consumerism."
19. On 7 November 1741, two waistcoats were received into the men's stock of clothing that had been "made of old things" (London Metropolitan Archives, hereafter LMA, P69/SEP/B/080/ MS 03252/004/fol. 37). An entry for 18 March 1741 lists four undercoats for girls made "of old things" (LMA P69/SEP/B/080/ MS 03252/004/fol. 236) and on 17 September 1742, one gown and one "undergown" [sic] for girls were received that were "made of old things" LMA P69/SEP/B/080/ MS 03252/004/fol. 240. I would like to thank Barbara Burman for bringing this reference to my attention.
20. LMA P69/SEP/B/080/ MS 03252/004/fol. 249.
21. LMA P69/SEP/B/080/ MS 03252/004/fol.260.
22. Fol. 167 lists a gown "made of 2 old gowns" LMA P69/SEP/B/080/ MS 03252/004/ fol. 167.
23. George Washington to Robert Cary & Company, 28 September 1760, in *Writings of Washington*, ed. John C. Fitzpatrick, (New York: Greenwood Press, 1970), vol. 2, 351. Cited in Baumgarten, *What Clothes Reveal*, 197.
24. 31 October 1782, Parson Woodforde, *The Diary of a Country Parson, 1758–1802*, ed. John Beresford (Oxford: Oxford University Press, 1924), vol. 2, 41.
25. 30 November 1782, *Diary of a Country Parson*, II, 46.
26. 11 December 1790, *Diary of a Country Parson*, III, 233.
27. 25 December 1790. *Diary of a Country Parson*, III, 238.
28. See Linda Baumgarten's drawing to explain these transformations in *What Clothes Reveal*, 195.
29. Platt Hall Gallery of English Costume, Manchester City Art Galleries. Photographed in Ann Buck, 165.
30. Martha Dodson Account Book, Museum of London, 80–71, passim.
31. Henry Mayhew, *London Labour and the London Poor*, ed. Robert Douglas Fairhirst (Oxford University Press, 2010), 150.
32. Peter Hayden, "Records of Clothing Expenditure for the Years 1746–79 Kept by E. Jervis of Leaford in Staffordshire," *Costume* 22 (1988): 38.
33. On the home as a recycling unit, see Margaret Ponsonby, *Stories from Home: English Domestic Interiors 1750–1850* (Aldershot: Ashgate, 2007), 79–102.
34. Priscilla Wakefield, *Reflections on the Present Condition of the Female Sex* (1798), 188.
35. Amanda Vickery, *The Gentleman's Daughter. Women's Lives in Georgian England* (London: Yale University Press, 1998), 151, 325.
36. Gertrude Saville, *Secret Comment. The Diaries of Gertrude Savile 1721–1757*, ed. Alan Saville (Nottingham: Kingsbridge History Society, 1997), 135.
37. Woodforde, *Diary of a Country Parson*, vol. 3, 143.
38. Vickery, *The Gentleman's Daughter*, 151.
39. Mary Jane Kilner, *The Adventures of a Pincushion. Designed Chiefly for the Use of Young Ladies* (London: J. Marshall & Co, 1780), 14, 17.

40. Ibid., 17.
41. See single pocket c. 1790 in the Gallery of Costume, Manchester City Galleries, MCAG 1947–1250.
42. Ann Conway, *The Correspondence of Anne Viscountess Conway, Henry More, and their Friends, 1642–1684*, ed. Marjorie Hope Nicolson (London: Oxford University Press, 1930), 134.
43. Margreta De Grazia, Maureen Quilligan, and Peter Stallybrass, eds., *Subject and Object in Renaissance Culture* (Cambridge: Cambridge University Press, 1996); Ann Rosalind Jones and Peter Stallybrass, *Renaissance Clothing and the Materials of Memory* (Cambridge: Cambridge University Press, 2000).
44. John Styles, *Threads of Feeling. The London Foundling Hospital's Textile Tokens, 1740–1770* (London: The Foundling Museum, 2010).
45. Heart motifs are a good common instance. See Ibid., 64–68.
46. LMA, A/FH/A/09/001/179.
47. Among the nontextile tokens the padlock and key symbol was often used—see Styles, *Threads of Feeling*, 17.
48. Barbara Kirshenblatt-Gimblett, "Objects of Memory: Material Culture as Life Review," in *Folk Groups and Folklore Genres, a Reader*, ed. Elliott Oring (Logan: Utah State University Press, 1989), 333. She also quotes a twentieth-century quilter talking about her work who articulates the mnemonic links between the scraps of fabric, family members, and history. "Now I have some ten big scrap bags. If someone else were to see them, they would seem like a pile of junk. [. . .] Different ones [people] of my family are always appearing from one of these bags. Just when you thought you'd forgotten someone, well like right here . . . I remember that patch. That was a dress that my grandmother wore to church. I sat beside her singing hymns, and that dress was so pretty to me then. I can just remember her in that dress now," Ibid., 334.
49. The workbasket (T.31–1935) worked by Hannah Downes at the end of the seventeenth century contains examples of needlework made by four generations of women from the seventeenth to the nineteenth century.
50. Ellen Weeton, *Miss Weeton's Journal of a Governess, 1807–1825*, ed. Edward Hall (Oxford: Oxford University Press, 1939), vol. 2, 325.
51. Thus Elizabeth Shackleton recorded in her diary the wearing and mending of her mother's old shifts and the distribution of her first husband's clothing to his sons—Vickery, *The Gentleman's Daughter*, 188.
52. Edmund Harrold's Diary (1712–16), MS A.2.137, 17–18 December 1712, Chetham's Library, Manchester; cited in Miles Lambert, "'Small Presents Confirm Friendship': The 'Gifting' of Clothing and Textiles in England from the Late Seventeenth to the Early Nineteenth Centuries," *Text: For the Study of Textile Art Design & History* 32 (2004–05): 31.
53. Vickery, *The Gentleman's Daughter*, 185.
54. Some surviving artefacts point to similar rituals of love although these sadly remain often undocumented. For instance, a woman's tie-on pocket, which will be discussed in a book-length study of women's pockets I am currently writing with Barbara Burman, was made from a soldier's cap, leaving the researcher to muse on how it might have been made and worn by the mother or the wife of the soldier, possibly after his death. See Barbara Burman and Ariane Fennetaux, *The Artful Pocket: Social and Cultural History of an Everyday Object* (Farnham: Ashgate, forthcoming).
55. Adam Smith, *The Wealth of Nations* [1776] (Harmondsworth: Penguin, 1997).
56. 13 June 1661, *The Diary of Samuel Pepys*, vol. 2, 120.

57. See Amélie Junqua's discussion of the *Spectator* in this volume for an example of this.
58. Styles, "Patchwork on the Page," in Sue Prichard, *Quilts, 1700–2010. Hidden Histories, Untold Stories* (London: V&A Publishing, 2010), 51.
59. Vickery, *The Gentleman's Daughter*, 151.
60. See for instance Old Bailey t17900915–51, or t17971025–5.

9 Science and Recycling in the Long Eighteenth Century

Simon Werrett

Historians of science have recently shifted their attention from studying innovation and the production of knowledge to its consumption, dissemination, and circulation.[1] Historians and sociologists of technology have similarly been keen to explore the ways technology is used rather than focus on the process of invention.[2] Such approaches point to the need for a better appreciation of everyday scientific and technical practices, and the ongoing significance they give to existing ideas, techniques, and objects. This essay argues that everyday scientific practice was often as much about preserving, repairing and reusing the old as it was about innovation, and eighteenth-century natural philosophers both participated in and contributed to the creation of a variety of such practices.

To describe these practices collectively, I shall use the term "stewardship," following the work of the American social historian Susan Strasser. She identifies a widespread concern with the maintenance, adaptation, and repair of materials in colonial America, which she calls the "stewardship of objects." As she puts it, Americans

> mended, reused, saved, and made do. They darned socks and fed food scraps to chickens and pigs. They dyed faded dresses and repaired rickety furniture. They handed things down to younger and poorer relatives or to servants; they turned old clothes and sewing scraps into rugs, quilts and other home furnishings.[3]

The goal of this essay is to think about stewardship in settings of natural philosophical inquiry. Stewardship might be thought of as one among many historical manifestations of recycling, to go along with the polysemic use of this term as it is defined by our approach in this book.[4] Nevertheless, this essay is a contribution to a broader history of recycling that is emerging in environmental studies and other disciplines. In addition to the essays in this volume, Martin Melosi, Sabine Barles, and Roland Ladwig have thus explored industries managing refuse and recycling in the United States, France, and Germany respectively.[5] Tim Cooper and Nicholas Goddard have highlighted the use of waste materials in agriculture and sanitation in

Victorian Britain, while Donald Woodward has shown forms of recycling to be widespread in early modern England.[6] This essay examines some of the ways materials were reused and stewarded in the natural sciences in the long eighteenth century. Practices of stewardship probably extended into diverse sciences in many regions, but here most of the examples will come from the history of physical and chemical natural philosophy in Britain and colonial North America. This is not because there was anything special about these sciences or locations. The choices merely reflect the limits of the author's expertise: this is an initial foray, rather than a comprehensive survey. Nevertheless I wish to argue that stewardship was a relevant aspect of eighteenth-century natural philosophy, and is worth further study, since it helped to shape philosophical practices, experimental agendas, and forms of apparatus. Enlightened science entailed not only the production and circulation of knowledge but also the reuse, repair, and adaption of the material culture used to create it.

THE STEWARDSHIP OF OBJECTS

Susan Strasser has pointed to the value placed on "the stewardship of objects" in the early modern American colonies.[7] The stewardship of objects refers primarily to a widespread thrift and care over materials which operated in American households, and to informal economies of used materials. Strasser points to the routine efforts of men and women to "make do" in this context, keeping domestic or workshop utensils in good repair, and reusing materials for other purposes. For most people, scarcity, and to a lesser extent poverty, dictated that such activities were a matter of course. As Strasser puts it, "Everyone was a *bricoleur*."[8] For most people, reuse was not a choice, an alternative to throwing things away, but the norm, a situation reflected in the fact that there was no special vocabulary for these practices in the early modern world. Making do was just what was done.

"The stewardship of objects," "bricolage," and "making do" are thus Strasser's categories, not contemporaries', but they do capture a form of life which was widespread. Indeed, the stewardship of objects also extended to the practitioners of science. If we associate the early modern period with a "*new* science" it was also one in which the sciences remained very much engaged, on a practical level, with the old, as philosophers routinely repaired, reused, and made do with material culture. They extended the scope of domestic stewardship from the household to the laboratory, which, of course, was itself typically an extension of domestic space, a converted kitchen, cellar, or parlour.[9] Household objects and practices were appropriated into novel laboratory practices. A variety of pots, pans, jugs, and bottles were used in early experiments, and this was part of a wider care for preserving and reusing material objects which early modern philosophers, and people in general, exhibited.[10]

Natural philosophers thus shared in the common practice of passing on clothes, books, and material possessions between friends and relations, or from one generation to the next. Samuel Pepys, president of the Royal Society, inherited his terrella magnet from William Barlow, and wore, he tells us, a "gray clothe suit and faced white coate, made of one of my wife's pettycoates."[11] Thrift pertained to the philosophical household as it did to any other. Robert Hooke routinely ordered his servants to mend his clothes, and he grumbled in his diary when his housemaids broke glassware.[12] Used books, of course, were regularly sold or exchanged among the learned, assisted by a variety of second-hand booksellers, and were also sold at numerous auctions, an important site for early modern natural philosophy. In England, the earliest of these auctions took place in coffee houses in the City of London, the same places where the virtuosi gathered to conduct experiments.[13] Hooke noted how he met friends and philosophical acquaintances at auctions, which he attended very regularly, so that besides supplying philosophers with books and later specimens and instruments, auctions were an important place for encouraging sociability, that key ingredient in seventeenth-century science.[14] In the provinces, taverns served as auction sites. In Cambridge, they took place in the Eagle and Child. In the 1680s, the Eagle hosted an auction of the library of Royal Society fellow Edmund Castell by the former bookseller Edward "Ned" Millington. Millington claimed he had started auctions on the authority of Herodotus, "who" as he put it "commends that way of sale for the disposal of the most exquisite and finest beauties to their amoroso's," a reference to the "bridal auctions" of the Babylonians described in the *Histories*.[15]

Like domestic goods, scientific goods were scarce, and so exchange was just as important, if not more so, than production or collection. The same was true in the case of repair. Philosophers often worked hard to preserve instruments and keep materials in good order, rather than make or buy new ones. When instruments broke, artisans routinely offered repair services, which became more prominent in places where instrument use was high and instrument makers were scarce: in the provinces, in ports, or colonial outposts, for example.[16] The concern to prolong the life of instruments also influenced their design and the effects they produced—experimental agendas were shaped by a concern over maintenance. Makers preferred robust, easily repairable instruments, and abandoned experiments if they threatened to damage the apparatus. In his version of the Torricellian experiment, Robert Boyle noted that warming the air increased the height to which a column of mercury in a glass tube was raised, yet, he wrote, "I made no doubt, that it might have been rais'd much higher, but I was unwilling by applying a less moderate heat to hazard the breaking of my Glasses, in the place I then was in, where such a mischance could scarce have been repair'd."[17] Glass, like other materials, was expensive and not to be thrown away. In the eighteenth century Joseph Priestley, Tiberius Cavallo, Benjamin Wilson, and other electricians agonised over the best ways to preserve the glass of Leyden jars, which were liable to crack during electric discharges.[18] Wilson described how to use wax, resin, turpentine, and olive oil to seal cracks in a Leyden jar, while the lecturer Cadogan Morgan advocated using lower charges in experiments to avoid this problem.[19]

Philosophers also "made do" by incorporating old and discarded materials into their labours. Glass and metals were expensive and probably many early modern instruments were made with recycled materials. It has been estimated that some 10 percent of all iron used in seventeenth-century England was recycled, and the trade in "old brass" was international. Galileo purchased old brass for his instrument maker Mazzoleni from Germany, for a third of the price of new, and made his first telescopes using organ pipes and lenses ground on a cannon ball.[20] Natural philosophers also adapted domestic waste to philosophical uses, a practice illustrated by the uses of playing cards. Because early modern playing cards were only printed on one side, the blank sides of defunct cards were used for a variety of purposes, as notepaper, as calling cards, or even as a form of currency. Dr John Morgan of the College of Philadelphia, later the University of Pennsylvania, thus advertised "A course of lectures on the *materia medica*" on a playing card in 1765.[21] Domestic space, Morgan's house, provided the venue for the lectures, while the card was made authoritative by applying Morgan's wax seal below his announcement. Botanists may have taken playing cards into the field to make notes on. In 1783 the French naturalist Jean-Pierre Bergeret proposed that the principles of his new system of botanical nomenclature "can be written on fewer than twelve playing cards."[22] Certainly Jean-Jacques Rousseau wrote his *Reveries of a Solitary Walker*, a series of philosophical contemplations, on playing cards, during countryside walks punctuated with botanizing.[23] Used cards also enabled new ways of organising knowledge. Edward Gibbon employed old playing cards to create one of the earliest card indexes, in this case of the books in his library.[24]

FRANKLIN AND PRIESTLEY

The thrifty stewardship of objects might affect the material culture of natural philosophy, experimental agendas, and methods of organising knowledge. It equally helped to shape new theories. Perhaps the thriftiest of early modern philosophers was Benjamin Franklin. From an early age Franklin extended the thrift common in American households to his philosophical pursuits. He often bought goods second-hand and valued the chance to borrow books from friends and acquaintances.[25] This desire to avoid buying new books led Franklin to establish Philadelphia's first library among his fellow members of the Junto, and following that he founded a popular subscription library which was copied throughout the United States.[26] Franklin also worked to bring order to the streets through the collection of waste. He carried out studies on efficient street-sweeping and introduced the first scavengers to Philadelphia, to pick up reusable waste materials.[27]

As he grew older, Franklin developed this thrift into what he called a "philosophy of virtue" encouraging industry and frugality, both in himself and others. "Frugality" he defined as "Make no expense but to do good to others or yourself; i.e. waste nothing."[28] Franklin exploited his skills as a printer to spread this philosophy, printing proverbial sentences on thrift in his journal *Poor Richard's Almanack*, which he collated into a famous essay, "The Way to Wealth," in 1757. Here he exhorted his audience not to waste money on superfluities, "The Art of getting Riches consists very much in Thrift."[29] Domestic thrift was thus conjoined with philosophy and with commerce, and Franklin's print shop, as an extension of his artisan household, was likewise a place of thrift. For example his wife helped in the printing shop by "purchasing old linen rags for the paper-makers."[30] Franklin was also a keen accountant, urging the need for careful bookkeeping, since even a tiny profit or loss could quickly turn into a significant one. As Otto Sibum has shown, Franklin's bookkeeping habits extended through his moral life, his commercial transactions, and his scientific inquiries. He kept careful accounts of his own virtues, entering dishonourable acts into a ledger which he made using a reusable ivory memorandum book written in pencil and rubbed out when necessary. He resolved arguments by drawing up a balance sheet of pros and cons, which he then matched and cancelled out until only one side predominated. To refine this method he proposed a more abstract "moral or prudential algebra" which gave a weighting to the different arguments. As Sibum shows, Franklin approached electricity in the same quantitative way, treating a surplus of electricity in a body as a credit, and a deficit as a debit, termed plus or minus. Electrical theory thus became "a bookkeeping problem that was to be solved algebraically."[31]

Franklin extended the arts of domestic thrift to the workplace, and to his moral and natural philosophy. No doubt thrift was also a part of the daily practice of many other natural philosophers, especially after the rise of public science encouraged a broader public to participate in scientific endeavours. In Britain, chemical experimenters made a virtue of thrift in the laboratory. Franklin's friend and correspondent Joseph Priestley was often short of money, and explained his turn to original experimentation as a result of not being able to afford the many books he needed to purchase in order to compile a history of vision, light, and colours.[32] Priestley turned to chemical experiments on airs because, as he put it, they were good for "keeping off such as would involve me in expense."[33] Like Franklin, Priestley extended domestic thrift to the new arena of experimentation. Priestley often adapted kitchen and household utensils to chemical ends, making an earthen trough to collect gases with a container "commonly used for washing linen," which he passed on to a friend after he had finished with it.[34] As Crosland notes, "mice, candles, and green plants also cost next to nothing."[35] Domestic interests and thrift also threatened Priestley's programs, however, and in 1772 he wrote to Franklin, "Frugality and an attention to a growing family will, at length get the better of experimenting, and I shall then write nothing but *Politicks* and *Divinity*."[36]

By redeploying common household items as chemical apparatus Priestley created an experimental culture open to a broad public, and so helped usher in the popular fascination with chemistry in the late eighteenth century.[37] This was also a geographically distinct enterprise, contrasting with French chemistry, which at this time was more concerned with distinction from the popular experimenter than with frugality. In Paris, novel and expensive instrumentation marked chemistry rather than pots and pans.[38] Nevertheless, the close links of domestic and laboratory stewardship remained salient in scientific practices of the nineteenth century. This is evident, for example, in Michael Faraday's *Chemical Manipulation*, first published in 1830 and based on a series of lectures given at the London Institution three years earlier.[39] *Chemical Manipulation* was filled with methods to avoid waste in the laboratory, based on Faraday's own experience and his observations of current chemical practice. Hints on how to preserve instruments from damage and how to reuse old materials were abundant. The remnants of kitchen frugality are evident in advice on how to use broken pots and jars, old metal saucepans, glass dishes, china cups, and damaged tobacco pipes in chemical inquiry. While he made clear that some instruments could not be reused—crucibles, for example, had to be discarded in case any remnants of their contents contaminated a subsequent experiment—Faraday urged that even the most expensive instruments could always be repaired or reused in some way. Air pumps, for example, should be sent to an instrument maker for repairs until they were unusable, and even then, Faraday wrote,

> When an instrument is absolutely bad, and cannot be replaced or repaired, the student must compensate for the imperfections as far as he can, by interposing a stop-cock between [the pump] and the retort, flask, or other vessel . . . and close the communication as soon as, by rapidly working the instrument, he has effected the best exhaustion he can attain.[40]

Scientific stewardship thus continued into the nineteenth century, and no doubt remained a part of laboratory practice whenever there was a need to deal with scarcity and economy. Stewardship certainly formed a common aspect of seventeenth- and eighteenth-century laboratory life. Domestic space might be adapted to scientific labours, while scarcity and economy prompted a busy economy of exchange and second-hand use of materials among philosophers. Domestic thrift and stewardship extended from the household into the laboratory, in practices of repair, reuse, and adaptation. Concerns over the maintenance and preservation of apparatus and materials influenced the direction of experimental investigations, and thrift could also inspire novel theoretical accounts of natural phenomena.

It remains to point out that stewardship should not be seen as the only way in which the sciences have been engaged with the reuse of materials. To conclude, another form of recycling might be briefly mentioned, which serves to clarify what was distinctive about practices of stewardship, both in terms of the scale and nature of practices and where they took place. While stewardship occurred at a domestic scale in laboratories and adapted rooms, the so-called "utilisation of waste products" which came to prominence in the nineteenth century entailed the industrial use of waste and by-products to manufacture new materials or products in factories on a massive scale. Coal tar, for example, was a waste product in the distillation of coal to produce coal-gas for lighting c. 1810, but by the close of the nineteenth century it was being used to manufacture medicines, antiseptics, smelling salts, fuels, and dyestuffs.[41] Such an enterprise was not pursued from a tradition of thrift or to meet scarcity, but was motivated by profit, and the profitable use of waste would come to be seen by figures such as Charles Babbage as a foundational element, along with mechanisation, of capitalism.[42] The utilisation of waste products also generated a substantial body of knowledge, as natural philosophers and industrialists sought to compile information on different materials and their potential as new products.[43] In contrast, stewardship practices, because they were just "what was done," were typically recorded only in passing, and most were probably not recorded at all. The Victorian literature on waste made waste into a problem for the nineteenth century, which was solved in part through new sciences of work, sanitation, hygiene, and thermodynamics.[44] The industrial use of waste in factories thus generated a quite different set of scientific practices and knowledge compared to the stewardship of the home and laboratory.

ACKNOWLEDGMENTS

Parts of this chapter were earlier published as "Recycling in Early Modern Science," *The British Journal for the History of Science*, 46, no. 4 (2013): 627–46. doi: 10.1017/S0007087412000696. © British Society for the History of Science, published by Cambridge University Press, reproduced with permission.

NOTES

1. On circulation, see James Secord, "Knowledge in Transit," *Isis* 95 (2004): 654–72; David Livingstone, *Putting Science in Its Place: Geographies of Scientific Knowledge* (Chicago and London: University of Chicago Press, 2003), 135–78.
2. David Edgerton, *The Shock of the Old: Technology and Global History since 1900* (Oxford and New York: Oxford University Press, 2007); Nelly Oudshoorn and Trevor Pinch, eds., *How Users Matter: The Co-Construction of Users and Technology* (Cambridge, MA: MIT Press, 2003).

3. Susan Strasser, *Waste and Want: A Social History of Trash* (New York: Metropolitan Books, 1999), 22.
4. Peder Anker discusses some of the history of the idea of recycling in the twentieth century. See Peder Anker, "The Ecological Colonization of Space," *Environmental History* 10 (2005): 239–68.
5. Strasser, *Waste and Want*; Martin V. Melosi, *Garbage in the Cities: Refuse, Reform, and the Environment* (Pittsburgh: University of Pittsburgh Press, 2004); Sabine Barles, *L'invention des déchets urbains: France 1790–1970* (Seyssel: Champ Vallon, 2005); Roland Ladwig, ed., *Recycling in Geschichte und Gegenwart: Vorträge* (Freiberg: Georg-Agricola-Gesellschaft, 2003); see also Carl Zimring, *Cash for Your Trash: Scrap Recycling in America* (New Brunswick, NJ: Rutgers University Press, 2005); Heather Rogers, *Gone Tomorrow: The Hidden Life of Garbage* (New York: New Press, 2005).
6. Tim Cooper, "Rags, Bones and Recycling Bins," *History Today* 56 (2006): 17–18; Nicholas Goddard, "Nineteenth-Century Recycling: The Victorians and the Agricultural Use of Sewage," *History Today* 31 (1981): 32–36; Donald Woodward, "Swords into Ploughshares: Recycling in Pre-Industrial England," *Economic History Review* 38 (1985): 175–91; see also Beverly Lemire, "Consumerism in Pre-Industrial and Early Industrial England: The Trade in Second-Hand Clothes," *Journal of British Studies* 27 (1988): 1–24; Erland Mårald, "Everything Circulates: Agricultural Chemistry and Recycling Theories in the Second Half of the Nineteenth Century," *Environment and History* 8 (2002): 65–84.
7. Strasser, *Waste and Want.*
8. Strasser, *Waste and Want*, 22–23.
9. Pamela H. Smith, "Laboratories," in *The Cambridge History of Science*, ed. Lorraine J. Daston and Katharine Park, *Vol. 3: Early Modern Europe* (Cambridge: Cambridge University Press), 290–305; Maurice Crosland, "Early Laboratories c. 1600–1800 and the Location of Experimental Science," *Annals of Science* 62 (2005): 233–53.
10. Elaine Leong has highlighted the use of cooking and household implements in the making of medicaments in early modern households. See her "Making Medicines in the Early Modern Household," *Bulletin of the History of Medicine* 82 (2008): 145–68, on 162.
11. Quoted in Woodward, "Swords into Ploughshares," 177–8; Patricia Fara, "'A Treasure of Hidden Vertues': The Attraction of Magnetic Marketing," *British Journal for the History of Science* 28 (1995): 5–35, on 16.
12. Henry W. Robinson and Walter Adams, eds., *The Diary of Robert Hooke, 1672–1680* (London: Wykeham Publications Ltd., 1968), 106, 144, 187.
13. Larry Stewart, "Other centres of calculation, or, where the Royal Society didn't count: commerce, coffee-houses and natural philosophy in early modern London," *British Journal for the History of Science* 32 (1999): 133–53; Giles Mandelbrote, "The Organization of Book Auctions in Late Seventeenth-Century London," in *Under the Hammer: Book Auctions Since the Seventeenth Century*, ed. Robin Myers, Michael Harris, and Giles Mandelbrote (New Castle, DE: Oak Knoll Press; London: British Library, 2001), 15–36; on the history of scientific auctions more generally, see J. M. Chalmers-Hunt, *Natural Historical Auctions 1700–1972: A Register of Sales in the British Isles* (London: Sotheby Parke Bernet, 1976).
14. *Diary of Robert Hooke*, 358–59, 414, 443; Leona Rostenberg, *The Library of Robert Hooke: The Scientific Book Trade of Restoration England* (Santa Monica, CA: Modoc Press, 1989), 66–81.
15. Mandelbrote, *Under the Hammer*, 31–32; John Nichols, *Literary Anecdotes of the Eighteenth Century*, 6 vols. (London, 1812), vol. 4, 29.

16. On colonial instrument-makers and repairs, see Silvio A. Bedini, *Thinkers and Tinkers: Early American Men of Science* (New York: Scribners, 1975), 184–204.
17. Robert Boyle, *A Continuation of New Experiments Physico-mechanical, Touching the Spring and Weight of the Air and Their Effects* (London: 1669), 13. Boyle heated the air with hot iron or tongs held near the receiver of the air-pump, but "without making it touch the Instrument, for fear of breaking it." Robert Boyle, *Animadversions upon Mr. Hobbes's Problemata de vacuo* (London: 1674), 72.
18. See e.g. Benjamin Wilson, "New Experiments upon the Leyden Phial, Respecting the Termination of Conductors," *Philosophical Transactions* 68 (1778): 999–1012, on 1011–12.
19. George Cadogan Morgan, *Lectures on Electricity*, 2 vols. (Norwich: 1794), vol. 2, 460.
20. Woodward, "Swords into Ploughshares," 185–86; Giorgio Strano, "Galileo's Telescope: History, Scientific Analysis, and Replicated Observations," *Experimental Astronomy* 25 (2009): 17–31, on 22.
21. General Collection of the University of Pennsylvania, 1740–1820. UPA 3. Matriculation and Lecture Ticket Collection 1620. Morgan, John. Materia. Medica and Practice of Physick: incomplete, 1765. Thanks for this reference to Karen Reeds.
22. Jean-Pierre Bergeret, *Phytonomatotechnie universelle* (Paris: 1783), 158. Thanks for this reference to Sara T. Scharf.
23. See Eli Friedlander, *J.J. Rousseau: An Afterlife of Words* (Cambridge, MA: Harvard University Press, 2004), 74, 163.
24. British Library Add Mss 34716; Geoffrey Keynes, ed., *The Library of Edward Gibbon*, 2nd ed. (Godalming: St. Paul's Bibliographies, 1980).
25. Benjamin Franklin, *Autobiography of Benjamin Franklin* (New York: Modern Library, 1944), 10, 17, 50.
26. Franklin, *Autobiography*, 87–89.
27. Franklin, *Autobiography*, 140–42, 145.
28. Franklin, *Autobiography*, 94.
29. Franklin, *Autobiography*, 209.
30. Franklin, *Autobiography*, 90.
31. H. Otto Sibum, "Nature's Bookkeeper: Benjamin Franklin's Electrical Research and the Development of Experimental Natural Philosophy in the 18th Century," in *Reappraising Benjamin Franklin: A Bicentennial Perspective*, ed. J.A. Leo Lemay, (Newark: University of Delaware Press, 1993), 221–46, on 228.
32. Maurice Crosland, "Priestley Memorial Lecture: A Practical Perspective on Joseph Priestley as a Pneumatic Chemist," *British Journal for the History of Science* 16 (1983): 223–38, on 231.
33. Quoted in Crosland, "Priestley Memorian Lecture," 232.
34. Crosland, "Priestley Memorian Lecture," 233.
35. Crosland, "Priestley Memorian Lecture," 234.
36. Crosland, "Priestley Memorian Lecture," 234.
37. Jan Golinski, *Science as Public Culture: Chemistry and Enlightenment in Britain, 1760–1820* (Cambridge: Cambridge University Press, 1992).
38. Lissa Roberts, "The Death of the Sensuous Chemist: The 'New' Chemistry and the Transformation of Sensuous Technology," *Studies in History and Philosophy of Science* 26 (1995): 503–29.
39. Michael Faraday, *Chemical Manipulation*, 3rd ed. (London: 1842).
40. Faraday, *Chemical Manipulation*, 376–77.

41. "The Waste Products of Coal." *Scientific American* 27, no. 7 (17 August 1872): 97.
42. Charles Babbage, *Economy of Machines & Manufactures*, 3rd ed. (London, 1846), 6, 11–12.
43. See e.g. Peter Lund Simmonds, *Waste Products and Undeveloped Substances: Or, Hints for Enterprise in Neglected Fields* (London, 1862); Timothy Cooper, "Peter Lund Simmonds and the Political Ecology of Waste Utilization in Victorian Britain," *Technology and Culture* 52 (2011): 21–44.
44. See Crosbie Smith and M. Norton Wise, "Work and Waste: Political Economy and Natural Philosophy in Nineteenth-Century Britain," *History of Science* 27 (1989): 263–301, 391–449; 28 (1990): 221–61.

10 Recycling the Sacred

The Wax Votive Object and the Eighteenth-Century Wax Baby Doll

Elizabeth Kowaleski Wallace

Among the dolls in the Victoria and Albert collection at Bethnal Green is a most extraordinary object: a wax effigy called Don Santiago de la Haza y Laguno (c. 1717–1720) (Figure 10.1).

Figure 10.1 Wax effigy dressed to represent a baby called Don Santiago de la Haza y Laguno, 1660–1690. Acc. No. T.239 to E-1917, Bethnal Green Museum of Childhood. © Victoria & Albert Museum, London.

Looking very much like a modern baby doll, the effigy is perfect as a mimesis of an actual infant. Still dressed in its costly linen, the "Don" has the heft of an actual baby, with one leg oddly bent at an angle, further suggesting a baby's natural pose. The back of the effigy's head shows sign of a trauma or injury, indicating to curators that it originally functioned as a votive object: presumably the wealthy parents of the injured child commissioned the effigy and placed it in a church to intercede for the child's speedy recovery. At the beginning of the nineteenth century, it was carried to Canterbury for unknown reasons and eventually it made its way to the museum collections, where it is currently stored among the other dolls and toys.[1] As both religious object and plaything, the "Don" holds kinship with other dolls, and in particular with an early English wax baby doll (c. 1801) (Figure 10.2), on display in the Bethnal Green Museum.[2]

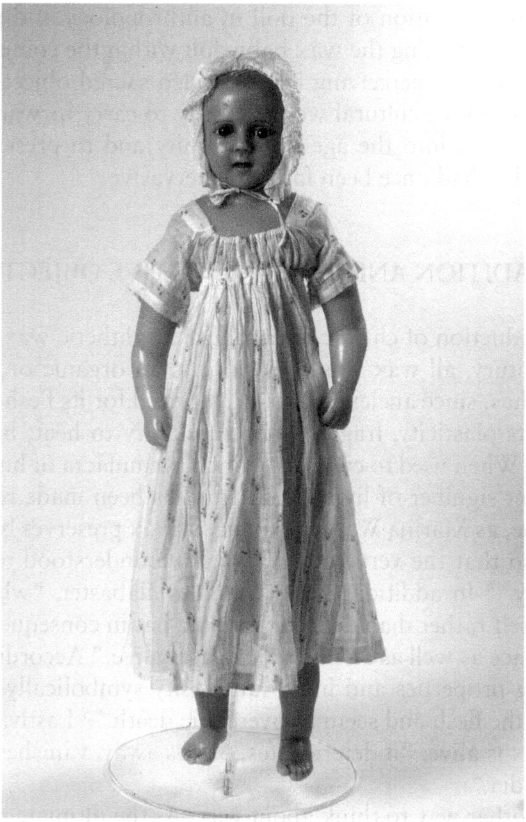

Figure 10.2 Wax-headed baby doll made in England between 1790–1805. Acc. No. MISC.750:1–1992. Bethnal Green Museum of Childhood. © Victoria & Albert Museum, London.

This second wax object exemplifies the category of wax dolls that were only coming into being at the end of the eighteenth century, and it provides one of the very first instances of the modern baby doll. This essay first situates the "Don" within the tradition of the wax votive and establishes how he recycles the otherworldly intensity that once permeated all votive objects. The story continues with the late eighteenth-century toy baby doll which, as we will see, initiates a second recycling of the magical power that the Don was once assumed to possess.

Before returning to the two dolls, this chapter explores the nature of wax as a medium, briefly explaining its special properties and associations. In part one, I address the question of why wax has proven to be such complicated medium of expression. This section is followed by a discussion of the wax votive object and its speedy evolution, over the course of the eighteenth century, into two related forms—the anatomical model and the popular waxwork. Both of these secularise a fundamentally sacred tradition, leaving the doll to carry on the tradition of the votive object. Part two resists a traditional interpretation of the doll in anthropology and philosophy to argue that only by placing the wax baby doll within the context to which it belongs—and only by perceiving it as recycled sacred object—do we fully comprehend its unique cultural work, namely to carry forward the magical associations of wax into the age of modernity and to preserve a form of mimetic play that had once been far more pervasive.

SACRED TRADITION AND THE WAX VOTIVE OBJECT

Until the introduction of chemically produced, synthetic waxes in the early nineteenth century, all wax was beeswax. As an organic or vegetal material, beeswax has, since ancient times, been prized for its flesh-like qualities, not only for its plasticity, fragility, and sensitivity to heat, but also for its translucence.[3] When used to create convincing simulacra of human life, wax can be a potent signifier of living flesh that has been made resistant to the passage of time, as Marina Warner explains: "wax preserves by sealing matter from air, so that the very substance can be understood to bring about imperishability."[4] In addition, wax resembles alabaster, "which holds the light within itself rather than deflecting it, and has in consequence a natural, glistening surface as well as an inner glow, as if alive." According to Warner, "its preserving properties and inner luminosity symbolically challenge the corruption of the flesh and seem to overcome death."[5] Lastly, as an organic substance, wax is alive: "it deteriorates, passes away, vanishes more easily" than other media.[6]

There is another way to think about wax. As the ultimate recycled material, it is malleable and can easily morph into almost any shape. Less coveted for its material status—for wax is not prohibitively expensive—its value lies instead in its symbolic associations, and in particular in the way it can signify enduring life. As it assumes its various shapes, wax recycles human sentiments. As we'll see, it can carry hope of health, cure, or immortality. However, it can also signify a disturbing capacity to change, and for this reason, it has also evoked negative emotions. In the realm of philosophy, wax has provoked meditation on the nature of human consciousness itself. For Descartes, wax, with its ever malleable and metaphoric capacities, challenges the notion that all knowledge can come through the senses and proves that "bodies are cognized not by the senses or by the imagination, but by the understanding alone."[7] Well into the twentieth century, wax continued to be a metaphoric material with the capacity to produce a physiological crisis. As Didi-Huberman explains, even though Sartre did not specifically reference wax in *Being and Nothingness*, his concept of the "viscous" as a sticky, unstable, and unbalanced material that threatens human subjectivity and haunts consciousness extends to wax itself. Because wax has the qualities of other viscous materials—evidencing "visible resistance," the tendency to deflate and then flatten out again in the possibility of "an annihilation that stops halfway through," for instance—wax has been "invested with the value of a haunting memory, a threat, a nightmare, a metamorphosis."[8]

In recent years, Didi-Huberman has been at the forefront of a group of scholars seeking to rescue wax objects from their status as unstable, nightmarish, or threatening and to restore them to a position of prominence within the Western aesthetic canon. He identifies the tendency of wax objects to resist their designation as mere things or inert signifiers: they always seem to signify something *more*.[9] As we will see, to reconsider the story of wax objects is to illuminate a cultural history of deep spiritual beliefs and practices that bespeak an ongoing relationship to the physical world and that defy rational explanation. This idea is best approached through one category of wax objects in particular—the wax votive object, also known as the ex-voto.

By definition, the ex-voto is an object that stands in for a living person or for part of a living person—an arm, a leg, an ear, a breast, or so on—in some kind of religious or mystical context. To be sure, not all ex-voti are made of wax, as can still be seen from a sizeable collection of metal votive objects in the Pitt River Museum in Oxford, among other places. Still, recent scholarship shows that the largest and most significant category of ex-voti was made of wax.[10] According to Roberta Panzanelli, in the past wax objects substituted for living persons in "ways not immediately evident and that appear related to the intrinsic characteristics of the material." She further contends, "Wax thus epitomizes a type of verisimilitude that does not merely portray or illustrate the image of the living but reproduces it, 'doubles' it, performing the donor according to conventions in the artistic vocabulary that are a precondition of shared social and visual practice."[11] In other words, wax objects not only imitate or copy, but they are thought *to substitute for human agency*, or in effect to enact human want, and this appears to have been the case for a very long time.

Egyptian papyri first testified to the use of wax in religious and magical rites. Later, Pliny the Elder catalogued the medical, cosmetic, industrial, and religious properties of wax in *Natural History.* Wax could be used to carry out the wishes of the living for good or ill. It is thought, for example, to have been used in the making of wax dolls—not unlike voodoo dolls—designed to carry out malevolent intentions. But wax was also used in rites involving the dead. For instance, ancient Roman patrician houses once featured wax "*cerae*" on their home altars.[12] Julius von Schlosser's seminal work on wax similarly begins with ancient Roman funerary practices that create simulacra of the dead, including wax heads and death masks.[13] However, it was under Catholicism that the custom of using wax votive objects became most widespread. In the early church, beeswax was used for church candles exclusively, until monasteries improved the art of apiculture, and then the use of the ex-voto appears to have expanded rapidly. In one especially intriguing example, Roberta Panzanelli describes how the use of the votive object reached its apotheosis during the seventeenth century in the Church of Annunziata, Florence:

> thousands of votive objects crowded the church [. . .] the life-size *voti* were dressed according to rank and arranged chronologically and in descending order of importance, starting with those closest to the altar. On one side were the effigies of the noble and notable Florentines [. . .] On the other side were illustrious foreigners: aristocrats, at least six popes [. . .] and cardinals dressed in purple [. . .] as well as emperors, kings, and nobles.

Also present were eminent warriors in full armour and a Turkish pasha attempting to guarantee his safe passage home. These ex-voti, also called *boti*, were created through a range of techniques, including both life and death casts and waxes modelled from portraits and medals.[14]

In the meantime, more common than the expensive, full-size human models were the innumerable ex-voti that replicated only a part of the human body. These appear to have been offerings, to be placed in a church or sacred setting, towards the cure or healing of an injury or illness: once again, the symbolic power of wax reinforced the idea of the resurrection of the flesh. Schlosser's essay includes early twentieth-century photographs of ex-voti in human shape, and Marina Warner claims to have seen votive objects for sale in Portuguese churches in the early twenty-first century, but their use seems to have fallen largely out of favour by the late seventeenth century.[15] And certainly, with the Reformation, the practice would have become suspect. During the English Civil War, Puritans smashed wax idols and drove wax modellers in England underground.[16] In addition, despite—or perhaps because of—their wide popular appeal, wax objects were increasingly viewed with suspicion by Catholic Church fathers who sought to control the authentication of sanctity.[17]

Yet continental wax modellers quickly found other outlets for their talents and skills, as their art took three different forms—the wax doll that is the subject of this essay, the anatomical model, and the popular waxwork. Developed to serve the requirements of emerging medical science during the eighteenth century, the wax anatomical body helped researchers to study the intricacies of the human body in a time when human body parts were difficult to obtain and otherwise perishable. To this day, the Museo di Specola in Florence offers stunning examples of not only excoriated, full-size human bodies—including an eighteenth-century "wax Venus" representing the body of a young woman—but also individual organs.[18] In Bologna, a city renowned for its medical science during the seventeenth and eighteenth centuries, Anna Morandi Manzolini (1714/6–1764) produced spectacular models of the human sense organs: her oversized wax model of the human ear, on view at the Palazzo Poggi, suggests how the artistic skill of the votive maker could be applied to objects that furthered a scientific purpose while simultaneously announcing the mystery of the human body.[19] Other wax modellers were quick to exploit the commercial possibilities of the wax model for a nonscientific elite. Most famously, Swiss physician turned entrepreneur Philippe Curtius (1737–1794) began his career by making anatomical models, but soon moved on to the more lucrative practice of displaying waxworks of notable French persons from both ends of the social spectrum, aristocrats and nobles on the one hand, and thieves and criminals on the other. The story of his famous "niece" (or possibly his daughter) Madame Tussaud (1761–1850) is well rehearsed: her earliest models are said to have been death masks of mutilated heads taken directly from the guillotine.[20]

What is important about these two, later ceroplastic traditions—the anatomical model and the popular waxworks—is that, while they carry on the technological skill once evinced in the votive object, they purposefully move away from an investment in the spiritual nature of the body. In the case of the popular waxwork, the aim is to celebrate not what we *cannot* know about a human being, but what we can capture, in precise and hyperrealistic form, about their public persona. In the popular waxwork, we approach not what is elusive or unknown, but to the contrary, what is known too well about a given personality. The ex-voto and the scientific model also work differently: like a wax votive object in the shape of a human arm, the anatomical wax arm precisely mimics human form. But the anatomical model objectifies that form: it fragments the body in order to render it into a series of discrete parts to be deciphered, laying open for inspection the inner workings of the human body.[21] Under such scrutiny, for example, the arm becomes a specimen to be mastered. The wax ex-voto arm, in contrast, does not yield up its secrets and it cannot be placed within a rational account of human physiology. Its purpose remains mystical. As we will see, at a time when other ceroplastic arts were being redeployed for secularised purposes, the wax doll uniquely resists dissection and challenges the notion that the boundary between dead and living, or embodied and disembodied, can be clearly drawn. As an object that exists in the space between human and nonhuman, it recycles a sacred practice into a dynamic, living form of play.

THE WAX BABY DOLL

Anthropologists and ethnographers have long asserted that dolls express a "primitive" impulse to imitate human form and to substitute representation for human life. Max von Boehn, for instance, maintains that the genealogy of dolls requires surveying the ancestor image, the idol, the fetish, the amulet, and the talisman, before arriving at the votive figure and, finally, the modern doll.[22] Similarly, Alice Early traces the ancestry of the doll to the Palaeolithic and Neolithic "Mother" figure, on through the image, the idol, the funeral image offered in lieu of human sacrifice, and finally to the expiatory wax figure.[23] Condescending to the "primitive" practices that remain hidden in the history of the modern doll, Boehn and Early express an obvious ethnocentrism that now dates their work, yet their approach reminds us how, in the wake of the Enlightenment, we have had few choices but to see the doll as taking us *backwards* to an earlier time in our human development: under modern psychoanalysis, the doll evokes the uncanny, which itself entails the return to an earlier moment in our psycho-sexual development.[24] However, here I propose that the appearance of the modern wax baby doll be considered not as a regressive inclination, but as a forward movement—in other words, as a creative recycling—which effectively isolated the magical thinking associated with the votive object and carried it *forward* into modernity.

As Juliette Peers points out, the "baby doll" as an infant is "anomalous in the total oeuvre of the European doll." In fact, "throughout earlier periods the adult fashionable doll was the norm."[25] The relatively rare, late eighteenth-century appearance of the wax baby doll most likely owed its genesis to the immigration of wax modellers from the continent, who turned skills that had once been used to create ecclesiastical objects towards the manufacture of secular things. Some—Peers among them—even see resemblance between "the idealized angel and cherubs from wax portraits and funerary effigies" and early wax dolls, and indeed the connection is close, as we will see.[26] The appearance of the wax baby doll, alongside other realistic playthings, participates in a "consumer revolution" that is commonly said to have occurred during the eighteenth century. As such, wax dolls belong to a proliferating catalogue of consumer items—the many "things," including clocks, china, furniture, fashionable clothing, even shaving equipment—that have drawn the attention of historians of the era.[27] Yet dolls are, of course, a particular kind of consumer item, with special cultural work to perform. There is good reason to link the appearance of the wax baby to the rise of an earlier, vast body of didactic literature insisting on the link between femininity and maternity. Roughly contemporaneous with medical treatises promoting maternal breast-feeding as the cornerstone of efficacious motherhood, perhaps the eighteenth-century wax baby doll encouraged young girls to imagine themselves at the scene of nurturing.[28]

To be sure, small children had long played at nurturing babies before the eighteenth century and the idea of the "baby" as plaything was scarcely new: the common use of the word "baby" for any doll, regardless of type, during the early modern period implies that many objects were often imagined as newborns. In addition, any object can stand in for a baby and an active imagination can animate any object.[29] However, before the eighteenth century, fashion dolls were the only manufactured dolls. Made by organised craft guilds, these dolls were highly stylised, with flattened faces devoid of individual expression and roughly fashioned torsos and limbs.[30] In fact, they were not dolls per se; rather they were adult objects—mini mannequins—used to convey important sartorial information. Perhaps some of these dolls, their usefulness over, were recycled as they found their way into the hands of children where they might be animated as ladies.

To inquire further about the significance of the wax baby doll, it is helpful to reflect on the nature of the doll as a mimetic object and to distinguish the different kinds of cultural work that can be performed by a doll: to what extent does a doll imitate human life? On what level does the mimesis occur? In the case of the fashion doll, the imitation occurs largely through the clothing: in this kind of mimesis, the doll's face is often highly stylised and relatively unimportant. Indeed the faces of wooden dolls tend to be painted to one common standard, regardless of the designated gender or age of the doll. The torso itself can also be unrealistic, reflecting not an actual human form, but a fashionable shape, in accordance with current understandings of the ideal. As a mimesis, the eighteenth-century fashion doll carried important messages about style and the nature of female subjectivity.[31] The fashion doll was, then, the appropriate toy for an age when status was to be telegraphed through the elaborate clothing of the female body. In the famous instance of Marie Antoinette's doll, visible in a 1762 portrait, the future queen not only imitates the far too grown-up fashion of her doll, but she also presages her own future role as living doll, as Caroline Weber's biography suggests.[32]

In other words, the mimetic work of the fashion doll distinguishes itself from the mimetic work of other dolls not by animating an interior life, but by featuring clothing that relates a story of how human life is lived through material practice. For example, fashion dolls commonly reflect the reality of a specific time and place through their various outfits, each one meant to convey something about an occasion for which the costume would be worn. In the case of fashion dolls, the body underneath the clothes is often both undeveloped and distorted. The hips of the dolls, for instance, are unnaturally wide, facilitating the sideways drape of the pannier. The doll itself (not unlike the modern Barbie doll) is largely an armature on which the telling potential of female fashion is to be hung.

Figure 10.3 Lord and Lady Clapham Dolls, wood, 1690–1700. Acc. No. T.846–1974 & T.847–1974. © Victoria & Albert Museum, London.

To be sure, some dolls from the earlier periods dolls do appear to be alive: the wooden dolls of Lord and Lady Clapham, for instance, which reside in the Victoria and Albert Museum (Figure 10.3), can be said to have personalities despite the relatively flat design of their features.[33]

But their connection to reality is still largely a function of their many outfits. Tiny gloves or miniature accessories, a sword, an amazingly precise mask with its bead to be held in a miniature doll mouth, stimulate the imagination and help animate the wooden forms, as the dolls appear to have places to go and ceremonies to attend—a life, as it were, elsewhere. Or, as Susan Stewart writes, miniature objects convey the daydream "that the world of things can open itself to reveal a secret life—indeed to reveal a set of actions and hence narrativity and history outside the given field of perception."[34] In the case of Lord and Lady Clapham both story and history are to be accessed through dress, as dress assigns them a place in a wider circle where, in a sort of parallel universe, they will be recognised as "real," through their clothes. The fact that their outfits (which the visitor views by pulling open a display case under the dolls) can be changed or adjusted—day wear to night wear, mask no mask—gives their story a narrative dimension. Although their frozen, painted faces give nothing away, their clothing places them in different imaginative settings and allows them to come alive.

In contrast to the fashion dolls, the baby doll shifts the focus of the mimesis from the clothing to the baby's face. This shift occurs when wax modellers begin to apply their skills, once applied to the ex-voto, to the making of playthings. In effect, the spiritual magic that had once been associated with the ex-voto was recycled into the form of the baby doll, with its realistic representation of a human face. A wax baby doll at the Victoria and Albert Museum of Childhood, dated at 1790–1805, provides one of the earliest examples of how the ex-voto evolved into a toy. This doll is unusual because it clearly intends to imitate an actual human infant: it has a small, delicate, well-proportioned face. Its mouth is detailed to show the hint of teeth and tongue; its hands and feet are well defined (Figure 10.2). Though its form does not perfectly reproduce an infant body, it nonetheless generally mimics a human physiology: its symmetrical shape, made out of soft cloth, is proportionate and relatively undistorted. Here the mimesis occurs in several places simultaneously—in the face that resembles a baby's, in its recognisably human form, and in its removable clothing that is a miniature version of actual baby dress. Here too wax is being used successfully to create the illusion of flesh. Its surface—as Marina Warner suggested is characteristic of wax—does indeed hold the light and give off an inner glow. Unlike the painted surface of a wooden doll, this doll's face has depth and provides the illusion of mysterious interiority. This wax face of a baby does seem to be both incorruptible and beyond time.

This wax doll moves us forward towards the recognition that the "infant" embodies a discrete moment of development, further testifying to the work of historians like Philip Ariès.[35] It also preserves its relationship to the votive object, as seen in its deep and soulful gaze within the realistic simulacrum of a human face. As a thing that retains its own thingness, the wax baby doll evokes "something" that proves elusive. Its gaze challenges the boundaries of selfhood by eliciting a series of possible emotions—tenderness, perhaps, or vulnerability. Unlike the stiff bodies of Lord and Lady Clapham, bodies that ask only to be posed in different ways, the body of the baby doll inspires interactive play. Where Lord and Lady Clapham tempt the mind to range over a series of social settings, the baby doll encourages the imagination to nurse the baby into life. Most importantly of all, it elicits human touch, and the importance of this invitation should not be underestimated. At a historical moment when, as Barbara Stafford quips, the bodily-kinaesthetic was "damned to the bottom of the Cave of humanities" or when the somatic was being systematically downgraded in favour of visual paradigms, the magic of the wax baby doll requires the deployment of other human senses.[36] In its invitation to smell and touch, and in its mock embodiment, it interrupts the wider Enlightenment tendency, as identified by Stafford, "to collapse the experience of the body into an assemblage of its projected optical effects."[37]

Looking at the wax baby in relation to the "Don" allows us to imagine how, in the moment when the artistry associated with the wax votive was recycled into the plaything, something more than technique was transferred—namely a spiritual investment in the idea of magical objects with the power to transcend death. As a recycled version of the ex-voto, the wax baby doll offers us an especially acute example of the power of mimesis. It appears at the moment when wax used in other hyperrealistic representations—the anatomical figure and the popular waxwork—also reaches an apotheosis. These other two uses of wax—the first to freeze the human body, to flay it, and to open it up to scientific inspection, the second similarly to immobilise human motion, to arrange it in all its peculiarities and to subject it to human curiosity—also engage in the art of copying. However, while the first representation banishes magic under the banner of scientific objectivism, the second circumscribes magic by relegating it to a popular spectacle known as "celebrity." Neither kind of wax representation invites or encourages sensual contact with an object to be held, cradled, or nursed into animation. Unlike the popular waxwork, the wax doll requires human touch to animate it. Unlike the anatomical dummy, it resists being dissected. Pull the baby apart, examine its sinews, and the point of the toy evaporates.

Unlike other uses of wax, the use of wax for the baby doll thus distinctively initiates and preserves the possibilities for mimetic play at a moment when such play was increasingly subject to legislation and control.[38] Yet child's play—and in particular playing with dolls—remains unpoliced or unregulated. With its connections to the ex-voto, the wax baby doll harkens back to a time of magical images, a world where the "dead" wax object interceded for the live human body. It thereby retains the agency once granted to certain kinds of objects, possessing a quality that is neither entirely rational nor subject to articulation. As a simulacrum of a living organism, the wax doll preserves an investment in the power of sacred objects to mend, heal, and restore. The wax baby doll is both human and not human: it mimics and reflects back to us a representation of our own transient existence.

This chapter has explored a singular history of recycling by considering how the deep spiritual practices associated with wax in forms that imitate the human body—and that were believed to extend its agency—were carried forward into the modern period. The early modern ceroplastic tradition would continue to evolve into the age of modernity, finding importance in both in medical science and popular culture. But the wax doll, as neither a medical specimen nor a life-size waxwork, would uniquely preserve the opportunity to encounter a "thing" with the capacity to awaken deep human sentiments. The wax baby doll deserves to be acknowledged, then, as more than a toy that helped little girls to imagine themselves as mothers, and its significance lies beyond the history of childhood. Consigned to the hands of little girls, the wax doll afforded an extraordinary power of creation—the ability to bring life out of what is apparently dead. It granted to the least powerful citizens the most enthralling command, making their play into most extraordinary work.

NOTES

1. I am grateful to curator Noreen Marshall, who first shared the Don and his history with me. This object, which is not currently on display in the museum, bears the listing "Lady Alwyne Compton File" (T. 239–1917) in the archives of the Victoria and Albert Museum. According to the unidentified writer of the note in the file, "About a hundred years ago or more, it was left at the 'Fountain Inn' at Canterbury by "some furriners" [sic] (which is very vague, isn't it?) They said that they would call for it but they never returned. It has passed from hand to hand during the last century and has been in the possession of my great aunt." Not immediately recognised for its value as a doll but prized for the needlework on the clothing, the Don was accepted by the textiles department of the V& A on 17 October 1917.
2. Item 750:1–1992 Caroline Serra, vendor 92/1294 (1790–1805 "large baby doll"). Victoria & Albert Museum.
3. Georges Didi-Huberman, "Wax Flesh, Vicious Circles," in *Encyclopedia Anatomica: A Complete Collection of Anatomical Waxes* (New York: Taschen, 1999), 65, 66. Michelle Bloom, *Waxworks: A Cultural Obsession* (Minneapolis: University of Minnesota, 2003), 265.
4. Marina Warner, "Waxworks and Wonderlands," in *Visual Display: Culture Beyond Appearances*, ed. Lynne Cooke and Peter Wollen (Seattle: Bay Press, 1995), 187.
5. Idem.
6. Didi-Huberman, "Wax Flesh, Vicious Circles," 155.
7. René Descartes, *Philosophical Writing,* trans. Norman Kemp Smith (New York: Modern Library, 1958), 190–91.
8. Georges Didi-Huberman, "Viscosities and Survivals: Art History Put to Test by the Material," in *Ephemeral Bodies: Wax Sculpture and the Human Figure*, ed. Roberta Panzanelli (Los Angeles: Getty Research Institute, 2008), 154–55.
9. Didi-Huberman, "Viscosities and Survivals," 155.
10. Roberta Panzanelli, "Compelling Presence: Wax Effigies in Renaissance Florence," in *Ephemeral Bodies*, 30.
11. Ibid., 31.
12. Didi-Huberman, "Wax Flesh, Vicious Circles," 64; Maria Grazia Vaccari, "Wax," in *Encyclopedia of Sculpture* (New York: Fitroy Dearborn, 2004), Vol. 3, 1750.
13. Julius Von Schlosser, *Histoire du portrait en cire*, 1997. Reprinted in English in *Ephemeral Bodies*, trans. James Michael Loughbridge, 175–80.
14. Panzanelli, "Compelling Presence," 15. The "boti" appear to be related to the Westminster waxes, analyzed by Joseph Roach in his article "Celebrity

Erotics: Pepys, Performance, and Painted Ladies," *Yale Journal of Criticism* 16 (2003): 211–30.

15. Schlosser, Figure 26; Marina Warner, *Phantasmagoria* (Oxford: Oxford University Press, 2006), 23.
16. Kenneth and Marguerite Faudry, *Pollock's History of English Dolls and Toys*, researched by Deborah Brown (London: Ernest Benn, 1979), 191.
17. Lucia Dacome, "Women, Wax and Anatomy in the Century of Things," *Renaissance Studies* 21 (2007): 541.
18. See Thomas N. Haviland and Lawrence Charles Parish, "A Brief Account of the Use of Wax Models in the Study of Medicine," *Journal of the History of Medicine and Applied Science* 25 (1970): 52–75; Marta Pioggesi, "The Wax Figure Collection in 'La Specola' in Florence," in *A Collection of Anatomical Waxes*, ed. Petra Lamers-Schutze and Yvonne Havertz (Cologne: Tashcen, 2006), 6–25; and Peter K. Knoefel, "Florentine Anatomical Models in Wax and Wood," *Medicina nei Secoli* (Rome: Institute for the History and Medicine, 1978), 329–41.
19. See Rebecca Messbarger, *The Lady Anatomist: The Life and Work of Anna Morandi Manzolini* (Chicago: University of Chicago Press, 2010) and Beth Kowaleski Wallace, "Representing the Corporal 'Truth' in the Work of Anna Morandi," in *Women and the Material Culture of Death*, ed. Beth Fowkes Tobin and Maureen Goggin (Burlington, VT: Ashgate Press, 2013), 283–210.
20. As Kate Berridge writes, a printed catalogue for Tussaud's collection in 1819 contained the assertion that "the [revolutionaries] carried the bleeding head [of Louis XVI] to Madame Tussaud, and ordered her to take a model of it which dreadful order more dead than alive she dared not refuse to obey," in *Madame Tussaud, A Life In Wax* (New York: HarperCollins, 2006), 140. See also Pamela Pilbeam, *Madame Tussaud and the History of Waxwork* (London: Hambledon and London, 2003).
21. See Barbara Maria Stafford, *Body Criticism: Imaging the Unseen in Enlightenment Art and Medicine* (Cambridge, MA: MIT Press, 1994), 103.
22. Max von Bœhn, *Dolls and Puppets*, trans. Josephine Nicoll (London: George G Harrap & Company Ltd.,1932).
23. Alice K. Early. *English Dolls, Effigies, and Puppets* (London: B. T. Batesford, 1955), 18.
24. See Julie Park, "Unheimlich Maneuvers: Enlightenment Dolls and Repetitions in Freud" *The Eighteenth century* 44 (2003): 45–68; Kitti Carriker, *The Miniature body of the Doll as Subject and Object* (Bethlehem, PA: Lehigh University Press, 1998); and Eva-Maria Simms, "Uncanny Dolls: Images of Death in Rilke and Freud," *New Literary History* 27 (1996): 663–77.
25. Juliette Peers, *The Fashion Doll from Bébé Jumeau to Barbie* (New York: Berg, 2004), 104, 122.
26. Ibid., 104.
27. McKendrick and Brewer.
28. On the rise of maternal discourse in the eighteenth century, see Elizabeth Kowaleski-Wallace, *Their Fathers' Daughters* (New York: Oxford University Press, 1991), chapter 4.
29. In a famous sociological study done in 1897, G. Stanley Hall and A. Caswell Ellis reported a range of substitute objects used by children as if they were dolls. Surprisingly, pillows were the most often reported items, followed by bottles, dogs, cats and kittens, clothespins, flowers—and even a piece of porterhouse steak! *A Study of Dolls* (New York: E.L. Kellogg & Co.: 1897), 8–9.

30. Caroline Goodfellow, *The Ultimate Doll Book*. (London: Dorling Kindersley, 1993), 10–11.
31. See Julie Park, *The Self and It: Novel Objects in Eighteenth-Century England* (Palo Alto: Stanford University Press, 2009), 79–122.
32. Caroline Weber, *Queen of Fashion* (New York: Picador, 2006), 14.
33. Lord and Lady Clapham Dolls, 1690–1700. T. 847–1974. Victoria and Albert Collections.
34. Susan Stewart, *On Longing: Narratives of the Miniature, the Gigantic, the Souvenir, the Collection* (Durham, NC: Duke University Press, 2005).
35. Philip Ariès, *Centuries of Childhood* (New York: Vintage Books, 1965).
36. Stafford, *Body Criticism*, 2.
37. Ibid., 28.
38. See Max Horkheimer and Theodor Adorno, *Dialectic of Enlightenment*, trans. Edmund Jephcott (Palo Alto: Stanford University Press, 2007).

Part III

Textual Recyclings

11 Inventive Mendicancy, Thrift, and Extravagance Manifested in Recirculated Material in an Eighteenth-Century Library

W. G. Day

Libraries such as the Fellows' Library at Winchester College, which has been accumulating books for over six hundred years, are model recycling units. Though in common parlance the notion of recycling has come to mean "to return (material) to a previous stage of a cyclic process"[1] there are alternative interpretations. The recycling effect seen in a library is generally a partial demonstration of the sense "to reuse." Books, and associated material, in a library are thus subject to these several definitions of recycling as the present chapter will attempt to illustrate.

The recataloguing of Winchester's Fellows' Library has entailed a meticulous search and survey of all readable material, and the numbering of all elements of the collection, including, in addition to books and manuscripts, papyri, boxes, and such oddities as a canopic urn for an ibis, given in 1764. Such detailed work—started in 2008 and estimated to be finished by the end of 2013—allows for some fascinating discoveries concerning the state, usage, and history of books over the course of several centuries. Thanks to the new catalogue, even fragments now have their own catalogue numbers—illuminated manuscript fragments, and the vellum and paper reinforcing strips which have been cut from earlier manuscripts, are now carefully collected and catalogued, as evidence of the "history of the book."

The present chapter therefore attempts to map recycling practices in the specific context of an extensive—in time as well as content—library, a topic that has seldom if ever been investigated. Recycling has always been a feature of libraries over the centuries, but this chapter will focus on a single library in a specific century to make the scope of the argument more manageable. The various types of recycling that are discernible in the library are variously enacted by readers as they donate or bequeath books; as they circulate the individual volumes that they read, sometimes leaving traces of their reading; by the authors themselves, or by the librarians, booksellers, and those in allied trades, such as bookbinding, who sometimes find their positions ambiguous, poised between destruction and preservation.

THE METATEXTUAL CHAIN OF READERS' NOTES AND RECYCLING

In the same way that donations to charity shops are a form of recycling, the books are given a new lease of life by acquiring possible new readers. In the library, readers' notes and bookmarks are two kinds of waste which history has recycled into valuable primary sources as evidence of reading rather than mere ownership. As part of the recataloguing programme, it has been decided wherever possible to record details of provenance, and what has become clear is that well over 80 percent of the collection is the result of gift or bequest, and in many cases of books which had themselves been the result of gift or bequest. As a typical example, for instance, there is a 1744 edition of James Thomson's *Seasons*. Inscriptions on the free endpaper indicate that this copy was given by the author, James Thomson, to Joseph Spence, an Old Wykehamist whose *Essay on Pope's 'Odyssey'* of 1726 brought him the lifelong friendship of Alexander Pope, while his theory of beauty as propounded in his *Polymetis* of 1747 brought him considerable wealth. Spence in turn gave the book to Thomas Henry Lowth, another Old Wykehamist and the son of Robert Lowth, the Bishop of London and grammarian. The volume was then acquired by the Reverend Peter Hall, the most indefatigable of collectors of wiccamical association copies and presented to the library in 1815.[2] There are many such examples where the chain of ownership and reuse can be thus traced.

Some texts are recycled in a different capacity. Loosely inserted into a copy of John Field's large folio two-volume Bible, printed in Cambridge in 1659–1660,[3] is to be found a unique and unrecorded copy of a printed bifolium headed: "London; January 1, 1781": this is an unsigned letter to "My Lord" which provides a synopsis of Benjamin Kennicott's "The general dissertation on the Hebrew Old Testament"; it has relevant page numbers added in the margins in ink. The reference here is to Benjamin Kennicott's *Dissertatio generalis in vetus testamentum Hebraicum; cum variis lectionibus, ex codicibus manuscriptis et impressis*.[4] This text has become a bookmark and appears to have survived as the only extant copy precisely because of having been recycled in this practical fashion. The Library subscribed to Kennicott's *Vetus testamentum Hebraicum, cum Variis Lectionibus. Edidit Benjaminus Kennicott, S.T.P. Aedes Christi Canonicus, et Bibliothecarius Radclivianus*,[5] and was bound in half calf and dark blue paper covered boards matching a copy of the *Dissertatio*. It appears to be a matter of pure chance that the bifolium is also in the collection, thus providing a unique record of levels of metatext.

The line of ownership and the material practices that books reveal also provide an invaluable facet to the investigation of eighteenth-century readership, its cultural codes, trends, or individual eccentricities. Readers often leave their marks of ownership on or in books, adding one more metatext—one more semantic layer, or occasion for deciphering—to an already multilayered artefact. Bookmarks or letters found within books may be considered as another form of palimpsest, as the bifolium bookmark has a noticeable effect on the reading experience of the book wherein it was inserted. Thus the mere presence of the former is inevitably a comment on the latter.

THE AUTHOR AS INVENTIVE MENDICANT

But within the library it is not only texts which are recycled. Elkanah Settle was an intermittently successful playwright and the Official Poet to the City of London between 1691 and 1708. From 1699 until his death in 1724 he supplemented his income by writing an increasing number of commendatory poems. Most of them were written in rhymed heroic verse, and some reworked similar lines for a range of occasions. F. C. Brown possibly the only scholar ever to have read Settle's complete works, observed: "Settle used many lines again and again in his eulogistic poems. When he hit upon what seemed to him a happy figure of speech he introduced it into perhaps a half-dozen different pieces. This repetition is most noticeable in his wedding-poems; in the three of these that I compared carefully two-thirds of the lines are common to all"[6]—arguably the most blatant of all examples of an author recycling his own work.

Settle made a practice of having copies specially bound with the individual arms of prospective patrons, to whom the volume would be sent in the hopes of financial return.[7] The Winchester copy of Settle's *A Pindaric Poem, on the Propagation of the Gospel in Foreign Parts, a Work of Piety, so Zealously Recommended and Promoted by Her Most Gracious Majesty* is bound in sheepskin over paste boards.[8] There is a gold-tooled rolled border with a decorative corner emblem, all surrounding an unidentified armorial-bearing stamped with individual tools (Figure 11.1).

We know that the bearer of these arms was a woman, as the arms are in a lozenge rather than a shield, and presumably she responded to Settle's approach. One can make a similar assumption about the acceptance of the copy of Settle's *A Funeral Poem to the Memory of the Honourable Sir John Buckworth, Kt and Bt*,[9] which has gold-tooled rolls with corner thistle emblems and a central coat of arms (**Figure 11.2**).

Settle comes across as a particularly opportunistic authorial or entrepreneurial figure, whose books were a commodity to be reworked and redistributed until such time as they generated an appropriate pecuniary benefit to himself.

Though these are known as "Settle" bindings, there is some evidence to suggest that Settle was not the only hack attempting to boost his income in this fashion. Winchester has a slim volume which contains three texts: William Harison's *Woodstock Park. A Poem*,[10] and two works by John Philips, *Blenheim, a Poem* and *The Splendid Shilling. An Imitation of Milton*.[11] The

Figure 11.1 Winchester copy of Elkanah Settle's *A Pindaric Poem, on the Propagation of the Gospel in Foreign Parts, a Work of Piety, so Zealously Recommended and Promoted by Her Most Gracious Majesty* (London: printed for the Author, 1721 [Bk8797]). Reproduced by permission of the Warden and Fellows of Winchester College.

binding is goatskin over paste boards. There is a single fine decorative rolled border around two typical seventeenth-century rolls, the outer with decorative corner pieces, the inner with rather clumsy combinations of skull and crossbones and a winged hourglass; all around a central crest surrounded by volutes, with a crown, a drawer handle, an inverted floral design, a winged cherub, and another skull and crossbones. Though none of these works is by Settle, the volume has all the hallmarks of a Settle binding, particularly the rather clumsily executed and entirely unsubtle *memento mori* decoration. Some of Settle's targets are known to have declined his advances and the book itself was returned, and there are copies of Settle's works where the

Figure 11.2 Elkanah Settle, *A Funeral Poem to the Memory of the Honourable Sir John Buckworth, Kt and Bt* (London: Printed for J. King at the Bible and Crown in Little-Britain, 1709 [Bk8798]). Reproduced by permission of the Warden and Fellows of Winchester College.

central armorial device has been cut out and replaced with those of another possible gull.[12] A close-up of the arms on this sammelband demonstrates the practice—the central shield on both boards of the latter has been (fairly neatly) replaced (Figures 11.3 and 11.4).

Close examination of the binding shows that the endpapers were replaced in the eighteenth century, and, bearing in mind that the decoration does not suit any of the texts bound within, an alternative explanation is that this was originally a Settle binding on a Settle poem, which was recycled from one prospective owner to another, and subsequently the binding itself was recycled and used to case this little collection of poems.

Figure 11.3 and Figure 11.4 Close-ups of the arms on the sammelband, of the central shield on both boards. Reproduced by permission of the Warden and Fellows of Winchester College.

The re-presentation of the individual copies of Settle's poems may thus seem as infinite as his opportunism. Through the manifold recycling of his works, what he created appears to be less a content than an endlessly variable form, as the poems he crafted mattered less than their bindings, decorations, and coats of arms; the putative benefactors Settle targeted being the sole *raison d'être* of the artefact. Thus, whether one considers books as contents or containers, a library may be said to keep track of the history of books or of their bindings, which reveal far more than may be expected about their readers and authors. The recycling of books in this particularly material and superficial regard provides fresh perspectives for the investigation of literary—and predominantly commercial—practices in the eighteenth century.

THRIFT IN THE BOOKSHOP AND BINDERY

Yet neither readers nor authors were the main driving force behind the practices of book recycling. From the earliest times recycling has been a fundamental feature of the manufacture of printed books. Very rapidly manuscripts and even certain types of printed materials were regarded as outmoded and were broken up and used as binders' waste both as endpapers and as reinforcements to the sewing. Neil Ker, in his seminal study of medieval manuscripts used as endpapers in Oxford bindings,[13] identified a surprising number of books in which this particular form of recycling had taken place. Clearly this is not a practice confined to the medieval period.

Winchester has evidence of an interesting variant on this practice. The Fellows' Library has six boxes which were constructed in the eighteenth century to hold specific legal documents relating to land the college owned. The bases and flat tops are made from rough-cut pine, which have then been attached using horn glue to side pieces which, on close inspection, prove to be made of thin laths of beech glued together to form a primitive plywood. The maker of these boxes was clearly using off-cuts of wood from another trade, possibly shipwrighting or wheelwrighting. Recycling is evident at every point. These simple wooden boxes were then covered with sheepskin, thus making very sturdy containers, some of which were secured by a strip of alum-tawed goatskin, used as a fastening. They were almost certainly made to order in the local stationer's shop, behind which there had been built a bindery. The bindery is still functioning in that building and still has a number of the eighteenth-century tools and one of the earliest known sample books of binding ornaments.

The pine is very rough-cut, and in order to protect the documents the interiors were lined with what, if they were books, would be called binders' waste, and this provides interesting evidence of the loose sheets which accumulated in an eighteenth-century provincial bookshop and bindery. Not all of the material has been identified. Content allows the researcher to limit the scope of the search, and running titles are further signposts, but even then there can be a surprisingly large number of candidates. For example, one of the texts is an account of the Babington Plot of 1586, which led directly to the execution of Mary, Queen of Scots, a major historical event which was written about extensively and frequently. This appears to be from an eighteenth-century text, but as yet it has not proved possible to identify the specific work. One of the other linings has proved more susceptible to identification. This lining sheet was taken from *The Lightless Starre: or, Mr. John Goodwin Discovered a Pelagio-Socinian: and This by the Examination of His Preface to His Book Entituled Redemption Redeemed. Together with an Answer to His Letter Entituled Confidence Dismounted. By Richard Resbury, Minister of the gospel at Oundle in Northampton-Shire. Hereunto Is Annexed a Thesis of that Reverend, Pious, and Judicious Divine, Doctor Preston, sometimes of Immanuel College in Cambridge, Concerning the Irresistibility of Converting Grace*. Rather surprisingly, given its title, which suggests a somewhat limited audience, this went to two editions, and these sheets are from the second.[14] Though this text ran to a second edition, it clearly did not sell out and the sheets may well have been sitting in the shop for the best part of a century before being employed as waste.

One of the more unusual pieces of waste found in these boxes is from a French commentary on the Psalms, which has not been identified. The importance of this is what it tells us about an eighteenth-century English provincial bookshop: at a period of English history during which Roman Catholics were viewed with considerable suspicion as the fomenters of plots against the Hanoverian monarchy, this appears to have been thought a title which would be of interest to the shop's customers in Winchester, the site of one of the most important Anglican cathedrals in the country, presumably on the principle of know-thine-enemy. As it is, the text does not allow us to conjecture when it might have been recycled. All we can say is that it was reused at some point during the eighteenth century. Since we have no clue as to its date of publication or acquisition by the Library, the intended reading public of such pieces and the motivation underlying its purchase by the bookshop, remain a mystery.

The most tantalising of the fragments preserved in this fashion is also still to be identified. In the largest of the boxes there is a remarkable large side-grain decorative woodcut inside the lid, together with a cut lining the base of three rather crudely drawn portraits with accompanying initials: DY, GM, and ML (Figure 11.5).

DY is the Duke of York, subsequently King James II; GM is George Monck, first Duke of Albemarle, who managed to fight for Charles I, Oliver Cromwell, and Charles II and was thus clearly a survivor. ML, clearly a woman, is something of a mystery. The only female with these initials to be found in a trawl of the Oxford Dictionary of National Biography for the post-Restoration period is Mary Lee, the actress who may, or may not, have been married to Sir Charles Slingsby—and there seems no reason to connect

Figure 11.5 Portraits with accompanying initials: DY, GM, and ML. Part of the lining of one of six Fellows' Library eighteenth-century boxes made to hold specific legal documents relating to land the college owned. Reproduced by permission of the Warden and Fellows of Winchester College.

her to either of the dukes.[15] The source of these portraits is unknown, but the quality of the paper suggests a single sheet broadside. If so, then this is likely to be another unique item. The surrounding text is from another as yet unidentified work. There has, of course, been a good deal of research, though rather dispersed, on binder's waste to be found in bindings. Antiquarian booksellers draw attention to such occurrences, and bibliographers use blogs to discuss the matter,[16] but there appears to have been virtually no discussion of waste used other than in bindings, not even in *Factotum*, the erstwhile newsletter of the eighteenth-century Short Title Catalogue, which dealt with a remarkable range of ephemeral examples of eighteenth-century printing.

EXTRAVAGANT DESTRUCTION

Perhaps the most remarkable instance in the Winchester Fellows' Library of an eighteenth-century manifestation of recycling is to be found in a manuscript Bible[17] which Walter Oakeshott described using the adjective "magnificent."[18] And indeed Ker thought it to be unique in that it is a fifteenth-century Bible which appears to have been written in England.[19] It must have been written early in that century as it appears in the inventory of 1433 as "Biblia cathenata"—the chained Bible.[20]

No longer chained—it was rebound in 1912—it is nonetheless a very distinguished volume, standing fifty-two centimetres tall; and the quality of the illumination, as seen in the initial to "Cantate Domine" in the Book of Psalms, is excellent, as is the rubrication. Though Oakeshott used the adjective "magnificent" to describe this volume, sadly he followed this compliment with the noun "wreck." "A magnificent wreck." Viewing the opening on which is found the initial to "Cantate Domine" it can be seen that another illuminated initial has been relatively neatly excised. This is not always the case: some of the initials have been removed by a real botcher (Figure 11.6).

James Willoughby, in his forthcoming British Academy volume on secular medieval libraries, records that Winchester is by far the most comprehensively and frequently catalogued such library in England. These lists reveal that the "magnificent wreck" became a wreck between 1697 and 1839. There were originally one hundred and forty five illuminated initials: there remains one. The manuscript is generally thought to have been reduced to this state by the college porters, during the long eighteenth century, who snipped out the initials to give to visitors as souvenirs. Cutting out souvenirs from a medieval manuscript had thus less to do with owning a small, yet material part of the library collection—a metonymy-like gesture—than with leaving Winchester with a pretty picture to remember the school by, rather than its books.

Whether these visitors were visiting the College as an institution, or specifically the Library, cannot be determined. It is known that British Grand Tourists visited libraries on their continental peregrinations: Samuel Johnson in his notes on his trip to Paris in 1775 recorded, "Oct. 24. Tuesday. We visited the King's library—I saw the *Speculum humanae Salvationis* [. . .], Thence to the Sorbonne.—The library very large, not in lattices like the King's [. . .] Oct. 30. Monday. We saw the library of St. Germain.—A very noble collection";[21] and Christopher Hibbert observes, that the Grand Tourist "was expected to see the theatre, of course (the largest in the world), the Brera Palace and the Ambrosian Library with its huge collection of books and manuscripts, its medals, antique sculpture and the mechanical drawings of Leonardo da Vinci, who had settled in Milan in 1482."[22] What is noteworthy is how little evidence there appears to be of library-visiting during this period, and this lacuna is not restricted to the Anglo-Saxon world. Roger

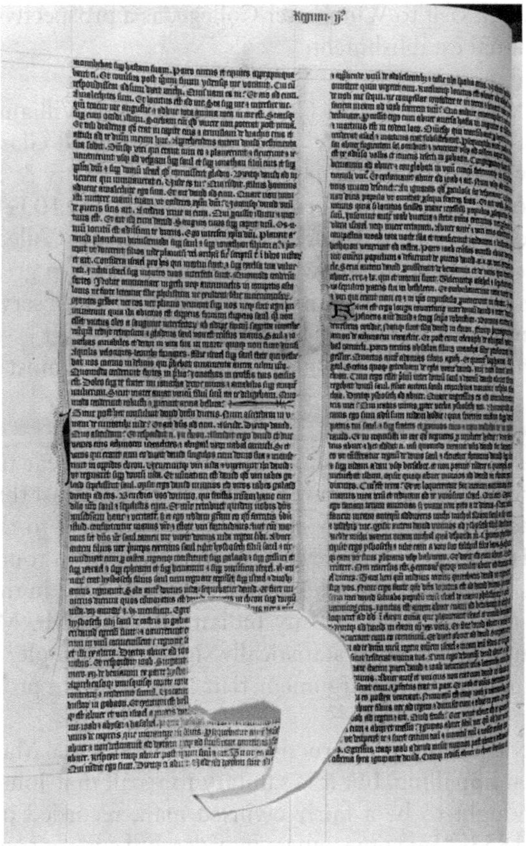

Figure 11.6 The Fellows' Library fifteenth-century Bible, written in England. Appears in the 1433 inventory as "Biblia cathenata"—the chained Bible. Reproduced by permission of the Warden and Fellows of Winchester College.

Chartier's *The Order of Books* deals admirably with the abstract concept of the library, but does not discuss the down-to-earth reality of visitors, presumably because of the paucity of evidence in this area.[23] "Library" does not even appear in the index of Peter Mandler's *The Fall and Rise of the Stately Home*; John Brewer, in his magisterial *The Pleasures of the Imagination: English Culture in the Eighteenth Century*, only considers circulating libraries; and in Robin Gard's survey of more than six hundred diaries of travellers in England, Wales, and Scotland held in the county record offices of England and Wales, references to libraries are conspicuous by their absence.[24] This is particularly noticeable in the account by John Ashburnham, first Earl of

Ashburnham, of a visit to Winchester College, as a prospective parent sizing up the educational establishment:

> After this we went to see the Colledge founded by William of Wykeham, There is a pretty Chappel & very good old painted Glasse Windowes, and a new School howse lately built extreamly pretty & convenient for that purpose They have a Warden underwarden and 10 Fellowes, and 60 or 70 Students, who are Chosen (when fitt) to New Colledge in Oxford, They have excellent Spring water in this Colledge in great abundance, and indeed the whole Town of Winchester is very well served with water, a River running through most of the Street Winchester is seated in a Bottom among the Hills and is one of the sweetest and most healthy places in Europe, I thinke to send my Sonne to School here.[25]

Even as a prospective parent Ashburnham does not appear to have considered the library worth a visit, or even a mention. Set against this one may put an almost exactly contemporary record of another visit to the College, on 25 February 1689, by Samuel Sewall, the first American tourist to Europe: "View'd Winchester Colledge, the Chapel, Library, built in the midst of the Green within the Cloisters. Left my Indian Bible and Mr. Mather's Letter there."[26] Though this is not a statistically significant sample, it may be that the evidence inclines to the argument that libraries, like prophets, are not valued in their own countries.[27]

The apparently wanton destruction of the Winchester Manuscript Bible may be thought appalling, but it is salutary to recall that John Ruskin, who is generally thought to be a fairly civilised man, recorded in his diary on 30 December 1853: "Set some papers in order and cut out some leaves from large missal; took me till 12 o'clock." And on 3 January 1854 he wrote: "Cut missal up in evening—hard work."[28] This, as Christopher de Hamel has pointed out, is a form of relic collecting and many libraries have fragments of medieval manuscripts as a result of this craze.[29] Perhaps the Winchester porters should not be too severely castigated for an exercise subsequently carried out by others supposedly more highly educated.

Though the activities of the eighteenth-century college porters may be regarded with a certain horror, librarians need to have a degree of pragmatism, an unsentimental materiality, in the treatment of the books under their care, which might be viewed similarly. Rather than simply accumulating and storing books, librarians must apply a certain ruthless application to the books of the requirements of space, reader demand, and commercial and material worth. Exigencies of space dictate that acquisitions and disposals policies be brought into operation: as recorded in his diary for 10 January 1668, Samuel Pepys famously got to the point where he decided he had to dispose of a similarly-sized volume whenever he acquired a new one.[30] That a library should play a destructive role in the histories of books and collections may seem paradoxical at first, yet materially necessary on second, and more sober, thoughts. One must not forget, however, that the selection process of sacrificed books will inevitably change over time, with the somewhat fickle evolution of cultural criteria. An interesting example of such variation may be found in Winchester with a twelfth-century manuscript of Palladius' *Philosophus de Agricultura*. This was bound, apparently when written, in a limp vellum cover which was part of an eighth-century manuscript of Rufinus' *Interpretatio S. Basili in Psalmo I.* Paradoxically this binding has now been removed and given its own binding, because its material worth has now been recognised. In this way a librarian may undo the well-meaning toil of his predecessors, by peeling away a protective layer and salvaging material previously regarded as inconsequential. Binding is a trade commonly considered to be protective of books, intended to add longevity to a volume by insulating it from dust, dampness and abrasion. Yet over the centuries libraries and binderies have used books and manuscripts to shield other books and manuscripts, defiling some volumes to preserve others. Libraries of long standing, as at Winchester, are historically and culturally important collections of palimpsests requiring decipherers as much as readers, testing the patience and flair of those who investigate its manifold, multilayered artefacts.[31]

NOTES

1. OED *recycle*, vb. I.1.a.
2. All manuscript and book numbers in this chapter refer to the Winchester Fellow's Library. James Thomson, *Seasons* (1744 [Bk9588]).
3. Bible, folio, 2 vols., (Cambridge: 1659–1660 [Bk129]).
4. Benjamin Kennicott, *Dissertatio generalis in vetus testamentum Hebraicum; cum variis lectionibus, ex codicibus manuscriptis et impressis* (Oxford: [no imprint but E Typographeo Clarendoniano], 1780).
5. Benjamin Kennicot, *Vetus testamentum Hebraicum, cum Variis Lectionibus. Edidit Benjaminus Kennicott, S.T.P. Aedes Christi Canonicus, et Bibliothecarius Radclivianus* (Oxford: E Typographeo Clarendoniano, 1776).
6. Frank Clyde Brown, *Elkanah Settle, His Life and Works* (Chicago: Chicago University Press, 1910), 109.
7. Settle bindings are discussed by W.E. Moss in three publications: "Elkanah Settle: The Armorial Binding Expert," *Book Collector's Quarterly* (1939): 722, 916, 1314; *A "Triumph" of Settle Bindings* (West Byfleet: W.E. Moss, 1938); and "Elkanah Settle," *Bodleian Library Review* (1944): 92–93. *Bookbinding in the British Isles Sixteenth to the Twentieth Century*, Maggs Bros Ltd, Catalogue 1212, part 1 (1996), 140–43, where Settle's binder is identified as either William Sparkes or George Chapman, predecessors of Christopher Chapman. Twenty-one Settle bindings are illustrated in the British Library Database of Bookbindings, see http://www.bl.uk/catalogues/bookbindings (accessed 9 July 2014), and there is an unusually magnificent example in *The Wormsley Library a Personal Selection by Sir Paul Getty, KBE* (London: published for the Wormsley Library, 1999), 144–45, item 57.
8. Elkanah Settle, *A Pindaric Poem, on the Propagation of the Gospel in Foreign Parts, a Work of Piety, so Zealously Recommended and Promoted by Her Most Gracious Majesty* (London: printed for the Author, 1721 [Bk8797]).

9. Elkanah Settle, *A Funeral Poem to the Memory of the Honourable Sir John Buckworth, Kt and Bt* (London: printed for J. King at the Bible and Crown in Little-Britain, 1709 [Bk8798]).
10. William Harison, *Woodstock Park. A Poem* (London: printed for Jacob Tonson, within Grays-Inn Gate next Grays-Inn Lane, 1706 [Bk4620]).
11. John Philips, *Blenheim, a Poem* (London: Printed for Tho. Bennet, at the Half-Moon in St. Paul's Church-Yard, 1705), *The Splendid Shilling. An Imitation of Milton* (London: Printed for Tho. Bennet, at the Half-Moon in St. Paul's Church-Yard, 1705).
12. There are two slightly different examples of this practice in the British Library collection, both copies of Elkanah Settle, *Eusebia Triumphans* (London: 1705), shelf-marks c67f14 and c67f15, where the coats of arms have been onlaid, probably covering an earlier, different coat of arms, rather than, as in the Winchester example, inlaid to replace arms which have been excised.
13. Neil R. Ker, *Pastedowns in Oxford Bindings with a Survey of Oxford binding c. 1515–1620*, NS Vol. V (Oxford: Oxford Bibliographical Society, 1954). Though one finds occasional references to seventeenth- and eighteenth-century examples of printed waste used in bindings in booksellers' catalogues, there does not appear to have been any extended study of this practice. For some examples of the various uses of waste see: http://libweb5.princeton.edu/visual_materials/hb/cases/bindingwaste/index.html (accessed 16 November 2012).
14. Richard Resbury, *The Lightless Starre* (London: Printed for John Wright at the Kings-Head in the Old-Bayly, 1652 [ESTC R18442]).
15. http://www.oxforddnb.com/view/article/25728?docPos=3 (accessed 16 November 2012)
16. See, e.g., http://antipodeanfootnotes.blogspot.com/2011/08/bound-but-not-forgotten-prospectuses-as.html (accessed 16 November 2012)
17. Manuscript Bible (MS28).
18. Walter Oakeshott, *Notes on the Medieval Manuscripts in Winchester College Library*, undated typescript in Librarian's office, 28.
19. Letter to Oakeshott, 3 February 1952, cited in Oakeshott's *Notes*, 28.
20. It was conventional in medieval libraries to chain books for security. The disadvantages were that books could only be consulted within the range of the chain: it was not possible to compare volumes which were, for example, in different book presses; and once a reader occupied a carrel no other reader could consult the adjacent texts. Most chained libraries started to de-chain their collections before the end of the seventeenth century. Winchester was very slow to do this: accounts show that chains were still being bought for the library in the eighteenth century and the books were not lettered (i.e. labelled on the spines following the removal of the chains and the repositioning of the books with the spine outwards) until 1747. See Walter Oakeshott, "Winchester College Library before 1750," in *The Library*, 5th series, vol. 9, no. 1 (March 1954), 3.
21. James Boswell, *Boswell's Life of Johnson*, edited by George Birkbeck Hill, revised and enlarged by L.F. Powell (Oxford: Clarendon Press, 1979), vol. 2, 397, 399.
22. Christopher Hibbert, *The Grand Tour* (London: Methuen, 1987), 114.
23. Roger Chartier, *The Order of Books: Readers, Authors and Libraries in Europe Between the Fourteenth and Eighteenth Centuries*, trans. Lydia G. Cochrane (Cambridge: Polity, 1994).
24. Peter Mandler, *The Fall and Rise of the Stately Home* (New Haven and London: Yale University Press, 1997), John Brewer, *The Pleasures of the Imagination: English Culture in the Eighteenth Century* (London: HarperCollins, 1997),

Robin Gard, ed., *The Observant Traveller: Diaries of Travel in England, Wales and Scotland in the County Record Offices of England and Wales* (London: HMSO, 1989).

25. Cited in Ibid., 14–15.
26. M. Halsey Thomas, ed., *The Diary of Samuel Sewall 1674–1729* (New York: Farrar, Straus and Giroux, 1973), Vol. 1, 197.
27. It might be worth noting that Jeremy Black in *The Grand Tour in the Eighteenth Century* has no reference to visits to libraries, which could suggest that Johnson is not a typical Tourist.
28. John Ruskin, *Diaries*, ed. Joan Evans and John Howard Whitehouse (Oxford: Clarendon Press, 1956–9), 486, 488; on 1 January 1854 Ruskin noted: "Put two pages of missal in frames," Ibid., 487.
29. Christopher De Hamel and Joel Silver, *Disbound and Dispersed: The Leaf Book Considered* (Chicago: Caxton Club, 2005). The library at Winchester has a folder of such fragments. See also J.J.G. Alexander, *Wallace Collection: Catalogue of Illuminated Manuscript Cuttings* (London: Trustees of the Wallace Collection, 1980).
30. "The truth is, I have bought a great many books lately, to a great value; but I think to buy no more till Christmas next, and these that I have will fill my two presses, that I must be forced to give away some to make room for them, it being my design to have no more at any time for my proper Library then to fill them." *The Diary of Samuel Pepys*, Robert Latham and William Matthews, eds. (London: G. Bell, 1970–87), vol. 9, 18.
31. I am grateful to the anonymous reviewers and to the editors of this volume for their helpful comments on an earlier version of this chapter. I must particularly thank Amélie Junqua for her patient and tactful advice.

12 Unstable Shades of Grey

Cloth and Paper in Addison's Periodicals

Amélie Junqua

> No Mortal Author, in the ordinary Fate and Vicissitude of Things, knows to what use his Works may, some time or other, be applied [. . .].
>
> (Joseph Addison, *Spectator*[1])

Paper is subjected to brutal changes—it is a versatile artefact, a material yet cultural object whose blank, unruffled surface belies the complexity of its nature. For the authors of the *Spectator* and *Tatler* the bonds uniting cloth, paper, and prose are far from simple. In the first column of *Spectator* 367 the reader encounters a carefully worded paragraph describing "Mean materials [. . .] wrought into Paper," then "Stained with News or Politicks."[2] These unnamed lowly products are precisely the subject of our study—the very matter of periodical prose, in the literal and figurative senses of the word. Joseph Addison, who penned this particular essay, is the only author in the group of contributors to the *Spectator* and *Tatler* to pay such explicit attention to the materiality of his work. By following the peregrinations of a single substance from the sheer whiteness of novelty to filth and obscurity, we shall ponder on the paradoxical reinvention of purity and dirt. If we agree with anthropologist Mary Douglas on dirt being "matter out of place" we may follow the displacement of paper as it shifts in space, acquires new shapes, colours, functions, and values.[3] The heap of rags, the vat of paper pulp, the gilded volume represent the successive aspects of one matter. They are the beginning and outcome of several recycling processes—of a complex circular journey. And as with any form of travel the question to be addressed remains the same: has anything been gained, or lost?

FROM FABRIC TO TEXT

Looking as far back as the thirteenth century one may observe how a chance evolution of taste fuelled the circulation of printed culture two centuries later.

> The first production of paper, as well as the printing press, Renaissance Humanism and the Modern period, were originally a matter of fashion.

> There would never have been enough cloth for the first paper mills nor enough paper for the new movable-type presses in the 15th century without a prior revolution that happened in an altogether different domain—a change in sartorial habits in the 13th century that suddenly popularised the taste for linen fabrics, the use of shirts and body linen.[4]

The coincidence and convenience of the process struck Addison no less deeply, and inspired him to devote a whole paragraph of *Spectator* 367, if not several other essays, to the phenomenon—what he himself describes as the "*Material* benefits" of the *Spectator*.

> Those Benefits which arise to the Publick from these my Speculations, as they consume a considerable quantity of our Paper Manufacture, employ our Artisans in Printing, and find Business for great Numbers of Indigent Persons.
>
> Our Paper Manufacture takes into it several mean Materials which could be put to no other use, and affords Work for several Hands in the collecting of them which are incapable of any other Employment. Those poor retailers, whom we see so busie in every Street, deliver in their respective Gleanings to the Merchant. The Merchant carries them in loads to the Paper-Mill, where they pass thro' a fresh Sett of Hands, and give Life to another Trade. Those who have mills on their Estates by this means considerably raise their Rents, and the whole Nation is in a great measure supplied with a Manufacture, for which formerly she was obliged to her Neighbours.[5]

The publication of this particular essay (1712) came at a time when England was enjoying a renewed production of paper—the beneficial consequences of Protestant migrations. After the revocation of the Edict of Nantes in 1685, highly qualified papermaking families had settled in the Netherlands and Germany, but also in England, close to urban centres and rivers, producing coarse brown or blue paper for manufacturing and industrial purposes. White paper was just starting to become an English commodity: "little paper of quality suitable for printing was made in England till the second decade of the eighteenth century, most of it until then being imported (directly or indirectly) from the Low countries, France, and Italy."[6] *Spectator* and *Tatler* papers were thus providing work for English papermills and were jointly printed in London by two publishers, Samuel Buckley for odd-numbered papers and Jacob Tonson for the even-numbered.

That material and body waste should turn into desirable matter, even a source of national profit and pride, that the "Indigent," "incapable," or "poor" should be turned into useful citizens almost equated papermaking with a form of magic. By using the word "magic," we mean to highlight how implicit pressures—i.e. visible through omissions, denial, and concealment—were at work in this description of the paper industry. A purely economic vision of papermaking cannot account for the wonder Addison expresses. As he leaps from nothingness to creation, from things "which could be put to no other Use" and people "which are incapable of any other employment" to the auspicious words of "Business" and "Life to another Trade," Addison ignores the dreary processes of purification that produced paper. If one excepts the epithet "mean," not a single adjective graces or disgraces the rags picked and collected. By contrast, the rag pickers are clearly ostracised by a double reference ("Indigent" and "poor retailers"). However, no such characterisation weighs on the "fresh Sett of Hands" working for the paper mills—the female workers who historians have shown were those washing and sorting out the rags are here given no individuality and their sex is not mentioned.

When one goes over the several processes of the paper manufacture, one cannot but notice how much knowledge—mainly feminine crafts—Addison prises away from the gaze of his readers. Linen or hemp fibres were scavenged from cast-off body and household linen—shirts, cravats, shifts, napkins, towels—or from the rags, ropes, and fragments of sails torn from disused ships. Their preparation was enacted by women, as it entailed traditionally female chores—washing and handling cloth stained with dirt. The process of washing was at that time close to a homely form of cooking, the rags being boiled or stewed over a number of hours with alkaline substances such as ashes. Dripping rags were then beaten and rinsed, dried, and whitened by exposure to the sun to obtain the whitest possible shade. The hems and seams were unpicked, buttons and hooks undone, leather, buttons, and other alien materials removed. Through these cleansing rituals requiring heat, water, and much toil, the grime and filth along with the status of rag were separated and shifted away from the cloth. All pieces, be they costly linen shirts or lowly towels, were democratically torn into large bandages, by the same "Sett of Hands" as above, before being minutely sorted out into categories depending on quality, thickness, and colour. In the early years of the eighteenth century—roughly when the Hollander beater was introduced in Great Britain—the rags were either beaten into a pulp by this same mechanical beater or else, in poorer and more traditional mills, submitted to a second preparation to ease up the process of pulp-making—eight to forty-two days of fermentation. In the dark confines of the paper mill, usually its cellar, dampened piles of rotting rags heated and softened up. The flaw of this second method was not its uncomfortable putridity but the fact that it produced a yellowish paper. Addison chose not to mention the menial and fetid trials rags had to undergo to become blank white paper. A frank description of the paper manufacture would have been outside the boundaries of taste—what may be properly and aesthetically perceived.

Yet one may find first-hand descriptions of papermaking processes elsewhere that do not shrink from mentioning most of the necessary processes, although olfactive perceptions are indeed omitted. The quotation below, an entry of John Evelyn's diary, tells of a visit to a paper mill in 1678—what is considered today as the first known account of a paper mill in England. Interestingly, papermaking is here also compared to a domestic craft: cooking and laundry-cleaning techniques.

> I went to see my L: St. Albon's house at Byfleete, an old large building; and thence to the Paper mills, where I found them making a Course white paper; First they cull the raggs (which are linnen for White paper, Wollen for browne) then they stamp them in troughs to a papp; with pestles or hammers like the powder mills; Then put it in a Vessel of Water, in which they dip a frame closely wyred, with wyer as small as an haire, & as close as a Weavers reede; upon this take up the papp, the superfluous water draining from it thro the wyres: This they dextrously turning shake out like a thin pan-cake on a smoth board, betweene two pieces of flannell; Then presse it, between a greate presse, the flanner sucking out the moisture, then taking it out ply and dry it on strings, as they dry linnen in the Laundry, then dip it in allume water, lastly polish, and make it up in quires: &c: note that the put some gumm in the water, in which they macerate the raggs into a pap [. . .].[7]

Evelyn's description of a paper sheet—"like a thin pan-cake," "as they dry linnen in the Laundry"—makes it obvious that the industry of paper had not yet been clearly defined, and lingered within the domestic, feminine sphere that provided it with workers, cleansing gestures, rituals, and metaphors. Women, as we have seen, enacted the first part of the metamorphosis, from rags to paper, but the final couching and drying of the sheets was traditionally men's work, the gender barrier clearly distinguishing matter from artefact. Addison lightly glosses over these distinctions and sums up the whole affair with a single verb ("wrought"), preferring to keep it veiled in "Mystery." "The Materials are no sooner wrought into Paper, but they are distributed among the Presses, where they again set innumerable Artists at Work, and furnish Business to another Mystery."[8]

Might it be that "dirt" is an unmentionable taboo for Addison's newspaper? According to The Spectator Project database[9] the word "dirty" is used ten times, both in *Tatler* and *Spectator*. Addison is responsible for two occurrences and Richard Steele, eight. One might retort that the adjective is neither shocking nor specific. In the above quoted *Spectator* 367, penned by Addison, one may find the only occurrence for both newspapers (and probably for all Addisonian prose) of the word "dung."

> The finest Pieces of Holland, when worn to tatters, assume a new Whiteness more beautiful than their first, and often return in the shape of Letters to their native Country. A Lady's Shift may be metamorphosed into Billets doux, and come into her Possession a second time. A Beau may peruse his Cravat after it is worn out, with greater Pleasure and

> Advantage than ever he did in a glass. In a word, a piece of Cloath, after having officiated for some years as a Towel or a Napkin, may by this means be raised from a Dung-hill, and become the most valuable piece of Furniture in a Prince's Cabinet.[10]

The Addisonian ellipse of all papermaking processes, while respecting the conventions of politeness, also heightens the mystery and surprise of the metamorphosis. The appearance of the word "Dung" enhances contrasts in the cycle of paper—from rags to riches. Yet by opposing two shades of white—"a new Whiteness more beautiful than their first"—Addison bestows different values on paper and cloth. Letters, billets doux, and books are receptacles of "greater Pleasure and advantage" while linen remains an inferior source of whiteness. One may wonder why, being made of the same matter, paper and cloth are not equal.

Shifts, cravats, shirts of Holland, towels, and napkins, share the common characteristic of being in contact with the body and skin. In Addison's time the notion of cleanliness, as shown by Georges Vigarello, did not necessarily imply the use of water but of daily, clean linen.[11] Addison illustrates this conception with an anecdote about a man who "chose to wear a Turban instead of a Perriwig; concluding very justly, that a Bandage of clean Linnen about his Head was much more wholsome, as well as cleanly, than the Caul of a Wig, which is soiled with frequent Perspirations."[12]

Defining dirt in Addisonian prose might thus prove more difficult than expected. If we are to believe certain descriptions of elegant beaux, a shirt itself need not be immaculately white, but only its visible parts—the collar, sleeves and adorned front. The same logic applies to the body—only the face, neck, throat, hands, and arms need usually be cleaned, being visible synecdoches of the whole body. Body linen was a perplexing textile paradox. It was expected to exhibit whiteness—often washed with a blue tint to enhance the optical illusion—and was supposed to embody purity. Yet it absorbed its symbolic opposite—body fluids and dirt. One might even offer the idea that since it materialised such a duality, the efforts with which filthy cloth was rejected as a rag equalled in intensity the visual attraction it enjoyed in its unsullied state. If we compare the status of paper to that of linen in the essays, an obvious asymmetry appears—paper, whether in its blank and used forms, is never subjected to such violent shifts in values. By the grace and toil of the paper mill, paper becomes a novel creation—reborn cloth, displaced, away from the body.

Yet many common characteristics remain. Both cloth and paper are surfaces that carry a visible meaning and contain, or hide, another message. Clothes outwardly express gender and social codes while indirectly revealing the body that wears them. Paper bears the written word to its reader but harbours invisible information in its weft—a watermark, a telltale shade of whiteness, a varying degree of pliancy, thickness, and softness. Paper betrays its users, just as any piece of clothing would. If the blue clothes of sailors became blue wrapping paper for the industries and trades that might have employed them, their fishing nets, ropes, and sails reflected their colour and ruggedness unto the coarse brown paper or board they were turned into. At the top of the paper hierarchy, the most distinguished writing paper came from the finer shirts and shifts of affluent beaux and ladies. The clothes of the upper classes performed a perfect recycling cycle—starting as fine white garments, falling into disuse, down the social ladder as they were traded, bartered, or exchanged, sojourning in the dung heaps as rags before experiencing reincarnation, revisiting their former milieu as white, velvety paper. When Addison had Mr Spectator cautiously wander into the unchartered territory of a lady's library, he describes a refined, intimate room where one such paper could be viewed: "a Quire of gilt Paper upon it, and on the Paper a Silver Snuff-box made in the Shape of a little Book."[13] Colours and textures not only survive the transformation from pulp to paper but continue to convey similar social information, especially as the quire is placed rather prominently on a "little Japan Table."

In an essay written by Richard Steele, Mr. Spectator receives a leaflet from a member of the "lower Order of *Britons*"& "whitish brown Paper put into my Hands in the Street."[14] The colour of the paper wordlessly introduces its owner as well as its futile content, being an advertisement for a fight in "the Bear-Garden at *Hockley in the* Hole." Steele uses the same correspondence between social status and paper quality in a love letter written to his spouse: "Madam, October 20, 1671. I Beg Pardon that my Paper is not Finer, but I am forced to write from a Coffee-house where I am attending about Business. There is a dirty Crowd of Busie Faces all around me talking of Mony, while all my Ambition, all my Wealth is Love."[15]

If the merchants' dusty clothes resemble the paper they write on, the ease with which the analogy is made can be explained by countless material similarities. When the papermaker's mould is lowered into a vat of diluted paper pulp, the mould's weft of chain and laid lines imprints into the sheet a texture similar to that of a woven fabric. Even the decorations adorning both cloth and paper may be found similar. When watermarks were imported from Europe by English papermakers in 1707, the continental models mimicked the designs of blasons and embroidery. Paper could also be tinted, scented, and gilt just as any expensive shirt. And when both products had been used, their end came to be described in interchangeable terms. A book, a newspaper, or a piece of fabric would fade, become stale, trite, or threadbare, materially and figuratively worn out by ill or exaggerated use. This sometimes even extended to text itself. "In the last place, you are to take notice of certain choice phrases scattered through the letter, some of them tolerable enough, till they were worn to rags by servile imitators."[16] That a phrase may be said to be "worn to rags" indicates that fabric, text, and paper are seen as one. And, as section IV of Swift's *Tale of the Tub* perfectly demonstrated, the metaphor was already a well-known *topos*.

AMBIVALENT PAPER—MATTER AND SURFACE

We may now consider paper a second time—not as an outcome, a finished product replete with intimations of its textile past—but as the beginning of the printing process.

> The Materials are no sooner wrought into Paper, but they are distributed among the Presses, where they again set innumerable Artists at Work, and furnish Business to another Mystery. From hence, accordingly as they are stained with News or Politicks, they fly thro' the Town in *Post-Men, Post-Boys, Daily-Courants, Reviews, Medleys* and *Examiners*.[17]

Through the "mystery" of printing—on which Addison has even less to say than papermaking—white paper is "stained" and soiled anew, to be yet again subsumed into a newspaper title. Paper becomes "a Paper" i.e. an essay. According to the Spectator Project database, one may find approximately seven hundred occurrences of the word in that sense. Regardless of the authorship of any essay, whenever Mr. Spectator appears to be in a metatextual mood, he refers to his own work as "my Paper." The synecdoche does not elicit any comments or puns—it is a stock phrase. Paper is a surface that carries a voice and stands for a spoken discourse. The fusion of paper and essay is what allows Mr Spectator to "print [him]self out."[18] The study of the same synecdoche in a religious context, when Addison is confronted to the divine written word, a Bible or a copy of the Alcoran, would exceed the scope of this article and has been confined to another.[19] By restricting the analysis to economic values, the essential ambiguity of printed paper comes to the fore.

Printed paper, by its double nature, is subjected to the erratic evolution of both cultural and material markets; it is produced, sold, circulated, over- and devalued. The recycling of fabric into paper provides a first deregulation of values. As underlined by Addison's essay, "a towel or a napkin" being "raised from the Dung-hill" to become "the most valuable piece of furniture in a Prince's Cabinet."[20]

Yet if the price of any piece of fabric slowly dwindles over time, till a final slump in its value consigns it to a dunghill, the cultural market of printed matter is ruled by different principles. The outward appearance and weight of the artefact remain the most relevant criteria—fat gilded octavos bound in fine leather easily ranking over lesser volumes or loose newspaper sheets—and the literary worth of a manuscript is seldom taken into account, its ephemeral fame or market value proving far more convincing for publishers. The popular ballad of the two children in the wood "one of the darling Songs of the common People" is thus scavenged "in a House in the Country" along with "several printed Papers which are usually pasted upon them."[21] Addison elsewhere bemoans the fate of sound yet slovenly printed works. "We have already seen the Memoirs of Sir William Temple published in the same character and volume with the history of Tom Thumb, and the works of our greatest poets shrunk into penny books and garlands. For my own part, I expect to see my lucubrations printed on browner paper than they are at present [. . .]."[22]

The *Tatler* was originally printed on a very brown paper called "tobacco paper." The *Spectator* was a whiter, half folio sheet (or foolscap) printed on both sides, the quality of which, however superior to the *Tatler*'s paper, must have left much to be desired.

> The new Edition which is given us of *Cæsar*'s Commentaries has already been taken notice of in Foreigh *Gazettes*, and is a Work that does Honour to the *English* Press [. . .]. The Beauty of the Paper, of the Character, and of the several Cuts with which this noble Work is Illustrated, makes it the finest Book that I have ever seen.[23]

Even when Addison celebrated somewhat enviously a rare occurrence of perfect balance between cultural and material values, he still had opportunities to deplore the indifference and vanity of the British reading public, when elegant ladies bought Locke's *Essay* only to impress visitors or use it to press a "Paper of Patches in it."[24] Between the crisp pages of sober Locke, a futile paper of cosmetics—the same substance carries vastly divergent meanings.

In Addison's essays, cloth and blank paper are versatile, fragile pieces of the same fabric. Yet printed paper is a crossbreed messenger, wavering between two separate identities—an abstract meaning and a material value. The archetype of such perilous mutability is undoubtedly paper money. On paper credit, on this fiducial invention, rests the health of Lady Credit and the country's entire financial system. "The great Heaps of Gold, on either side of the Throne, now appeared to be only Heaps of Paper, or little Piles of notched Sticks, bound up together in Bundles, like Bath-Faggot [. . .]. The Lady reviv'd, the Bags swell'd to their former Bulk, the Piles of Faggots and Heaps of Paper changed into Pyramids of Guineas."[25]

Printed paper defines its meaning through the perception or esteem of its reader. Mr Spectator, a fictional *persona*, is made of this very paper, just as any member of the Spectator club. "Mr Spectator, It is with inexpressible Sorrow that I hear of the Death of good Sir *Roger*, and do heartily condole with you upon so melancholy an Occasion. I think you ought to have blacken'd the Edges of a Paper which brought us so ill News, and to have had it stamped likewise in Black."[26]

When a whimsical reader reacts to the announcement of Sir Roger de Coverley's death by expressing the wish for a corresponding change of the printed paper, the idea that is entertained here is that Mr Spectator could be made to wear mourning clothes by the simple act of a matching paper colour, in a manner that anticipates Sterne's marbled or darkened pages. Yet Mr Spectator differs from Roger de Coverley in that he is made of a thicker, more complexly layered paper—not only is he a "Paper," he is also fiat money, firstly because his renewed existence relies on the continued belief and support of his readers and secondly because a *Spectator* paper corresponds to a fixed monetary value—a penny, and two pence after the stamp tax of August 1712.

The mutable status of paper had been noticed long ago, almost as soon as it was circulated. As far back as Horace's *Epistles* the condition of paper or in Horace's case, papyrus, already raised an amused jibe on the material fate of a mediocre poet's work.

> For easier 'tis to learn and recollect
> What moves derision than what claims respect.
> He's not my friend who hawks in every place
> A waxwork parody of my poor face;
> Nor were I flattered if some silly wight
> A stupid poem in my praise should write:
> The gift would make me blush, and I should dread
> To travel with my poet, all unread,
> Down to the street where spice and pepper's sold,
> And all the wares waste paper's used to fold.[27]

In this conclusion to Horace's *Epistles to Augustus* wax tablets (*cereus*) are indeed associated to the written word, but in the Latin original *chartis* provides the final pun: it refers to papyrus which, by the adjective *ineptis*, is emptied of any meaning, thus aptly preparing it to be used as wrapping or packet paper. The same reference is used in Addison's essay: "my Landlady often sends up her little Daughter to desire some of my old *Spectators*, and has frequently told me, that the Paper they are printed on is the best in the World to wrap Spices in."[28] Addison and his educated male readers obviously knew Horace's passage. Addison protracted the joke into two entire essays, *Spectator* 85 and 367.

> I remember in particular, after having read over a Poem of an Eminent Author on a Victory, I met with several Fragments of it upon the next rejoicing Day, which had been employ'd in Squibs and Crackers, and by that means celebrated its Subject in a double Capacity [. . .]. For this Reason, when my Friends take a Survey of my Library, they are very much surprised to find, upon the Shelf of Folios, two long Band-Boxes standing upright among my Books, till I let them see that they are both of them lined with deep Erudition and abstruse Literature. I might likewise mention a Paper-Kite, from which I have received great Improvement; and a Hat-Case, which I would not exchange for all the Beavers in Great-Britain.[29]

When printed paper swiftly evolves from text to meaningless object, Mr Spectator either contemplates its "double capacity," material and abstract, or gleefully enacts the return travel, scavenging the text back from material oblivion or fragmentation—a forerunner of other, more adventurous and metatextual decipherers, such as Laurence Sterne's heroes and readers. Critics have voiced the idea that Addison exorcises the fate of his own work by writing about it.[30] By spinning out the inglorious material fate of his work into a story, Addison writes, and sells, a whole essay. Emphasising the recyclable qualities of his work as well as the recycled quality of his writing materials, Addison comfortingly reasserts that his work is nothing more than a rewriting of familiar ideas, well- or lesser-known authors, past events and fictions. Addison consigned his notes and possible essay subjects in two large folios, these and Pierre Bayle's *Dictionnaire* providing him with a semi-inexhaustible source of writing materials.[31] Addison not only found inspiration in his travel diary, books, and his readers' letters, but all over London, on the papered walls of public places, in the polite conversations of his distinguished Whig friends at Button's and in the yarns of tavern customers. The very fact of such serendipity is exploited in a clever metatext.

> When I want Materials for this Paper, it is my Custom to go abroad in quest of Game; and when I meet any proper Subject, I take the first Opportunity of setting down an Hint of it upon Paper. At the same time I look into the Letters of my Correspondents, and if I find any thing suggested in them that may afford Matter of Speculation, I likewise enter a Minute of it in my Collection of Materials. By this means I frequently carry about me a whole Sheetful of Hints, that would look like a Rhapsody of Nonsense to any Body but myself.[32]

This cheerful paragraph would lead us to believe there is everything to be gained from the recycling of matter and ideas. When in *Spectator* 435 Addison himself composes the fiction of a future and laudatory criticism, he draws a metaphor from another infinitely recyclable substance—silver. "When I think on the Figure my several Volumes of Speculations will make about a Hundred years hence, I consider them as so many Pieces of old Plate, where the Weight will be regarded, but the Fashion lost."[33] The comparison is meant to uphold the intrinsic value of his writing, that is to say, its content. However, the word "lost" rings a melancholy note—with the transformation of time Addison acknowledges that a part, at the very least, of his work will come to be ignored.

WASTE PAPER, REINVENTION, AND LOSS

Cast-off paper is never lost or wasted upon Addison. In one of the humorous inventories Addison wrote for the *Spectator* and *Tatler* he muses on the shredded paper London theatres cast on the scene to create the semblance of snow and distinguishes a subtle difference. "One shower of snow in the whitest French paper. Two showers of a browner sort"—the whiteness of these fake snowflakes is the only remnant of their past status as paper since it continues to indicate a foreign or national origin.[34]

As raw material, paper retains an objective, stable value, however small. It preserves the univocal identity of paper pulp, bereft of symbolic depth or mutations. The wealth of layered uses, the manifold meanings it had once possessed—paper as textile, screen, text—have all been flattened out. Its past, its former place in the literary hierarchy, have vanished. In a later *Spectator* essay Addison enacts a similar vengeance on a literary critic.

> [London theatres] are also provided with above a Dozen Showers of Snow, which, as I am informed, are the Plays of many unsuccessful Poets artificially cut and shredded for that Use. Mr *Rimer*'s *Edgar* is to fall in Snow at the next acting of King *Lear*, in order to heighten, or rather to alleviate, the Distress of that unfortunate Prince; and to serve by way of Decoration to a Piece which that great Critick has written against.[35]

Addison appears to delight in the ironic meeting of text and metatext, to highlight the double death of an obnoxious work—both as discourse and as paper. One might see in the pleonastic pair of words, "cut and shredded," either a characteristic example of the symmetrical Addisonian prose or else a pleasurable insistence on the act of annihilation itself. Mr Spectator twice admits using his own papers as tobacco stopper and lighter for his pipe, and apart from the other inventive uses he records—snow showers, paper crackers, kites, pie foundation, spice wrapper, wallpaper, candlestick fringe, lining for hat-cases and band-boxes—fire seems to be the most frequent fate he conceives for printed paper. "I have lighted my Pipe more than once with the Writings of a Prelate; and know a Friend of mine, who, for these several Years, has converted the Essays of a Man of Quality into a kind of Fringe for his Candlesticks," can be read in *Spectator* 85. Then in *Spectator* 46: "After having cast a cursory Glance over it, and shook my Head twice or thrice at the reading of it, I twisted [my innocent Paper] into a kind of Match, and litt my Pipe with it" and finally in *Spectator* 367: "I must confess, I have lighted my Pipe with my own Works for these Twelve-months past."[36]

That the same fate be attributed to printed paper in three distinct essays seems to point at a larger significance. Fire, we propound, might stand here for another voracious element—novelty. The all-consuming principle was interpreted both as the driving force and pitfall of a periodical.[37] The insatiable appetite for new subjects impels Addison to transform old materials into new essays whilst being aware that these will only last as long as they are read. His essay on occasional papers as opposed to "fixt, immutable" subjects (the above-mentioned *Spectator* 435) openly admits the dangers of novelty whilst optimistically highlighting the permanence of his prose.

Yet once again Addison omits underlying texts and realities. Purposely obscuring his all-powerful vision, Mr Spectator avoids contemplating the ultimate and most degrading transformations of a printed text. No *Tatler*, *Spectator*, or even *Guardian* essay ever mentions the fate of paper once it has lost its status and can no longer be read, even as a soiled, yet decipherable fragment.

Paper being a precious, albeit familiar, commodity, bookbinders often reused printed papers that were thrown away by publishers, to laminate or glue them together into a stiff, board-like cover for their books. Thus neglected works routinely disappeared to help the birth of others. The scarcity of materials created countless palimpsests—bibliophagous books swallowing their unlucky predecessors as illustrated by Geoffrey Day's essay in this collection. Paper as protean paste, or *papier mâché*, was also a possible fate for *Spectator* papers. Robert Boyle first sang the praise of this last recycling process using—yet again—cooking terms and similes. Paper is soaked, beaten, and dried in a second enactment of its initial transformation, rendering it "fit for new, and perhaps unthought of purposes."

> Though paper be one of the commonest bodies that we use, yet there are a very few, that imagine it is fit to be employed other ways than about writing, or printing, or wrapping up of other things, or about some such obvious piece of service, without dreaming, that frames for pictures, and divers fine pieces of embossed work, with other curious moveables, may, as trial has informed us, he made of it, after this or the like manner. First, soak a convenient quantity of whitish paper, that is not fine, about two or three days in water, till it be very soft; then mash it in hot water, and beat or work it in large mortars or troughs, (much after the manner used in some places to churn butter) till it be brought to a kind of thin pap [. . .].[38]

The use of paper as hygienic tissue—"some such obvious piece of service," euphemises Robert Boyle—is one that neither Addison nor other "polite" authors dare broach. Only Grub Street hacks and bold satirists such as Swift or Pope master enough impertinence or wit to allude, albeit chastely, to this ultimate transformation.[39]

The lexicon of dirt recurrently defines the subclass of Grub Street writers, likening them to parallel trades—the first, plagiarizing texts, and the second, recycling clothes. Addison, contrary to Steele, usually writes off Grub Street imitators and pamphleteers as parasites with clearly the same idea of unwanted yet organic exploitation.[40] Similarly in the Republic of Letters, Grub Street was viewed as a literary dump—malodorous yet necessary. For polite authors such as Addison and Steele, mentioning typical Grub Street subjects must have dangerously steered the *Spectator* towards this pestilential, forbidden ground. Only issue 238 of the *Tatler* dared make an incursion there, thanks to Swift's sharp wit, when Isaac Bickerstaff opened his columns to the poetic contemplation of a city shower.[41]

Such bold matter will not be presented to readers ever again, especially not in the more refined *Spectator* and *Guardian*. Similarly, the cycle of paper in periodical prose is left open to interpretation and innuendos. The polite discourse of the author, like a fashionable garment revealing only chosen parts of the body, hides the processes and practices that are outside the scope of propriety. Addison must have favoured fire as the best end of printed paper because he dared not, before his readers, perform its return to original dirt and its first function, absorbing and hiding what is rejected as rubbish or excreta.

As described elliptically in the periodical prose, the paper cycle signals a new perception of the body and the shifting boundaries of dirt in the eighteenth century. Paper and cloth symbolically help purge body and mind of meaning and matter. They act as a double skin—a flexible, cellulose husk—absorbing all personal signs, be it the productions of the mind or the smells and traces of the body. Between the symbolic locus of cleanliness and the displacement of refuse, cloth and paper act as discreet carriers and protective shields that are shunned or celebrated according to their colour, to the message they bear. Whenever these go-betweens wax into whiteness or wane into obscurity, they trace and retrace the line between purity and dirt.

NOTES

1. *Spectator* 85, vol. 1, 61. All references to the *Spectator* are taken from Donald F. Bond's edition in 5 vols (Oxford: Clarendon Press, 1965); for the *Tatler*, his edition in 3 vols (Oxford: Clarendon Press, 1987).
2. *Spectator* 367, vol. 3, 379–80.
3. Mary Douglas, *Purity and Danger* [1966] (London: Routledge, 2002), 36.
4. "Les premières productions de papier—et avec elles l'imprimeries, l'humanisme, les Temps Modernes—ont été à l'origine une affaire de mode. Il n'y aurait jamais eu assez de chiffons pour les premiers moulins ni assez de papier pour les nouvelles presses à caractères mobiles au XVe siècle sans une révolution préalable dans un tout autre domaine: un revirement dans les habitudes vestimentaires qui, au XIIIe siècle, a brusquement généralisé le goût pour les tissus de lin, l'usage de la chemise et du linge de corps." Pierre-Marc de Biasi, Karine Douplitzky, *La Saga du papier* (Paris: Adam Biro, 1999), 109.
5. *Spectator* 367, vol. 3, 379–80.
6. Terry Belanger, "Publishers and Writers in Eighteenth-Century England," in *Books and their Readers in Eighteenth-Century England*, ed. Isabel Rivers (Leicester: Leicester University Press, 1982), 7.
7. *Papermaking in 17th century England*, Peter and Donna Thomas, eds. (Santa Cruz: Peter and Donna Thomas, 1990).
8. *Spectator* 367, vol. 3, 380.
9. *The Spectator Project*, a supremely useful database of all *Spectator* and *Tatler* issues, may be found on http://www2.scc.rutgers.edu/spectator/project.html (accessed 9 July 2014).

10. *Spectator* 367, vol. 3, 380.
11. Georges Vigarello, *Le propre et le sale. L'hygiène du corps depuis le Moyen-âge* (Paris: Seuil, 1985).
12. *Spectator* 576, vol. 4, 571.
13. *Spectator* 37, vol. 1, 153.
14. *Spectator* 436, vol. 4, 30.
15. *Spectator* 142, vol. 2, 63.
16. *Tatler* 230, vol. 3, 194.
17. *Spectator* 367, vol. 3, 380.
18. *Spectator* 1, vol. 1, 5.
19. Amélie Junqua, "Destruction and survival of the written word in Joseph Addison's periodical prose," in "Revue de la Société d'Etudes Anglo-Américaines des XVIIe et XVIIIe siècles, La diffusion de l'écrit / Spreading the written word," edited by Anne Bandry-Scubbi and Jean-Jacques Chardin, special issue, *Revue de la Société d'études anglo-américaines des XVIIe et XVIIIe siècles* 1, no. 2. (2010): 197–219.
20. *Spectator* 367, vol. 3, 381.
21. *Spectator* 85, vol. 1, 362.
22. *Tatler* 101, vol. 2, 119.
23. *Spectator* 367, vol. 3, 381–82.
24. *Spectator* 37, vol.1, 155.
25. *Spectator* 3, vol. 1, 16.
26. *Spectator* 518, vol. 4, 342.
27. Discit enim citius meminitque libentius illud
Quod quis deridet, quam quod probat et veneratur.
Nil moror officium quod me gravat, ac neque ficto
n peius vultu proponi cereus usquam,
Nec prave factis decorari versibus opto,
Ne rubeam pingui donatus munere, et una
Cum scriptore meo, capsa porrectus operta,
Deferar in vicum vendentem tus et odores
Et piper et quidquid chartis amicitur ineptis.
John Conington, trans., *Epistles,* Book II
(London: George Bell, 1892), vol. 1, 163.
28. *Spectator* 367, vol. 3, 380.
29. *Spectator* 85, vol. 1, 361.
30. Alain BONY, *Joseph Addison et la création littéraire. Essai périodique et modernité* (Lyon: Université Lumière, CERAN-Diffusion, 1979).
31. Donald Bond, preface to the *Spectator* edition, xxvi: "Tickell, in the preface to the *Works* of 1721, observed that Addison could not have contributed so largely to the *Spectator* 'if he had not ingrafted into it many pieces, that had lain by him in little hints and minutes, which he from time to time collected, and ranged in order and moulded into the form in which they now appear.'"
32. *Spectator* 46, vol. 1, 195–96.
33. *Spectator* 435, vol. 4, 27.
34. *Tatler* 42, vol. 1, 303.
35. *Spectator* 592, vol. 5, 26.
36. *Spectator* 46, vol. 1, 198; *Spectator* 85, vol. 1, 361, and *Spectator* 367, vol. 3, 380.
37. Alain Bony, *Joseph Addison et la création littéraire.*
38. Robert Boyle, *Of Men's Great Ignorance of the Uses of Natural Things, or, That there is Scarce any one Thing in Nature, whereof the Use to human Life*

are yet thoroughly understood, in *Works of the Honourable Robert Boyle* (London, 1772), vol. 3, section 4, 485–86.

39. "Clinket: Thou destroyer of learning, thou worse than a bookworm; thou hast put me beyond patience. Remember how my lyrick ode bound about a tallow-candle; thy wrapping up snuff in an epigram; nay, the unworthy usage of my hymn to Apollo, filthy creature!" John Gay, Alexander Pope, Arbuthnot, *Three Hours After Marriage* [1717], *Burlesque Plays of the Eighteenth century*, ed. Simon Trussler (Oxford: Oxford University Press, 1969), 101.
40. *Tatler* 229, vol. 3, 186.
41. *Tatler* 238, vol. 3, 227.

13 Black Transactions

Waste and Abundance in Samuel Richardson's *Clarissa*

Rebecca Anne Barr

Twenty-first century readers are accustomed to superabundance. Texts once obscure and forgotten, rare and unobtainable are available online in numerous vast virtual libraries: their contents searchable and hyperlinked, connections and cross-references expanding exponentially. Yet this sense of textual plenitude is not new. As Alberto Manguel has argued, "the new sense of infinity created by the Web has not diminished the old sense of infinity inspired by the ancient libraries—merely lent it a sort of tangible intangibility."[1] Such sense of infinity, tangible or otherwise, can provoke either exhilaration or anxiety. In the eighteenth century, as in the twenty-first, technology's proliferation of texts problematizes not merely knowledge acquisition but knowledge itself. Diderot's *Encyclopédie*, which attempted to shape information into a critical instrument, was based upon the premise that though knowledge was *not* infinite, the number of books was. This generative capacity threatened to overwhelm knowledge, since "the number of books will grow continually, and one can predict that a time will come when it will be almost as difficult to learn anything from books as from the direct study of the whole universe."[2] Paradoxically, abundance of print threatened to waste meaning as an "excess of writing piled up useless texts and stifled thought beneath the weight of accumulating discourse, creating a peril no less ominous than the threat of disappearance."[3] Yet print-glut's auxiliary was material vulnerability: the eighteenth-century culture of wholesale recycling subjected books to waste and reuse "through the regular commercial practices of the day," with volumes routinely "dismembered, dispersed, and humiliatingly used for purposes other than those for which they were first intended."[4] Ironically, books were recycled due to a strict economy of materials—paper being a limited resource—in a marketplace where there was no scarcity of writing. Literary value could be broken down, reprocessed, rendered detritus, and subsumed by a culture of ephemera. Swift, Pope, and their Romantic successors worried about the extinction of the book (and civilisation itself) by textual supersaturation, a cultural nightmare in which the marketplace's labile appetites would consume texts without distinction: textual superabundance threatened intellectual inanition.

Despite such cultural pessimism, however, textual culture based around recycling print always held forth the "promise of possible retrieval"—the salvaging of text, the recuperation of useful fragments from a broken whole.[5] As much as eighteenth-century writers feared the repurposing of their work in ignominious forms, they also displayed a fascination for the ways in which textual meaning could be exhumed from wreckage, with the potential of re-absorption into literary culture. Textual salvage often exerts a sentimental appeal, as in Henry MacKenzie's *The Man of Feeling* (1777), where the local curate cheerfully recycles Harley's pathetic story. The medley of papers has been torn and crumpled as "excellent wadding" for guns, but the papers are sufficiently legible to garner curiosity and prevent total destruction.[6] Saved from loss, these fragments provide affecting matter for the sensible reader: their derelict status amplifying their emotional power. Presenting these recovered texts for publication, MacKenzie's obtuse editor compares their affecting scenes to Samuel Richardson's epic *Clarissa, or the History of a Young Lady* (1748–1749): "had the name of a Marmontel, or a Richardson, been on the title-page—'tis odds that I should have wept.'"[7]

The comparison is apt, for at the heart of Richardson's novel lies an assortment of literary debris. Midway through the fifth volume of the first edition is the notoriously remarkable Paper X (Figure 13.1). This is the last of a sequence of "mad papers" from the heroine, Clarissa Harlowe, following her violation by the libertine Robert Lovelace. "What she writes, she tears, and throws the papers in fragments under the table, either not knowing what she does, or disliking it: Then gets up, wrings her hands, weeps, and shifts her seat all around the room: Then returns to the table, sits down, and writes again."[8] "Papers" rather than letters, these are abortive scraps in a novel of letters. Lovelace's enveloping missive situates the papers as recovered texts, transcribed copies of "scraps and fragments"; Paper I is marked as "torn in two pieces" while Paper II is "scratched through, and thrown under the table";[9] many are "blistered" with the tears of their transcriber.

The bizarre *mise-en-page* of Paper X has bestowed it with a peculiar iconic persistence: warranting reproduction in discussions such as this, simulation in the popular Penguin edition edited by Angus Ross, and image inclusion in online hypertext versions of the novel. The academic database *Literature Online* (LION), for instance, supplements its online text of the novel with a linked image of 1748 edition. Such editorial decisions confirm that Paper X is fantastic—textually excessive. It is "exorbitant [. . .] beyond the scope of the possible, the tolerable, the thinkable [. . .] [it] cannot be assimilated."[10] In a novel famous for textual proliferation these scraps of waste exert a curious power. These pieces of detritus occlude the decisive narrative action that has occurred so that Clarissa Harlowe's violation is delivered in a mere six words: "the affair is over. Clarissa lives."[11] Editorial deferral highlights the narrative lacuna, as the reader is informed that the "whole of this black transaction is given by the injured lady to Miss

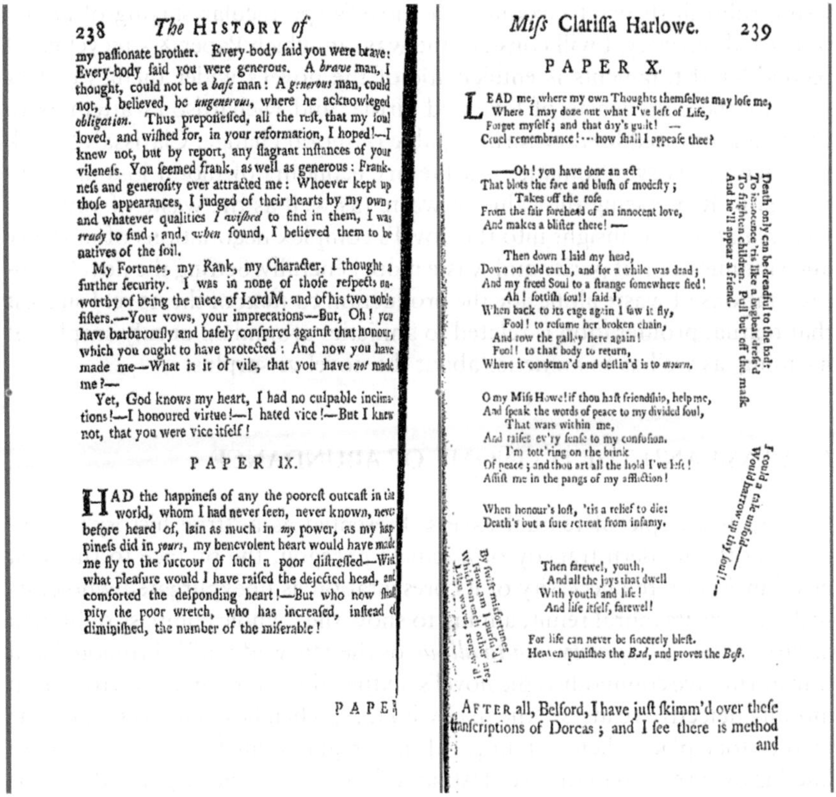

Figure 13.1 Paper IX and X from Richardson's first edition of *Clarissa, or the History of a Young Lady* (1748). © The British Library Board, C.71.bb.1 vol.5, page 238–39.

Howe in her subsequent letters [. . .] to which the reader is referred."[12] Chronological and epistemological disruption makes Clarissa's textual waste crucial to the novel's meaning. Clarissa's fragments act as "signs of the peculiar transformations that take place in literary texts," significant rubbish that demonstrate "meaning has been made."[13] Richardson's novel reclaims and elevates Clarissa's epistolary detritus, altering the value of waste and the moral status of a fallen woman.

This chapter will argue that this recuperation of waste and loss is of central importance to *Clarissa*. Reclaimed text in *Clarissa* is symbolic of its project of literary innovation, moral reform, and the paradoxes of novelty and waste. If waste is always dynamic and relational, *Clarissa*'s waste is both textual and metaphorical; what Clarissa discards is enthusiastically taken up by her readership, and the novel's proliferation is predicated on its heroine's physical dissolution and (posthumously burgeoning) textual remains.[14]

Using rubbish theory to examine the novel's spectacular staging of an act of textual recovery, I will consider the ways in which Paper X's recycling of second-hand fragments is emblematic of the novel's wider themes of loss of innocence, the waste of love and virtue, and Richardson's attempts to create a renovated literary form capable of moral change: Clarissa's "black transaction" is symptomatic of a literary economy of moral loss and textual gain. Reassessing the value of waste (as well as the waste of value) in *Clarissa* allows us insight into the novel's complex negotiations of morality and sinfulness, or of purity and waste more generally. Setting the novel's representations of waste alongside the production context of the novel I suggest that textual proliferation is related to anxieties around an unruly surplus of meaning, as well as to anxieties about the novel *as* surplus.

CLARISSA AND THE ECONOMY OF ABUNDANCE

Clarissa is an epic of textual excess. Presented as a "true history" documenting the modern tragedy of a female paragon, the preface to this vast novel insists on the necessity of its presentation as unexpurgated whole. Its scale reflects its moral remit, aiming to show the "whole compass of human nature, as far as *Capacity would allow*, or the *Story admit*."[15] Promoted as a transformative commodity, the novel's textual abundance purports to retrain morally defective readers: "the man who [. . .] when he comes to revolve the whole story placed before him [. . .] may regulate his future actions as to find his own reward in the ever-lasting welfare."[16] Despite arguing that literary surplus would produce personal restraint, the principle of inclusion and fidelity to an interminable epistolary impulse produced authorial anxiety. *Pamela's* (1740–1742) unprecedented success had fomented mass adulation and market success as well as parody and a profusion of impolite "sequels" and these unauthorised extensions of the fictional Pamela Andrews caused significant moral stress for her valetudinarian creator.[17] Eighteenth-century readers' craving for *more* of a character frequently resulted in creative appropriation of literary characters in unlicensed continuations or alternative endings; a phenomenon that David Brewer has titled "imaginative expansion," a precursor of twentieth-century slash fiction.[18] Lack of property rights governing imaginative fiction, authority, and copyright meant that once in the public domain fictional works were a kind of common property, particularly if they claimed to tell "real" stories. Such imaginative expansion is characteristic of what Simon Stern has called the eighteenth-century "economy of abundance."[19] Rather than conceiving of literary property as "a zero-sum game: [in which] a reader's gain must mean an author's loss," the plenitude of imaginative expansion means that characters are perpetually available, constantly renewing in the minds of an ever-expanding audience.[20] Richardson's more proprietorial conception of his works saw him attempting to sequester his creation from promiscuous imaginations;

revising and reforming *Pamela*'s colloquial liveliness in subsequent editions, barricading his story of rustic "virtue rewarded" behind puff letters, prefaces, and recommendations, and ultimately neutering the original through the stolid antidote *Pamela in her Exalted Condition* (1742).[21] Anxiety about fiction's imaginative excess continues to operate in *Clarissa*, as the epic novel seeks to exhaust the means of imaginative expansion (as well as its readers). *Clarissa's* abundance, therefore, is partly a defensive formal strategy but also a symptom of the reflexivity of Richardson's writing—perpetually revising, recalibrating, expanding: saving the novel from going to waste.

Such self-reflexivity is inextricable from Richardson's profession as a master printer, which granted him direct access to the means of production as well as considerable economic and aesthetic independence.[22] Professional autonomy bolstered perceptions of his moral authority, confirming the printed output's integrity: as one admirative encomium asserted "His Virgin-sheets no prostitution stains, / His moral ink no venom'd fall profanes [. . .] From his pure Press, see, hallow'd incense rise! / As from an Altar, grateful to the skies!"[23] Despite this unique position as author and producer Richardson's first edition of *Clarissa* refuses "to assert the prerogatives of authorship [. . .] [showing] an avowed willingness to bow to the views of readers" in both public and private consultation.[24] This "consultatory" style of composition made his works "endlessly malleable [. . .], always mutable" but did not seem to concentrate their meaning.[25] So his readers "might be less frighted at the Bulk" Richardson removed the blank pages interleaving *Clarissa's* draft, and once published he bewailed that the novel was "unconscionably long" and therefore potentially unsaleable.[26] In Richardson's case fear of misinterpretation (and love of praise) catalysed textual superabundance. Postscripts, prefaces, editorial notes, and typographical amendments were added to subsequent editions; "Clarissa Harlowe's" *Meditations Collected from the Sacred Books* (1750)—a limited edition "spin off," a substantially altered third edition of the novel, and the supplement *Letters and Passages Restored from the Original Manuscripts of the History and Clarissa* (1751). A paratextual index, *Moral and Instructive Sentiments, Maxims, Cautions, and Reflections from Pamela, Clarissa, and Sir Charles Grandison* (1755), was also compiled.[27] As Leah Price has argued, the frequency and scale of intervention in the "final" work suggests that despite its claims to unity Richardson defined it "as an aggregate of modular parts rather than an indissoluble whole."[28]

Yet *Clarissa*'s expansive dynamic invokes the spectre of its own desuetude, its textual surplus generated by the loss of its heroine. The painful culmination of the novel also had a deleterious effect on the sales, as more than a third of customers who purchased the first four volumes did not go on to complete their set.[29] Richardson's attempt to sustain *Clarissa*'s moral authority is a symptom of a marketplace reaching saturation: the process of recycling and renovating implying possible obsolescence through an over-eager assertion of infinite moral relevance.[30] John Scanlan has shown that the inescapable consequence of capitalist "progress" is waste—the creation of devalued or redundant materials.[31] *Clarissa*'s reincarnations and commitment to *novelty* embody the capitalist process of dynamic change in which the market must periodically transcend its current productions, thus condemning itself to a Sisyphean renovation. In making itself "new," Richardson's work betrays its commodity status: literary surplus on the brink of becoming waste.

PRODUCTIVE WASTE

The paradoxically procreative capacities of waste are nowhere clearer than in the textual "paroxysm" that signals the loss of Clarissa's bodily integrity. Paper X's "patchwork of derelict quotation" is seen as synonymous with the mental abjection of the heroine—the fragments equivalent to the desolate and confused discards of a damaged subjectivity.[32] Paper X's cento of deracinated texts is itself culled from literary remains salvaged from Edward Bysshe's *Art of English Poetry* [1706]. Although Richardson's mode of quotation has been called "pedestrian, didactic, and artless," reader response confirms that its "borrowed social languages [. . .] [and] combinatorial forms" successfully catalysed sentimental identification with the heroine's abjection.[33] These broken texts are dramatically repurposed to reclaim Clarissa's virtue by diverting disgust toward libertine action, an act of literary recycling. Hamlet's speech against Gertrude's inconstancy (*Hamlet*, III.iv.44–44) is redirected against Lovelace and untrammelled sexual appetite: "You have done an act / that blots the face and blush of modesty; / Take off the rose / From the fair forehead of a innocent Love, / And makes a blister there!"[34] Rendering burning as *mourning* ("Fool! To that Body to return, / Where it condemn'd and destin'd is to burn") Richardson recalibrates Abraham Cowley's courtly love lyric "The Despair" as an condemnation of aristocratic excess.[35] As Tom Keymer notes, the mad papers signal "a new literary form, marking the point of a shift from realism to abstraction."[36] G. Gabrielle Starr has argued that this abstraction is more precisely generic absorption, as the novel adapts the familiar mode of lyrical poetry. Lyric provides Richardson with "models of emotional consensus imagined, lost and ultimately reconstructed," a formal means of "melding public and private experience."[37] This graphic "harrowing" signals "the destruction of the old position and the formation of a new one," a reformation of reading habits and literary form.[38] *Clarissa* dismembers the coherent texts it plunders for aesthetic effects as the novel form assimilates the anthology. However, while Clarissa's "poetical flights"[39] imagine community through sentimental overflow Richardson's *mise-en-page* strenuously contains figurative abjection. The page layout contains fragmentation, confining the material state of the originals to parentheses, retaining the pages' drop capitals and sustaining the bounds of margin. *Clarissa*'s exemplary production value converts waste into a moral commodity.

Within the novel itself Clarissa's vivid "images of hermeneutic fragmentation [. . .] the salvos of dementia and despair" generate sufficient curiosity for their inclusion within the network of epistolary circulation.[40] Framed by coherent letters, their status as waste matter is explicit:

> I sat down, intending [. . .] to give thee a copy of [Clarissa's "delirious" letter]: but, for my life, I cannot; 'tis so extravagant. And the original is too much an original to let it go out of my hands. But some of the scraps and fragments, as either torn through, or flung aside, I will copy for the novelty of the thing, and to show you how her mind works now she is in this whimsical way.[41]

"Too affecting"[42] to transcribe initially, Lovelace's attempts to reserve or restrict the heroine's extravagances adds to their sentimental impact. Delegating transcription to his maidservant Dorcas, the mediated fragments accumulate further emotional value through circulation, becoming "blistered with the tears of even the hardened transcriber."[43] The lachrymal effusions produced by the fragments (and "overlaying" their copies) testify to the abundance of affect created by loss: exchanging these fragments increases their meaning, so that "the sum of values is greater afterward than it was before, and this implies that each party gives the other more than he had himself possessed."[44] Clarissa's waste produces an emotional surplus in excess of the literal value of her writing. Yet this emotional profit depends on narrative arrest. At least one contemporary critic complained that there was "something trifling in the incoherences, which *Clarissa* writes in her delirium," a product of the novel's excessive typographical "affectation."[45] In defence, Richardson's friend Jane Collier emphasised the role of the reading subject in supplementing meaning with *feeling*:

> To those who are not affected by the Pathetic Incoherence of those Scattered Pieces of Paper, they *may perhaps* appear Trifling; nor can any other Answer be given to any Objections which might be raised to those Passages which are addressed intirely to the Heart, and not to the Head [. . .] [these are] uncommon and surprisingly pathetic Passages.[46]

For Collier the economy of sensibility ("the heart") re-evaluates these discards and compensates for their epistemological disorder with sighs, tears, sympathy: representational incoherence, or *lack* of meaning, extracts subjective responsiveness. But that responsiveness—the very sign of sensibility—arrests rational language: "no Answer can be given" if the critic is "unaffected."[47] This is "the sublimity of waste [. . .] a unique blend of attraction and repulsion arousing an equally unique mixture of awe and fear."[48] Textual fragments, like the novel itself, become objects whose worth is an index to, and product of, the individual. Thus, the novel's "black transaction" becomes productive through the value of its exchange.

The surfeit of emotional energy generated by this waste, by this abjection, opposes the dynamic libertinism of Robert Lovelace. Lovelace's behaviour carries "strong associations of aristocratic excess" and can be "aesthetically alluring" to readers "precisely because of its economic inefficiency."[49] His rhetorical and dramatic abilities augment an aristocratic status further bolstered by personal attractiveness and wealth. Claiming the motto "*debellare superbos*"[50] [to humble the proud], Lovelace's sense of entitlement rests upon others' acknowledgement of, and submission to, his potency: "many and many a pretty rogue had I spared, whom I did not spare, had my power been acknowledged and my mercy been in time implored,"[51] he boasts to Belford. This appetite feeds upon the subjection of others, as Colonel Morden warns Clarissa "Prayers, tears and the most abject submission are but fuel to his pride."[52] In this zero-sum conception of power, dominance depends upon the subjugation and deprivation of others. Displaying a Hobbesian "perpetuall and restlesse desire of Power after power," Lovelace can "put no other bound to the views than what want of power gives [him] [. . .] from one advantage gained, [he] wouldst proceed to attempt another."[53] His appetite suggests a boundless energy, a limitless and annihilating vitality. However, though Lovelace argues that rape is merely a "common theft, a private larceny"[54] his "rake's creed" does not necessarily devalue female chastity but is rather an extreme expression of an economy of moral scarcity. Rakes "*seldom* meet with the stand of virtue in the women whom they attempt [. . .] by those they have met with, they judge of all the rest."[55] Thus unassailable female virtue becomes an elusive premium whose imagined worth is enhanced by comparative lack. Indeed, Lovelace argues with characteristic irony that he brings virtue "to the touchstone with a *view to exalt it*, if it come out to be virtue."[56] Clarissa's "trial" becomes, in effect, the proof of womankind: "if I have not found a virtue that cannot be corrupted, I will swear that there is not one such in the whole sex [. . .] [for] What must that virtue be which will not stand a trial?" (429–30). The heroine's seduction would confirm that women's "natural" state was morally worthless; "*once subdued, and always subdued.*"[57] Within the negative terms of a libertine economy, then, Clarissa's fall simply adduces the rake's power and divests womankind of worth.

In order to repudiate the maxim that "*a reformed rake makes the best husband*"[58] the novel must reconfigure Lovelace's zero-sum conception of power and Clarissa's "pathetic passages" effect just such a redistribution of aesthetic power. Their dialectical figuration of appetite and devastation, consumption and rot, produces an indictment of the moral profligacy that performs (and sustains) its potency through the annihilation of virtue. Paper III sees a beast savage the young woman who has fed it from infancy; "neglecting to satisfy its hungry maw" the beast returns to its savagery and "on a sudden fell upon her, and tore her in pieces,"[59] the fleshy fragments recalling the torn paper of Clarissa's papers. The heroine's decline is described in terms of spectacular vegetal blight, "Blooming, yet declining in her blossom!"[60] Such "bloom" is a grim parody of fecundity, a spectacle of deformation and contagion.

> Thou pernicious caterpillar, that preyest upon the fair leaf of virgin fame, and poisonest those leaves which thou canst not devour! Thou fell blight, thou eastern blast, thou overspreading mildew, that destroyest the early promises of the shining year! [. . .] Thou eating canker-worm, that preyest upon the opening bud, and turnest the damask rose into livid yellowness![61]

Putrefaction is "deathly life," a conflation of waste and profusion in which appetite transforms plenitude into detritus.[62] Clarissa's lyrical disgust fuses moral and visual opposites, "death infecting life"—a boundary transgression characteristic of the Kristevan abject.[63] If it is "not lack of cleanliness or health that causes abjection but what disturbs identity, system, order [. . .] the in-between, the ambiguous, the composite," the mad papers' queasy oscillation between coalescing matter and physical disintegration suggests a collapse of order and uncontainable moral indifference. The novel's claim for the "generative, recuperative power of literature" rests upon the power of degeneration and decay to create an abundance of sympathy.[64]

EXCHANGING PROFIT FOR LOSS

The reversal of fortune sees Lovelace's social prestige and power decline, the rape rendering him a "wretch, *who could rob himself of his wife's virtue.*"[65] Not merely an individual loss but "a loss likewise to the world!"[66] her ruin "has increased, instead of diminished, the number of the miserable!"[67] The chiastic logic of Lovelace's despair—"O Belford! Belford! Whose the triumph now!—Hers, or MINE?"[68]—encapsulates his conception of "emotional scarcity [. . .] where the emotional wealth of one social agent necessarily comes at the expense of another."[69] Within such a zero-sum economy only one victor is possible. Clarissa's refusal to acquiesce in her degradation triggers a paradoxical expansion in Lovelace's correspondence and appetite. His sexual desire proliferates aggressively, manifesting itself in schemes of baroque obscenity, projects of "a *new* kind."[70] As "variety has irresistible charms" and Clarissa "has no passions; that is to say, none of the passions that I want her to have,"[71] Lovelace aims to revenge himself upon three women who obstructed his attempts upon her. Proposing a gang rape involving Belton, Mowbray, Tourville, and himself, this "frolic" will give the women "knowledge" of the wicked ways of town rakes. Such exorbitant fantasies testify to the aggression of Lovelace's hypersexuality and feigned indifference to the objects of his desire. Such dissipation leads to physical dissolution as Lovelace and his associates die violently, expiring from "surfeits," "salivations," lanced and quartered by surgeons. Lovelace's dying words, "Let this expiate!"[72] acknowledge the terminal point of libertine extravagance; both his death and his words redundant in plot terms.

By contrast, the plenitude of Clarissa's holy dying is based on her withdrawal from reciprocity, as meditations, legal documents, and testament substitute for correspondence. But as Clarissa's body wastes, so the novel increases. Starvation may annihilate her body, but it generates concern, distress, forgiveness, and admiration: her hunger is not wasted. Clarissa's "whole story" must be reassembled and rearticulated by John Belford, the agent who "will indeed re-produce Clarissa as *Clarissa*."[73] Following her escape from debtor's prison, Belford finds her in a house whose ramshackle construction conveys her reclamation of marginalised spaces and alliance with outcasts and damaged individuals. Clarissa's surroundings are decaying around her.

> A horrid hole of a house . . . within broken walls . . . the ceiling was smoked with a variety of figures, and initials of names . . . [a bed] with coarse curtains tacked up at the feet to the ceiling . . . plaguily in tatters, and the corners tied up in tassels, that the rents in it might go no farther. [. . .]
>
> An old, tottering, worm-eaten table, that had more nails bestowed in mending it to make it stand . . . an old looking-glass, cracked through the middle, breaking out into a thousand points; the crack given it, perhaps, in a rage, by some poor creature, to whom it gave the representation of his heart's woes in his face. [. . .]
>
> An old, broken-bottomed cane couch, without a squab, or coverlid, sunk at one corner, and unmortised, by the failing of one of its worm-eaten legs, which lay in two pieces under the wretched piece of furniture it could no longer support[74]

At the centre of this misery and chaos Clarissa is pure and coherent: "Her dress was white damask, exceeding neat [. . .] the kneeling Lady, sunk with majesty too in her white, flowing robes [. . .] spreading the dark, tho' not dirty, floor, and illuminating that horrid corner; her linen beyond imagination white [. . .] I thought my concern would have choaked me. Something rose in my throat."[75] Amid the surrounding debris and degeneration Clarissa maintains a purity "beyond imagination." But Belford's reverence, his role as executor and Richardsonian "editor" cannot fully distract the reader from his investment in the heroine's loss. Despite commending her beauty, intelligence, and virtue, Belford is queasily complicit in Lovelace's schemes; regarding Clarissa's ruin he ruminates "how effectually would her story, were it generally known, warn all the sex."[76] The transformative possibilities of Clarissa's story justify her waste. Richardson's commitment to his heroine's fate means that the imaginative exorbitance of the novel is accompanied by critical anxiety about waste of meaning exemplified in his "superfluous" postscript. Here the author defends his refusal of "*poetical justice*," a system of "*equal distribution* of *rewards* and *punishments*,"[77] which would dictate a happy ending to the novel. Richardson's refusal of a zero-sum economy leaves the textual residue of its own excess in his numerous supplements to the novel, in passionate reader response and in the wealth of critical studies. *Clarissa*'s "black transactions" have yet to be exhausted.

NOTES

1. Alberto Manguel, *The Library at Night* (New Haven: Yale University Press, 2008), 322.
2. Denis Diderot (1755) in *The Old Regime and the French Revolution,* ed. Keith Michael Baker (London: University of Chicago Press, 1987), 85.
3. Roger Chartier, *Inscription and Erasure: Literature and Written Culture from the Eleventh to the Eighteenth Century*, trans. Arthur Goldhammer (Philadelphia: University of Pennsylvania Press, 2007), vii.
4. Ian Donaldson, "The Destruction of the Book," *Book History* 1, no. 1 (1998): 1–10, on 8, 7.
5. Elizabeth L. Eisenstein, *Divine Art, Infernal Machine: The Reception of Printing in the West from First Impressions to the Sense of an Ending* (Oxford: University of Pennsylvania Press, 2011), 237.
6. Henry MacKenzie, *The Man of Feeling* [1777], ed. Brian Vickers (Oxford: Oxford University Press, 2001), 4.
7. Ibid., 5.
8. Samuel Richardson, *Clarissa; or, The History of a Young Lady* [1747–48], ed. Angus Ross (Harmondsworth: Penguin, 1985), 889.
9. Richardson, *Clarissa*, 892.
10. Julia Kristeva, *Powers of Horror: An Essay on Abjection*, trans. Leon S. Roudiez (New York: Columbia University Press, 1994), 1.
11. Richardson, *Clarissa*, 883.
12. Idem.
13. Sophie Gee, *Making Waste: Leftovers and the Eighteenth-Century Imagination* (Princeton NJ: Princeton University Press, 2010), 17.
14. John Scanlan, *On Garbage* (London: Reaktion, 2004), 69.
15. Samuel Richardson, *Meditations Collected from the Sacred Books: And Adapted to the Different Stages of a Deep Distress* (London: 1750), ii.
16. Richardson, *Clarissa*, 1176–77.
17. See John Carroll, ed., *Selected Letters of Samuel Richardson* (Oxford: Clarendon Press, 1964), 42–45; T. C. Duncan Eaves and Ben D. Kimpel, *Samuel Richardson: A Biography* (Oxford: Clarendon, 1971), 135–39.
18. David Brewer, *The Afterlife of Character, 1726–1825* (Pennsylvania: University of Pennsylvania Press, 2005), 1.
19. Simon Stern, "Tom Jones and the Economies of Copyright", *Eighteenth-Century Fiction*, vol. 9, no. 4 (1997), 429–444: 430.
20. Ibid., 11.
21. See the introduction to *Pamela*: *Or, Virtue Rewarded* [1740], Tom Keymer and Alice Wakely, eds. (Oxford: Oxford University Press, 2000).
22. John A. Dussinger, "Richardson, Samuel (*bap.* 1689, *d.* 1761)," *Oxford Dictionary of National Biography*, Oxford University Press, September 2004; online edition, January 2008. http://www.oxforddnb.com/view/article/23582 (accessed 21 January 2010).

23. "A Poem on the Invention of Letters and the Art of Printing" (March 1758), in *Clarissa: The Eighteenth-Century Response, 1747–1804*, vol. 1, *Reading Clarissa,* ed. Lois E. Bueler (New York: AMS Press, 2010), 263.
24. *Samuel Richardson's Published Commentary on Clarissa, 1747–1765*, ed. Tom Keymer (London: Pickering and Chatto, 1998), vol. 1, 1.
25. David McKitterick, *Print, Manuscript, and the Search for Order, 1450–1830* (Cambridge: Cambridge University Press, 2003), 224; Lisa Maruca, *The Work of Print: Authorship and the English Text Trades, 1660–1760* (Seattle: University of Washington Press, 2008), 134.
26. Richardson to Aaron Hill, 20 January 1745/6, Carroll, *Selected Letters*, 63; Richardson to Aaron Hill, 26 January 1746/7, Carroll, *Selected Letters*, 83.
27. See Keymer, *Published Commentary*, vol. 3.
28. Leah Price, *The Anthology and the Rise of the Novel* (Cambridge: Cambridge University Press, 2000), 24.
29. See Thomas Keymer, "Clarissa's Death, Clarissa's Sale, and the Text of the Second Edition," *Review of English Studies* 45 (1994): 389–92; and Adam Budd, "Why Clarissa Must Die: Richardson's Tragedy and Editorial Heroism," *Eighteenth-Century Life* 31, no. 3 (Fall 2007): 1–28.
30. For the numerous abridgements and adaptations of Richardson's works see Leah Price, "Reading (and Not Reading) Richardson," *Studies in Eighteenth Century Culture* 29 (2000): 87–103 and Leah Price's *The Anthology and the Rise of the Novel*, 13–42.
31. Scanlan, *On Garbage*, 37.
32. Margaret Anne Doody and Florian Stuber, "'Clarissa' Censored," *Modern Language Studies* 18, no. 1 (Winter 1988): 74–88, on 81.
33. Michael E. Connaughton, "Richardson's Familiar Quotations: *Clarissa* and Bysshe's *Art of English Poetry*," *Philological Quarterly* 60 (1981): 194; Helen Vendler, *The Art of Shakespeare's Sonnets* (Cambridge, MA: Harvard University Press, 1997), 2.
34. Richardson, *Clarissa*, 893.
35. *The Collected Works of Abraham Cowley*, Thomas O. Calhoun, Laurence Heyworth, and J. Robert King, eds. (London and Toronto: Associated University Press, 1993), vol. 2, 44.
36. Tom Keymer, "Richardson's *Meditations*: Clarissa's *Clarissa*," in *Samuel Richardson: Tercentenary Essays*, Margaret Doody and Peter Sabor, eds. (Cambridge: Cambridge University Press, 1989), 89–109, 93–94.
37. G. Gabrielle Starr, *Lyric Generations: Poetry and the Novel in the Long Eighteenth Century* (Baltimore: Johns Hopkins University Press, 2004), 16.
38. Julia Kristeva, *Revolution in Poetic Language*, trans. Margaret Waller (New York: Columbia University Press, 1984), 59.
39. Richardson, *Clarissa*, 894.
40. Terry Castle, *Clarissa's Ciphers: Meaning and Disruption in Richardson's 'Clarissa'* (Ithaca and London: Cornell University Press, 1982), 119.
41. Richardson, *Clarissa*, 889.
42. Ibid., 894.
43. Richardson, *Clarissa*, 896.
44. Georg Simmel, "Exchange," in *On Individuality and Social Forms*, trans. Donald Levine (Chicago: University of Chicago Press, 1971), 44.
45. Albrecht von Haller, Review of *Clarissa* with Richardson's annotations (*Gentleman's Magazine*, 19, June and August, 1749), in Keymer, *Published Commentary*, vol. 1, 152.
46. Jane Collier to Edward Cave, 19 September 1749, in Keymer, *Published Commentary*, vol. 1, 143.

47. Collier's response is echoed by many others, including the critic James Beattie, who claimed that Clarissa's frenzied letter could not be read "without sensible emotion. The starts of frenzy, of frenzy in such a person, under such circumstances, are I think hit off in such a manner as would not have been unworthy of Shakespeare himself." Bueler, ed., *Reading Clarissa*, 420.
48. Zygmunt Bauman, *Wasted Lives: Modernity and Its Outcasts* (Cambridge: Polity, 2004), 22.
49. Yota Batsaki, "Clarissa; or, Rake Versus Usurer," *Representations* 93 (Winter 2006): 22–40, 37, my italics.
50. Richardson, *Clarissa*, 162.
51. Idem.
52. Richardson, *Clarissa*, 564.
53. Richardson, *Clarissa*, 714; Thomas Hobbes, *Leviathan*, ed. Richard Tuck (Cambridge: Cambridge University Press, 1996), 70.
54. Ibid., 1439.
55. Ibid., 426, my emphasis.
56. Ibid., 427, my emphasis.
57. Ibid., 430.
58. Ibid., 36.
59. Ibid., 897.
60. Ibid., 1124.
61. Ibid., 892.
62. Aurel Kolnai, cited in Gee, *Making Waste*, 8.
63. Kristeva, *Powers of Horror*, 4.
64. Gee, *Making Waste*, 17.
65. Richardson, *Clarissa*, 901.
66. Ibid., 180.
67. Ibid., 893.
68. Ibid., 901.
69. Daniel M. Gross, *The Secret History of Emotion: From Aristotle's Rhetoric to Modern Brain Science* (Chicago: University of Chicago Press, 2007), 46.
70. Richardson, *Clarissa*, 897.
71. Idem.
72. Richardson, *Clarissa*, 1488.
73. Deirdre Shauna Lynch, *The Economy of Character: Novels, Market Culture, and the Business of Inner Meaning* (Chicago: University of Chicago Press, 1998), 45.
74. Richardson, *Clarissa*, 1064–65.
75. Idem.
76. Ibid., 713.
77. Ibid., 1495.

14 "Never Was a Thing Put to So Many Uses"

Transfer and Transformation in Laurence Sterne's Fiction (1759–1768)

Brigitte Friant-Kessler

> "This vile, dirty planet of ours,—which o' my conscience, with reverence be it spoken, I take to be made up of the shreds and clippings of the rest."
>
> (Laurence Sterne, *The Life and Opinions of Tristram Shandy, Gentleman*[1])

Laurence Sterne (1713–1768) is well known for incorporating in his prose fiction "shreds and clippings" from works as diverse as Chamber's *Cyclopaedia*, Swift's *Tale of a Tub*, or Montaigne's *Essays*, to name but a few, but his rewritings extend beyond that use. He deliberately played with borrowing to the point of mocking it in a self-derisive fashion as, for instance, in *Tristram Shandy*, at the beginning of volume V, when Tristram, the narrator, laments the lack of originality with which book production is plagued: "Shall we for ever make new books, as apothecaries make new mixtures, by pouring only out of one vessel into another?"[2] While this is a question directly addressed to the reader it is equally an allusion in which the learned reader was expected to identify a lift from Robert Burton's *Anatomy of Melancholy*. By tapping into other writers' sources Sterne fed cycles of novelty and created a new type of "cento," precisely in the manner of Burton.[3] Thus Sterne turned recycling of past works into an essential feature of his writings.[4] But contrary to the vast body of verbal borrowings, the reshaping of material things is a facet of Sterne's fiction to which little critical attention has hitherto been given.[5] To cast the net a little wider, this chapter enquires into the type of recycling which affects the material world in *The Life and Opinions of Tristram Shandy, Gentleman* (1759–1767) and *A Sentimental Journey* (1768). In those novels recycling is not so much a way to prolong use value and salvage discarded objects as a means to endow inanimate elements, such as clothes and everyday household objects, with a spirit of empirical, creative, and often game-like experimentation. The circulation of things and the various transformative processes to which things are submitted neatly echo the formulation of Yorick, the narrator in *A Sentimental Journey*, whose "There is nothing unmixt in this world" serves both as a philosophical guideline and aesthetic manifesto.[6]

By looking at the multiple functions of objects in the two novels several aspects related to transfer and transformation will be discussed. First I will explain how the circulation of dress illustrates social mobility as well as the possible connections between recycling and memory. I will then show how and why transformation is a nostalgia-driven game, and discuss the impact of recycling as both structural and emotional. My overall argument is that the way things are circulated and altered affects the fictional characters and their surroundings as well as language and the reader's perception. As Sterne's fiction is governed by a perpetual motion pattern, of which recycling is an essential point, it will then be shown that transfer and transformation underpin the link between recycled matter and the materiality of the book itself. The transformative craze at work is inseparable from the plasticity of the text. Thus the recycling of objects lies at the foundation of a narrative in which the lack of stability is staged so as to be partly plausible in a real world yet ideal as a tool for the author's humorous treatment of fictionalised lives and opinions.

THINGS IN MOTION AND RECYCLING *IN ABSENTIA*

In eighteenth-century Britain, the lives and afterlives of objects were as diverse as their circulation, and the latter easily spread across social and generic boundaries, thus supporting views according to which this was a dynamic society. Dress is a case in point, and in *Tristram Shandy* what falls into the category of domestic and social recycling is illustrated by an episode set in the kitchen where all the servants have gathered. Obadiah, a male domestic of the Shandy household, has just broken the news of the death of Bobby Shandy, the elder son of the family. Tristram narrates how Susannah, the maid, knowing fully well that during mourning period coloured clothes will have to be discarded, hopes that most of the wardrobe will come to her, and how she launches into a visionary survey of the wardrobe of her mistress:

> A green sattin night-gown of my mother's, which had been twice scoured, was the first idea which *Obadiah*'s exclamation brought into *Susannah*'s head [. . .] the word *mourning*, notwithstanding *Susannah* made use of it herself—failed also of doing its office; it excited not one single idea, tinged either with grey or black,—all was green.—The green sattin night-gown hung there still.[7]

Though at this stage still in the possession of Tristram's mother, the green gown conjures a powerful envisioning of a green-tinted world, as well as a whole series of animated garments literally dancing before Susannah's eyes: "My mother's whole wardrobe followed.—What a procession! her red damask,—her orange-tawny,—her white and yellow lutestrings,—her brown taffata,—her bone-laced caps, her bed-gowns, and comfortable under-petticoats.—Not a rag was left behind."[8] The passage as such combines visual—largely emphasised by the colours and the dash after each garment—with material elements, and signs of a common social practice, at least in households where servants were reasonably well treated. To be noted is a touch of humour and a degree of ribaldry as the expression "green gown" was slang for sexual intercourse so that the morbidity of the mourning be counteracted by the comic effect of a superimposed imagery.[9] The transfer of the gown being conditioned by social conventions it was destined to circulate according to the preestablished pattern that governed most master-servant relationships.[10] However, passing on the gown to Susannah may not have been performed without applying changes, for even though the narrator does not dwell on the subject, the garment is likely to have generated either waste or want of fabric, be it only to alter it so that it should fit the maid's body.[11] As this scene draws on a fantasy rather than on the proper transfer of the garment it epitomises a mode of recycling *in absentia*.[12] The garment, and indeed the whole wardrobe which is imagined point to the maid's anticipation of wearing her mistress's clothes and imitating those of another social rank. As noted by Jean Hecht, eighteenth-century Britain was "a relatively dynamic society" in terms of social mobility between classes. Moving up and down the social ladder involved the circulation of objects and dress, either by loss or gain.[13] But the type of transfer described in this passage of *Tristram Shandy* also aptly illustrates the pleasures of the imagination, more precisely those which Addison termed "secondary pleasures" because they "flow from the ideas of visible objects, when the objects are not actually before the eye, but are called up into our memories, or formed into agreeable visions of things that are either absent or fictitious."[14]

About clothes in fiction narratives, Clair Hughes argues that "references to dress for both reader and writer contribute to the 'reality effect': they lend tangibility and visibility to character and context."[15] As a piece of dress, the green nightgown is concrete because it is said to exist in Mrs Shandy's wardrobe yet it remains intangible all at once if one takes into consideration that the representation bursts into the narrative and is described as "an idea brought into Susannah's head." With Susannah's inventory we move toward intangibility and the gown is closer to Chloe Wigston-Smith's definition of an "autonomous garment."[16] Isolated and pinned down in the mindscape of the reader, the gown however sets all manner of ideas into motion, in contravention of the expected sobriety due to the mourning circumstances.

Another absence-related case of sartorial transfer occurs when a character, Corporal Trim, is given the regimental coat of Le Fever, who had served in the army during the same wars.[17] Le Fever's demise—one of the most sentimental passages in the *Tristram Shandy*—is dwelt on at length so as to elicit a strong emotional response on the part of the reader, and the reference to the dead soldier's uniform echoes the pathos of the Story of Le Fever: "There remained nothing more in my uncle *Toby*'s hands, than an old regimental coat and a sword; [. . .] The coat my uncle *Toby* gave the corporal;—Wear it, *Trim*, said my uncle *Toby*, as long as it will hold together, for the sake of the poor lieutenant."[18] Unlike the maid's desired gown, which symbolises her failure to enter into the proper spirit of mourning, the coat doubles as sentimental memorabilia and a relic of Le Fever's military past. This attachment to one piece of dress thus reinforces the role of group-bonding objects among war veterans. The coat is being offered another life in Trim's wardrobe, and as such it connects all the veterans beyond a lifespan. With the aim of prolonging the life of clothes, transfer is a means to strengthen family or friendship ties. But in Sterne's second novel there is an example of recycled clothes that takes place in the context of an economic transaction outside household and family relationships. In the course of Yorick's travels through France the Englishman narrates how he hires a French servant, La Fleur, and gives the reader a detailed account of the acquisition of a second-hand outfit:

> He had purchased moreover a handsome blue sattin waistcoat, fancifully enough embroidered—this was indeed something the worse for the services it had done, but 'twas clean scour'd—the gold had been touch'd up, and upon the whole was rather showy than otherwise—and as the blue was not violent, it suited with the coat and breeches very well: he had squeez'd out of the money, moreover, a new bag and a solitaire; and had insisted with the *fripier*, upon a gold pair of garters to his breeches knees.[19]

This description underscores ways of making over different garments so that they would look aesthetically pleasing. Although details such as "embroidered," "gold pair of garters" sound fairly extravagant, it was frequently the case that servants dressed well, under the proviso they were given garments that had belonged to their masters.[20] While Yorick expresses the wish that La Fleur's clothes should be bought new he is glad that his valet did not act spendthriftly with the money he had received from him. The servant's outfit is detailed so as to emphasise cleanliness but also elements of luxury, for instance with the repetition of "gold," though "touch'd up." There are also clues to good colourfastness. Furthermore with the mention of the French "*fripier*" Yorick eulogises La Fleur's frugality. Recycling is thus more than a case of external appearance—it becomes a way to display moral values. However, the emphasis on the scouring suggests that the overall effect was one that could only ever be next best to the more desirable new.

Outside dress, other material elements are circulated, and *A Sentimental Journey* is rife with circulating objects. The thing that probably best epitomises this circulating pattern is a trivial piece of paper primarily used to wrap a pat of butter, but which turns out to be one of several fragments from sheets meant to form a mysterious narrative:

> When I had finish'd the butter, I threw the currant leaf out of the window, and was going to do the same by the waste paper—but stopping

> to read a line first, and that drawing me on to a second and third—I thought it better worth; so I shut the window, and drawing a chair up to it, I sat down to read it.[21]

When the narrator realises that the sequel is missing he finds out it has been used to form a makeshift wrapping around a nosegay. While one half is solely used for a practical purpose the other half is recycled by La Fleur to serve his sentimental enterprise: "he told me there were only two other sheets of it which he had wrapt round the stalks of a *bouquet* to keep it together, which he had presented to the *demoiselle* upon the *boulevards*." There is no stopping the incessant transfer of the object from one individual to the next: "his faithless mistress had given his *gage d'amour* to one of the Count's footmen—the footman to a young sempstress—and the sempstress to a fiddler, with my fragment at the end of it,"[22] and we can safely assume that by the time the wrapping paper and the bouquet had come into the possession of the fiddler the handling of such an ephemeral thing had resulted into an inevitable state of decay, only to chime in with the sense of loss experienced by La Fleur in the role of the dejected lover.

Though endowed with a sense of novelty and desire to prolong life recycling partly originates from the individual's experience of absence. While forming part of conventional interactions in society, the motion of the objects is equally linked to an owner's (or would-be owner's) emotional response. Objects, particularly in sentimental fiction, signify remembrance of things past as well as attitudes to death. The latter can be ambivalent, as with Susannah's imagined wardrobe. The scene is presented so that fancy may prevail over speech and act while the maid's incapacity to keep her attention on mourning forms the inception of a micronarrative that has all the characteristics of a reverie. In the case of the recycling of the regimental coat, the reverie percolates through the object as a souvenir. That the coat is offered a second life—a new wearer makes for a new aspect of the garment—is perhaps not as important as the fact that, by being transferred, its material aspect is transcended. Whereas both examples seem to indicate that there is a careful treatment of the material world in Sterne's novels, several sections in *Tristram Shandy* however revolve around things that are prone to being either neglected or disassembled in order to satisfy an urge for transformation that simultaneously affects the objects, the characters, and the validity of words.

OBJECTS AND WORDS: (UN)FORTUNATE RECYCLING ?

Nostalgia is undoubtedly the motivation behind a series of transformations performed at Shandy Hall, in particular all those related to Toby's and Trim's re-enactment of the battles, in which compulsive transformation contaminates not only their minds but the whole of the material world which surrounds them. Indeed Proteus appears to be actively at work in the wings, something that results in amusing *quid pro quo* situations but is also the cause of disasters, for instance, when Trim takes off the weights of a sash-window to recycle the lead and make cannons. While this may demonstrate Trim's ingenious capacity to transform matter it is also an unfortunate transformation as the mechanism of the window is seriously damaged. The alteration affects the whole structure, which, devoid of its pulleys, brutally falls down on the penis of five-year old Tristram when the boy tries to urinate from the window and is then almost castrated.

Another corporeal accident linked to recycling combines inventiveness and linguistic instability when Tristram is delivered with the help of a pair of forceps at the hands of one Dr Slop. "In bringing him into the world with his vile instruments, he has crush'd his nose, *Susannah* says, as flat as a pancake to his face, and he is making a false bridge with a piece of cotton and a thin piece of whalebone out of *Susannah*'s stays, to raise it up."[23] This scene is one which best illustrates the connection between object, transformation, and language.[24] From a medical viewpoint the whalebone in the maid's stays is meant to be a makeshift splint for Tristram's nose. The recycling of this piece of dress shows the multiple uses an object, or part of it, may be put to. Simultaneously, the word "bridge," used to describe Dr Slop's use of Susannah's stays, is highly polysemous since it evokes a drawbridge in Uncle Toby's warfare-obsessed mind. The punning on "bridge" is a comic device that reinforces the parallelism between semantic unreliability, the ever-widening gap between signifier and what is signified. The link of the word "bridge" with recycling connects the plastic dimension of the body and the material plasticity of words, only to show more blatantly the latter's weakness.

Words, body parts, and material recycling are also associated in the episode of the "papilliotes" in volume VII, a fine example of how change in function and semantic transformation go hand in hand. The shift in the function of the thing conflates with the polysemous verb "twist." Volume VII presents the reader with an adult Tristram who has set off on a Grand Tour, and the scene is set in France.[25] Having just lost a number of manuscript remarks in a chaise, Tristram complains about that loss and decides to retrieve them by visiting the chaise-vamper's home. Upon his encounter with the wife of the chaise-vamper, he notices, almost accidentally, that his remarks have been recycled into curlpapers and that they elegantly adorn the lady's hair: "The wife of the chaise-vamper step'd in, I told you, to take the papilliotes from off her hair—the toilet stands still for no man—so she jerk'd off her cap, to begin with them as she open'd the door, in doing which, one of them fell upon the ground—I instantly saw it was my own writing."[26] In order to act as an efficient curling device Tristram's recorded remarks had to be twisted, hence transformed and distorted. Since the verb "twist" applies both to the meaning of the remarks and to what is actually inflicted to the paper, language and matter become intertwined. Though there is no detailed account of corporeal contact between Tristram and the chaise-vamper's wife, these remarks establish a contact between the two bodies, i.e. between what came out of his head and what landed on hers. The staged recycling of remarks into curlpapers serves as a manifestation of Sterne's art to enhance the importance of snippets in print and to bring forth a vestigial representation of the self, while "twist" may also remind the reader of the spiralling structure of the narrative.[27]

Much to the reader's entertainment, the most spectacular transformations are those effected by Toby and Trim on the bowling green where the veterans display their talents in warfare while re-enacting battles, past and present. The first example is narrated in volume III, the second in volume VI. The episode in volume III revolves around a pair of boots that stirs a major row between the two brothers. While Walter Shandy, uncle Toby's brother and Tristram's father, considers the boots to be a family heirloom, the footwear becomes a bone of contention the moment Trim announces that the boots have been turned into mortars to be used for a re-enactment game: "May it please your honour, cried *Trim*,—they are two mortar-pieces for a siege next summer, which I have been making out of a pair of jack-boots, which *Obadiah* told me your honour had left off wearing.—By heaven! cried my father, springing out of his chair, as he swore."[28] More than a mere act of recycling of a cast-off object the transformation to which the boots are subjected is perceived as a mutilation and a desecrating act, at least from Walter Shandy's point of view. But in spite of the shift in function that triggers Walter Shandy's outburst of anger, the boots retain most of their original appearance. Toby, on the contrary, is described as elated and insensitive to the idea of cutting off the top of the boots that have been in the family for several generations: "Sir *Roger Shandy* wore them at the battle of *Marston-Moor.*—I declare I would not have taken ten pounds for them.—I'll pay you the money, brother *Shandy*, quoth my uncle *Toby*, looking at the two mortars with infinite pleasure, and putting his hand into his breeches-pocket, as he viewed them."[29] By using the term "mortars" we are made aware that the old soldier's imaginative eye and performative act of speech have operated a complete transformation, and that indeed the footwear has been recycled into an explosive device.[30] As Richard Lanham put it, re-enactment is part of the many games of pleasure experienced on the bowling green.[31] So is recycling. It is the transformative craze that generates chaos in the household but enables the veteran to expand the scope of their games. Transformative activities can affect objects in antagonistic ways. They can induce confusion in the value scale and alter the importance given to a particular object. Both the transformed boots and Le Fever's regimental coat see their value increased in Toby's view, hence the offer to pay £10 for them.[32] However as a symbolic act the change in shape and function lays emphasis on Toby's solipsistic obsession with his former battles, his individual manner of confronting his own past, and the fact that, according to Walter Shandy, the same boots are worthless as a family heirloom when the tops are removed.

Overall, transformation is part of a host of comic devices that entail a constant reshaping of the environment. Objects, like the pair of jack-boots, are transformed but the narrative itself yields little as to the final state of those boots, which in turn gives illustrators plenty of leeway to represent them. In Charles Catton's illustration to *Tristram Shandy* published in Cooke's series of Pocket Novels in 1793 (Figure 14.1) the viewer may notice in the foreground a pair of boots awkwardly mounted on wheels.

Although such explosive devices could indeed be seen fixed on wheels the dominating effect is one that enhances the function of boots as children's toys.[33] While the recycled jack-boots reinforce the theatricality with which those wooing scenes are endowed, the visual representation of the boots duplicates the military metaphors in the amorous discourse.

Figure 14.1 Charles Catton Jr., "The Widow Wadman making love to Uncle Toby in the sentry box," *Tristram Shandy* (Cooke's Pocket Edition of Select Novels, 1797). Private collection. Reproduced with permission.

When examining makeshift weapons for the bowling green two further important material elements spring to mind. They are both described as having been sent from Lisbon to Corporal Trim by his brother Tom, which again connects recycling to family relationships: a pair of water pipes and a Montero cap. The latter is a multipurpose headwear that lends itself to recycling by nature: "never was a Montero-cap put to so many uses; for in all controverted points, whether military or culinary, provided the corporal was sure he was in the right,—it was either his *oath*,—his *wager*,—or his *gift.*"[34] This cap fits well his owner, a character epitomised by his multiple competences, as indicated in the first volumes: "Toby took him for his servant, and of excellent use was he, attending my uncle Toby in the camp and in his quarters as valet, groom, barber, cook, sempster, and nurse."[35] In volume VI the tobacco pipes are turned into succedaneum of field battery. The result of this transformation is best perceived in the depiction of Toby and Trim's mutually enhanced satisfaction that leads to a climactic sense of gratification. Recycling acts as a substitute, rather like a euphemism would in language, particularly when Tristram makes clear that none of the explosive devices on the bowling green would have been safe had they been activated by real powder: "I say proper ammunition—because his great artillery would not bear powder; and 'twas well for the *Shandy* family they would not—For [. . .] so heated was my uncle *Toby*'s imagination with the accounts of them, that he had infallibly shot away all his estate."[36] Be it the battles or the construction of additional parts to the fortifications erected on the bowling green, Toby and Trim's activities are executed in a ritualised manner.[37] Jonathan Lamb argues that Toby "constructs a scene that is supposed never to change, since it has no other purpose from his point of view than the regular rhythm of its being built and then demolished. The story of the bowling green is less like a narrative than a rite, with Toby the priest and the works the sacrifice."[38] But such a rationale does not take into account the dynamics entailed by the rite of construction and deconstruction, as both offer numerous possibilities of recycling and taking advantage of the plasticity of the material world. On the bowling green there is only one town yet "the town was a perfect *Proteus* [. . .] Surely never did any TOWN act so many parts, since *Sodom* and *Gomorrah*, as my uncle *Toby*'s town did."[39]

Between volume II and VI there has been a shift from recycling boots interpreted as an act of desecration to a Scriptural evocation in which recycling plays an essential role. In an analogous fashion the Montero cap is an accessory that can be put to many uses so that the fixity of ritualization in the scenes in which the cap appears (often story-telling passages) is largely undercut. As materiality and language become one, recycling is made part of the dynamics of the narrative. Words and things at once collide and coalesce so as to constitute the main contact point between material transformation and Sterne's aesthetics in general. Transforming objects is an essential element of an overarching pattern of subversion, and from this perspective recycling fits into the broader picture of a narrative that claims to be emblematically paradoxical, or as Tristram himself explains to the reader his work is "digressive, and it is progressive too,—and at the same time."[40]

RECYCLING MADE EMBLEMATIC

At the crossroads of the inanimate object and the animated living being stands the animal. Out of all animals, caged birds show that it is a thin line between object and animal, indeed one that proves hard to draw.[41] With its transformation from bird into visual design, the starling in *A Sentimental Journey* raises exactly this question. While travelling in France Yorick comes across a cage with a speaking bird that begs to be set free.[42] Further to this encounter Yorick's mind is haunted by images of captivity. The original story of the bird reveals that it is a highly itinerant object of desire, much circulated in all kinds of social strata. As a trapped animal, the starling passes from being a talking bird in his cage to that of a still (life) detail when the reader discovers the crest of Yorick's coat of arms embellished with a representation of that same bird.[43] Not only is the starling's engraved immobility turned into immortality but the emblematic value of the bird is further emphasised by the interwoven play on the author's name.[44] An emblem, in the heraldic sense, is both an intangible symbol and a visible sign on a real escutcheon. Sterne frequently draws the reader's attention to the book as a physical object, particularly in passages which create an effect of substitution between object and book: "We'll not stop two moments, my dear Sir,—only, as we have got thro' these five volumes, (do, Sir, sit down upon a set—they are better than nothing)."[45] Although transformation is only achieved by way of words, the image that is conjured is not one of books appreciated for their contents but of a material object, part of a set of furniture, or perhaps even a chair recycled into reading material. It has been argued that the Shandean body may be read—and so, it appears, can objects.[46]

As formulated by Tom Keymer, Sterne "digests and reworks."[47] In both novels objects are not only circulated but they also undergo minor and major changes. Single parts and fragments are put to many uses. At the same time recycling and putting objects to a variety of uses is an act of preservation whose chief purpose is to defy Time's and Death's relentless assaults. Thus the spectrum covered by what may then be seen as a pattern based on a series of cycles in Sterne's fiction ranges from the down-to-earth, trivial, and concrete things in everyday life to more abstract and philosophical concepts, such as life and death. In *Tristram Shandy* recycling is part and parcel of what Keymer calls "the dynamics of communication." But instead of words being exchanged, objects are passed round, an element of Sterne's fiction which is well illustrated in volume III when Tristram refers to, and simultaneously derides, eloquence and its classical rhetorical devices: "It is a singular stroke of eloquence (at least it was so, when eloquence flourished at *Athens* and *Rome*, and would be so now, did orators wear mantles) not to mention the name of a thing, when you had the thing about you, *in petto*, ready to produce, pop, in the place you want it."[48] This example of word-thing substitution is an aspect of what Lynn Mary Festa terms a "befetished word."[49] Central to any transformation is its association with imagined worlds, as well as words, a fundamental principle made clear in Tristram's allegorical description of Fancy which has "the power to turn straws and bulrushes into masts and bowsprits," thus making small things look larger and more impressive.[50]

Cycles of novelty in the material world of Sterne's fiction echo the way the author frequently compares his writings to a vehicle in constant motion. The circulation of objects may be seen as accidental yet entirely part of an overall pattern that affects both the animate and the inanimate. Metamorphosis is given preference over stasis as the latter would petrify memory and cause the narrative vehicle to grind to a halt. Trim appropriates not only the transformation of the boots but is forever associated with the final recycled product itself. In the same way Slop's recycling of the whalebone in Susannah's stays implants a tripartite object-subject relationship in the reader's brain: Susannah and stays/Slop and bridge/Toby and fortifications. Yet while most recycling aims at prolonging the life of the object, or even life as such, it often does so in a fragmented way, especially as separate parts are put to a variety of ends.[51] In *Tristram Shandy*, in particular, the dismantling goes hand in hand with the constant urge to create. More important still is the idea that re-creation is but another name for entertainment, which means that recycling is a game, and that an essential aspect of such playful activities is to perceive objects like toys in the hands of children.

The game dimension of recycling is aptly illustrated by the two nostalgic veterans Toby and Trim, who transfer and transform small parts of the Shandy Hall household (spouts, a shaving basin, sash-window weights and pulleys) and who thus demonstrate imaginative albeit solipsistic ways of improving the installations on the bowling green. Examples of clothes made over speak for an approach of objects that are not discarded but rather salvaged. The garments (the green gown, the regimental coat) are circulated and lightly transformed for preservation purposes. However a concomitant experience of loss and gain is inevitable as both *Tristram Shandy* and *A Sentimental Journey* revolve a great deal around gaps to be filled in and blanks left to trigger perplexity and elicit an active response from the reader. Fragments of text as well as tangible things are continuously generated, gathered, dislocated, and reassembled to the point of becoming emblematic of the writer's style. Recycled shreds and clippings of the material world are in keeping with an overall pattern that fosters cycles of novelty and partakes of a constant sense of regeneration. Recycling in Sterne's fiction is not only a matter of aesthetics but a means for objects to flesh out an organic perception of metamorphosis. Elizabeth Harries argued in her essay on Sternean fragments: "Saint Paraleipomenon, the patron of things left out does indeed watch over Sterne's novels, with the God Muddle, Sterne's gaps, leaps, blank pages, and fragments equally call to fulfil the command 'that nothing be lost.'"[52] But rather than looking at things as if left in the hands of a god named Muddle, let Proteus be the divinity called upon to order and recycle the matter, for better or worse.

NOTES

1. *The Life and Opinions of Tristram Shandy, Gentleman* 1.5.9. Unless otherwise specified all references are to *The Life and Opinions of Tristram Shandy, Gentleman*, ed. Ian Campbell Ross (Oxford: Oxford University Press, 2009). Throughout this chapter the title will henceforth be referred to in its abridged form *TS*. The first number corresponds to the volume (in Roman numerals in the text), the second to chapter numbers, the third to page number in the OUP edition. As the novel was published in serialised form, with intermittent pauses due to Sterne's travels to France and ill health, the complete set of nine volumes took eight years to come out. All references to Sterne's second novel *A Sentimental Journey through France and Italy* correspond to *A Sentimental Journey* and *Continuation of Bramine's Journal, with Related Texts*, Melvyn New and W. G. Day, eds. (Indianapolis: Hackett Publishing, 2006). This work will henceforth be referred to in its abridged form as *ASJ*.
2. *TS* 5.1.275
3. In the introduction to *The Anatomy of Melancholy*, first published in 1621, Burton uses the word "cento" to provide the reader with an explanatory definition of his work: "I have laboriously collected this cento out of divers writers, and that *sine injuria*, I have wronged no authors, but given every man his own." T. C. Faulkner, N. K. Kiessling, and R. L. Blair, eds., *The Anatomy of Melancholy* (Oxford: Oxford University Press, 1989), vol. 1, 11.
4. Sterne's borrowings were first pointed out in 1792, in a paper delivered to the Manchester Literary and Philosophical Society by Dr. John Ferriar, the physician to the Manchester Infirmary's lunatic asylum. The subsequent version of this lecture entitled *Illustrations of Sterne*, published in 1798, became the seedbed for a long-lasting trend of plagiarism charges levelled at Sterne, although Ferriar does also indicate that previous authors amply and continuously borrowed.
5. Recent scholarship on the so-called "it-narratives" has endeavoured to establish connections between objects in Sterne's novels and experimental fiction in the 1740s and 1750s. See for instance Deirdre Lynch's essay: "Personal Effects and Sentimental Fictions," in *The Secret Life of Things. Animals, Objects and It—Narratives in Eighteenth-Century England*, ed. Mark Blackwell (Cranbury, NJ: Associated University Presses, 2007), 63–91.
6. *ASJ* 126.
7. *TS* 5.7.288.
8. *TS* 5.7.288.
9. For a definition that points to the sexual connotation of "green gown" see, for instance, Francis Grose, *A Dictionary of the Vulgar Tongue*, repr. 1811: "to give a girl a green gown; tumble her on the grass."
10. For a detailed study of the relationship between masters and servants see Jean Hecht, *The Domestic Servant Class in Eighteenth-Century England* (London: Routledge and Kegan, 1956); Bridget Hill, *Servants: English Domestics in the Eighteenth Century* (New York: Clarendon Press, Oxford University Press, 1996).

11. Hecht cites the account of a German traveller impressed by the costume of female servants in England: "They are usually clad in gowns well adjusted to their shapes, and hats adorned with ribbands. There are some who even wear silk, sattin, when they are dressed." Jean Hecht, *The Domestic Servant,* 119.
12. Shortly after this episode the gown is effectively described as having changed owner, as might have been expected in a genteel household like the Shandys': "after affairs were a little settled in the family, and *Susannah* had got possession of my mother's green sattin night-gown" (*TS* 5.16.445). A similar view is expressed by Kirstin Olsen: "Servants also inherited clothes when employers dies, or were given cast off to wear or sell." Kirstin Olsen, *Daily Life in Eighteenth-Century England* (Westport: Greenwood Press, 1999), 126.
13. Jean Hecht, *The Domestic Servant*, 209–15.
14. For the complete essay, see Joseph Addison, "The Pleasures of the Imagination," *The Spectator* no. 411, 21 June 1712.
15. Clair Hughes, *Dressed in Fiction* (Oxford: Berg, 2006), 2.
16. For a detailed discussion of the notion of when and how a garment becomes autonomous, see Chloe Wigston-Smith, who offers the following definition for the notion of "autonomous garment": "By autonomous clothes, I mean unworn garments that are represented as detached from the body, the kind of clothes capable of thwarting their owner's agency, of circulating beyond the owner's grasp." Chloe Wigston-Smith, "Clothes without Bodies: Objects, Humans, and the Marketplace in Eighteenth-Century It-Narratives and Trade Cards," *Eighteenth-Century Fiction* 23, no. 2 (2011): 348.
17. Tristram's uncle, Captain Tobias Shandy, and Corporal Trim fought in the wars of the Spanish Succession during the reigns of King William and Queen Anne. Ian Campbell Ross depicts them as: "[. . .] good-old natured uncle Toby, a retired army captain, grievously wounded in the groin at the 1695 siege of Namur, who plays elaborate war-games on his bowling-green with his servant, Corporal Trim, a soldier with an unusual capacity for oratory (and a brother in a Portuguese prison)." Introduction to *The Life and Opinions of Tristram Shandy, Gentleman,* ed. Ian Campbell Ross, (Oxford: Oxford World's Classics, 2009), xviii.
18. *TS*. 6. 12. 346.
19. *ASJ* 139.
20. Conversely Hecht underlines that some masters and mistresses may have deemed it inappropriate to see their servants too well-dressed, and worried about the domestics being mistaken for them because of their exceedingly fine clothes. In such a chain of emulation it was essential to find an acceptable middle ground between an acknowledged sense of advancement and the aping of a social class above one's rank.
21. *ASJ* 141.
22. *ASJ* 147.
23. *TS* 3.27.170.
24. Slop's technique for mending Tristram's crushed nose seems inadequate in more ways than one. The first report of such an operation or "Curious Chirurgical Operation," was published in a letter in *The Gentleman's Magazine* 64, no. 4 (October 1794): 891–92.
25. As noted by Ross, in this volume of the book we have both the viewpoint of Tristram as an adult who flees from the menace of Death and of Sterne's as a Grand Tourist, a detail which is later to be given much more scope in *A Sentimental Journey* as the second novel is entirely devoted to this topic. For more details on the "narrative virtuosity" of volume VII, see Ian Campbell Ross's introduction, xxi–ii. For the tight links between volume VII in *Tristram Shandy* and *A Sentimental Journey,* see the appendix to *A Sentimental*

Journey and the Continuation of the Bramine's Journal, ed. Melvyn New and W. G. Day (Indianapolis: Hackett, 2006).

26. *TS* 7.38. 425–26.
27. For an illuminating anthropological and literary view on spirals and circular patterns in Sterne's *Tristram Shandy*, see Mary Douglas, *Thinking in Circles: An Essay on Ring Composition* (Yale: Yale University Press, 2007).
28. *TS* 3.22.162.
29. *TS* 3.22. 163.
30. The term "act of speech" is used in the Austinian sense of how to do things with words, mainly to suggest that the act of recycling is brought about by language as well as by change in shape and function.
31. For a discussion applying game theory to Uncle Toby, defined as *homo ludens*, see Richard Lanham, *Tristram Shandy. The Games of Pleasure* (Berkeley: University of California Press, 1973).
32. Comparatively, and to provide an order of magnitude, we may bear in mind that although Toby's proposition relates to Britain in the first quarter of the century, Sterne's annual salary as an assistant curate of a Yorkshire parish in 1738 was of £30 (Ian Campbell Ross, introduction, xi).
33. See the plate on fortifications and warfare in Ephraïm Chambers's *Cyclopaedia: Or, an Universal Dictionary of Arts and Sciences* (London: 1741) from which Sterne borrowed extensively, and which is reproduced in *The Life and Opinions of Tristram Shandy, Gentleman, The Florida Edition of the Works of Laurence Sterne. Vol. 3. The Notes, ed.* Melvyn New, Richard Davies, and W. G. Day (Gainesville: University Press of Florida, 1984), 554.
34. *TS* 6. 24. 361.
35. *TS* 2.5.77.
36. *TS* 6. 23–24. 360.
37. Trim is said to be able to recite the first five commandments of the Bible much in the same way he executes a military drill with a firearm.
38. Jonathan Lamb, *The Things Things Say* (Princeton: Princeton University Press, 2011), 20.
39. *TS* 6. 23. 359.
40. *TS* 1. 22.58.
41. The French scholar René Demoris makes a similar point in his essay "L'oiseau et sa cage en peinture." In "Esthétique et poétique de l'objet au dix-huitième siècle," ed. Christophe Martin and Catherine Ramond, special issue, *Lumières* 5 (2005): 29–47.
42. *ASJ* 100–01. The caged starling is a symbol of slavery and allows the narrator to launch into a moving antislavery oratory, which in turn triggered a response by Ignatius Sancho, a former slave.
43. For a detailed discussion of the starling added on the crest of Yorick's arms and the possible origins of Sterne's coat of arms, see *ASJ* 106, note 2.
44. Michael O'Shea notes the canting effect in this crest. "Heraldic canting is the practice of adopting emblems that pun on the name of the bearer." Michael O'Shea, "Laurence Sterne's Display of Heraldry," *The Shandean* 3 (1991): 62.
45. *TS* 6.1.329.
46. On the issues raised by Sterne's fiction and reading bodies, see Juliet McMaster, *Reading the Body in the Eighteenth-Century Novel* (Basingstoke: Palgrave Macmillan, 2004).
47. Keymer Casebook 52.
48. *TS* 3.14.146. I am indebted to W. G. Day for correction of the first draft of this chapter and making many insightful suggestions.
49. Lynn Mary Festa, *Sentimental Figures of Empire in Eighteenth-Century Britain and France* (Baltimore: Johns Hopkins University Press, 2006), 92.

50. *TS* 8.5.438.
51. Susan Strasser begins her book with the example of a seventeenth-century bottle that has been recycled by reusing each component for a different purpose. See Susan Strasser, *Waste and Want. A Social History of Trash* (New York: Metropolitan Books, 1999), 21–67.
52. God Muddle is an allusion to E.M. Forster's 1927 criticism of Sterne's lack of narrative structure. St Paraleipomenon is a lift from *Tristram Shandy* in volume III (*TS* 3.36.180). The quotation is from Elizabeth Harries, "Sterne's Novels: Gathering Up the Fragments," *English Literary History* 49, no. 1 (Spring 1982): 35–49, 48.

15 Recycling a Medical Case
The Walpoles' Stone and Gravel

Sophie Vasset

The recycling of previous papers for the elaboration of a new one is a taboo practice among contemporary academics. The originality of sources, methodologies, and interpretations are elementary criteria for the evaluation of academic research in any field. Any scholar filling in the application for a grant needs to write about innovation, initiative, and creativity, and show the specificity of their research project, which needs to be carried out to explore new territories in the ever-expanding realm of knowledge. And yet, recycling seems to be a structural component of knowledge: forgotten ideas are given a new life, cultural transfers and belated translations enable us to discuss the same ideas at different times and in different contexts, old concepts are transformed and revisited with each new discovery. On a more individual level, recycling is the art of reusing the material we have gathered in libraries and archives, and adapting this material in storage for new conferences or book proposals. Just like chipped pots and make-do, however, academics feel this type of academic recycling needs to be hidden for added value, and we conceal what is considered a professional fault behind a new argumentative structure. The increased value attributed to originality is traditionally perceived as a romantic concept in literature.[1] In science, it is usually associated with nineteenth-century scientific journals, which promoted the circulation of scientific knowledge, and thus emphasised the originality of their contributions.[2] In these contexts, recycling practices—whether literary or scientific—became gradually associated with negligence and idleness.

The status of originality is rather difficult to determine in eighteenth-century medical writings. On the one hand, the encyclopaedic trends of medical doctors and natural historians valued repetition, rewriting, and summaries of other works—which all enter into the category of textual recycling—as part of the synthesising process needed for such work in which tracing back one's sources was secondary. On the other hand, the originality of medical discovery was valued and rewarded by the institutions. Renowned European physicians competed for the primacy of physiological discoveries, and the various controversies on these subjects are a sign of a growing anxiety for newness in medicine or natural history.[3] However, the guidelines for research and experiment in these two fields were not as clear as in other sciences, and the development of observation-based science coexisted with the exhumation of past cases taken from older medical texts. Case studies, as they exemplify a particular theory, stand at the intersection of observation-based medicine—as the cases were often singled out of the doctor's practice—and of more theoretical medicine based on the knowledge of ancient authors. Traditionally, case studies were compiled in textbooks to teach diagnosis: medical authors had to browse through them, and single out the case they needed as an illustration for their new treatise. Even though many case studies derived from the observation and practice of eighteenth-century doctors, several cases were still taken from such compilations in their medical treatises.

The epistemological function of such textual recyclings will be studied in the context of eighteenth-century medical writings, when originality and newness were not the only criteria for the reception of medical works. My reflection will start from the articulation between the immutable specificity of a narrative and the variation of its interpretations in various contexts, as I will focus on what I call the "recycling" of a particular medical case. The cases that are attached to a particular—famous—name are often easier to trace in medical corpuses, first because family names were not always published in case studies, and secondly because famous patients tend to be more discussed by doctors than unknown ones, as their fame could be a means of self-promotion.[4] I will take into account this celebrity bias in my present analysis of the case of Horace Walpole—not the man of letters and art *connoisseur*, whose Strawberry Hill is an example of an altogether different type of recycling—but the man he was named after, his more modest uncle, brother to the first prime minister of England, Robert Walpole. I will investigate the case of Horace Walpole's stone and gravel, which was reported when he suffered from several acute crises of the disease, and chose to start a lime-water treatment. This will help me to understand how what started as a first-hand observation of a patient by himself was reused and rewritten throughout the eighteenth century. By following the evolution of Walpole's case, I would like to show how recycling case studies was part of medical knowledge in the making.

I will present the various metamorphoses of Walpole's case throughout the treatise, but I have compiled them all in a chart, that details all the different steps in the case study's evolution. I will give the context of each new publication to show how Walpole's initial letter to Baron Edlin, his well-meaning friend who advised him on his treatment options, was turned into a text of medical interest and debate.

HORACE WALPOLE'S STONE AND GRAVEL—A CASE IN THREE PARTS

When the surgeons opened Horace Walpole's dead body, they found three little stones in his bladder, which were described thus: "The two first were very much alike, being of the shape and size of the kernel of a Spanish nut; only the sides were irregularly flattened, but without forming any sharp angle."[5] The stone and gravel was a disease widely written about in the eighteenth century, first because many male patients suffered from its acute pains, secondly because it could, to some extent, be treated. It could be cured by "cutting," also called lithotomy, but the operation was excruciating and the stone could come back, in spite of the skill of quick, able surgeons who sometimes acquired a reputation throughout Europe, as was the case for the London-based surgeon William Cheselden (1688–1752).[6] The pain and danger of the operation often terrified patients, who looked for other options available to relieve them. If they did not want to face lithotomy, they could turn to popular remedies such as "Joanna Stephen's Remedy" or Dr Jurin's "Lixivium."[7] These treatments remained the object of angry debates among physicians for or against the use of lime-water and soap (lye and oil) to dissolve the stone. Lime-water and soap smoothed the sharp edges of the stone, which no longer irritated the mucous membrane of the bladder, and stopped the presence of blood in the patient's urine (which was typically of "coffee water" colour).[8] It could even cut the stone into smaller pieces, and the patient usually voided small stones after an acute crisis.

Sir Robert Walpole died of the stone and gravel in 1745.[9] Horace Walpole, who worked in the administration as secretary to the Treasury in Sir Robert Walpole's first government and occupied various other positions afterwards, suffered from the same disease. Horace died in 1757, and even though he apparently did not die of the stone and gravel directly, he had his first painful crises just after his brother's death, in 1746. Like many other patients at the time, Robert and Horace Walpole refused to submit their bodies to the hands of a lithotomist, fearing that the consequences of the operation—or the mere pain—might be worse than the disease. Robert was treated by a group of doctors—a common practice among members of the upper classes—which included the famous physician James Jurin, who became popular for his work on inoculation, and the Royal Surgeon John Ranby. Jurin had concocted a medicine for the cure of the stone called *Lixivium Lithotronpticum*.[10] He published a pamphlet on the cure of his own stone and gravel, in which he explained his own positive reaction to the treatment, even though he acknowledged that he needed a few other positive responses to prove the efficiency of his medicine. This *Lixivium* was made of lime-water and soap, and he prescribed it to Sir Robert Walpole. According to the Royal surgeon John Ranby who was Jurin's main competitor on the treatment of the stone, the prescribed medicine had been good for nothing, highly offensive to the prime minister's health, and hastened him towards his painful death. Ranby made his opinion known in *An Account of the Disease of the Late Earl of Orford*, in 1745.[11] I have previously studied the furious pamphlet war ensuing the publication of Ranby's pamphlet, in a dozen publications by various authors, some anonymous authors claiming to be in the medical profession, others, like Jurin himself, writing under their own names.[12] All the pamphleteers questioned Ranby's incoherent conclusions and reacted to his insulting innuendos, while discussing further the symptoms of the Late Earl of Orford (Sir Robert Walpole's title after he retired from Parliament). The various pamphlets in this controversy are very hybrid in their genre as they mingle medical science, descriptive techniques, emotional reactions, and structural patterns of obstacles and resolutions. The account of Robert Walpole's case evolves from one pamphlet to another, and the debates over the understanding and the treatment of a particular disease pivots around the details of the story, but more particularly, around the narrative strategies at work in the various texts.

When Horace Walpole sat down to describe his own case in a letter to Baron Edlin in 1750, the controversy about his brother's case was still fresh in his memory, especially as John Ranby was also his doctor. In the letter, he refers to Robert's case to account for his initial refusal of the lime-water treatment:

> Lord Barrington, hearing of my Complaint, was so good as to send me the Volume of *Scotch Medical Essays* containing Dr *Whytt's* Account of the good Effects which taking Soap and Lime-water had had in Cases similar to mine, with ingenious Reflexions and directions relating to that cruel Disease, and the Remedy for it. I read them with great Satisfaction, and would have immediately fallen into that Method; but my Relations, touched with the fatal Effect which Dr. Jurin's *Lixivium* had had upon the late Lord Orford would not suffer me to follow my inclinations.[13]

Horace Walpole's first-hand account of his disease stages the disease as a bodily and social event. Neither Walpole nor Lord Barrington had any training in medicine, and yet, they exchange their thoughts on a rather technical medical treatise. This quotation illustrates how treatments were then negotiated between doctors and their patients, and remained an object of debate and discussions within the circle of the patient's close relations.

I would like to take a step back, and follow the movements of Walpole's letter as it evolves in the realm of medical publications throughout the eighteenth century (Figure 15.1)

It was first written as a letter to one of his peers, Baron Edlin Chancellor of the Exchequer in Scotland. Horace Walpole kept a copy of this letter, and sent it to the Royal Society, who published the paper in Volume 47 of the *Philosophical Transactions*.[14] It would be tempting to see this publication as a major shift from a personal report—a letter to Baron Edlin—to a public, scientific testimony. But the status of personal letters in the eighteenth century, especially those of public figures, was always more than personal. If a letter was not necessarily intended for publication when being written, letters routinely circulated among relatives and friends, and letter writers often kept copies as a trace of their own writing.[15] Letters could be read publicly and found their way into publication

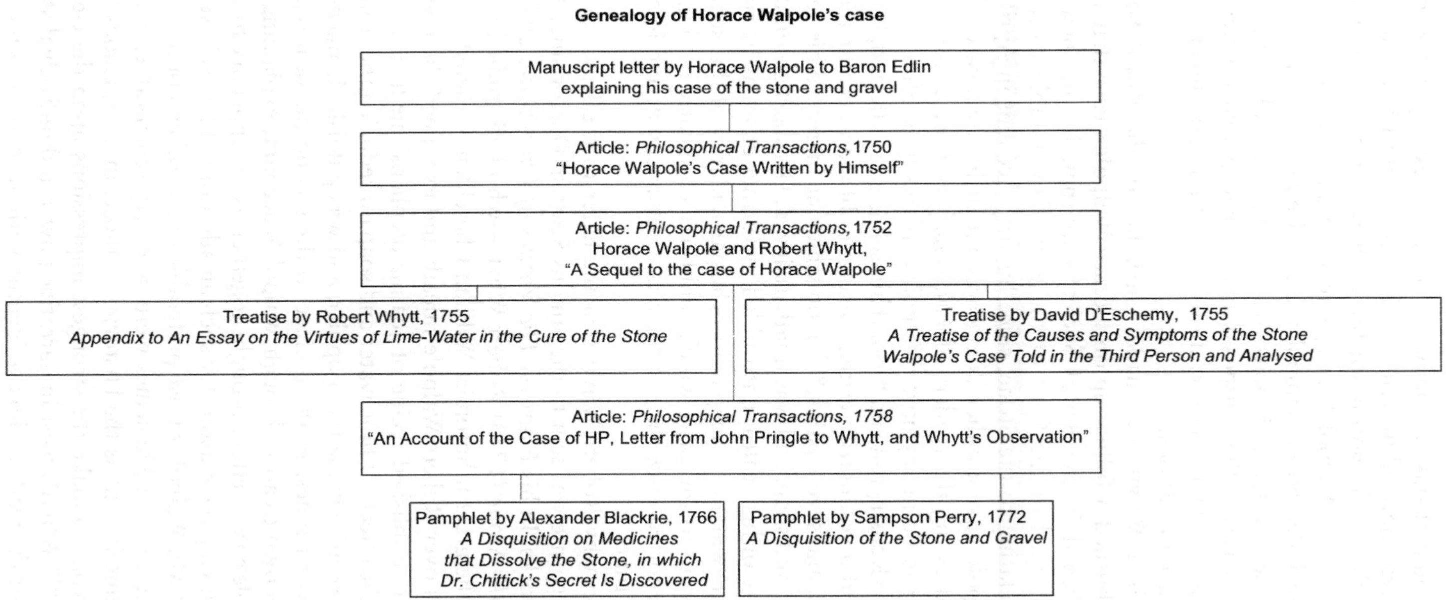

Figure 15.1 Genealogy of Horace Walpole's case

when the account at stake could be of public interest. Epistolary practices have often been analysed in terms of circulation, but I find that recycling is a particularly fruitful notion for the study of letter-writing in the eighteenth century. As in Walpole's case, letters could be copied or rewritten in order to be included into a pamphlet, a treatise or an article. As medical consultations were often given in correspondence, several medical authors had a pool of cases at their disposal among their patients' letters, which could be reused as clinical observations, case studies, or illustrative anecdotes for their publications.[16]

When Robert Whytt was made a member of the Royal Society in 1752, he published a follow-up on Horace Walpole's case that was previously published in the Royal Society's journal. In this new article, entitled "A Sequel of the Case of the Right Honourable Horace Walpole, Esq.; relating to the Stone, since his first Account in April 1750," Horace Walpole gave another direct account of his own case, this time officially addressing the readers of *Philosophical Transactions*, and not his friend Baron Edlin anymore. Walpole explains how, after his last fits, he travelled to Kensington and "found himself greatly affected, by making frequently and involuntarily water, sometimes bloody, accompanied with sudden stops, and severe pains,"[17] upon which he increased his daily take of lime-water and soap, and was finally relieved. His short account asserts the equal state of his health, untroubled by further crises as he continues taking his lime water and soap daily. The particularity of this sequel is to give a follow-up to the case, which could not frequently be done: cases were often reported once the patient was dead or cured, and in any case never in real time.

The reason why Robert Whytt sent the letter to the Royal Society, is that the first epistle was sent to the famous Scottish Doctor since Walpole quoted his works. In his *Essay on The Virtues of Lime-Water and Soap in the Cure of the Stone* (1743) Robert Whytt—who had studied under the direction of the great lithotomist William Cheselden—reacted to the previous debates over Robert Walpole's death and examined the ingredients in the recently published recipe of Joanna Stephens' medicine,[18] he gave evidence on the effects of lime water and soap on reducing the stone in the bladder. The treatise made him popular, and was published, amended and expanded several times. In the preface to the second publication, Whytt advertises his own treatise through Walpole's account, explaining that he added Walpole's two letters brought together as an appendix to the new edition, and giving the reasons for such an addition: "I have chosen, however, to insert Mr. Walpole's Case preferable to any other, not only because the good effects of the Medicines were here very remarkable, but as it is written by himself, and as the Histories of those, in conspicuous Stations of Life, are wont to make the strongest Impressions upon the Generality of Mankind."[19] Whytt's trust in narrative power and individual stories as an example for the reader, who can identify with the patient, is reminiscent of the prefaces of novels of the times. Take for example, the preface to *Roderick Random*, written by another medical doctor and author, Tobias Smollett:

> The reader gratifies his curiosity in pursuing the adventures of a person in whose favour he is prepossessed; he espouses his cause, he sympathises with him in his distress, his indignation is heated against the authors of his calamity: the humane passions are inflamed; the contrast between dejected virtue and insulting vice appears with greater aggravation, and every impression having a double force on the imagination, the memory retains the circumstance, and the heart improves by the example.[20]

The narrative of a case, especially as it is presented in Walpole's letter, written in the first person and with no particular medical authority from the narrator, is thus acknowledged as a strong example for nonmedical readers, a story that will appeal to their imagination—and compassion, as they identify with the patient—just like the fiction of the times. The addition of Walpole's case as an appendix to Dr Whytt's treatise, one year after the publication of its sequel in *Philosophical Transaction*, is an example of textual reuse and transformation. Walpole's case had initially been published in the Royal Society's journal to illustrate the effects of lime-water on stones, as an observation leading to scientific debate. It now had a different status: the two initial narratives (the letter to Baron Edlin and the follow-up on clinical observations by the patient) are brought together in one longer narrative aiming at provoking "a strong impression"—in other words, more emotion than observation. Although it was published again in a scientific context, and remained the same as the original, the function and genre of the narrative had shifted from one publication—where it stood as one article among other observations on physics and natural history—to another, since it came after the medical treatise, singled out at the periphery of the main text. Thus placed, it both attracted the reader's attention while altering his or her horizon of expectations.

Walpole's narrative did not lose any of its interest for medical readers, as it was remembered by Sir John Pringle five years later, when he wrote to the Royal Society after Walpole's death in 1757. The final elements added to the case are composed of a letter from John Pringle to Robert Whytt, giving the details of the autopsy, and Robert Whytt's answer to Dr. Pringle with several remarks relating to the effects of lime-water and soap on Walpole's body. The case is thus very complete once the three publications are juxtaposed, as the patient describes his sensations at full-length, but the narrator changes after his death, as his physician analyses the opening of his body and lists the stones in Walpole's bladder. It ends on the medical conclusion of the most renowned specialist on that question. The members of the Royal Society are therefore given a double internal description of the disease: one through the sensations of the patient, and the other, through the objective description of the internal organs. Pringle's description of the autopsy was not a first-hand account, however: he received the description from John Graham, who attended the autopsy with John Ranby, the surgeon involved in the controversy over Sir Robert Walpole's case that I mentioned at the beginning.[21] The account focuses on the stones discovered in the bladder: "The two first were very much alike, being of the shape and size of the kernel of a Spanish nut; only the sides were irregularly flattened, but without forming any sharp angle."[22]

Pringle then discloses Whytt's commentary on the shape of the stones, and his conclusion on the effects of lime-water:

> It is highly probable, nay, I think, altogether certain, that the soap and lime-water not only relieved Lord Walpole of the painful symptoms occasioned by the stones in his bladder, but also prevented their increase.
>
> If these stones came into the bladder in 1734, they must, in so many years as his Lordship lived after this, have acquired a very great bulk: nay, if we suppose them not to have been lodged in the bladder above a year when they began to occasion frequent inclination to make urine, with pain, and sometimes sudden stoppages of urine, yet, from 1746 to 1757, they ought to have grown to a much larger size than that of the kernel of a Spanish nut.[23]

Autopsies at the end of a case, as it had been done with Robert Walpole are often presented as the moment of truth validating the diagnostic of the author. They are, in that sense, the scientific climax of the narrative, the outcome of their inquiry into the patient's body: Pringle shifts the reader's point of view on Walpole's body, giving the ocular proof, through the material description of the stones, of Whytt's earlier medical reasoning and deductions on Walpole's case through clinical observation. The three little stones were seen as the sign of a larger, more painful one that had been broken in several pieces by daily intake of lime-water.

RECYCLING WALPOLE'S CASE IN MEDICAL TREATISES

Very thorough and complete cases such as Walpole's are rare enough to become a reference. Whytt's treatise was translated into French and German, and so were the *Philosophical Transactions*, which must have contributed to make soap diluted in lime-water "a popular lithontriptic until the second part of the nineteenth century," according to Roger French.[24] I have found some references to Walpole's case in other English treatises on the stone, which either use Whytt's analysis to prove their point, or continue to argue about the relevance of lime-water prescriptions for the stone and gravel.

Before the outcome of the dissection was made public in *Philosophical Transactions*, Walpole's case had already been published in French by David D'Escherny, whose treatise *Traité des causes et symptômes de la pierre et des principaux remèdes en usage pour guérir cette maladie* was published in 1755 both in French and English.[25] In the preface to his treatise, David D'Escherny—a French Doctor practicing in London—owns that he is brother-in-law to Mrs Stephens, and offers to review the benefits of the remedy, clearly an advertisement for his sister-in-law's product.[26] D'Escherny's aim is to determine what is the best lithontriptic available for patients suffering from the stone, which, unsurprisingly, is confirmed to be Mrs Stephens's Remedy. He mentions therefore Jurin's Lixivium, and both Robert and Horace Walpole's cases. His reaction to Horace Walpole self-applied treatment focuses on the quantity that the patient had to ingest daily:

> It is a very melancholy Consideration that such a Gentleman as this, should find himself in so uncertain a Situation, as not to know what Medicines to choose, and in the mean while to suffer so cruelly, as he did. We cannot doubt but he had all the Assistance that a Person in his Circumstances, of his Rank and Fortune could have; and yet it was all to no Purpose. And had it not been for Lord Barrington, he must not only have suffered a lingring [sic], but extreme painful Death. Can any one who reads this, and has the least Grain of Humanity left, refrain from Tears?

D'Escherny's sentimental reading of Walpole's case turns the original account into a pathetic scene, appealing to the reader's emotions rather than his scientific reasoning. The case comes early in the treatise, and is followed by a series of letters from patients witnessing the benefits of Joanna Stephens's medicine. D'Eschemy's argumentative strategy is based on accumulation, and this case history is yet another proof of the superiority of the remedy he is promoting.

Alexander Blackrie, a Scotch surgeon-apothecary, turned to Walpole's case eight years later since his own motivation to write a treatise on the stone and gravel also tackled the question of the disclosure of secret remedies. In that sense, his purpose resembled Robert Whytt's "Essay on the virtues of lime-water and soap in the cure of the stone" in many respects.[27] In the spirit of antiquackery that led Whytt to analyse the contents of Joanna Stephen's medicine to understand the active ingredients in it, Blackrie aims at ridiculing the commercial strategies of one of his fellow doctors who will not deliver the recipe of a secret remedy which has been proved to be very efficient to cure the stone and gravel: "He will not dispense this remedy but upon such terms as must exclude all but the rich from the benefit of it, and in such a manner as must exclude even the rich themselves, if they cannot reside in the small circle that will admit a personal communication with him every day."[28] Blackrie's purpose is therefore to analyse the contents of the medicine to make it public, and expose the quackery of his fellow physician. He concludes that the medicine examined is nothing but a light veal broth with soap lye, and expands his article in a treatise published three years later, in which he quotes the case of the late Lord Walpole, who "took only one pint of lime-water, and one third part of an ounce of soap daily, by which means he was not only relieved from the painful symptoms of the stone, but had his health greatly improved in other respects."[29] Blackrie enlivens the description of the patient with a personal commentary, portraying the patient as if he had met him: "his appetite, healthful look, and a degree of spirits uncommon to his age (he was then in his seventy-eighth year)."[30] He therefore adds his own touch to the portrait of the patient, recycling this first-person account in a second-person narrative, slightly bent towards his own critical purpose. The initial narrative is not transformed very much, but rather selected and diminished, so that only its useful remains can be appointed a new textual use.

Interestingly, the exact same fact—Walpole's regular drinking of one pint of lime-water—is not praised but mocked in 1772 by Perry Sampson. This physician claimed to have found a treatment for the stone and gravel, and would later be involved in a group of radical politicians. Perry looks back on the amount of lime-water ingurgitated by Lord Walpole:

> It appears, that his Lordship took no less than one 180 pounds of weight of Soap [81 kg], and 1200 gallons [5455 L] of Lime-water! a quantity so prodigious as might stagger the faith of any one, if no authenticated by his own hand writing, and further corroborated by the testimony of Doctor Pringle F.R.S. as related in the Philosophical Transactions.[31]

Sampson's overview of the case echoes Blackrie's concern for Walpole's painful treatment, but the tone of the narrative is entirely different. Even though the measurements sound scientific, the excess in quantity makes the treatment look wrongly dosed at best, but most probably ridiculous, and tormenting the patient to no avail. This, I think, is to be read in the humanitarian context of the second part of the eighteenth century. Several enlightened medical doctors throughout Europe reflected on the side effects of medicines, and did consider that the pain of the patient was unnecessary for the treatment and should be avoided when possible. Such ethics questioned the cultural context in which pain and healing went hand in hand so that the patient sometimes had to "deserve" his cure, so to speak. In Sampson's words, Walpole's case has now become a reference for what should not be prescribed, and an example of heavy and cumbersome treatment. The author still expects the reader to identify with the patient, although his comments now deter the reader from going into such a barbarous practice.

As it was being recycled from one treatise to another, the case history of Walpole's disease mostly changed genres, from a personal letter to a scientific report at the Royal Society, to medical treatises. It travelled from

England to France, and back to England again, with several layers of interpretation each time. Such recycling enabled the physicians to contrast their interpretation with that of other doctors, and sometimes with famous doctors in the past. This is why case histories were so crucial to medical learning and teaching in the eighteenth century: a case is resistant to interpretation, it is not the narrative of a disease but the narrative of an individual manifestation of this disease, always differing from the typical pathology. Giving new life to an old case, for the sake of medical teaching, learning, or further research, was therefore constitutive of scholarly practices. This epistemological function of textual recycling makes me consider medical writing in the eighteenth century differently. One is indeed tempted to radically oppose the methods of observation inherited from the New Science to more obvious recycling modes of medical writings, such as quoting the ancients or compiling previous works, that we tend to associate with early modern medicine. However, various modes of recycling still exist within eighteenth-century medical writings, whether referential, translations, copies of letters from patients or fellow doctors, or even compilations of previous case studies. This shows how repetition and the recycling of previous works is constitutive of a scholarly discipline, as it is based on past scholarly work, and shows signs of repetition and regress, as much as it produces new knowledge. Considering recycling as a constitutive part of knowledge in the making might help to relieve the intense anxiety we feel to produce new knowledge from our contemporary academics, who loved jazz standards and its repetitive patterns in the seventies and eighties, and are now turning to rap and its samples when they enjoy a little free time, and who should know better than discarding or hiding their own recycling. Even though novelty is a decisive part of our research, it often remains more of an aesthetic construction than the reflection of the way we think and write, and recycling older forms of knowledge, repeating previous works, or, as we say, "re-reading" forgotten studies, seems to be structurally constituent of collective thinking.

NOTES

1. Thomas McFarland argues that eighteenth-century authors and critics started to question imitation, and praise originality in literary and essay writing. Thomas McFarland, "The Originality Paradox," *New Literary History* 5, no. 3 (1974): 448. He quotes from Edward Young's *Conjectures on Original Composition* (1749): "The pen of an *original* writer like *Armida*'s wand, out of a barren waste calls a blooming spring." This image of a writing process as a transformation of waste echoes Amélie Junqua's chapter 12 on writing and recycling in the eighteenth century. On the questions of originality and composition in the eighteenth century, see also Forest Pyle, *The Ideology of Imagination: Subject and Society in the Discourse of Romanticism* (Stanford: Stanford University Press, 1995).
2. The requirement of originality also comes from nineteenth-century research training in science, as Jan Golinski shows in *Making Natural Knowledge:*

Constructivism and the History of Science (Chicago: University of Chicago Press, 1998), see especially chapter 2, "Identity and Discipline," 47–66.

3. In *Leviathan and the Air-Pump* (Princeton: Princeton University Press, 1985), Schaffer and Shapin delineate the conventions at stake for writing the account of an experiment, but the research that has been made so far on conventions of medical cases by Giana Pomata ("Sharing Cases: The *Observationes* in Early Modern Medicine," *Early Science and Medicine* 15, no. 3 [2010]: 193–236) and Philip Rieder (*La figure du patient au XVIIIe siècle* [Geneva: Droz, 2010]) show no such convention for reporting a case history in the eighteenth century.
4. This is mentioned in the controversy about Robert Walpole's stone and gravel, in which a pamphleteer doubts the motivation of Walpole's surgeon, John Ranby, for making Walpole's case public—"It looks, as if you intend to put in for Fame, and make your Name immortal; especially when we consider who has been the Occasion of your writing," *Advice to John Ranby, Esq.; Principal Surgeon to His Majesty and F.R.S. with some Observations on his Narrative of the Last Illness of the Right Honourable The Earl of Orford* (London, 1745), 2.
5. John Pringle, Lord Walpole, and Robert Whytt, "An Account of the Case of the Late Right Honourable Horace Lord Walpole; Being a Sequel to His Own Account Published in the *Philosophical Transactions*, Vol. XLVII., pages 43. and 472," *Philosophical Transactions* 50 (1757–58): 206.
6. William Cheselden, *A Treatise on the High Operation for the Stone* (London, 1723).
7. As I will explain further down, both treatments contain lime-water, an active principle that dissolved the stone and smoothed its sharp angles.
8. Horace Walpole knows this symptom as he notes: "altho' I did not always make bloody or Coffee-water, yet my Provocations to Urine (which, after a Gush of a Spoonful of Water, suddenly stopped with excessive Pain) were more frequent, and were attended with a Tenesmus and irritation at the end of my Yard."
9. His body was also dissected in 1745 by John Ranby, who gave a full account of his dissection in *A Narrative of the Last Illness of the Earl of Orford* (London, 1745).
10. Literally, "soap-water for cutting the stone." It is presented in a pamphlet by James Jurin: *An Account of the Effects of the Soap Lye taken internally for the stone in the case of James Jurin, M.D., written by himself* (London, 1744).
11. John Ranby, *A Narrative of the Last Illness of the Right Honourable The Earl of Orford* (London, 1745).
12. On the narratives strategies at stake in the controversy over Sir Robert Walpole's case, see my article "How to Narrate a Medical Case: The Controversy about John Ranby's *Narrative of the Last Illness of the Earl of Orford*, 1745," in *Medicine and Narration in the 18th century*, ed. Sophie Vasset (Oxford: SVEC, 2013).
13. Horace Walpole, "An Account of the Right Honourable Horace Walpole Esq; Drawn up by Himself," *Philosophical Transactions* 47 (1751–52): 44–45.
14. "An Account of the Right Honourable Horace Walpole," 43–48.
15. On epistolary circulation see for example James How, *Epistolary Spaces: English Letter-Writing from the Foundation of the Post Office to Richardson's Clarissa* (Aldershot: Ashgate, 2003).
16. On medical letter-writing in the eighteenth century see Wayne Wild, *Medicine-by-Post: The Changing Voice of Illness in Eighteenth-Century British Consultation Letters and Literature* (Amsterdam: Rodopi, 2006) and Philip Rieder, *La Figure du patient Au XVIIIe Siècle* (Geneva: Droz, 2010).

17. Horace Walpole and Robert Whytt, "A Sequel of the Case of the Right Honourable Horace Walpole, Esq; Relating to the Stone, since His First Account in April 1750," *Philosophical Transactions* 47 (1751–52): 472.
18. Philip K. Wilson sums up the transaction between Joanna Stephens and the Parliament of England for the publication of her recipe: "In his 1738 publication Hartley announced that Mrs Stephens had proposed to make her medicine known to the public for the benefit of all who suffered from 'this wrath.' In exchange for this benevolence to her compatriots, Stephens demanded £5,000 for disclosing her remedy. She advertised her intentions in the *Gentleman's Magazine* between April and December 1738. By December, 189 people had contributed a total of £1,356. Short of the remaining amount Stephens petitioned parliament in March 1739 for the full £5,000. A parliamentary vote of 105 to 62 prompted the formation of a committee to consider her petition. The committee approved her request on 10 April 1739, agreeing to pay the whole sum if her remedy proved to be as efficacious as she claimed. In June 1739 Stephens delivered the secret recipe to the archbishop of Canterbury, who, in turn, presented it to the other twenty-eight trustees appointed by parliament for this investigation. The recipe was also sent to the editors of the London Gazette, where it was published in its entirety on 16 June 1739." in "Stephens, Joanna (d.1774)," Philip K. Wilson in the *Oxford Dictionary of National Biography*, online ed., Oxford: OUP, http://www.oxforddnb.com/view/article/40525 (accessed 6 July 2012).
19. Robert Whytt, *Essays on the Virtues of Lime-Water* (London, 2nd edition, 1752).
20. Tobias Smollett, *Roderick Random* (London, 1748), preface.
21. "Mr Ranby and Mr Hawkins, surgeons, with Mr Graham, were present at the opening of the body; and from the two lasts I received the account of the dissection." *Philosophical Transactions* 50 (1757–58): 207. Pringle was a key figure among the members of the Royal Society at the time, and it seems logical that such an account would have been sent to him.
22. Pringle, "An Account of the Case of the Late Right Honourable Horace Lord Walpole," 207.
23. Ibid., 211.
24. Roger French, "Whytt, Robert (1714–1766)," *Oxford Dictionary of National Biography*, Oxford University Press, 2004; http://www.oxforddnb.com/view/article/29345 (accessed 8 May 2012)
25. David D'Escherny, *A Treatise of the Causes and Symptoms of the Stone; and of the Chief Remedies now in use to Cure this Distemper* (London, 1755) and *Traité des causes et symptômes de la Pierre: et des principaux remèdes en usage pour guérir cette maladie* (Dublin, 1755).
26. D'Escherny's advertising of Stephens' remedy might sound strange, because the patent had been sold fourteen years before, and everyone could make the recipe, but he still obviously helped to sell it: "What a great comfortable change have not those found, who, after taking this lime-water, have entered upon a course of Mrs Stephens' remedy? [. . .] They have acknowledged that ours is an elegant preparation compared to this Lime-Water." Ibid., 32.
27. *Observations and Essays in Medicine by a Society in Edinburgh* 2 (1743): 2.
28. *The Gentleman's Magazine* (October 1763): 471.
29. Alexander Blackrie, *A Disquisition on Medicines that Dissolve the Stone. In which Dr. Chittick's Secret is Considered and Discovered* (London, 1766), preface.
30. Idem.
31. Perry Sampson, A *Disquisition of the Stone and Gravel, and Other Diseases of the Bladder, Kidney*, (London, 1772), 50.

Contributors

Rebecca Anne Barr is a lecturer in English Literature at the National University of Ireland, Galway. She has previously published on Samuel Richardson's *Sir Charles Grandison* in the journal *The Eighteenth Century: Theory and Interpretation* and elsewhere on twentieth-century poetry and film. Her research interests include literary representations of masculinity and the eighteenth-century novel.

Laurent Châtel is a senior lecturer at Paris-Sorbonne University and currently a research fellow at the University of Oxford (CNRS, Maison Française, USR 3129). His main areas are eighteenth-century British visual culture (landscape gardening and painting), William Beckford and the reception of the *Arabian Nights*—with a recent contribution to the Paris Institut du Monde Arabe exhibition catalogue on the *Arabian Nights* (Hazan, 2013). Aside from *Jardins et paysages* [*Gardens and Landscapes in Eighteenth-Century Britain* (Paris: CNED, 2001)], he is the author of numerous studies on Enlightenment gardens in Britain, examining questions of national rhetoric, utopia, and cultural transfers between France and Britain.

Natacha Coquery is a professor of early modern history at the University of Lyon 2 (France) and a member of the IUF (Institut Universitaire de France). Her work focuses on the luxury and semi-luxury market in eighteenth-century Paris, and, most recently, in the French Revolution. She is the author of *L'Hôtel aristocratique. Le marché du luxe à Paris au XVIIIe siècle* (Publications de la Sorbonne, 1998) and *Tenir boutique. Luxe et demi-luxe à Paris au XVIIIe siècle* (Comité des Travaux historiques et scientifiques, 2011). She is the coeditor of several books, including most recently, with Bruno Blondé, Eugénie Briot, and Laura Van Aert, *Retailers and Consumer Changes in Early-Modern Europe. England, France, Italy and the Low Countries* (Presses Universitaires François-Rabelais, 2005) and with Bruno Blondé, Jon Stobart, and Ilja Van Damme, *Fashioning Old and New. Changing Consumer Patterns in Western Europe (1650–1900)* (Brepols, 2009).

W. G. Day is Fellows' and Eccles Librarian at Winchester College, where he was formerly head of the English department. He has completed recataloguing the library and was the cocurator of a major exhibition of bibles in the summer 2011 to commemorate the quatercentenary of the translation of the King James Bible, much of the New Testament of which was carried out in one of the library's rooms. Principally a Sternean, he is one of the editors of the Florida Sterne, the review editor of *The Shandean* and, together with Anne Bandry, he edited *The Clockmakers Outcry against the Author of Tristram Shandy*. He has published notes and articles on diverse eighteenth-century topics.

Ariane Fennetaux is a senior lecturer in eighteenth-century studies at the University of Paris Diderot. Her area of specialisation is eighteenth-century material culture with a particular emphasis on dress and textile. Her publications have addressed topics such as undress garments, portable objects, women's pockets, or most recently the female practices of "bricolage" and mourning jewellery. She is currently cowriting a book on women's tie-on pockets in eighteenth-and nineteenth-century Britain with Barbara Burman to be published by Ashgate.

Brigitte Friant-Kessler is a senior lecturer in English at the University of Valenciennes (France). Her teaching and research cover a range of visual media and genres. Mainly a Sternean, she has published on illustrations to *Tristram Shandy*, as well as comic book and film adaptations. Most recently she has explored the notion of "graphic afterlife" in visual satire, eccentricity in headdresses, and humorous animals. Her current interests centre on developments in the artistic practice of British women engravers, caricaturists, and illustrators in the eighteenth and nineteenth centuries. She is also in charge of the iconographic material for the scholarly journal *Revue de la Société des Etudes Anglo-Américaines des XVII*e *et XVIII*e *Siècles*, for which she designs covers.

Olivia Fryman completed her doctorate at Kingston University and Historic Royal Palaces in 2011. Based at Hampton Court Palace her research explored housekeeping practices, and in particular the role of servants in caring for royal bedchambers between 1689 and 1737. During a two-year MA in the history of design at the Royal College of Art and the Victoria and Albert Museum, Olivia specialised in eighteenth-century interior design and furniture, and spent time working as an assistant curator. She is currently a researcher for Historic Royal Palaces at Hampton Court and Kensington Palace.

Amélie Junqua is a senior lecturer in English at the University of Amiens (France). She has studied Joseph Addison, his periodical prose and relation to language in the course of a doctorate thesis obtained in 2007 at the University of Paris Diderot. She is now researching on eighteenth-century literary and material culture and the status of the *Spectator* papers in particular. Addison's interest in paper and more generally the materiality of his own prose has led her to the idea of studying recycling through the particular media of textile, paper, and text.

Elizabeth Kowaleski Wallace is a professor at Boston College. She specialises in British eighteenth-century literature and culture and feminist and cultural theory. She is also interested in contemporary British culture, including drama, the novel, and film. She has published on eighteenth-century women writers, eighteenth-century consumer culture, and mostly recently on the way that the British slave trade has been remembered and represented in the popular imagination. Her monographs include *The British Slave Trade and Public Memory* (New York: Columbia University Press, 2006), *Consuming Subjects: Women, Shopping and Business in the 18th Century* (New York: Columbia University Press, 1997) and *Their Fathers' Daughters: Hannah More, Maria Edgeworth, and Patriarchal Complicity* (Oxford University Press, 1991).

Sara Pennell is a senior lecturer in early modern British history at the University of Roehampton, London. She thinks and writes about historic domestic knowledge and its applications in the long "early modern" (c. 1600–1850), especially in relation to foodways and material culture. She has published most recently on household sales of domestic goods in early modern England; on "mundane" material culture in seventeenth century Britain; and on recipe collections, in a coedited volume (with Michelle DiMeo), *Reading and Writing Recipe Books 1550–1800* (Manchester University Press, 2013).

Allan Potofsky is a professor at the Université Paris Diderot. He is the author of *Constructing Paris in the Age of Revolution* (Basingstoke: Palgrave Macmillan, 2009). His research interests include eighteenth-century Atlantic history, France in America in the eighteenth century, the French Revolution, and the history of Paris. He is the coeditor with Trevor Burnard of "The Political Economy of the French Atlantic World and the Caribbean before 1800" (*French History* 25, no. 1 [March 2011]). He also edited "New Perspectives on the Atlantic" (*History of European Ideas* 34, no. 4 [December 2008]). He is currently working on the book tentatively entitled *Architectes, ingénieurs et entrepreneurs—Paris, 1750–1850* (Paris: Editions Vendémiaire, collection Révolutions).

Jon Stobart is a professor of history at the University of Northampton. He has written extensively on retailing and consumption in eighteenth-century England, covering topics such as fashion and taste, leisure, shopping practices, advertising, and second-hand trading. His current research centres on consumption and the country house, and on the retailing and consumption of groceries in the period 1650–1850. He has recently published *Sugar and Spice: Grocers and Groceries in Provincial England, 1660–1830* (Oxford University Press, 2013).

Ilja Van Damme is professor of urban history at the University of Antwerp. He wrote and presented research on such diverse topics as consumption preferences, fashion and taste, advertising and shopping. He is currently conducting research into the urban history from the eighteenth through to the twentieth century.

Sophie Vasset is a senior lecturer at the Université Paris Diderot, where she teaches British literature and eighteenth-century subjects. Her monograph on eighteenth-century medicine and literature (*Décrire, Prescrire, Guérir: médecine et fiction dans la Grande-Bretagne du XVIIIe siècle*, PUL, 2011) was awarded the French prize for anglophone research in 2012. She has also published a study guide to Smollett's *Roderick Random* (Paris: Presses Universitaires de France, 2009) and *Medicine and Narration in the 18th Century* (SVEC, 2013:04). Her current research focuses on the history of infertility.

Simon Werrett is a lecturer in the Science and Technology Studies Department at University College London, where he teaches the history of science. Previously he was an associate professor in the Department of History at the University of Washington, Seattle. His work explores historical and geographical relationships between the sciences and the arts in Europe and Russia, principally in the early modern period. His monograph *Fireworks: Pyrotechnic Arts and Sciences in European History* was published by the University of Chicago Press in 2010. Werrett's current research examines the history of arts of recycling and repair in early modern science.

Works Cited

Adamson, Glenn, Paola Antonelli, and Jane Pavitt, eds. *Postmodernism—Style and Subversion, 1970–1990*. London: Victoria and Albert Museum Publications, 2011.

Addison, Joseph, and Richard Steele. *The Spectator*, edited by Donald F. Bond. Oxford: Clarendon Press, 1965.

———. *The Tatler*, edited by Donald F. Bond. Oxford: Clarendon Press, 1987.

Alder, Ken. *Engineering the Revolution. Arms and Enlightenment in France, 1763–1815*. Princeton: Princeton University Press, 1997.

Alexander, J. J. G. *Wallace Collection: Catalogue of Illuminated Manuscript Cuttings*. London: The Trustees of the Wallace Collection, 1980.

Allerston, Patricia. "Clothing and Early Modern Venetian Society." *Continuity and Change* 15, no. 3 (2000): 367–90.

———. "Reconstructing the Second-Hand Clothes Trade in Sixteenth-and Seventeenth-Century Venice." *Costume* 33 (1999): 4–56.

———. "The Market in Second-Hand Clothes and Furnishings in Venice, c.1500–c.1650." PhD. diss., European University Institute Florence, 1996.

Anon. "Adventures of a Quire of Paper." in *The London Magazine or Gentleman's Monthly Intelligencer*, 1779.

———. *Advice to John Ranby, Esq.; Principal Surgeon to His Majesty and F.R.S. with some Observations on His Narrative of the Last Illness of the Right Honourable The Earl of Orford*. London: Printed for W. Bickerton, 1745.

———. *Almanach d'Anvers et du département des deux-nethes*. Antwerp: Chez Allebé, 1806.

———. *Almanach du Dauphin, ou Tableau du vrai mérite des artistes célebres, et d'indication générale des principaux Marchands Négocians, Artistes et Fabricans des Six Corps Arts et Métiers de la Ville et Fauxbourgs de Paris et autres Villes du Royaume*. Paris: Dumas, 1776.

———. *Auction Catalogue of Joseph Sansot*. Brussels: Poppens, 1739.

———. *Essai sur l'Almanach général d'indication d'adresse personnelle et fixe, des Six Corps, Arts et Métiers*. Paris: Veuve Duchesne, 1769.

———. *Valuable Secrets Concerning Arts and Trades or approved directions from the best artists*. London, 1775.

———. "The Waste Products of Coal." *Scientific American* 27, no. 7 (17 August 1872): 97.

Anker, Peder. "The Ecological Colonization of Space." *Environmental History* 10 (2005): 239–68.

Appadurai, Arjun. "Introduction: Commodities and the Politics of Value." In *The Social Life of Things: Commodities in Cultural Perspective*, edited by Arjun Appadurai, 3–63. Cambridge: Cambridge University Press, 1986.

Aries, Philip. *Centuries of Childhood*. New York: Vintage Books, 1965.

Arnout, Anneleen. "Het adres van de kunst of de kunst van het adres. Locatiepatronen en de verschuivingen op de scène van de Brusselse kunst-en antiekhandel, 1830–1914." *The Low Countries Journal of Social and Economic History* 9 (2012): 30–56.

Avcioglu, Nebahat. "A Palace of One's Own: Stanislaus I's Kiosks and the Idea of Self-Representation," *Art Bulletin* 85, no. 4 (December 2003): 662–84.

———. *'Turquerie' and the Politics of Representation, 1728–1876*. Farnham: Ashgate, 2011.

Babbage, Charles. *Economy of Machines & Manufactures*. 3rd ed., London, 1846.

Backhouse, Alison. *The Worm Eaten Waistcoat*. York: Backhouse, 2003.

Backouche, Isabelle. *La trace du fleuve. La Seine et Paris (1750–1850)*. Paris: EHESS, 2000.

Bann, Stephen. *The Inventions of History: Essays on the Representation of the Past*. Manchester: Manchester University Press, 1990.

Baker, Malcolm, Michale Snodin, and Tim Shroder. *Beckford and Hamilton Silver from Brodick Castle*. London: Spink & Son, 1980.

Baker, Keith Michael, ed. *The Old Regime and the French Revolution*. London and Chicago: University of Chicago Press, 1987.

Ballaster, Ros. *Fables of the East—Selected Tales from the East*. Oxford: Oxford University Press, 2005.

Barles, Sabine. *La ville délétère: médecins et ingénieurs dans l'espace urbain, XVIIIe–XIXe siècle*. Seyssel: Champs Vallon, 1999.

———. *L'Invention des déchets urbains: France 1790–1970*. Seyssel: Champ Vallon, 2005.

Bastet, Frederic L. "Reizigers en oudheden." In *Herinneringen aan Italië. Kunst en toerisme in de 18de eeuw*, edited by Ronald De Leeuw, 35–41. Zwolle: Waanders, 1984.

Batchelor, Jennie, and Cora Kaplan, eds. *Women and Material Culture 1660–1830*. Basingstoke: Palgrave Macmillan, 2007.

Batsaki, Yota. "Clarissa; or, Rake Versus Usurer." *Representations* 93 (Winter 2006): 22–40.

Bauman, Zygmunt. *Wasted Lives. Modernity and Its Outcasts*. Cambridge: Polity, 2004.

Baumgarten, Linda. *What Clothes Reveal: The Language of clothing in Colonial and Federal America, the Colonial Williamsburg Collection*. London and New Haven: Yale University Press, 2002.

Beard, Geoffrey. "Thomas and Richard Roberts: Royal Chair-Makers." *Apollo* 148 (1998): 46–48.

———. *Upholsterers and Interior Furnishing in England, 1530–1840*. London and New Haven: Yale University Press, 1997.

Béaur, Gérard. *L'Immobilier et la revolution: marché de la pierre et mutations urbaines, 1770–1810*. Paris: Cahiers des Annales, 1994.

Beckford, William. *Dreams, Waking Thoughts, and Incidents* [1783], edited by Robert J. Gemmett. Stroud: Nonsuch, 2006.

———. *The Journal of Beckford in Portugal and Spain, 1787–1788*, edited by Boyd Alexander. London: Rupert Hart-Davis, 1954.

———. *Life at Fonthill 1807–1822. From the Correspondence of William Beckford*, translated and edited by Boyd Alexander. Stroud: Nonsuch, 2006.

Bedini, Silvio A. *Thinkers and Tinkers: Early American Men of Science*. New York: Scribners, 1975.

Belanger, Terry. "Publishers and Writers in Eighteenth-Century England." In *Books and their Readers in Eighteenth-Century England*, edited by Isabel Rivers, 5–25. Leicester: Leicester University Press, 1982.

Bending, Stephen. "Every Man Is Naturally an Antiquarian: Francis Grose and Polite Antiquities." *Art History* 25 (2002): 520–30.

———. "The True Rust of the Barons' Wars: Gardens, Ruins and the National Landscape." In *Producing the Past. Aspects of Antiquarian Culture and Practice 1700–1850*, edited by Martin Myrone and Lucy Peltz, 83–93. Aldershot: Ashgate, 1999.

Berg, Maxine. *The Age of Manufactures, 1700–1820. Industry, Innovation and Work in Britain.* London: Routledge, 1994.

———. *Luxury and Pleasure in Eighteenth-Century Britain.* Oxford: Oxford University Press, 2005.

———. "New Commodities, Luxuries and their Consumers in Eighteenth-Century England," in *Consumers and luxury. Consumer culture in Europe 1650–1850*, edited by Maxine Berg and Helen Clifford, 63–85. Manchester: Manchester University Press, 1999.

Berg, Maxine, and Helen Clifford, eds. *Consumers and Luxury: Consumer Culture in Europe 1650–1850.* Manchester: Manchester University Press, 1999.

Bergeret, Jean-Pierre. *Phytonomatotechnie universelle.* Paris: 1783.

Bermingham, Ann, and John Brewer, eds. *The Consumption of Culture 1600–1800.* London: Routledge, 1995.

Bergvelt, Ellinoor, Debora J. Meijers, and Mieke Rijnder, eds. *Verzamelen. Van rariteitenkabinet tot kunstmuseum.* Heerlen: Open Universiteit, 1993.

Bertholon de Saint-Lazare, Pierre. *De la salubrité de l'air des villes et en particulier des moyens de la procurer par M. l'abbé Bertholon.* Montpellier, 1786.

Berridge, Kate. *Madame Tussaud: A Life in Wax.* New York: HarperCollins, 2006.

Bœhn, Max von. *Dolls and Puppets*, translated by Josephine Nicoll. London: George G. Harrap & Company Ltd., 1932.

Biasi, Pierre-Marc de, and Karine Douplitzki, eds. *La Saga du Papier.* Paris: Adam Biro, 1999.

Black, Jeremy. *The Grand Tour in the Eighteenth Century.* Stroud: Sutton Publishing, 1992.

Blackrie, Alexander. *A Disquisition on Medicines that Dissolve the Stone. In which Dr. Chittick's Secret is Considered and Discovered.* London: 1766.

Blackwell, Mark, Liz Bellamy, Christina Lupton, and Heather Keenleyside, eds. *British It-Narratives, 1750–1830*, 4 vols. London: Pickering & Chatto, 2012.

Blondé, Bruno. "Art and Economy in Seventeenth- and Eighteenth-Century Antwerp: A View from the Demand Side." In *Economia e arte secc. XIII-XVIII*, edited by Simonetta Cavaciocchi, 379–91. Firenze: Monnier, 2002.

Blondé, Bruno, Peter Stabel, Jon Stobart and llja Van Damme, eds. *Buyers and Sellers. Retail Circuits and Practices in Medieval and Early-Modern Europe.* Turnhout: Brepols, 2006.

Blondé, Bruno, Natacha Coquery, Jon Stobart and llja Van Damme, eds. *Fashioning Old and New: Changing Consumer Patterns in Western Europe (1650–1900).* Turnhout: Brepols, 2009.

Bloom, Michelle. *Waxworks: A Cultural Obsession.* Minneapolis: University of Minnesota, 2003.

Bodinier, Bernard, and Eric Teyssier. *L'Evénement le plus important de la Révolution. La vente des biens nationaux.* Paris: Société des Études Robespierristes, 2000.

Bonnet, Jean-Claude. *Naissance du Panthéon: Essai sur le culte des grands hommes.* Paris: Fayard, 1998.

Bony, Alain. *Joseph Addison et la création littéraire. Essai périodique et modernité.* Lyon: Université Lumière, CERAN-Diffusion, 1979.

Boswell, James. *Boswell's Life of Johnson*, edited by George Birkbeck Hill, revised and enlarged by L. F. Powell. Oxford: Clarendon Press, 1979.

Bottin, Jacques, and Nicole Pellegrin, eds. "Échanges et cultures textiles dans l'Europe pré-industrielle. Actes du colloque de Rouen, 17–19 mai 1993." *Revue du Nord* 12 (1996): 91–109.

Bowett, Adam. *English Furniture 1660–1714, From Charles II to Queen Anne.* Woodbridge: Antique Collectors Club, 2002.

Bowie, Karen, ed. *La modernité avant Haussmann: Formes de l'espace urbain à Paris, 1801–1853.* Paris: Éditions Recherches, 2001.

Boyle, Robert. *Animadversions upon Mr. Hobbes's Problemata de vacuo.* London: 1674.

———. *A continuation of new experiments physico-mechanical, touching the spring and weight of the air and their effects.* London: 1669.

———. *Works of the Honourable Robert Boyle.* London: 1772.

Braudel, Fernand. *Civilisation and Capitalism 15th–18th Century, vol. II: The Wheels of Fortune*, translated by S. Reynolds. London: Fontana, 1982.

Brewer, David. *The Afterlife of Character, 1726–1825.* Pennsylvania: University of Pennsylvania Press, 2005.

Brewer, John. *The Pleasures of the Imagination: English Culture in the Eighteenth Century.* London: HarperCollins, 1997.

Brewer, John, and Roy Porter, eds. *Consumption and the World of Goods.* London and New York: Routledge, 1993.

Brewer, John, and Frank Trentmann, eds. *Consuming Cultures, Global Perspectives: Historical Trajectories, Transnational Exchanges.* Oxford: Berg, 2006.

Brown, Frank Clyde. *Elkanah Settle, His Life and Works.* Chicago: Chicago University Press, 1910.

Burney, Fanny. *Cecilia. Memoirs of an Heiress* [1782]. London: Virago, 1986.

Buys, Susan, and Victoria Oakley. *The Conservation and Restoration of Ceramics.* Oxford: Butterworth-Heinemann, 1993.

Bucholz, Robert, and John Sainty. *Officials of the Royal Household 1660–1837, Part One: Department of the Lord Chamberlain and Associated Offices.* London: Institute of Historical Research, 1997.

Budd, Adam. "Why Clarissa Must Die: Richardson's Tragedy and Editorial Heroism." *Eighteenth-Century Life* 31, no. 3 (Fall 2007): 1–28.

Lois E. Bueler, ed. *Clarissa: The Eighteenth-Century Response, 1747–1804.* New York: AMS Press, 2010.

Burman, Barbara, and Ariane Fennetaux. *The Artful Pocket: Social and Cultural History of an Everyday Object.* Farnham: Ashgate, forthcoming.

Burstin, Haim. *Une révolution à l'œuvre. Le faubourg Saint Marcel (1789–1794).* Seyssel: Champ Vallon, 2005.

Burton, Robert. *The Anatomy of Melancholy*, edited by T.C. Faulkner, N.K. Kiessling, and R.L. Blair. Oxford: Oxford University Press, 1989.

Büttner, Nils. "De verzamelaar Abraham Ortelius." In *Abraham Ortelius (1527–1598): cartograaf en humanist*, edited by Dirk Imhof, 169–80. Turnhout: Brepols, 1998.

Cabestan, Jean-François. *La conquête du plain-pied. L'immeuble à Paris au XVIIIe siècle.* Paris: Picard, 2004.

Campbell, R. *The London Tradesman*, London: T. Gardner, 1747.

Carriker, Kitti. *The Miniature Body of the Doll as Subject and Object.* Bethlehem, PA: Lehigh University Press, 1998.

Carvais, Robert. "La force du droit: Contribution à la définition de l'entrepreneur parisien du bâtiment au XVIIIe siècle." *Histoire, économie et société* 2 (1995): 163–89.

———. "Le statut juridique de l'entrepreneur du bâtiment dans la France moderne," *Revue historique de droit français et étranger* 74 (1996): 221–52.

Castle, Terry. *Clarissa's Ciphers: Meaning and Disruption in Richardson's 'Clarissa.'* Ithaca and London: Cornell University Press, 1982.

Cavaciocchi, Simonetta, ed. *Economia e arte secc. XIII-XVIII*. Florence: Monnier, 2002.

Chalmers-Hunt, J.M. *Natural Historical Auctions 1700–1972: A Register of Sales in the British Isles*. London: Sotheby Parke Bernet, 1976.

Chartier, Roger. *Inscription and Erasure: Literature and Written Culture from the Eleventh to the Eighteenth Century*, translated by Arthur Goldhammer. Philadelphia: University of Pennsylvania Press, 2007.

———. *The Order of Books: Readers, Authors and Libraries in Europe Between the Fourteenth and Eighteenth Centuries*, translated by Lydia G. Cochrane. Cambridge: Polity, 1994.

Chassin, Charles-Louis, ed. *Les élections et les cahiers de Paris en 1789*. Paris: Imprimerie nationale, 1888–9.

Châtel, Laurent. "Les sources des contes orientaux de William Beckford (*Vathek* et la 'Suite des contes arabes'): bilan de recherches sur les écrits et l'esthétique de Beckford." *Etudes Epistémé* 7 (2005): 93–106.

———. "The Lures of Eastern Lore: William Beckford's Oriental Dangerous Supplements," *RSEAA* 67 (2011): 127–44.

———. "'One Must Become Half-Catholic.' William Beckford (1760–1844) as 'Impolite and Uncommercial' Aesthete" in *Marketing Art in the British Isles, 1700 to the Present. A Cultural History* edited by Charlotte Gould and Sophie Mesplède, 195–211. Aldershot: Ashgate, 2012.

———. "Orientalist Translations, Grafts and Outgrowths: New Perspectives on the *Complete Works* of William Beckford." *The Beckford Journal* 5 (2005): 39–49.

———. "Re-Orienting William Beckford: Translating and Adapting the Thousand and One Nights." In *The Arabian Nights: Encounters and Translations in Literature and the Arts*, edited by Philip Kennedy and Marina Warner, 53–69. New York: New York University Press, 2013.

———. "Utopies paysagères: Les sublimes 'progrès' de William Beckford," *RSEAA* 51 (2000): 281–322; http://www.persee.fr/web/revues/home/prescript/article/xvii_0291-3798_2000_num_51_1_1529

———."Utopies paysagères: vues et visions dans les écrits et dans les jardins de William Beckford." PhD diss., Université Paris III, 2000.

Chambers, Ephraïm. *Cyclopaedia: Or, an Universal Dictionary of Arts and Sciences*. London: 1741.

Charpy, Manuel. "The Auction House and its Surroundings: The Trade of Antiques and Second-Hand Items in Paris During the Nineteenth Century." In *Fashioning Old and New. Changing Consumer Patterns in Western Europe (1650–1900)*, edited by Bruno Blondé, Natacha Coquery, Jon Stobart and llja Van Damme, 217–33. Turnhout: Brepols, 2009.

Cheselden, William. *A Treatise on the High Operation for the Stone*. London: 1723.

Christie, Christopher. *The British Country House in the Eighteenth Century*. Manchester: Manchester University Press, 2000.

Clifford, Helen. "A Commerce with Things: The Value of Precious Metalwork in Early Modern England." In *Consumers and Luxury. Consumer Culture in Europe, 1650–1850*, edited by Maxine Berg and Helen Clifford, 147–68. Manchester: Manchester University Press, 1999.

Coekelberghs, Dennis, and Pierre Loze. *Om en rond het neo-classicisme in België, 1770–1830*. Brussels: Gemeentekrediet, 1986.

Cohen, Deborah. *Household Gods. The British and Their Possessions*. London and New Haven: Yale University Press, 2006.

Coleman, Donald Cuthbert. *The British Paper Industry, 1495–1860*. Oxford: Clarendon Press, 1958.
Connaughton, Michael E. "Richardson's Familiar Quotations: Clarissa and Bysshe's Art of English Poetry." *Philological Quarterly* 60 (1981): 183–95.
Conway, Ann. *The Correspondence of Anne Viscountess Conway, Henry More, and their Friends, 1642–1684*, edited by Marjorie Hope. London: Oxford University Press, 1930.
Cooke, Lynne, and Peter Wollen, eds. *Visual Display: Culture Beyond Appearances*. Seattle: Bay Press, 1995.
Cooper, Tim. "Modernity and the Politics of Waste in Britain." In *Nature's End: History and the Environment*, edited by Sverker Sörlin and Paul Warde, 247–72. Basingstoke: Palgrave Macmillan, 2009.
———. "Peter Lund Simmonds and the Political Ecology of Waste Utilization in Victorian Britain." *Technology and Culture* 52 (2011): 21–44.
———. "Rags, Bones and Recycling Bins." *History Today* 56 (2006): 17–18.
———. "Recycling Modernity: Waste and Environmental History," *History Compass* 8, no. 9 (2010): 1114–24.
Coquery, Natacha. "Fashion, Business, Diffusion: An Upholsterer's Shop in Eighteenth-Century Paris." In *Furnishing the Eighteenth Century: What Furniture Can Tell Us about the European and American Past*, edited by Dena Goodman and Kathryn Norberg, 63–79. London and New York: Routledge, 2006.
———. *L'Hôtel aristocratique. Le marché du luxe à Paris au XVIIIe siècle*. Paris: Publications de la Sorbonne, 1998.
———. *Tenir boutique à Paris au XVIIIe siècle. Luxe et demi-luxe*. Paris: éditions du Comité historique et scientifique, 2011.
Corbin, Alain. *Le miasme et la jonquille: l'odorat et l'imaginaire social aux XVIIIe et XIXe siècles*. Paris: Flammarion, 1982.
Cornelis Lens, Andreas. *Le costume ou essai sur les habillements et les usages de plusieurs peuples de l'antiquité prouvé par les monuments*. Luik: Chez J.F. Bassompierre, 1776.
Cowan, Brian. "An Open Elite: The Peculiarities of Connoisseurship in Early-Modern England." *Modern Intellectual History* 1 (2004): 151–83.
Cowley, Abraham. *The Collected Works of Abraham Cowley*, edited by Thomas O. Calhoun, Laurence Heyworth, and J. Robert King. London and Toronto: Associated University Press, 1993.
Crosland, Maurice. "Early Laboratories c.1600–1800 and the Location of Experimental Science." *Annals of Science* 62 (2005): 233–53.
———. "Priestley Memorial Lecture: A Practical Perspective on Joseph Priestley as a Pneumatic Chemist." *British Journal for the History of Science* 16 (1983): 223–38.
Dacome, Lucia. "Women, Wax and Anatomy in the Century of Things." *Renaissance Studies* 21 (2007): 522–50.
Dagognet, François. *Des détritus, des déchets, de l'abject: une philosophie écologique*. Paris: Empêcheurs de Penser en Rond, 1997.
Davis, Richard H. *Lives of Indian Images*. Princeton: Princeton University Press, 1997.
De Bast, Martin-Jean. *Recueil d'antiquités romaines et gauloises, trouvées dans la Flandre proprement dite, avec désignation des lieux où elles ont été découvertes*. 2nd ed. Ghent: Stéven, 1808.
Deceulaer, Harald. "Second-Hand Dealers in the Early-Modern Low Countries: Institutions, Markets, and Practices," in *Alternative Exchanges. Second-Hand Circulations from the Sixteenth Century to the Present*, edited by Laurence Fontaine, 13–42. New York and Oxford: Berghahn, 2008.

De Grazia, Margreta, Maureen Quilligan, and Peter Stallybrass, eds. *Subject and Object in Renaissance Culture*. Cambridge: Cambridge University Press, 1996.

De Hamel, Christopher, and Joel Silver, eds. *Disbound and Dispersed: The Leaf Book Considered*. Chicago: Caxton Club, 2005.

De Leeuw, Ronald, ed. *Herinneringen aan Italië. Kunst en toerisme in de 18de eeuw*. Zwolle: Waanders, 1984.

De Marchi, Neil, and Hans J. Van Miegroet, eds. *Mapping Markets for Paintings in Europe 1450–1750*. Turnhout: Brepols, 2006.

———. "Transforming the Paris Art Market, 1718-1750," in *Mapping Markets for Painting in Europe 1450–1750*, edited by Neil De Marchi and Hanz J. Van Miegroet, 383–402. Turnhout: Brepols, 2006.

Deming, Mark. "Le Panthéon révolutionnaire," in *Le Panthéon: symbole des révolutions: de l'Eglise de la Nation au Temple des grands hommes*, 97–150. Paris: Picard, 1989.

De Mot, Jean. "Collectionneurs et collections d'antiques en Belgique." *La Belgique artistique et littéraire* 4 (1906): 526–51.

Descartes, René. *Philosophical Writing*, translated by Norman Kemp Smith. New York: Modern Library, 1958.

D'Escherny, David. *Traité des causes et symptômes de la Pierre: et des principaux remèdes en usage pour guérir cette maladie*. Dublin: 1755.

———. *A Treatise of the Causes and Symptoms of the Stone; and of the Chief Remedies now in use to Cure this Distemper*. London: 1755.

Deseure, Brecht. "Ouvrez l'Histoire. Revolutionary Historical Politics in the Southern Netherlands (1792–1799)." *Low Countries Historical Review* 125 (2010): 25–47.

De Vries, Jan. *The Industrious Revolution. Consumer Behaviour and the Household Economy, 1650 to the Present*. Cambridge: Cambridge University Press, 2008.

DiCaprio, Lisa. *The Origins of the Welfare State. Women, Work and the French Revolution*. Urbana and Chicago: University of Illinois Press, 2007.

Didi-Huberman, Georges. "Wax Flesh, Vicious Circles." In *Encyclopedia Anatomica: A Complete Collection of Anatomical Waxes*, edited by Monika Von Düring, Marta Poggesi, and Georges Didi-Huberman, 154–69. New York: Taschen, 1999.

Donaldson, Ian. "The Destruction of the Book." *Book History* 1, no. 1 (1998): 1–10.

Doody, Margaret Anne, and Florian Stuber. "'Clarissa' Censored." *Modern Language Studies* 18, no. 1 (Winter 1988): 74–88.

Douglas, Mary. *Purity and Danger* [1966]. London: Routledge, 2002.

———. *Thinking in Circles: An Essay on Ring Composition*. London and New Haven: Yale University Press, 2007.

Ducoudray, Emilie, Raymonde Monnier, Daniel Roche, and Alexandra Laclau, *Atlas de la Révolution française*. Vol. 11. Paris: EHESS, 2000.

Earle, John. "Genji Meets Yang Guifei: A Group of Japanese Export Lacquers." *Transactions of the Oriental Ceramic Society* 47 (1984): 45–76.

Early, Alice K. *English Dolls, Effigies, and Puppets*. London: B.T. Batesford, 1955.

Eaton, Natasha. "The Art of Colonial Despotism. Portraits, Politics and Empire in South India, 1750–1795." *Cultural Critique* 70 (Fall 2008): 363–92.

Eaves, Duncan, and Ben D. Kimpel. *Samuel Richardson: A Biography*. Oxford: Clarendon, 1971.

Eden, Sir Frederick Morton. *The State of the Poor or an History of the Labouring Classes in England*. 3 vols. London, 1797.

Edgerton, David. *The Shock of the Old: Technology and Global History since 1900*. Oxford and New York: Oxford University Press, 2007.

Edwards, Clive. *Encyclopaedia of Furniture Materials, Trades and Techniques*. Aldershot: Ashgate, 2000.

Eisenstein, Elizabeth L. *Divine Art, Infernal Machine: The Reception of Printing in the West from First Impressions to the Sense of an Ending*. Oxford: University of Pennsylvania Press, 2011.

Elias, Norbert. *The Civilizing Process, Volume I. The History of Manners*. Oxford: Blackwell, 1969.

Elsner, John, and Roger Cardinal, eds. *The Cultures of Collecting*. London: Reaktion Books, 1997.

Fairchilds, Cissie. "The Production and Marketing of Popular Goods in Eighteenth-Century Paris." In *Consumption and the World of Goods*, edited by John Brewer and Roy Porter, 228–48. London and New York: Routledge, 1993.

Fara, Patricia. "'A Treasure of Hidden Vertues': The Attraction of Magnetic Marketing." *British Journal for the History of Science* 28 (1995): 5–35.

Faraday, Michael. *Chemical Manipulation* [1827]. 3rd ed. London: 1842.

Faudry, Kenneth and Marguerite. *Pollock's History of English Dolls and Toys*. Researched by Deborah Brown. London: Ernest Benn, 1979.

Festa, Lynn Mary. *Sentimental Figures of Empire in Eighteenth-Century Britain and France*. Baltimore: Johns Hopkins University Press, 2006.

Friedlander, Eli. *J.J. Rousseau: An Afterlife of Words*. Cambridge, MA: Harvard University Press, 2004.

Fine, Ben, and Ellen Leopol. "Consumerism and the Industrial Revolution." *Social History* 15, no. 2 (May 1990): 151–79.

Findlen, Paula. "Possessing the Past: The Material World of the Italian Renaissance." *The American Historical Review* 103 (1998): 83–114.

Fitzpatrick John C., ed. *The Writings of Washington*. 39 vols. New York: Greenwood Press, 1970.

Filipczak, Zirka Z. *Picturing Art in Antwerp 1550–1700*. Princeton: Princeton University Press, 1987.

Fontaine, Laurence. "Le colportage et la diffusion des 'galanteries' et 'nouveautés."' In "Échanges et cultures textiles dans l'Europe pré-industrielle. Actes du colloque de Rouen, 17–19 mai 1993," edited by Jacques Bottin and Nicole Pellegrin. Special issue, *Revue du Nord* 12 (1996): 91–109.

———, ed. *Alternative Exchanges: Second-Hand Circulations from the Sixteenth Century to the Present*. New York and Oxford: Berghahn, 2008.

———. "The Exchange of Second-Hand Goods Between Survival Strategies and 'Business' in Eighteenth-Century Paris," in *Alternative Exchanges*, edited by Laurence Fontaine, 97–114. New York and Oxford: Berghahn, 2008.

Furetiere, Antoine. *Dictionnaire universel contenant tous les mots français tant vieux que modernes et les termes de toutes les sciences et des arts* [1690]. Paris: SNL-Le Robert, 1978.

Franklin, Benjamin. *Autobiography of Benjamin Franklin*. New York: Modern Library, 1944.

Fryman, Olivia. "Making the Bed: The Practice, Role and Significance of Housekeeping in the Royal Bedchambers at Hampton Court Palace, 1689–1737." PhD diss., Kingston University, 2011.

———. "Rich Pickings: The Royal Bed as a Perquisite, 1660–1760." *Furniture History* 68 (2014, forthcoming).

Gallet, Michel. *Demeures parisiennes*. Paris: Editions du Temps, 1964.

Gallo, Daniela. "Verzamelingen van oudheden van 1750 tot heden." In *Verzamelen. Van rariteitenkabinet tot kunstmuseum,* edited by Ellinoor Bergvelt, Debora J. Meijers, and Mieke Rijnders, 279–316. Heerlen: Open Universiteit, 1993.

Gard, Robin, ed. *The Observant Traveller: Diaries of Travel in England, Wales and Scotland in the County Record Offices of England and Wales*. London: HMSO, 1989.

Garrioch, David. *The Making of Revolutionary Paris*. Berkeley: University of California Press, 2002.

Gay, John, Alexander Pope, and Arbuthnot. *Burlesque Plays of the Eighteenth Century*, edited by Simon Trussler. Oxford: Oxford University Press, 1969.

Gee, Sophie. *Making Waste: Leftovers and the Eighteenth-Century Imagination*. Princeton: Princeton University Press, 2010.

Gemmett, Robert J. "'The Tinsel of Fashion and the Gewgaws of Luxury': The Fonthill Sale of 1801." *The Burlington Magazine* 40 (2008): 381–88.

George, Edwin, and Stella George, with the assistance of Peter Fleming, eds. *Bristol Probate Inventories, Part III: 1690–1804*. Vol. 60. Bristol: Bristol Record Society, 2008.

Getty, Paul. *The Wormsley Library a Personal Selection by Sir Paul Getty, KBE*. London: published for the Wormsley Library, 1999.

Gilmour, Samuel Carter. *Paper, its Making, Merchanting and Usage*. London: Longmans, Green and Co, 1955.

Ginsburg, Madeleine. "Rags to Riches: The Second-Hand Clothes Trade 1700–1978." *Costume* 14 (1980): 121–35.

Glasse, Hannah. *The Servant's Directory or the Housekeeper's Companion: Wherein the Duties of the Chambermaid, Nursery Maid, Housemaid, Laundry-Maid, Scullion, or Under-Cook are Fully and Distinctly Explained*. London, 1760.

Gleeson, Janet. *The Arcanum: The Extraordinary True Story of the Invention of European Porcelain*. London: Bantam Press, 1998.

Glorieux, Guillaume. *À l'Enseigne de Gersaint. Edme-François Gersaint, marchand d'art sur le pont Notre-Dame (1694–1750)*. Seyssel: Champ Vallon, 2002.

Goddard, Nicholas. "Nineteenth-Century Recycling: The Victorians and the Agricultural Use of Sewage." *History Today* 31 (1981): 32–36.

Golinski, Jan. *Making Natural Knowledge: Constructivism and the History of Science*. Chicago: University of Chicago Press, 1998.

———. *Science as Public Culture: Chemistry and Enlightenment in Britain, 1760–1820*. Cambridge: Cambridge University Press, 1992.

Goodfellow, Caroline. *The Ultimate Doll Book*. London: Dorling Kindersley, 1993.

Goodman, Dena, and Kathryn Norberg, eds. *Furnishing the Eighteenth Century: What Furniture Can Tell Us About the European and American Past*. London and New York: Routledge, 2006.

Gourlier, Charles, and Charles-Auguste Questel. *Notice historique sur le Service des Travaux et sur le Conseil Général des bâtiments civils à Paris et dans les départements, depuis l'an IV (1795) jusqu'en 1886*. Paris: 1886.

Gregg, Edward. *Queen Anne*. London: Routledge and Kegan and Paul, 1980.

Gregson, Nicky, and Louise Crewe, eds. *Second Hand Cultures*. Oxford: Berg, 2003.

Greig, Hannah. "Leading the Fashion: The Material Culture of London's *Beau Monde*." In *Gender, Taste and Material Culture in Britain and North America 1700–1830*, edited by John Styles and Amanda Vickery, 293–313. London and New Haven: Yale University Press, 2006.

Grell, Chantal. *Le dix-huitième siècle et l'antiquité en France, 1680–1789*. Oxford: Voltaire Foundation, 1995.

Grose, Francis. *A Dictionary of the Vulgar Tongue*. London: 1811.

Gross, Daniel M. *The Secret History of Emotion: From Aristotle's Rhetoric to Modern Brain Science*. Chicago: University of Chicago Press, 2007.

Gubel, Eric, ed. *Egypte onomwonden: Egyptische oudheden van het museum Vleeshuis*. Antwerp: Pandora, 1995.

Guichard, Charlotte. *Les amateurs d'art à Paris au XVIIIe siècle*. Paris: Seyssel, Champ Vallon, 2008.

———. "From Social Event to Urban Spectacle: Art Auctions in Late Eighteenth-Century Paris." In *Fashioning Old and New: Changing Consumer Patterns in*

Western Europe (1650–1900), edited by Bruno Blondé, Natacha Coquery, Jon Stobart and llja Van Damme, 203–16. Turnhout: Brepols 2009.
Guillerme, André. *Bâtir la ville:* révolutions industrielles dans les matériaux de construction: France-Grande-Bretagne, 1760–1840. Seyssel: Champ Vallon, 1995.
———. *La naissance de l'industrie à Paris. Entre sueurs et vapeurs 1780–1830.* Seyssel: Champ Vallon, 2007.
Guillerme, André, Anne-Cécile Lefort, and Gérard Jigaudon. *Dangereux, insalubres et incommodes: paysages industriels en banlieue parisienne (XIXe–XXe siècles).* Seyssel: Champ Vallon, 2005.
Hall, G. Stanley, and Alexander Caswell Ellis. *A Study of Dolls.* New York: E.L. Kellogg & Co., 1897.
Halsey Thomas, M., ed. *The Diary of Samuel Sewall 1674–1729.* New York: Farrar, Straus and Giroux, 1973.
Hamling, Tara, and Catherine Richardson, eds. *Everyday Objects: Medieval and Early Modern Material Culture and Its Meanings.* Farnham: Ashgate, 2010.
Harison, William. *Woodstock Park. A Poem.* London: printed for Jacob Tonson, within Grays-Inn Gate next Grays-Inn Lane, 1706.
Harouel, Jean-Louis. *L'Embellissement des villes. L'urbanisme français au XVIIIe siècle.* Paris: Picard, 1993.
Harries, Elizabeth. "Sterne's Novels: Gathering Up the Fragments." *English Literary History* 49, no. 1 (Spring 1982): 35–49.
Harvey, Karen. "Barbarity in a Teacup? Punch, Domesticity and Gender in the Eighteenth Century." *Journal of Design History* 21, no. 3 (2008): 205–21.
Haviland, Thomas N., and Lawrence Charles Parish. "A Brief Account of the Use of Wax Models in the Study of Medicine." *Journal of the History of Medicine and Applied Science* 25 (1970): 52–75.
Hawkins, Gay. *The Ethics of Waste: How We Relate to Rubbish.* Oxford: Rowman and Littlefield, 2006.
Hayden, Peter. "Records of clothing expenditure for the years 1746–79 kept by E. Jervis of Leaford in Staffordshire." *Costume* 22 (1988): 32–38.
Hayward, Maria. "Repositories of Splendour: Henry VIII's wardrobes of the Robes and Beds." *Textile History* 29 (1998): 134–56.
Hazlitt, William. "Fonthill Abbey." *The London Magazine* 6, no. 35 (1822): 405–09.
Hecht, Jean. *The Domestic Servant Class in Eighteenth-Century England.* London: Routledge & Kegan, 1956.
Hefford, Wendy. '"Bread, brushes and brooms,' Aspects of Tapestry Restoration in England, 1660–1760.' In *Acts of the Tapestry Symposium*, edited by A. Bennett, 64–75. San Francisco: Fine Arts Museum of San Francisco, 1979.
Hibbert, Christopher. *The Grand Tour.* London: Methuen, 1987.
Hill, Bridget. *Servants: English Domestics in the Eighteenth Century.* New York: Clarendon Press, Oxford University Press, 1996.
Hitchcock, Tim. *Down and Out in Eighteenth-Century London.* London: Hambledon and London, 2004.
Hobbes, Thomas. *Leviathan*, edited by Richard Tuck. Cambridge: Cambridge University Press, 1996.
Hoffman, Philip T., Gilles Postel-Vinay, and Jean-Laurent Rosenthal. *Des marchés sans prix: une économie politique du crédit à Paris, 1660–1870.* Paris: EHESS, 2001.
Hooke, Robert. *The Diary of Robert Hooke, 1672–1680*, edited by Henry W. Robinson and Walter Adams. London: Wykeham Publications Ltd, 1968.
Horace. *Epistles*, translated by John Conington. London: George Bell, 1892.
Horkheimer, Max, and Theodor Adorno. *Dialectic of Enlightenment*, translated by Edmund Jephcott. Palo Alto: Stanford University Press, 2007.
How, James. *Epistolary Spaces: English Letter-Writing from the Foundation of the Post Office to Richardson's Clarissa.* Aldershot: Ashgate, 2003.

Hughes, Clair. *Dressed in Fiction*. Oxford: Berg Publishers, 2006.
Hunter, J. Paul. *Before Novels, The Cultural Contexts of Eighteenth-Century English Fiction*. New York: Norton, 1990.
Impey, Oliver, and John Whitehead, "Observations on Japanese Lacquer in the Collection of William Beckford." In *William Beckford, An Eye for the Magnificent*, edited by Ostergard, 217–27. New Haven: Yale University Press, 2001.
Jackson Downing. Andrew, *The Architecture of Country Houses*. London: D. Appleton, 1850.
Jackson-Stops, Gervase. "The Court Style in Britain." In *Courts and Colonies: The William and Mary Style in Holland, England, and America*, edited by Renier Baarsen, Jenny Greene, Leslie Geddes-Brown and Clive Aslet, 36–61. New York: Cooper Hewitt Museum, distributed by the University of Washington Press, 1988.
———. "William III and French Furniture." *Furniture History* 7 (1971): 121–26.
Jameson, Frederic. *Postmodernism: The Cultural Logic of Late Capitalism*. Durham, NC: Duke University Press, 1991.
Jamieson, Elizabeth, and Peter Kidd. "Report on the James II bed." Unpublished document. The National Trust, July 2009.
Jencks, Charles. *What Is Post-Modernism?* London: Academy, 1986.
Jones, Ann Rosalind, and Peter Stallybrass. *Renaissance Clothing and the Materials of Memory*. Cambridge: Cambridge University Press, 2000.
Jourdain, Margaret. *Stuart Furniture at Knole*. London: Country Life, 1952.
Junqua, Amélie. "Destruction and Survival of the Written Word in Joseph Addison's Periodical Prose." In "La diffusion de l'écrit / Spreading the written word," edited by Anne Bandry-Scubbi and Jean-Jacques Chardin. Special issue, *Revue de la Société d'études anglo-américaines des XVIIe et XVIIIe siècles* 1, no. 2. (2010): 197–219.
Juratic, Sabine. "Mobilités et populations hébergées en garni." In *La ville promise. Mobilité et accueil à Paris*, edited by Daniel Roche, 175–220. Paris: Fayard, 2000.
Kaplan, Steven. "Les corporations, les faux ouvriers et le faubourg Saint-Antoine." *Annales: ESC* 40 (March–April 1988): 253–78.
Kaufmann, Thomas Dacosta. "Antiquarianism, the History of Objects, and the History of Art before Winckelmann." *Journal of the History of Ideas* 62 (2001): 523–41.
Kennicott, Benjamin. *Dissertatio generalis in vetus testamentum Hebraicum; cum variis lectionibus, ex codicibus manuscriptis et impressis*. Oxford: [no imprint but E Typographeo Clarendoniano], 1780.
———. *Vetus testamentum Hebraicum, cum Variis Lectionibus. Edidit Benjaminus Kennicott, S.T.P. Aedes Christi Canonicus, et Bibliothecarius Radclivianus*. Oxford: E Typographeo Clarendoniano, 1776.
Ker, Neil R. *Pastedowns in Oxford Bindings with a Survey of Oxford Binding c. 1515–1620*. Oxford: Oxford Bibliographical Society, 1954.
Keymer, Thomas. "Clarissa's Death, Clarissa's Sale, and the Text of the Second Edition." *Review of English Studies* 45 (1994): 389–92.
———. "Richardson's *Meditations*: Clarissa's *Clarissa*." In *Samuel Richardson: Tercentenary Essays*, edited by Margaret Doody and Peter Sabor, 89–109. Cambridge: Cambridge University Press, 1989.
Keynes, Geoffrey, ed. *The Library of Edward Gibbon*. Godalming: St. Paul's Bibliographies, 1980.
Kilner, Mary Jane. *The Adventures of a Pincushion. Designed Chiefly for the Use of Young Ladies*. London: J. Marshall & Co, 1780.
Kirkham, Pat. *The London Furniture Trade 1700–1870*. London: Furniture History Society, 1988.
Kirshenblatt-Gimblett, Barbara. "Objects of Memory: Material Culture as Life Review." In *Folk Groups and Folklore Genres, a Reader*, edited by Elliott Oring, 329–38. Logan: Utah State University Press, 1989.

Knoefel, Peter K. "Florentine Anatomical Models in Wax and Wood." *Medicina nei Secoli.* (1978): 329–41.

Koch, Ebba. "'The Moghuleries' of the Millionenzimmer, Schönbrunn Palace, Vienna." In *Arts of Mughal India: Studies in Honour of Robert Skelton*, edited by Rosemary Crill, Susan Stronge, and Andrew Topsfield, 153–67. London: Victoria & Albert Museum; Ahmedabad, India: Mapin Publishing, 2004.

Koob, Stephen. "Obsolete Fill Materials Found on Ceramics." *Journal of the American Institute for Conservation* 37, no. 1 (1998): 49–67.

Kopytoff, Igor. "The Cultural Biography of Things: Commoditization as Process." In *The Social Life of Things. Commodities in Cultural Perspective*, edited by Arjun Appadurai, 64–91. Cambridge University Press, 1986.

Kowaleski Wallace, Elizabeth. *Their Fathers' Daughters*. New York: Oxford University Press, 1991.

———. "Representing the Corporal 'Truth' in the Work of Anna Morandi." In *Women and the Material Culture of Death*, edited by Beth Fowkes Tobin and Maureen Goggin. Burlington, VT: Ashgate Press, forthcoming.

Kristeva, Julia. *Powers of Horror: An Essay on Abjection*, translated by Leon S. Roudiez. New York: Columbia University Press, 1994.

———. *Revolution in Poetic Language*, translated by Margaret Waller. New York: Columbia University Press, 1984.

Ladwig, Roland, ed. *Recycling in Geschichte und Gegenwart: Vorträge*. Freiberg: Georg-Agricola-Gesellschaft, 2003.

Lamb, Jonathan. *The Things Things Say*. Princeton and Woodstock: Princeton University Press, 2011.

Lancaster, Charles. *Seeing England: Antiquaries, Travellers & Naturalists*. Stroud: Nonsuch, 2008.

Langereis, Sandra. "Antiquitates: voorvaderlijke oudheden." In *Erfgoed. De geschiedenis van een begrip*, edited by Frans Grijzenhout, 57–84. Amsterdam: Amsterdam University Press, 2007.

———. *Geschiedenis als ambacht: oudheidkunde in de Gouden Eeuw: Arnoldus Buchelius en Petrus Scriverius*. Hilversum: Verloren, 2001.

Lanham, Richard. *Tristram Shandy. The Games of Pleasure*. Berkeley: University of California Press, 1973.

Laugier, Marc-Antoine. *Essai sur l'architecture*. Paris, 1755.

Le Camus de Mézières, Nicolas. *Le guide de ceux qui veulent bâtir*. 2 vols. Paris, 1781.

Lefebvre, Georges. *Etudes sur la révolution française*. Paris: Presses Universitaires de France, 1959.

Leith, James A. *Space and Revolution. Projects for Monuments, Squares, and Public Buildings in France, 1789–1799*. Montréal: McGill-Queen's University Press, 1991.

Lemire, Beverly. "Consumerism in Pre-Industrial and Early Industrial England: The Trade in Second-Hand Clothes." *Journal of British Studies* 27 (1988): 1–24.

———. "Developing Consumerism and the Ready-Made Clothing Trade in Britain, 1750–1800." *Textile History* 15, no. 1 (1984): 21–44.

———. *Fashion's Favourite: The Cotton Trade and the Consumer in Britain 1660–1800*. Oxford: Oxford University Press, 1991.

———. "Peddling Fashion: Salesmen, Pawn-Brokers, Taylors, Thieves and the Second-Hand Clothes Trade in England, c.1700–1800." *Textile History* 22, no. 1 (1991): 67–82.

———. "Second-Hand Beaux and 'Red-Armed Belles': Conflict and the Creation of Fashions in England, c.1660–1800." *Continuity and Change* 15 (2000): 391–417.

———. "The Theft of Clothes and Popular Consumerism in Early Modern England." *Journal of Social History* 24 (Winter 1990): 255–76.

Leong, Elaine. "Making Medicines in the Early Modern Household." *Bulletin of the History of Medicine* 82 (2008): 145–68.

Le Roux, Thomas. *Le laboratoire des pollutions industrielles, Paris, 1770–1830.* Paris: Albin Michel, 2011.

Lévi-Strauss, Claude. *The Savage Mind*. Chicago: University of Chicago Press, 1966.

Lipski, Louis, and Michael Archer. *Dated English Delftware*. Woodbridge: Antique Collectors' Club, 1984.

Livingstone, David. *Putting Science in Its Place: Geographies of Scientific Knowledge*. Chicago and London: University of Chicago Press, 2003.

Llewellyn, Nigel, and Michael Snodin, eds. *Baroque. Style in the Age of Magnificence 1620–1800*. London: V&A Publications, 2009.

Logan, Annie-Marie S. *The 'Cabinet' of the Brothers Gerard and Jan Reynst*. Amsterdam: North-Holland Publishing Company, 1979.

Lunsingh Scheurleer, Theodoor Herman. "Documents on the Furnishing of Kensington House," *The Walpole Society* 38 (1960–62): 15–58.

Lüsebrink, Hans-Jürgen, and Rolf Reichardt. *The Bastille: A History of a Symbol of Despotism and Freedom*. Durham, NC: Duke University Press, 1997.

Lyna, Dries. "Changing Geographies and the Rise of the Modern Auction. Transformations on the Second-Hand Markets of Eighteenth-Century Antwerp." In *Fashioning Old and New: Changing Consumer Patterns in Western Europe (1650–1900)*, edited by Bruno Blondé, Natacha Coquery, Jon Stobart and llja Van Damme, 169–84. Turnout: Brepols, 2009.

Lyna, Dries. "Power to the Broker. Shifting Authorities over Public Sales in Eighteenth-Century Antwerp." In *Modernity and the Second-Hand Trade: European Consumption Cultures and Practices, 1700–1900*, edited by Jon Stobart and Ilja Van Damme, 158–74. Basingtoke: Palgrave, 2010.

Lyna, Dries, and Ilja Van Damme. "A Strategy of Seduction? The Role of Commercial Advertisements in the Eighteenth-Century Retailing Business of Antwerp." *Business History* 51 (2009): 100–21.

Lyna, Dries, Filip Vermeylen, and Hans Vlieghe, eds. *Art Auctions and Dealers: The Dissemination of Netherlandish Art during the Ancien Régime*. Turnhout: Brepols, 2009.

Lynch, Deirdre Shauna. *The Economy of Character: Novels, Market Culture, and the Business of Inner Meaning*. Chicago: University of Chicago Press, 1998.

Lynch, Deirdre. "Personal Effects and Sentimental Fictions." In *The Secret Life of Things. Animals, Objects and It—Narratives in Eighteenth-Century England*, edited by Mark Blackwell, 63–91. Cranbury, NJ: Associated University Presses, 2007.

MacArthur, Rosie, and Jon Stobart. "Going for a Song? Country House Sales in Georgian England." In *Modernity and the Second-Hand Trade. European Consumption Cultures and Practices, 1700–1900*, edited by Jon Stobart and Ilja Van Damme, 175–95. Basingstoke: Palgrave, 2010.

MacKenzie, Henry. *The Man of Feeling* [1777], edited by Brian Vickers. Oxford: Oxford University Press, 2001.

MacGregor, Arthur. *Curiosity and Enlightenment. Collectors and Collections from the Sixteenth to the Nineteenth Century.* New Haven: Yale University Press, 2007.

Mandelbrote, Giles. "The Organization of Book Auctions in Late Seventeenth-Century London." In *Under the Hammer: Book Auctions Since the Seventeenth Century*, edited by Robin Myers, Michael Harris, and Giles Mandelbrote, 15–36. New Castle, DE: Oak Knoll Press; London: British Library, 2001.

Mandler, Peter. *The Fall and Rise of the Stately Home*. New Haven and London: Yale University Press, 1997.

Manguel, Alberto. *The Library at Night*. New Haven: Yale University Press, 2008.

Mann, Theodore-Augustin. *Description de la ville de Bruxelles ou etat présent tant ecclésiastique que civil de cette ville*. Brussels: Chez Lemaire, 1785.

Manzalaoui, Mahmoud. "Pseudo-Orientalism in Transition: The Age of Vathek." In *William Beckford of Fonthill 1760–1844: Bicentenary Essays*, edited by Moussa-Mahmoud, 123–50. Port Washington: Kennikot, 1964.

Mårald, Erland. "Everything Circulates: Agricultural Chemistry and Recycling Theories in the Second Half of the Nineteenth Century." *Environment and History* 8 (2002): 65–84.

Margadant, Ted W. *Urban Rivalries in the French Revolution*. Princeton: Princeton University Press, 1992.

Margairaz, Dominique. "L'Invention du 'Service Public' entre 'changement matériel' et 'contrainte de nommer.'" *Revue d'histoire moderne et contemporaine* 52–53 (July–September 2005): 10–32.

Marschner, Joanna. "Mary II: Her Clothes and Textiles." *Costume* 34 (2000): 44–50.

Martin, Christophe, and Catherine Ramond, eds. "Esthétique et poétique de l'objet au dix-huitième siècle." Special issue, *Lumières* 5 (2005).

Maruca, Lisa. *The Work of Print: Authorship and the English Text Trades, 1660–1760*. Seattle: University of Washington Press, 2008.

Mayhew, Henry. *London Labour and the London Poor*, edited by Robert Douglas Fairhirst. Oxford: Oxford University Press, 2010.

Meganck, Tine L. "Erudite Eyes: Artists and Antiquarians in the Circle of Abraham Ortelius (1527–1598)." PhD diss., Princeton University, 2003.

Messbarger, Rebecca. *The Lady Anatomist: The Life and Work of Anna Morandi Manzolini*. Chicago: University of Chicago Press, 2010.

McFarland, Thomas. "The Originality Paradox." *New Literary History* 5, no. 3 (1974): 447–76.

McKeon, Michael. *The Origins of the English Novel 1600–1740*. Baltimore: Johns Hopkins University Press, 1987.

McKendrick, Neil. "Josiah Wedgwood: An Eighteenth-Century Entrepreneur in Salesmanship and Marketing Techniques." *Economic History Review* 12, no. 3 (April 1960): 408–33.

———. "Josiah Wedgwood and Thomas Bentley: An Inventor-Entrepreneur Partnership in the Industrial Revolution." *Transactions of the Royal Historical Society*, fifth series, 14, (1964): 1–33.

———. "Josiah Wedgwood and the Commercialisation of the Potteries." In *The Birth of a Consumer Society, The Commercialization of Eighteenth-Century England*, edited by Neil McKendrick, John Brewer, and J. H. Plumb, 100–45. London: Europa Publications Limited, 1982.

McKendrick, Neil, John Brewer, and J. H. Plumb. *The Birth of a Consumer Society: The Commercialisation of Eighteenth-Century England*. London: Europa Publications Limited, 1982.

McKitterick, David. *Print, Manuscript, and the Search for Order, 1450–1830*. Cambridge: Cambridge University Press, 2003.

McLeod, Bet. "A Celebrated Collector." In *William Beckford, An Eye for the Magnificent*, edited by Derek E. Ostergard, 155–75. New Haven: Yale University Press, 2001.

McMaster, Juliet. *Reading the Body in the Eighteenth-Century Novel*. Basingstoke: Palgrave Macmillan, 2004.

Melosi, Martin V. *Garbage in the Cities: Refuse, Reform, and the Environment*. Pittsburgh: University of Pittsburgh Press, 2004.

Mercier, Louis-Sébastien. *Tableau de Paris*, edited by Jean-Claude Bonnet. Paris: Mercure de France, 1994.

Meuvret, Jean. "Circulation monétaire et utilisation économique de la monnaie dans la France du XVIe et du XVIIe siècle." In "Études d'histoire économique. Recueil d'articles." Special issue, *Cahier des Annales* 32 (1971): 127–38.

Milliot, Vincent. Un policier des Lumières, suivi de Mémoires de J.C.P. Lenoir, ancien lieutenant de police de Paris, écrits en pays étrangers dans les années 1790 et suivantes. Seyssel: Champ Vallon, 2011.

Mokyr, Joel. *The Enlightened Economy: An Economic History of Britain 1700–1859*. London and New Haven: Yale University Press, 2009.

Momigliano, Arnoldo. "Ancient History and the Antiquarian." *Journal of the Warburg and Courtauld Institutes* 13 (1950): 285–315.

Morand, Jean-Antoine. Projet d'un plan général de la ville de Lyon et de son agrandissement en forme circulaire dans les terrains des Brotteaux. Lyon, 1775.

Morgan, George Cadogan. *Lectures on Electricity*. Norwich: 1794.

Morrison, Alfred, ed. *Collection of Autograph Letters and Historical Documents*, second series, privately printed, 1893.

Moss, W. E. "Elkanah Settle." *Bodleian Library Review* (1944): 92–93.

———. "Elkanah Settle: The Armorial Binding Expert." *Book Collector's Quarterly* 1 (1939): 722, 916, 1314.

———. *A 'Triumph' of Settle Bindings*. West Byfleet: W.E. Moss, 1938.

Muller, Jeffrey M. *Rubens, the Artist as a Collector*. Princeton: Princeton University Press, 1989.

Murdoch, Tessa. "Jean Rene and Thomas Pelletier, a Huguenot Family of Carvers and Gilders in England 1682–1726, Part 1." *The Burlington Magazine* 139, no. 1136 (November 1997): 732–42. Part 2, *The Burlington Magazine* 140, no. 1143 (June 1998): 363–74.

Murhem, Sophia, Göran Ulväng, and Christina Lilja. "Tables and Chairs under the Hammer: Second-Hand Consumption of Furniture in the Eighteenth and Nineteenth Centuries in Sweden." In *Modernity and the Second-Hand Trade: European Consumption Cultures and Practices, 1700–1900*, edited by Jon Stobart and Ilja Van Damme, 211–12. Basingstoke: Palgrave, 2010.

Nenadic, Stena. "Middle-Rank Consumers and Domestic Culture in Edinburgh and Glasgow 1720–1840." *Past and Present* 145 (1994): 122–56.

———. "Romanticism and the Urge to Consume in the First Half of the Nineteenth Century." In *Consumers and Luxury. Consumer Culture in Europe 1650–1850*, edited by Maxine Berg and Helen Clifford, 208–27. Manchester: Manchester University Press, 1999.

Nichols, John. *Literary Anecdotes of the Eighteenth Century*. 6 vols. London, 1812.

North, Michael, and David Ormrod, eds. *Art Markets in Europe, 1400–1800*. Aldershot: Ashgate, 1998.

Oakeshott, Walter. *Notes on the Medieval Manuscripts in Winchester College Library*. undated typescript. Winchester College Fellows' Library.

———. "Winchester College Library before 1750." *The Library*, 5th series,9, no. 1 (March 1954): 1–16.

O'Connell, Lauren Marie. "Redefining the Past: Revolutionary Architecture and the Conseil des Bâtiments Civils." *The Art Bulletin* 77, no. 2 (June 1995): 207–24.

Oliver, John W. *The Life of William Beckford*. London: Oxford University Press, 1910.

Olsen, Kirstin. *Daily Life in Eighteenth-Century England*. Westport: Greenwood Press, 1999.

O'Shea, Michael. "Laurence Sterne's Display of Heraldry." *The Shandean* 3 (1991): 61–69.

Ostergard, Derek E., ed. *William Beckford-An Eye for the Magnificent*. New Haven: Yale University Press, 2001.

Oudshoorn, Nelly, and Trevor Pinch, eds. *How Users Matter: The Co-Construction of Users and Technology*. Cambridge, MA: MIT Press, 2003.

Panzanelli, Roberta, ed. *Ephemeral Bodies: Wax Sculpture and the Human Figure.* Los Angeles: Getty Research Institute, 2008.
Papayanis, Nicholas. *Planning Paris Before Haussmann.* Baltimore, London: Johns Hopkins University Press, 2004.
Pardailhé-Galabrun, Annick. *La Naissance de l'intime.* Paris: Presses Universitaires de France, 1988.
Park, Julie. *The Self and It: Novel Objects in Eighteenth-Century England.* Palo Alto: Stanford University Press, 2009.
———. "Unheimlich Maneuvers: Enlightenment Dolls and Repetitions in Freud." *The Eighteenth Century* 44 (2003): 45–68.
Peck, Linda Levy. *Consuming Splendor. Society and Culture in Seventeenth-Century England.* Cambridge: Cambridge University Press, 2005.
Peers, Juliette. *The Fashion Doll from Bebe Jumeau to Barbie.* New York: Berg, 2004.
Peltz, Lucy, and Martin Myrone, eds. *Producing the Past: Aspects of Antiquarian Culture and Practice.* Aldershot: Ashgate, 1999.
Pennell, Sara. "For a Crack or Flaw Despis'd: Thinking about Ceramic Durability and the 'Everyday' in Late Seventeenth and Early Eighteenth-Century England." In *Everyday Objects: Medieval and Early Modern Material Culture and Its Meanings*, edited by Tara Hamling and Catherine Richardson, 27–40. Farnham: Ashgate, 2010.
———. "Material Culture in Seventeenth-Century 'Britain': The 'Matter of Domestic Consumption." In *The Oxford Handbook of the History of Consumption*, edited by Frank Trentmann, 64–84. Oxford: Oxford University Press, 2012.
Perry, Graham. *The Trophies of Time: English Antiquarians of the Seventeenth Century.* Oxford: Oxford University Press, 1995.
Pearce, Susan. *Visions of Antiquity: The Society of Antiquaries of London 1707–2007.* London: Society of Antiquaries of London, 2007.
Pepys, Samuel. *The Diary of Samuel Pepys*, edited by Robert Latham and William Matthews. London: G. Bell, 1970–87.
Philips, John. *Blenheim, a Poem.* London: Printed for Tho. Bennet, at the Half-Moon in St. Paul's Church-Yard, 1705.
———. *The Splendid Shilling. An Imitation of Milton.* London: Printed for Tho. Bennet, at the Half-Moon in St. Paul's Church-Yard, 1705.
Pietri, Valérie. "Uses and the Used. The Conventions of Renewing and Exchanging Goods in French Provincial Aristocracy," in *Alternative Exchanges: Second-Hand Circulations from the Sixteenth Century to the Present,* edited by Laurence Fontaine, 115–26. New York and Oxford: Berghahn, 2008.
Pilbeam, Pamela. *Madame Tussaud and the History of Waxworks.* London: Hambledon and London, 2003.
Pioggesi, Marta. "The Wax Figure Collection in 'La Specola' in Florence." In *A Collection of Anatomical Waxes*, edited by Petra Lamers-Schutze and Yvonne Havertz, 6–25. Cologne: Taschen, 2006.
Pomata, Giana. "Sharing Cases: The Observationes in Early Modern Medicine." *Early Science and Medicine* 15, no. 3 (2010): 193–236.
Pomian, Krzysztof. *Collectionneurs, amateurs et curieux. Paris, Venise: XVI*^e^*-XVIII*^e^ *siècle.* Paris: Gallimard, 1987.
Ponsonby, Margaret. *Stories from Home. English Domestic Interiors, 1750–1850.* Farnham: Ashgate, 2007.
Potofsky, Allan. *Constructing Paris in the Age of Revolution.* Basingstoke and New York: Palgrave Macmillan, 2009.
———. "Paris-on-the-Atlantic, from the Old Regime to the Revolution." *French History* 25, no. 1 (March 2011): 89–107.

Pradère, Alexandre. *Les ébénistes français de Louis XIV à la Révolution*. Paris: Chêne, 1989.

Price, Leah. *The Anthology and the Rise of the Novel*. Cambridge: Cambridge University Press, 2000.

———. "Reading (and Not Reading) Richardson." *Studies in Eighteenth Century Culture* 29 (2000): 87–103.

Pringle, John, Lord Walpole, and Robert Whytt. "An Account of the Case of the Late Right Honourable Horace Lord Walpole; Being a Sequel to His Own Account Published in the *Philosophical Transactions*." *Philosophical Transactions* 50 (1757–58): 205–386.

Pyle, Forest. *The Ideology of Imagination: Subject and Society in the Discourse of Romanticism*. Palo Alto: Stanford University Press, 1995.

Raven, John. *The Business of Books. Booksellers and the English Book Trade, 1450–1850*. Cambridge: Cambridge University Press, 2007.

Ranby, John. *A Narrative of the Last Illness of the Right Honourable The Earl of Orford*. London: 1745.

Reddy, William M. *The Rise of Market Culture. The Textile Trade and the French Society, 1750–1900*. Cambridge: Cambridge University Press, 1984.

Resbury, Richard. *The Lightless Starre*. London: Printed for John Wright at the Kings-Head in the Old-Bayly, 1652.

Reynard, Pierre Claude. *Ambitions Tamed: Urban Expansion in Pre-revolutionary Lyon*. Montreal and Kingston: McGill-Queen's University Press, 2009.

Richard, Camille. *Le Comité de Salut Public et les fabrications de guerre sous la Terreur*. Paris: Rieder, 1921.

Richards, Sarah. *Eighteenth-Century Ceramics: Products for a Civilised Age*. Manchester: Manchester University Press, 1999.

Richardson, Samuel. *Clarissa; or, The History of a Young Lady* [1747–48], edited by Angus Ross. Harmondsworth: Penguin, 1985.

———. *Meditations Collected from the Sacred Books: And Adapted to the Different Stages of a Deep Distress*. London: 1750.

———. *Pamela, Or, Virtue Rewarded* [1740], edited by Tom Keymer and Alice Wakely. Oxford: Oxford University Press, 2000.

———. *Samuel Richardson's Published Commentary on Clarissa, 1747–1765*, edited by Tom Keymer. London: Pickering and Chatto, 1998.

———. *Selected Letters of Samuel Richardson*, edited by John Carroll. Oxford: Clarendon Press, 1964.

Richter, Anne Nellis. "Spectacle, Exoticism, and Display in the Gentleman's House: The Fonthill Auction of 1822." *Eighteenth Century Studies* 41 (2008): 643–64.

Rieder, Philip. *La figure du patient au XVIIIe siècle*. Geneva: Droz, 2010.

Rittersma, Rengenier C., ed. *Luxury in the Low Countries*. Brussels: Pharo Publishing, 2012.

Roberts, Hugh. "Beckford, Vulliamy and Old Japan." *Apollo* 124, no. 296 (October 1986): 338–41.

Roberts, Jane. *George III and Queen Charlotte: Patronage, Collecting and Court Taste*. Exhibition catalogue, Queen's Gallery, Buckingham Palace, London, The Royal Collection, 2004.

Roberts, Jane, ed. *Royal Treasures, A Golden Jubilee Celebration*. London: Royal Academy, 2002.

Roberts, Lissa. "The Death of the Sensuous Chemist: The 'New' Chemistry and the Transformation of Sensuous Technology." *Studies in History and Philosophy of Science* 26 (1995): 503–29.

Roche, Daniel. *The Culture of Clothing. Dress and Fashion in the 'Ancien Régime.'* Cambridge: Cambridge University Press, 1994.

———. *The People of Paris. An Essay in Popular Culture in the Eighteenth Century.* Berkeley and Los Angeles: University of California Press, 1987.
Rogers, Heather. *Gone Tomorrow: The Hidden Life of Garbage.* New York: New Press, 2005.
Rostenberg, Leona. *The Library of Robert Hooke: The Scientific Book Trade of Restoration England.* Santa Monica, CA: Modoc Press, 1989.
Rowell, Christopher. "The Kings Bed and its Furniture at Knole." *Apollo* 160, no. 513 (2004): 58–65.
Ruskin, John. *Diaries*, edited by Joan Evans and John Howard Whitehouse. Oxford: Clarendon Press, 1956–59.
Sampson, Perry. *A Disquisition of the Stone and Gravel, and other Diseases of the Bladder, Kidney.* London: 1772.
Sargentson, Carolyn. *Merchants and Luxury Markets: The Marchands Merciers of Eighteenth-Century Paris.* London: V&A Museum, 1996.
Savary des Bruslons, Jacques. *Dictionnaire universel de commerce.* Paris: Veuve Estienne, 1741.
Savile, Gertrude. *Secret Comment. The Diaries of Gertrude Savile 1721–1757*, edited by Alan Saville. Nottingham: Kingsbridge History Society, 1997.
Scanlan, John. *On Garbage.* London: Reaktion Books, 2005.
Schaffer, Simon, and Steven Shapin. *Leviathan and the Air-Pump.* Princeton: Princeton University Press, 1985.
Schnapper, Antoine. *Le géant, la licorne, la tulipe. Collections françaises au XVIIe siècle.* Paris: Flammarion, 1988.
Schwoerer, Lois. "Images of Queen Mary, 1689–1695." *Renaissance Quarterly* 42 (1989): 717–48.
Secord, James. "Knowledge in Transit." Isis 95 (2004): 654–72.
Settle, Elkanah. *A Funeral Poem to the Memory of the Honourable Sir John Buckworth, Kt and Bt.* London: printed for J. King at the Bible and Crown in Little-Britain, 1709.
———. *A Pindaric Poem, on the Propagation of the Gospel in Foreign Parts, a Work of Piety, so Zealously Recommended and Promoted by Her Most Gracious Majesty.* London: printed for the Author, 1721.
Shammas, Carole. "Changes in English and Anglo-American Consumption from 1550 to 1800." In *Consumption and the World of Goods*, edited by John Brewer and Roy Porter, 177–205. London and New York: Routledge, 1993.
———. *The Pre-Industrial Consumer in England and America.* Oxford: Clarendon Press, 1990.
Shaw, William A., ed. *Calendar of Treasury Books.* Vol. 29, Part 2. London, 1957.
Shorter, Alfred H. *Studies on the History of Papermaking in Britain*, edited by Richard L. Hills. Variorum Collected Studies Series: CS425. London: Ashgate Variorum, 1993.
Sibum, H. Otto. "Nature's Bookkeeper: Benjamin Franklin's Electrical Research and the Development of Experimental Natural Philosophy in the 18th Century." In *Reappraising Benjamin Franklin: A Bicentennial Perspective*, edited by J. A. Leo Lemay, 221–46. Newark: University of Delaware Press, 1993.
Signe Morrison, Susan. *Excrement in the Late Middle Ages, Sacred Filth and Chaucer's Fecopoetics.* New York, Palgrave Macamillan, 2008.
Silvestre, Hubert. "Commerce et vol de reliques au moyen âge." *Revue Belge de Philologie et d'Histoire* 30 (1952): 721–39.
Simmel, Georg. "Exchange." *On Individuality and Social Forms*, translated by Donald Levine. Chicago: University of Chicago Press, 1971.
Simmonds, Peter Lund. *Waste Products and Undeveloped Substances: Or, Hints for Enterprise in Neglected Fields.* London: 1862.

Simms, Eva-Maria. "Uncanny Dolls: Images of Death in Rilke and Freud." *New Literary History* 27 (1996): 663–77.

Smollett, Tobias. *Roderick Random*. London: 1748.

Smith, Adam. *The Wealth of Nations* [1776]. Harmondsworth: Penguin, 1997.

Smith, Crosbie, and Norton M. Wise. "Work and Waste: Political Economy and Natural Philosophy in Nineteenth-Century Britain." *History of Science* 27 (1989): 263–301, 391–449; 28 (1990): 221–61.

Smith, John Graham. *The Origins and Early Development of the Heavy Chemical Industry in France*. Oxford: Clarendon Press, 1979.

Smith, Pamela H. "Laboratories." In *The Cambridge History of Science, Vol. 3: Early Modern Europe*, edited by Lorraine J. Daston and Katharine Park, 290–305. Cambridge: Cambridge University Press, 2003.

Smuts, Robert Malcolm. "Art and the Material Culture of Majesty in Early Stuart England." In *The Stuart Court and Europe: Essays in Politics and Political Culture*, edited by Robert Malcolm Smuts, 86–112. Cambridge: Cambridge University Press, 1996.

Snodin, Michael, and Malcolm Baker, "Beckford's Silver I & II." *The Burlington Magazine* 122, no. 932 (November 1980): 734–48, 820–34.

Somerset, Anne. Queen Anne: The Politics of Passion. London: Harper Collins, 2012.

Spring, Eileen. "The Strict Settlement: Its Role in History." *The Economic History Review*, 41 (1988): 454–60.

Stafford, Barbara Maria. *Body Criticism: Imaging the Unseen in Enlightenment Art and Medicine*. Cambridge, MA: MIT Press, 1994.

Starr, G. Gabrielle. *Lyric Generations: Poetry and the Novel in the Long Eighteenth Century*. Baltimore: Johns Hopkins University Press, 2004.

Stern, Simon. "Tom Jones and the Economies of Copyright." *Eighteenth-Century Fiction*, vol. 9, no. 4 (1997): 429–444.

Sterne, Laurence. *The Life and Opinions of Tristram Shandy, Gentleman, The Florida Edition of the Works of Laurence Sterne*, edited by Melvyn New, Richard Davies, and W. G. Day. Gainesville: University Press of Florida, 1984.

———. *The Life and Opinions of Tristram Shandy, Gentleman*, edited by Ian Campbell Ross. Oxford: Oxford World's Classics, 2009.

———. *A Sentimental Journey and Continuation of Bramine's Journal, with Related Texts*, edited by Melvyn New and W. G. Day. Indianapolis: Hackett Publishing, 2006.

Stewart, Larry. "Other Centres of Calculation, or, Where the Royal Society Didn't Count: Commerce, Coffee-Houses and Natural Philosophy in Early Modern London." *British Journal for the History of Science* 32 (1999): 133–53.

Stewart, Susan. *On Longing: Narratives of the Miniature, the Gigantic, the Souvenir, the Collection*. Baltimore: Johns Hopkins University Press, 1984.

Stobart, Jon, and Ilja Van Damme, eds. *Modernity and the Second-Hand Trade: European Consumption Cultures and Practices, 1700–1900*. Basingstoke: Palgrave, 2010.

Stobart, Jon. "Clothes, Cabinets and Carriages: Second-Hand Dealing in Eighteenth-Century England." In *Buyers and Sellers. Retail Circuits and Practices in Medieval and Early-Modern Europe*, edited by Bruno Blondé, Peter Stabel, Jon Stobart and llja Van Damme, 225–44. Tournhout: Brepols, 2006.

———. "Gentlemen and Shopkeepers: Supplying the Country House in Eighteenth-Century England." *Economic History Review* 64 (2011): 885–904.

———. "The Language of Luxury Goods: Consumption and the English Country House, c.1760–1830." *Virtus* 18 (2011): 89–104.

Strano, Giorgio. "Galileo's Telescope: History, Scientific Analysis, and Replicated Observations." *Experimental Astronomy* 25 (2009): 17–31.

Strasser, Susan. *Never Done: A History of American Housework*. New York: Pantheon Books, 1982.

———. *Waste and Want: A Social History of Trash*. New York: Metropolitan Books, 1999.

Stronge, Susan. *Tipu's Tigers*. London: V&A Publishing, 2009.

Styles, John, and Amanda Vickery, eds. *Gender, Taste and Material Culture in Britain and North America 1700–1830*. London: Yale University Press, 2006.

Styles, John. "Clothing the North: The Supply of Non-élite Clothing in the Eighteenth-Century North of England." *Textile History* 25, no. 2 (1994): 139–66.

———. "Custom or Consumption? Plebeian Fashion in Eighteenth-Century England." In *Luxury in the Eighteenth Century. Debates, Desires and Delectable Goods*, edited by Maxine Berg and Elizabeth Eger, 103–15. Basingstoke: Palgrave Macmillan, 2003.

———. "Patchwork On the Page." In *Quilts, 1700–2010. Hidden Histories, Untold Stories*, edited by Sue Pritchard, 48–51. London: V&A Publishing, 2010.

———. *Threads of Feeling. The London Foundling Hospital's Textile Tokens, 1740–1770*. London: The Foundling Museum, 2010.

Storer, James. *A Description of Fonthill Abbey, Wilts*. London, 1812.

Stynen, Herman. *De onvoltooid verleden tijd. Een geschiedenis van de monumenten- en landschapszorg in België 1835–1940*. Brussels: Stichting Vlaams Erfgoed, 1998.

Suda, Tomoko. "Eighteenth-Century Glass Bonding Repairs to Porcelain." *Transactions of the English Ceramic Circle* 19, no. 3 (2007): 419–28.

Swain, Margaret. "Loose Covers, or Cases," *Furniture History* 33 (1997): 128–33.

Sweet, Rosemary. *Antiquaries: The Discovery of the Past in Eighteenth-Century Britain*. London: Hambledon and London, 2004.

Swift, Jonathan. *Directions to Servants* [1745]. London: Hesperus Press, 2003.

Symonds, R. W. "Gerrit Jensen, Cabinet Maker to the Royal Household." *Connoisseur* 95 (1935): 268–74.

Szambien, Werner. *Les projets de l'An II. Concours d'architecture de la période révolutionnaire*. Paris: Ecole nationale supérieure des beaux-arts, 1986.

Teyssot, Georges. "Planning and Building in Towns: The System of the Bâtiments civils in France, 1795–1848." In *The Beaux-Arts and the Nineteenth-Century French Architecture*, edited by Robin Middleton, 34–49. Cambridge, MA: MIT Press, 1982.

Tharp, Lars. *Hogarth's China: Hogarth's Paintings and Eighteenth-Century Ceramics*. London: Merrell Holberton, 1997.

Thirsk, Joan. *Economic Policy and Projects. The Development of a Consumer Society in Early Modern England*. Oxford: Oxford University Press, 1978.

Thomas, Donna and Peter, eds. *Papermaking in 17th century England*. Santa Cruz: Peter and Donna Thomas, 1990.

Thomas, M. *Almanach des marchands, négocians et commerçans de la France et du reste de l'Europe*. Paris: Valade, 1770.

Thompson, Michael. *Rubbish Theory: The Creation and Destruction of Value*. Oxford: Oxford University Press, 1979.

Thomson, James. *Seasons*. 1744.

Thurley, Simon. *Hampton Court Palace, A Social and Architectural History*. London, New Haven: Yale University Press, 2003.

Timmermans, Bert. "Networkers and Mediators in the 17th-Century Antwerp Art World: The Impact of Collectors-Connoisseurs on Artistic processes of Transmission and Selection." In *Luxury in the Low Countries*, edited by Rengenier C. Rittersma, 109–34. Brussels: Pharo Publishing, 2010.

Tollebeek, Jo. *De ijkmeesters. Opstellen over de geschiedschrijving in Nederland en België*. Amsterdam: Bakker, 1994.

———. "Geschiedenis en oudheidkunde in de negentiende eeuw. De *Messager des sciences historiques* 1823–1896." *Bijdragen en mededelingen betreffende de Geschiedenis der Nederlanden* 113 (1998): 23–55.

———. "Het verleden in de negentiende eeuw. Arthur Merghelynck en het kasteel van Beauvoorde." *Verslagen en Mededelingen van de Koninklijke Academie voor Nederlandse Taal-en Letterkunde* 109 (1999): 107–47.

Trentmann, Frank. "Materiality in the Future of History: Things, Practices and Politics." *Journal of British Studies* 48, no. 2 (2009): 283–307.

Trotter, David. *Cooking with Mud: The Idea of Mess in Nineteenth-Century Art and Fiction*. Oxford: Oxford University Press, 2000.

Tournon, Antoine. *Moyens de rendre parfaitement propres les rues de Paris, ainsi que les quais, places, culs de sacs, atteliers, cours, allées, manufactures, halles & boucheries . . . dans toutes les villes, bourgs & autres lieux du royaume*. Paris, 1789.

Tsingarida, Athena, and Donna Kurtz, eds. *Appropriating Antiquity. Saisir l'antique. Collections et collectionneurs d'antiques en Belgique et en Grande-Bretagne au XIXe siècle*. Brussels: Le Livre Timperman, 2002.

Turpin, Adriana. "'Filling the Void': The Development of Beckford's Taste and the Market in Furniture." In *William Beckford, An Eye for the Magnificent*, edited by Derek Ostergard, 177–202. New Haven: Yale University Press, 2001.

Vaccari, Maria Grazia. "Wax." In *Encyclopedia of Sculpture*, edited by Antonia Boström, vol. 3, 1749–50. New York: Fitroy Dearborn, 2004.

Van Damme, Ilja, and Reinoud Vermoesen. "Second-Hand Consumption as a Way of Life: Public Auctions in the Surroundings of Alost in the Late Eighteenth Century." *Continuity & Change* 24 (2009): 275–305.

Van Damme, Ilja. "Changing Consumer Preferences and Evolutions in Retailing. Buying and Selling Consumer Durables in Antwerp (c. 1648–1748)." In *Buyers and Sellers. Retail Circuits and Practices in Medieval and Early Modern Europe*, Bruno Blondé, Peter Stabel, Jon Stobart and llja Van Damme, eds. 199–223. Turnhout: Brepols, 2006.

———. "Second-Hand Dealing in Bruges and the Rise of an Antiquarian Culture." In *Modernity and the Second-Hand Trade. European Consumption Cultures and Practices, 1700–1900* Jon Stobart and Ilja Van Damme, 73–92. Basingtoke: Palgrave, 2010.

Van Cleven, Jean. *Neogotiek in België*. Tielt: Lannoo, 1994.

Van der Veen, Jaap. "Vorstelijke en burgerlijke verzamelingen in de Nederlanden vanaf het einde van de zestiende eeuw tot omstreeks 1700." In *Kabinetten, galerijen en musea. Het verzamelen en presenteren van naturalia en kunst van 1500 tot heden*, edited by Ellinoor Bergvelt, Debora J. Meijers, and Mieke Rijnders, 101–28. Zwolle: Waanders, 2005.

Vasset, Sophie, ed. *Medicine and Narration in the 18th century*, Oxford: Studies in Voltaire and the Eighteenth Century, 2013.

Vendler, Helen. *The Art of Shakespeare's Sonnets*. Cambridge, MA: Harvard University Press, 1997.

Verhoeven, Gerrit. *Anders reizen? Evoluties in vroegmoderne reiservaringen van Hollandse en Brabantse elites (1600–1750)*. Hilversum: Verloren, 2009.

Verlet, Pierre. "Le commerce des objets d'arts et les marchands-merciers à Paris au XVIIIe siècle." *Annales ESC* 1 (January–March 1958): 10–29.

Verley, Patrick. *L'Echelle du monde. Essai sur l'industrialisation de l'Occident*. Paris: Gallimard, 1997.

Verschaffel, Tom. *Historici in de Oostenrijkse Nederlanden (1715–1794). Proeve van repertorium*. Brussels: Facultés Universitaires Saint-Louis, 1996.

———. *De hoed en de hond. Geschiedschrijving in de Zuidelijke Nederlanden*. Hilversum: Verloren, 1998.

Vickers, Michael. "Value and Simplicity: Eighteenth-Century Taste and the Study of Greek Vases." *Past & Present* 116 (August 1987): 98–137.

Vickery, Amanda. *Behind Closed Doors. At Home in Georgian England.* London and New Haven: Yale University Press, 2009.

———. *The Gentleman's Daughter. Women's Lives in Georgian England.* London and New Haven: Yale University Press, 1998.

Vigarello, Georges. *Le propre et le sale. L'hygiène du corps depuis le Moyen-âge.* Paris: Seuil, 1985.

Voltaire, *Des embellissements de Paris. Œuvres complètes de Voltaire / Complete works of Voltaire*, edited by Theodore Besterman. Vol. 31B, 199–233. Genève, Banbury, Oxford: Voltaire Foundation, 1968.

Wainwright, Clive. *The Romantic Interior*. London and New Haven: Yale University Press, 1984.

Wakefield, Priscilla. *Reflections on the Present Condition of the Female Sex*. 1798.

Walker, Robin B. "Advertising in London Newspapers, 1650–1750." *Business History* 15, no. 1 (January 1973): 112–30.

Wall, Cynthia. "The English Auction: Narratives of Dismantlings." *Eighteenth-Century Studies* 31 (1997): 1–25.

Walpole, Horace. "An Account of the Right Honourable Horace Walpole Esq; Drawn up by Himself." *Philosophical Transactions* 47 (1751–52): 44–45.

Walpole, Horace, and Robert Whytt. "A Sequel of the Case of the Right Honourable Horace Walpole, Esq; Relating to the Stone, since His First Account in April 1750." *Philosophical Transactions* 47 (1751–52): 472–73.

Warner, Marina. *Phantasmagoria*. Oxford: Oxford University Press, 2006.

Watson, Francis. "Beckford, Mme de Pompadour, the Duc de Bouillon and the Taste for Japanese Lacquer in the Eighteenth Century." *Gazette des Beaux-Arts* 61 (1963): 101–27.

Weatherill, Lorna. *Consumer Behaviour and Material Culture in Britain 1660–1760.* London and New York: Routledge, 1988.

Weatherill, Lorna, and Gillian Wilson. *Oriental Mounted Porcelain*. Los Angeles: J. Paul Getty Trust, 1999.

Weber, Caroline. *Queen of Fashion*. New York: Picador, 2006.

Weeton, Ellen. *Miss Weeton's Journal of a Governess, 1807–1825*, edited by Edward Hall. Oxford: Oxford University Press, 1939.

Westgarth, Mark. *A Biographical Dictionary of Nineteenth-Century Antique & Curiosity Dealers*. Glasgow: Regional Furniture Society, 2009.

———. *The Emergence of the Antique and Curiosity Dealer 1815–1850: The Commodification of Historical Objects*. Aldershot: Ashgate, 2011.

Westman, Annabel, and Geoffrey Beard. "A French Upholsterer in England: Francis Lapiere 1653–1714." *The Burlington Magazine* 135, no. 1085 (August 1993): 515–24.

———. "A Royal Bed at Chatsworth, The Puzzle of the 4th Duke's Perquisite." *Apollo* 167, no. 555 (1 June 2008): 68–75.

Whytt, Robert. *Essays on the Virtues of Lime-Water*. 2nd ed. London: 1752.

Wild, Wayne. *Medicine-by-Post: The Changing Voice of Illness in Eighteenth-Century British Consultation Letters and Literature.* New York, Amsterdam: Rodopi, 2006.

Williams, Nigel. "Ancient Methods of Repairing Pottery and Porcelain." In *British Museum Occasional Paper 65: Early Advances in Conservation*, edited by Vincent Daniels, 147–50. London: British Museum, 1988.

Willis, Alfred. "Flemish Renaissance Revival in Belgian Architecture (1830–1930)." PhD diss., Ann Arbor University, 1984.

Willoughby, James. *The Libraries of Collegiate Churches*. London: The British Academy, forthcoming.

Wigston-Smith, Chloe. "Clothes without Bodies: Objects, Humans, and the Marketplace in Eighteenth-Century It-Narratives and Trade Cards." *Eighteenth-Century Fiction* 23, no. 2 (2011): 347–80.

Wilson, Benjamin. "New Experiments upon the Leyden Phial, respecting the Termination of Conductors." *Philosophical Transactions* 68 (1778): 999–1012.

Wischermann, Clemens, and Elliott Shore, eds. *Advertising and the European City. Historical Perspectives*. Aldershot: Ashgate, 2000.

Wittman, Richard. *Architecture, Print Culture, and the Public Sphere in Eighteenth-Century France*. New York and London: Routledge, 2007.

Wohlfarth, Irving. "Et Cetera? The Historian as Chiffonier." *New German Critique* 39 (1986): 142–68.

Wolvesperges, Thibaut. *Le meuble français en laque au XVIIIe siècle*. Paris: L'Amateur, 2000.

Wood, Lucy. "A Royal Relic: The State Bedroom Suite at Warwick Castle." *Furniture History* 48, 67 (2012): 45–104.

———. *The Upholstered Furniture in the Lady Lever Art Gallery*. New Haven and London: Yale University Press, 2008.

Woodforde, James. *The Diary of a Country Parson, 1758–1802*, edited by John Beresford, 5 vols. Oxford: Oxford University Press, 1924.

Woodward, Donald. "Swords into Ploughshares: Recycling in Pre-Industrial England." *Economic History Review* 38 (1985): 175–91.

Woolf, Daniel. "Images of the Antiquary in Seventeenth-Century England." In *Visions of Antiquity: The Society of Antiquaries of London 1707–2007*, edited by Susan Pearce, 11–43. London: Society of Antiquaries of London, 2007.

———. *The Social Circulation of the Past. English Historical Culture 1500–1730*. Oxford: Oxford University Press, 2003.

Woronoff, Denis. "Le charbon épuré vers 1780: un essai manqué." In *La houille avant le coke*, edited by Paul Benoit and Catherine Verna, 169–175. Liège: Université de Liège, 1999.

Wylie, John Capie. *The Waste of Civilization*. London: Faber and Faber, 1959.

Yates, Joshua, and James Davison Hunter, eds. *Thrift and Thriving in America: Capitalism and Moral Order from the Puritans to the Present*. Oxford: Oxford University Press, 2011.

Yonan, Michael A. *Empress Maria Theresa and the Politics of Habsburg Imperial Art*. Philadelphia: Penn State University Press, 2011.

———. "'Veneers' of Authority: Chinese Lacquers in Maria Theresa's Vienna." *Eighteenth-Century Studies* 37, no. 4 (2004): 652–72.

Young, Edward. *Conjectures on Original Composition*. London: Millar and Dodsley, 1749.

Young, Hilary. *English Porcelain 1745–1795: Its Makers, Design, Marketing & Consumption*. London: V&A Publications, 1999.

Zimring, Carl. *Cash for Your Trash: Scrap Recycling in America*. New Brunswick, NJ: Rutgers University Press, 2005.

Index

[illegible]
[illegible] Taylor & Francis
Verlag GmbH, Kaufingerstraße 24, 80331 München, Germany